Geraldine Hackett-James
— Sept. 1993

In Conall's Footsteps

In Conall's Footsteps

Lochlann McGill

Foreword by Brian Friel

BRANDON

First published in 1992 by
Brandon Book Publishers Ltd
Dingle, Co. Kerry

British Library Cataloguing in Publication Data
McGill, Lochlann
In Conall's Footsteps
I. Title
941.693

ISBN 0 86322 151 3

The maps in this book are reproduced by kind permission of the Ordnance Survey, Dublin.

Photographs on back cover show: Drumboghill lanula; Loughadoon; Evie Hone stained-glass window, Ardara.

Typeset by Brandon
Cover design by John Brady
Printed by Colour Books Ltd, Dublin

To my wife, Carmel, who traced my footsteps since I was fifteen years old, and to our beautiful daughters – Eleanor, Olivia, Genevieve and Lucienne.

CONTENTS

MAPS

FOREWORD

I HAVE NEVER met Lochlann McGill of Falcarragh, nor do I know anything about the genesis of this book. But I can imagine it began as a modest notion. He would compile a record or catalogue of all the sites and pilgrimages in West Donegal associated with St. Conall; his area of exploration would lie between Doochary and Glencolmbkille; and he would write a brief history of each place and explain in what ways it was similar to and differed from other Conall sites. The exercises would be compact and engaging and would be pursued in a leisurely fashion in McGill's spare time – an ideal hobby for a country doctor with an alert interest in his native county.

But what seemed at first to be modest turned out to be complex and took on a vision and scale of huge ambition. And what was embarked on with an amateur's love became, I suspect, a compulsion. Because the recording and cataloguing of these Conall sites refused to be a mere listing and demanded that archaeological, social, religious, historical and folklore elements be explored and analysed. And before he was a year into his task McGill must have realised that he was involved in a book whose ambition was infinitely greater than that first modest notion, and that he was caught up in practices and disciplines and passionate histories that could not be accommodated by lists and catalogues. The ideal hobby had become close to a profession.

More than 150 years ago the great John O'Donovan faced a similar drama when he began working for the Ordnance Survey. Would he clinically map and measure and name in obedience to his civil service brief, or would he open his job up to embrace a full acknowledgement and celebration of the rich culture that every small field in every townland hoarded between its stone walls? O'Donovan chose celebration. And McGill thankfully takes the same route; goes even further. Because his area of scrutiny is only a tiny fraction of O'Donovan's he has more time to linger and listen and study and gossip. He can weigh historical fact against personal belief. He can pursue a biography that takes him far off his stated itinerary for no better reason than that the biographee fascinates him. He can compare archaeological theory with local experience and adjudicate wisely and gently. He can acknowledge residual pagan customs and quietly note their absorption into current religious exercise. And, at least as importantly, he tells kind stories about old friends of his now dead – just because they were his friends. The result is that within their given terms McGill is more comprehensive and better company than O'Donovan, and, as befits his professional training, much more caring.

In Conall's Footsteps, besides being scrupulous in its scholarship and affectionate in its attitude, is truly a labour of love. And all those stone-walled fields between Doochary and Glencolmbkille are now even richer because of the book they inspired.

Brian Friel

ACKNOWLEDGEMENTS

MY FATHER, BEING a Fellow of the Royal Society of Antiquaries of Ireland, instilled a love of archaeology in all his children, and with my mother hailing from Co. Laois our family spent many happy summer days dawdling around the historical sites of Ireland. I must know every Romanesque and Gothic doorway in the country.

My own interest is archaeology/topography – anything that gets one outdoors examining the landscape. To convey a sense of being outdoors I required a cartographer/illustrator and in Brian Fleury I had the assistance of a craftsman of the highest order. His talents adorn and enrich this book and I would like to thank him most sincerely. Indeed the entire Fleury family has been most supportive of the project from its inception

Words cannot express my thanks to Brian Friel for his generosity in contributing the foreword to this book. Despite being an intensely busy man he took the time to read my manuscript when it was in its early, rough form – not an easy task. His genius is universally acknowledged and if nothing else I will be glad to be remembered as the man who wrote the book which contained a foreword written by Brian Friel!

When I took my first faltering steps in research outside of Donegal I went to the Department of Irish Folklore at University College, Dublin. Professor Séamas Ó Catháin welcomed me with an extraordinary warmth; he went through the indexes himself and brought all the relevant manuscripts to my reading table. I thought his personal involvement was most supportive and I interpret his actions as being his way of saying "thank you" to the many Donegal people who have contributed, over the years, to the archives of his department.

I owe a great debt to the staff of the County Library, Letterkenny – the progressive county librarian Liam Roynane, Mary Monaghan and Mary McCole. I have always admired Liam's professionalism but it is his generosity I wish to thank him for on this occasion: much of the early manuscript form of this book was typed by the library staff under his guidance. The ubiquitous Mary Monaghan was always available and though I must have tested her patience severely she was never anything other than helpful and co-operative. Her vast knowledge of books proved most valuable and she also made many corrections which would otherwise have gone unnoticed.

I must also thank Mary Hughes of the Linenhall Library, Belfast, who always made me feel welcome – and we generally conversed in Gaelic. I also extend my thanks to the staff of the library of the Royal Irish Academy and the staff of the National Library in Dublin. At the National Library Brian McKenna, Keeper of Manuscripts, kindly allowed me to view maps of south-west Donegal on a number of occasions. All of these maps – mostly estate maps of the 18th and 19th centuries – had come into my father's possession over the years and he had wisely deposited them with the library.

In attempting to interpret the decorated slabs on Inishkeel island I had the good fortune to approach Cormac Bourke of the Department of Antiquities of the Ulster Museum, Belfast. Minute for minute the time I spent with Cormac was the most instructive of all the enquiries I had undertaken.

In the field of hagiography Rev. Dr. John J. Silke and Arthur Spears were very responsive to my correspondence and I would like to thank Professor Pádraig Ó Riain of U.C.C. for his advice.

In the study of placenames I badgered Dónall Mac Giolla Easpaig of the Ordnance Survey, Phoenix Park, Dublin. His advice was freely given in the most scholarly manner. However, I did not always take Dónall's advice and on occasions went off to find my own conclusions. Because the interpretation of many placenames is so equivocal the amateur will always feel the urge to have his own stab at it!

I hope that this book will engender a re-awakening of interest in historic Inishkeel island and I am very grateful to the members of *Cumann Oidhreachta Inis Caoil* – the Inishkeel Heritage Project – who have assisted me. I would like to acknowledge, too, the ready support which *Údarás na Gaeltachta* has given to the *Cumann*.

I would like to thank Dr. Donald Martin for contributing two photographs and Brian Fleury for contributing two others; to Denis Verschoyle and the British Museum and National Library for the use of a number also. The remainder of the photographs in the book were taken by the author. I am also grateful to Francis Harvey for allowing me to use his poem, "Heron," in this book.

As we travel along through the book various people are mentioned in the text and footnotes at different locations. I will not repeat these names. However, I would like to thank the following: Enda Cunningham, Cathach Books, Dublin; Angelique Day, Institute of Irish Studies, Queen's University, Belfast; Mrs Geri Taggart, Coleraine University Library; Rev. Canon Bernard Treanor, Dallán Ave, Warrenpoint, Co. Down; Séamus Ó Dolain, Belturbet, Co. Cavan; Dr. Leslie Lucas, Carrigart; Brian Cannon, Lettermacaward; Jim Boyle, Loughfad; Danny McHugh, Laconnell; Breid McGill, Maghera; John

Francis Gallagher, Glengesh; Vincent O'Donnell, Inver; Patrick Dunleavy, Dungloe; Lucuis Emerson, Ballyshannon; Ralph Sheppard, Raphoe; Harry Johnson, Rosbeg; Brendan Twomey and Tommy Francis, Falcarragh; Clement Sweeney, Beagh; Kathleen O'Donnell N.T., Narin Road, Ardara; Sylvie Gallagher, Ardara, and my niece Orlaith McBride.

The text of this book has been revised on many occasions and I would like to thank the following typists for assisting me: Nancy McHugh-Yates, Eileen McGarvey, Jacquette Fleury, Margaret Doherty and in particular Áine McLoughlin who did Trojan work for me over the past year.

As a country doctor one is often visited by representatives of pharmaceutical companies. On realising that I was attempting to write a book this fine body of people was uniform in giving me constant encouragement over the years ("Keep at it, doc") and I would like to acknowledge that I found their support a great spur to finish the work.

My research called for many trips to Dublin and I would like to thank Teresa Andreucetti whose generosity I courted on numerous occasions when in the capital. Research for a book of this magnitude is slow and expensive and I would like to thank the following Patrons of the Arts who supported my research: Johnny and Christine Boyle, Highlands Hotel, Glenties; Con and Nessa Molloy, Nesbitt Arms Hotel, Ardara; John and Nancy Yates, Woodhill House, Ardara; John Neil and Peggie O'Donnell, Ardara; Ulster Bank, Ardara (manager: Des Sheridan); Charles McHugh, Nancy's Bar, Ardara; Donal and Anne McBride, Ballybofey; Dr. Donald and Anna Martin, Killybegs; Nicholas McGill (my brother); Connell Kennedy, Kennedy of Ardara (Knitwear); Micheál and Adele Melley, Óstan na Fearthainne (Narin Inn).

ABBREVIATIONS

A.F.M.   *Annala Rioghachta Eireann. Annals of the Kingdom of
             Ireland* by the Four Masters
A.S.D.   *Archaeological Survey of County Donegal*
A.U.   *Annals of Ulster*
B.A.R.   *British Archaeological Reports*
Corpus   *Corpus Genealogiarum Sanctorum Hiberniae*
D.A.   *Donegal Annual: Journal of the Donegal Historical Society*
H.D.R.   *History of the Diocese of Raphoe*
H.P.A   *History of the Parish of Ardara*
J.C.H.A.S. *Journal of the Cork Historical and Archaeological Society*
J.R.S.A.I. *Journal of the Royal Society of Antiquaries of Ireland*
Kenny   *The Sources for the Early History of Ireland: Ecclesiastical*
M.O.D.   *Martyrology of Donegal: A Calender of the Saints of Ireland*
O.G.   *Onomasticon Goedelicum*
P.R.I.A.   *Proceedings of the Royal Irish Academy*
U.J.A.   *Ulster Journal of Archaeology*

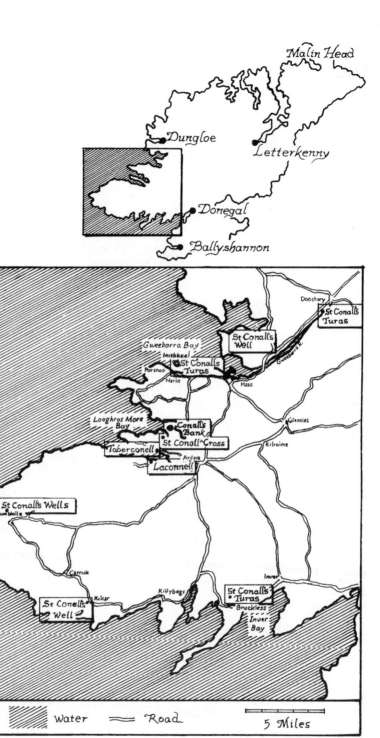

Malin Head

Dungloe

Letterkenny

Donegal

Ballyshannon

Doochary

St Conall's Turas

St Conall's Well

Gweebarra Bay
Inishkeel
St Conall's Turas
Portnoo
Narin
Maas

Gweebarra R.

Glenties

Loughros More Bay
Conall's Bank
St Conall Cross
Toberconell
Ardara
Laconnell

Kilraine

St Conall's Wells
Glencolumbkille

Carrick

Killybegs

Inver

St Conall's Turas
Bruckless
Inver Bay

Kilcar

St Conall's Well

Sites of St Conall

Water

Road

5 Miles

B. FLEURY 1991

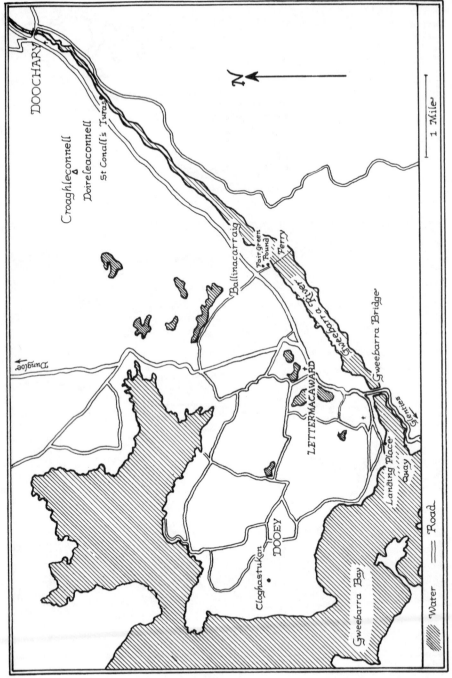

DOOCHARY

Croaghleconnell △
Doireleaconnell △
St Conall's Turas △

Ballinacarraig

Dungloe →

Fair green
Pound
Ferry

Gweebarra River

Gweebarra Bridge

LETTERMACAWARD

Landing Place

Cloghastukan ·
DOOEY

Gweebarra Bay

Glenties →
Quay

N

1 Mile

B. FLEURY 1991

▨▨▨ Water   ═══ Road

I

DOOCHARY TO GWEEBARRA BRIDGE

"I PICK UP SEVEN pebbles around about the house or on the road on my way down. Once I go inside the little wooden gate and into the field I take off my shoes and stockings. On my way down through the field I say the Creed. When I get to the place where the stones are with the tracks of St. Conall's knees and elbow on them I walk around the cairn in a clockwise direction three times saying the seven decades of the rosary as I go. I throw one of the pebbles into the centre of the cairn as I start each decade. If I haven't the seven decades of the rosary finished when I have walked around the cairn three times, then I kneel down at any spot outside the cairn and finish the decades. Then I kneel beside the stone which has the marks of his knees and I say five Our Fathers and Hail Marys. Then I go up under the tree to the little place we call 'the altar' and I say another five Our Fathers and Hail Marys.

"I always have to take something of my own with me to tie on to the tree. This is usually a bit of clothing of some kind. If somebody has written to me and asked me to do the *turas* for them, or for one of their relations, then they always have to send me some item of clothing belonging to that person. I always attach that item to the tree at 'the altar'. It is always a very good sign if the birds are hopping about when I am doing the *turas*. The robin is the bird that I like to see the best. I always know that my request is going to be granted if I see the birds flying about. If I don't see birds when I am doing the *turas* then I know that my request will not be granted.

"The most important thing of all if you are doing the *turas* is to have faith. When my brother was a baby the doctors said that he only had a fifty-fifty chance of being alive by morning. My mother stayed up all night and noticed that at about six o'clock in the morning he was starting to improve. In fact my aunt, who lived near by, was doing the *turas* to St. Conall for the sick child at that exact time. That's my brother you saw going down the road on a tractor just now when you arrived at the house.

"If people ask me to do the *turas* for them I usually fill up a little bottle of water from the stone with the elbow-mark on it. Sometimes I can get water from that stone even though it might not have rained for two months. The well with the knee-marks sometimes could be dried up completely and only full of leaves, but the elbow-stone always seems to have a little water that I can send to the person who asked me to do the *turas* for them.

"Not many people do the *turas* now, only myself and a few of the neighbours. My mother used to say that there used to be very large crowds doing the *turas* on the 15th August every year. The young people nowadays don't have the same interest in it.

"In olden times people always did the *turas* before their breakfast. They often left home in their bare feet and did the *turas* and came back to have their breakfast. Of course in those days there were no rosary beads and that is why people collected seven little pebbles before going down into the field, so that they could count when they were starting each of the seven decades of the rosary."

This is how Sophie Devenney of Derryleconnell, near Doochary, describes the local *turas*. The *turas* is done around a mound (cairn) at the bottom of a field, right on the edge of the Gweebarra river. A few steps down into the mound there is a well made of two deep round indentations in stone, and this is known as the knee-stone. On the other side is a small portable basin-stone with a depression in it. This is known as the elbow-stone.

Elbow-stone of St. Conall

In relation to this site Sophie heard the following legend from the older generation: St. Conall had committed a grave sin and was doing penance by immersing himself in the cold waters of the sea. A *péist mhór* (sea-serpent) attacked him and Conall swam frantically to avoid it; the sea miraculously opened up through the land in front of St. Conall while he was swimming to avoid the sea-monster, and that is how the Gweebarra river was created. Conall managed to scramble ashore at Derryleconnell and lay there exhausted for a year and a day. It was the pressure of St. Conall's elbow and knees while he lay there for such a long time that caused the depression in the stones at the *turas* site.

There is an old song in Gaelic, referring to another location, and one of the lines in it is "*Tá aoibhneas i nDoire Leac Chonaill nach raibh ariamh san áit seo* – There is an enchantment in Derryleconnell that never existed in this place". I would agree with these sentiments, having experienced the serenity that one feels at this site beside the flowing river. It is a delight also to converse with Sophie and her brother, Francey Doogan. Listening to Francey's beautiful Gaelic is a pleasure. I am a moderate Gaelic speaker myself, but everyone delights in hearing one whose Gaelic is music to the ears because of the sweetness of its pronunciation and the range of its vocabulary. This is how I feel about Francey's Gaelic.

Before heading west for Gweebarra Bay and Inishkeel island we will briefly go east, down the road a few miles to Doochary [*An Dubh Choraidh*; *dubh*: black; *cora*: a weir, here indicating a natural weir where salmon jump up-river]. The Roman Catholic church here in Doochary is called St. Conall's, there is a Gaelic-speaking summer college called St. Conall's and the Doochary band (no longer in existence) was called St. Conall's Band.

If one were to go eastward from Doochary in the direction of Churchill one would come into the territory dominated by the prince of early Irish ecclesiastical saints – St. Columba (Colmcille). A friend of mine was recently telling me that he was having a drink in a pub in Doochary when a Scottish visitor came in. A local man struck up a conversation with the visitor and during the course of the conversation the local remarked: "And we sent a 'quare' man over to you there one time." (In Donegal "quare" means "great".) The visitor enquired who the "quare" man might be, possibly thinking that he would know him himself, and the local replied, "St. Colmcille." Colmcille went to Iona, off the Scottish coast, in 563 A.D. but his legend exists so strongly in the lives of the people of the area that he could be talked about in such a present-day form in a pub in Doochary almost 1,500 years after his death.[1]

We will now turn and go back through Derryleconnell [*Doire Leac*

Chonaill; doire: an oakwood, from *dair*, an oak; *leac*: a flagstone; and of course Chonaill refers to Conall Caol, the saint whom we normally associate with Inishkeel island]. The "Doire"[2] that most people would know is Doire Colmcille, the present city of Derry, Colmcille referring to St. Columba who was baptized under the name Colm (*cille*: of the churches).

Oak woods were very important to the druids. We read that "In pagan Ireland the druids had a pre-eminence of their own in Celtic society. And it is interesting to note that 'Druid', as a word, is considered to derive from roots meaning 'knowledge of the oaks'.[3] And so oak sanctuaries and sacred woods were common here as well as in Celtic Europe. ... Oak was the most common species (of wood in Ireland) and the anglicised form (derry) is included in many townland names. There are about 62,200 townland names in Ireland, and about 1,600 contain *derry* in one form or another."[4]

There are few statistics relating to Irish woodland before the 17th century. In 1600 about one-eighth of Ireland was forested; by 1800 the proportion had been reduced to a fiftieth as a result of the commercial exploitation of the Irish woodlands following on the establishment of English control over the whole country.[5] On the evidence available it does not appear that Donegal was very extensively wooded at the end of the 16th century. There were intermittent areas of wood along the western seaboard from Ballintra to Killybegs. Tongues of woodland stretched inland up the river valleys and encompassed Lough Eske. The western side of Lough Derg was also wooded. The triangle of country between Ardara, Glenties and Narin was tree-covered with an extension of these woods stretching up the Gweebarra river to Lough Barra.[6]

The song entitled *"Na Buachaillí i nAlbain"* which has the reference to the *aoibhneas* in Derryleconnell which we have already quoted appears in a Gaelic book of songs entitled *Céad de Cheoltu Uladh*. In introducing the song Énrí Ó Muirgheasa says: "This is another song from the pleasant area of the Gweebarra. There were once twelve oak woods along the Gweebarra between Glen Domhan and the sea, and it is said that Fionn, when he tasted the venison, could tell by its flavour in which of these woods the deer was killed. But there is hardly a bush to be seen over most of this district at present.[7] Doire Leac Chonaill, mentioned in this song, was one of these woods. It gets its name from St. Conall's flagstone at the holy well where no doubt he baptized the huntsmen and fishermen who then dwelt along the Gweebarra. St. Conall Caol, though hardly known at present outside west Donegal, fills a large place in the traditions and the folklore of his native district."[8]

I found the story which Sophie Devenney narrated, about St. Conall trying to evade the sea-serpent and finally scrambling ashore at Derryleconnell, intriguing. Sophie also added that when St. Conall then slept for a year and a day he awoke to find that a bird had nested in the palm of his hand and that the eggs had hatched. It is because of this legend associating birds with St. Conall that she feels it is a good omen if birds are overhead when she is doing the *turas*. In the archives of the Department of Irish Folklore in Belfield, Dublin, there are numerous stories related to St. Conall. In a collection obtained in the 1930s from Roise Brennan of Shallogans national school[9] there are numerous stories of enemies coming in from the sea and attacking St. Conall on Inishkeel island. In this collection we are again told of how, while he evaded his enemies, the sea followed Conall from Narin and opened up miraculously through the land towards Doochary and that that is how the Gweebarra estuary was formed. Roise Brennan states that people would leave in the morning before breakfast, go barefoot and do the Inishkeel *turas* and then walk back the nine miles from Narin and do the Derryleconnell *turas*. She describes how, when finishing the latter *turas*, one would take a bottle of water from the elbow-stone and say three Our Fathers and Hail Marys. One could take as many bottles of the water as one liked but one had to say three Our Fathers and Hail Marys in lieu of each bottle.

Sophie Devenney was in the company of a party of people who did the *turas* on Inishkeel island when she was a child. She does not remember much about the "stations" performed but she does remember that there was a particular well on the far side of the island and the belief was that if the water turned red when wading through this well then one of the people doing the *turas* would be dead within the year. Roise Brennan also refers to this legend. She states that many years ago, when a young girl from the Lettermacaward area was doing the *turas* on Inishkeel island, the water in this particular water-hole turned red and she died within the year.

We now proceed westwards towards Lettermacaward and the Gweebarra bridge; on our right the peak of Croaghleconnell is visible, further evidence of the influence of St. Conall on the nomenclature of this area. We leave Derryleconnell Near and on our right we pass Glenaltaderry and Derryhenny, these "derrys" supporting the tradition that this area was once densely wooded with oak trees. We now pass through the townland of Ballinacarralg (the town of the rocks). In the past, being situated on the river ford, the main road from Glenties to Dungloe passed through it. It was once the hub of the Lettermacaward area, with its fair day on the 20th of each month.[10] A fair green and a pound are marked on the Ordnance Survey maps. It was the site of the upper Gweebarra ferry before the building of the Gweebarra bridge.

Leaving Ballinacarraig we come to the townland of Boyoughter,[11] where the present road from Dungloe comes in from the right. What of earlier travellers coming from the Dungloe direction? The Rev. Dr. Pococke, passing through here in 1752, got into difficulties at Glasbeginmill and writes: "We came to a boggy part of the Country... but the guide went to the mill and brought a board and an Oxes skin; So laying sods and heath, the skin and the board on that, and sods on each side of it to keep the horses from slipping in, we cross'd on them safely, and passing on still over bog, when we came to any narrow passes, the horses leap'd them; And taking another guide we came to Letter McWard, a hamlet of three or four houses."[12]

Lettermacaward is known locally as Leitir.[13] The name is a direct borrowing from the Gaelic *Leitir-mic-a-bhaird* which translated means "hillside of the son of the bard". Folklore has it that the bard in question was of the O'Donnell clan and that he was given Lettermacaward as payment for favours rendered.[14] To anyone who wishes to know more about the Lettermacaward area I would recommend the booklet entitled *A Tour Of Lettermacaward*, written by my colleague Karl Cannon in 1985.

Before leaving the Gweebarra we will visit Dooey [from *dumhach*: a sandbank]. John O'Donovan, travelling through this area in 1835, "veered a little to the south west with an intention of visiting the Townlands of Mín A Ghóbhann and Dúmhaidh where the most intelligent of the natives of the Parish reside, and to cross the Mouth of the ferry near Gaoth Beara Bay."[15]

At Dooey there is another well dedicated to St. Conall, but it is no longer visited by the people. Rev. Dr. Maguire, writing in 1920, and echoing the "bird tradition" associated with St. Conall, states: "There is however, a remarkable well in Dooey, connected by tradition with St. Conall's first visit to these parts. He had travelled a long distance in search of a site for a monastery, and having slept soundly, after a refreshing drink from this well, he awoke to find a seagull's egg in his outstreched hand. Then raising his eyes, he discerned the gull hovering over him, and slowly directing her flight to Inniskeel, whither he followed, and was rewarded for his pains by the concession of a generous grant of land for his contemplated monastery." Dr Maguire continues: "The western portion of Lettermacaward was very intimately associated with the island of Inniskeel, till the extinction of St. Conall's Monastery. Some old people relate that their parents used to describe as eye-witnesses the spectacle of a whole fleet of boats crossing the estuary of the Gweebarra, on Sunday, conveying the Letter folk to Mass. It is more than probable, however, that this description was applied to the scene of an annual pilgrimage."[16] (Very likely they were doing the *turas* to Inishkeel island.)

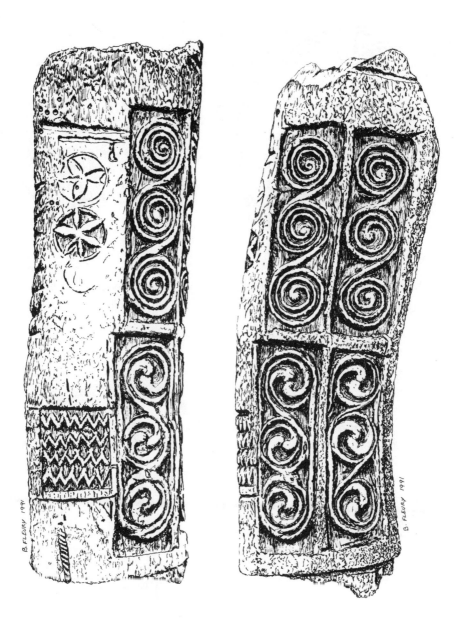

Two views of the antler motif piece (after "The Work of Angels")

*Model of brooch pin from Dooey
(after "The Work of Angels")*

*Mould-value for penannular
Dooey brooch
(after "The Work of Angels")*

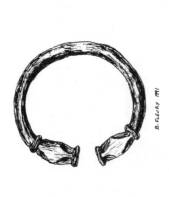

*Representation of brooch
from Dooey mould*

*Example of a penannular brooch
(after "The Work of Angels")*

Dooey's place in history is firmly established because of the archaeological excavation which took place here a few decades ago. A sandhill site at Dooey marked "Cloghastuckan" on the Ordnance map was excavated in the months of May to September 1959. Finds suggest that the whole period of occupation belonged to the early centuries A.D. About 2,000 items were found during the excavation. Iron pins, iron ring brooches and iron belt-buckles were found, as were bronze pins and several bronze belt-buckles. Delicate carving was a feature of the pins, needles, combs, spindle-whorls, knife-handles and other objects of bone which came from the site. Evidence suggests that the site was inhabited by a community of craftsmen who also practised agriculture and kept domestic animals. The animal bones found show that cattle, sheep and pigs were kept while the presence on the site of much antler, worked and unworked, and fish-bones demonstrates that the food supply was augmented by hunting and fishing, parallel evidence for which is supplied by finds of flint arrow-heads and iron fish hooks. Large middens of the shells of oysters, mussels, clam, periwinkle and limpets proved that shellfish were an important item in the common diet.[17] A large number of shells of the white dog-whelk (*Nucella [Purpura] lapillus L*) found at various middens suggest that they were used to produce a purple or crimson dye. But the most interesting discovery, found in the lowest or primary phase of habitation, was a small very finely decorated piece of antler, 12 cm. long by 4.4 cm. in maximum diameter.[18] It is covered with panels of carving executed in chip carving (*kerbschnitt*) technique. Four of these are filled with beautiful scroll work, four with tightly packed rows of chevrons, while two small circular panels are each filled with a marigold. This piece, regarded as the earliest of the Irish motif pieces, is thought to date to the 5th or 6th century.[19] Motif pieces, which were a distinctive feature of Celtic workshops, were used mostly for trying out designs before the real object was made, but they were also sometimes used as models or dies which could be used to impress a design, in foil for instance, or in a clay mould. The decoration on this early piece recalls the designs found reserved against red enamel in 5th-7th century metalwork.

In 1990 a major exhibition of Celtic artwork – entitled The Work of Angels – was held in the British Museum in London and it then transferred to the National Museum, Dublin. It included Celtic pieces from as far away as Scandinavia and Italy. The antler motif-piece from Dooey was part of the exhibition (item no. 152) and there were two further items (nos 180. and 185) from Dooey in the exhibition: one was a 7th-8th century valve of a two-piece clay mould for casting a penannular brooch[20] (a brooch type current in western Scotland and the north of Ireland from the 7th to the 8th centuries);

the other was an 8th-9th century lead and alloy brooch-pin model.[21] This model would have been used for impressing the mould from which the finished object was cast, was re-usable, and would itself have been cast from a mould bearing the impression of a (lost) wax model.

The next time you admire modern design, aided by graphics and computers, spare a thought for these craftsmen, living out here in sand dunes on the edge of the Atlantic, carving their intricate designs on bones, a millenium and a half ago.

Notes

1   J. F. Kenney, *The Sources for the Early History of Ireland: Ecclesiastical* (hereafter Kenney), pp. 425-26 writes: "Columba died about 597. We possess records of his life written by three eminent churchmen who flourished within a century of that date, two at least of whom possessed unusual facilities for acquiring information – Cuimine Ailbe, Abbot of Iona 657-669, Adamnán, Abbot 679-704, and the Venerable Bede, who was born in 673 and died in 735. The result is that Columba stands out as a clear-cut historical personality against a background wherein his associates in sanctity, including the legend-encrusted Patrick and the half-mythical Brigit, move as shadows in a land of twilight."

However Columba, too, gathered legend around him with the passing centuries, much of which is related by Manus O'Donnell in his book *Betha Colaim Chille*, written in 1532. Indeed in recent years some unease has arisen concerning some of the earlier writings on Columba and this will be touched on when we reach Kilkenny, on the Gweebarra estuary.

2   Adamnán, *Vitae Columbae*, ed. Reeves, pp. 160, 277. The present city of Derry, before being called *Doire Colmcille*, was known as *Daire Calgaich*. The name was derived from *calg*, a "sword" or "thorn", and as an adjective denotes sharp or angry; hence *calgach*, genetive *calgaich*, became a proper name in the sense of "fierce warrior". The original church of Colm in Derry was called the *Dubh-Regles* – the black church.

3   T.G.E. Powell, *The Celts*, p. 156.

4   *Donegal Annual* (hereafter *D.A.*) (1972), pp. 216-17.

5   McCracken, *The Irish Woods Since Tudor Times*, p. 15.

6   Eileen McCracken, "The Woodlands of Donegal, 1660 to 1840," in the *D.A.* (1958), p.62.

7   1915.

8   p. 296, n. 82.

9   Ms. 948, pp. 27-33.

10   Karl Cannon, *A Tour of Lettermacaward*, p. 31.

11   I was interested in the translation of the *Boy-* element in this placename be-

cause of the -*boy* which crops up in the townland names of Crannogeboy and Cloghboy on the Loughros peninsula near Ardara. This Boy is translated as *baigh*, a bay, while the Ardara *boys* are translated as *buidh*, yellow.

12   Richard Pococke, *Dr. Pococke's Irish Tour*, p.66. Richard Pococke, D.D., L.L.D., born 1704, was the son of a clergyman. The doctor travelled extensively and, at the time of his Irish tour, was Archdeacon of Dublin. He later became Bishop of Ossory, but died within three months of his transition to the See of Meath in 1765. (D.A. (1979), p. 444.) I make this note of him here because we will be running into him now and then on our travels.

13   *Leitir*: a hillside. Joyce, *The Origin and History of the Irish Names of Places* (3 vols. 1891; 1893; 1913) (hereafter Joyce) tells us (vol. I, p. 404) that John O'Donovan translates it as a "hillside with the tricklings of water" and that in the ancient *Cormac's Glossary* it is thus explained: "Leitir, i.e. *leath tirim agus leath fliuch*: half dry and half wet"; from which it appears that Cormac considered it derived from *leath-tirim*, half dry.

14   Cannon, *A Tour of Lettermacaward*, p. 1.

15   O.S. Letters (1835), p. 109.

16   *History of the Diocese of Raphoe* (hereafter *H.D.R.*), vol. II, p. 241.

17   The above is abridged from the National Museum of Ireland *Archaeological acquisitions in the year 1959* (1961) pp. 58-64.

18   National Museum of Ireland, E 33: 1385.

19   The Work of Angels Exhibition, Item 152.

20   Ibid., Item 180, pp. 190-91. National Museum of Ireland, E 33: 621.

21   National Museum of Ireland, 1963: 18.

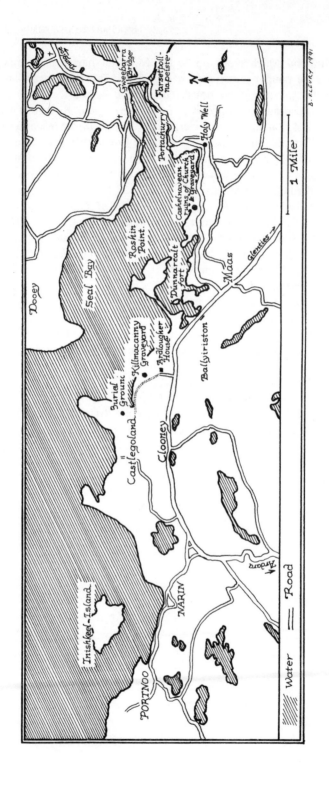

Portnoo · Narin · Inishkeel Island · Portinoo · Clooney · Castlegoland · Burial Ground · Killmacanny Graveyard · Ardlougher House · Ballyiriston · Dooey · Seal Bay · Roshin Point · Dunnarealt Fort · Maas · Glenties → · Castlenaveen ruins of Church & graveyard · Holy Well · Portachurry · Farsetpoll-na-peiste · Gweebarra Bridge · Ardara →

B. FLEURY 1991

N

1 Mile

≈ Water   Road

II

From the Gweebarra Bridge to Narin

E NOW CROSS the Gweebarra river. The present Gweebarra bridge was built in 1953, replacing an iron bridge which had served the people for the previous fifty years.[1] This iron bridge was built by the Congested Districts Board "in order to shorten by something like seven miles the drive for the country folk from the far side to Glenties".[2] Before the present bridge was built passengers had to get out of their cars when crossing the old iron bridge; the driver of the car then drove across while the passengers walked over and got back in the car on the far side. So my older brothers and sister tell me anyhow: I would not be old enough to re-member that far back! Before the time of the present bridge and certainly before the time of the iron bridge, crossing the Gweebarra was not so easy. When Pococke, in 1752, came to the Gweebarra he crossed it in a curragh while the horses swam the river. John O'Donovan, crossing in 1835, gives a vivid account: "We made towards the ferry; and the tide being far out, we had to walk over a considerable extent of strand. ... But the water being shallow they could bring the boat not nearer than a perch to the dry sand. We had not time to strip, and stripping off shoes and stockings was useless, as we saw that the depth of the water required more, so on we dashed with shoes and clothes into the brine and embarked vexatiously wet. We soon ap-proached the Iniskeel side, but the ferry boat which is of considerable size, could not be brought very near the bank. Taking my bundle of papers, I sprang out of the boat with an intention of gaining dry land, but landing on my left leg on a round stone I sprained my ankle."[3]

The difficulties presented to earlier travellers by rivers such as the Gweebarra is referred to by McParlan in 1802: "As the mountain region com-

mences at Killybegs, and accompanies the ocean all around those parts of
the county, it would be nearly endless to numerate all the rivers that have indented their traces on its face; most of these indentures are dry in fair
weather, but in times of rain and flood are not only full, but overflowing. The
largest of those are Gweedore and Gweebarra, and are of all the rest the
most remarkable for annoying those who have the good fortune of travelling
this region."[4]

Travelling was obviously difficult in those days but improvements were
being made; from 1786 we read: "There are neither roads, quays or other
conveniences in the road to the Rosses; it is true that the road is scarcely
passable from Killybegs to the Rosses, but Col. B. Conyngham has made a
new road across the mountains from Mount Charles, by the ford of
Guybarrow, which shortens the distance 15 miles. In the course of the
summer a bridge will be built over this river."[5]

The bridge was built; it was part of the grandiose improvement plan carried out by William Burton Conyngham (1733-96) who had inherited the
Conyngham properties in Donegal. The bridge was built at Doochary and the
Mount Charles road continued on to Burtonport (i.e. Burton's Port). The
road when completed was declared to be one of the finest in Ireland. Its
building had been regarded by all the gentry of the county as impractical,
and its sucessful completion gained for Burton Conyngham the reputation of
being a very excellent engineer.[6] Along the new road Burton Conyngham established three inns at, apparently, Doochary (25km from Mount Charles),
Dungloe, and Leckbeg; and at Dungloe he built a market town to serve the
Rosses.[7]

By William Burton Conyngham's time the English had gained control
over this area. However, until the Flight of the Earls in 1607 which brought
an end to the old Gaelic order, they knew very little of their social domain.
At Inquisitions, held to gather information on the old Gaelic way of life, in
Derry on 16 April 1611, we see that they had heard of the Gweebarra ferry,
but didn't know much about it: "Of the several ferrys called Portnunker and
Goybera al' Gothbera the jury knowe nothinge." They then grant to a John
Browne the power and authority "To settle and establish several ferries or
passages" including "One other ferry at or near Litter Mc Warde in the said
co' of Donegall, over the lough or river of Govbera al' Gothbera in
Dallilogh".[8]

When one has come off the Gweebarra bridge the road veers to the right
and almost immediately there is a second bridge under which the seawater
goes and forms a pool away over amongst the trees on the left. This large
lagoon is called *Farset-poll-na-péiste* [*fearsaid*: a sandbar formed near the

mouth of a river, by the opposing currents of tide and stream; *poll*: a hole; topographically it usually means a very deep spot in a river or lake; *péist*: a worm, a beast, in this case a sea-serpent]. Legend has it that one day St. Conall and St. Brendan (Brennain) were travelling up the Gweebarra on a boat and they were attacked by a sea-serpent. The serpent struck St. Brendan with its tail and killed him instantly. The spot where St. Brendan is reputedly buried is still known as *Uaimh Naomh Brennain*: the grave of St. Brendan. The sea-monster then made its way into the deep hole now known as *Poll Na Péiste* and "she sunk there because they say there is no bottom to it".[9]

Dragon-creatures, such as this *péist mhór*, "all originally of serpent nature and spawned by the sea, swarm in popular myth from remotest antiquity to the present, from the far eastern ocean to the western". In Ireland these dragons or *péisteanna* were, according to Christian legend, not driven from Erin by Patrick like the lesser reptiles but were imprisoned by his order, apparently not always obeyed, in the waters where they lived.[10]

It is unlikely[11] that there was a St. Brendan in this area. His name probably crept into oral folklore here as part of the saint's legend – a large body of fabulous and incredible stories surrounding the maritime adventures of St. Brendan, who was the patron saint of the *Ciarraige* or ancient people of Kerry, but whose chief monastery was founded at Clonfert, just west of the Shannon, in Co. Galway. We are dealing here with the cult of Brendan the Navigator, founded on written works[12] of approximately the 9th century, and spread among all the maritime people of the west. However I would like to point out that a St. Conall is honoured at Killconnell, also at Clonfert in Co. Galway. Coincidence?

There are a number of interesting references to sea-monsters which resemble whales in Manus O'Donnell's book on the life of Colmcille – *Betha Colaim Chille*[13] – which he wrote in the year 1532. This book is full of vivid and imaginative stories about St. Columba which do not exist in the much earlier book entitled *The Life of St. Columba*[14] written by Adamnán (Eunan), the 9th abbot of Iona (Hy), towards the end of the 7th century and edited by William Reeves, D.D., in 1875. Many of these stories about St. Colmcille are obviously works of imagination, layers of legend which attached to Colmcille over the centuries; however, they make interesting reading.

In Manus O'Donnell's book we read: "There is a frightful beast in the sea called Rochuaidh, and when it speweth to landward it is a sign that there will be sickness and disease in every land that year. And when it belcheth upward it is a sign that there will be great storms that year and many deaths among the birds in the air; and when it disgorgeth downward into the sea there will be many deaths that year among the fishes and the beasts of the sea."[15]

We further read, when Colmcille and his companions were on the way to Iona: "and then they saw a monstrous beast rising out of the sea; and not more vast to them seemed a mountain peak than seemed she; and she raised a storm and a great tempest in the sea round about them, so that the boat was in peril of sinking therefrom. And great fear fell on Colmcille's folk, and they besought him to pray God for them to bring them out of the great danger that they were in."[16]

We continue along the Gweebarra and where the road turns suddenly to the left there is a little minor road going off down to the right. This goes down to the quay which was the site of the lower ferry across the Gweebarra, before the bridge was built. This quay-side was called Portachurry (Port of Curraghs – remember that the "ferry" originally consisted of your being rowed across in a curragh). Patrick MacGill, the writer who was born near by in the townland of Kilkenny, refers to this ford in his book *The Rat-Pit*. He describes the heroine, Nora Ryan, crossing with other women from Dungloe to Glenties[17] with their knitting.

"The kneeling women rose from their knees and hurried towards the channel in the bay, now a thin string of water barely three yards in width. The wind, piercingly cold, no longer carried its burden of sleet, and the east, icily clear, waited, almost in suspense, for the first tint of the sun. The soil, black on the foreshore, cracked underfoot and pained the women as they walked. None wore their shoes, although three or four carried brogues tied round their necks. Most had mairteens (double-thick stockings) on their feet, and these, though they retained a certain amount of body heat, kept out no wet. In front the old woman, all skin and bones and more bones than skin, whom Norah had wakened, led the way, her breath steaming out into the air and her feet sinking almost to the knees at every step. From her dull, lifeless look and the weary eyes that accepted everything with fatalistic calm it was plain that she had passed the greater part of her years in suffering.

"All the women had difficulty with the wet and shifty sand, which, when they placed their feet heavily on one particular spot, rose in an instant to their knees. They floundered across, pulling out one foot and then another, and grunting whenever they did so. Norah Ryan, the child, had little difficulty; she glided lightly across, her feet barely sinking to the ankles...

"The sun was nearing the horizon, and the women, now on the verge of the channel ... stood in silence looking at the water. It was not at its lowest yet; probably they would have to wait for five minutes, maybe more. And as they waited they came closer and closer to one another for warmth...

"'It's time that we were trying to face the water in the name of God,' said one of the women, who supported herself against a neighbour's shoulder whilst she took off her mairteens. 'There is a low tide now.'

"All mairteens were taken off, and raising their petticoats well up and tying them tightly around their waists they entered the water. The old woman leading the party walked into the icy sea placidly; the others faltered a moment, then stepped in recklessly and in a second the water was well up to their thighs. They hurried across shouting carelessly, gesticulating violently and laughing loudly. Yet every one of them, with the possible exception of the woman in front, was on the borderland of tears. If they had spoken not they would have wept."[18]

Continuing, we descend a steep hill, at the bottom of which, on the left, is a little sign marked "Holy Well". This is *Tobar na Faoileoige* [*tobar*: a well; *faoileog*: a seagull; the well of the seagulls. A little inlet of the sea almost encroaches on to the road on the right-hand side here]. People from along the Gweebarra, while on their way home after doing the Inishkeel *turas*, usually stopped here to pray. This well was frequented by earlier generations in the hope of gaining relief from toothache, giving rise to the local suggestion that its proper name is *Tobar na Fiacaile* [*fiacal*: a tooth].

Our next stop is in the townland of Kilkenny. Taking the dirt track at the side of Quinn's house, and closing the gates behind you, you come down at the water's edge to the remains of an old church and graveyard, surrounded by the partial remains of an enclosure, marked "Cashelnavean" on the Ordnance Survey map - a name - *Caiseal na bhFiann* - which reminds us of the legendary epic warrior Fionn, of *na Fianna* fame, whom we noted earlier having a taste for the venison from the woods further up the Gweebarra.

The Archaeological Survey informs us: "To the N. and W. of this graveyard is the outline of a curving enclosure. Most of a semicircle can be seen. No sign of the enclosure could be found to the E. and S. but the modern graveyard and church would have stood roughly at the centre of such a circle had this been originally complete."[19] This later church may well have been built on the site of an early Christian habitation, since, as we will note again later, early Christians often built their basic hermitages within existing enclosures, making use of the protection - against nature and possible foe - afforded by such as the cashel which stood here. Since we assume that our early Christian missionaries travelled along the coast in small boats, this site would have been attractive to them.

But who built his hermitage here and left us the name Kilkenny [*Cill Chainnigh*, the Church of Cainnech]? Dr. Maguire, writing in 1920, felt it was the same person who gave his name to Kilkenny city:

"That St. Cainech was identical with the patron of Ossory is more than probable, for his association with Columba in Clonard and in Iona, and the meagre facts known to us of his early life, are suggestive and confirmatory of the assumption that he founded a monastery here. This famous saint was born in Kianacht, near Dungiven, in 517, and next to Baithen was Columba's most intimate and favoured companion. While Columba was founding monasteries in all parts of Tirconaill, St. Canice settled down in the neighbourhood of Conal Caol's celebrated monastery, to prepare himself and his disciples for their projected mission among the Scottish Picts. 'Eighty-four years was his age when he sent his spirit to heaven, A.D. 598,'[20] says O'Clery in the *Donegal Martyrology*, at his feast-day, the 11th of October, but he is careful to add, 'There are three other Cainechs'..."[21]

This last statement, "There are three other Cainechs",[22] allied to the fact that there are Kilkennys also in counties Westmeath and Sligo, leads us into deep water. Suffice to say here that over the centuries the monks who wrote and rewrote the lists of Irish saints' feast-days, coming across references to saints with the same name in very different areas of the country, presumed them to be different people. What they were often dealing with, and possibly what we have here at Kilkenny, is a cult system, whereby an illustrious saint's reputation was spread to various outlying areas by his later followers, and because these followers used the example and acts and miracles of the saint to help spread the word, the great man's name was immortalised in folklore and legend while his followers, who actually toiled in the area, were consigned to oblivion.

So who is celebrated here? Is it Cainnech, born in Co. Derry, companion of St. Columba (Colmcille), and patron of Kilkenny city (Ossory). Possibly; his cult may have spread to this area, leaving us the placenames Kilkenny and Kilmacanny - the latter is another old ecclesiastical site further along this coast which we will reach soon. But in an intriguing piece of writing[23] in 1983, Pádraig Ó Riain, one of the foremost experts on early Irish saints, goes back into the mists of time and concludes that Cainnech was an alias for Colmcille. He states that Cainnech "was clearly the subject of a widespread cult among the early Ulaid"[24] - an ancient people who inhabited counties Down and Antrim - and that his supposed Derry origin "may simply reflect the fact that this district had become the principal northern centre of Cainnech's cult". He argues that the name Cainnech originated as Colm and that the cult of the latter, as it spread, divided into many names: Colmán, otherwise Mocholmóc (mo-cholm-óc)[25]; Cumma(e), Mochumma(e), Caimme; Cuimmín; Conna(e), a hypocoristic form of Colmán; Mochanna (mo-chonna); Conna, Coinne, Caine, Cainnech.

The names which we nowadays give to some of our early saints are often different from the names attached to them in their own lifetime. Many of them, while they lived, were known by the hypocoristic or "pet" form of their names. But why did Adamnán [Eunan], who died *c.* 704, not refer to these alternative forms of Colm's (died *c.* 597) name in his book *Life of St. Columba*? Because when Adamnán received his linguistic training the formation of hypocoristic forms of names had already died out. Adamnán's *Life of St. Columba* has always been seen as a solid rock in the sea of uncertainty which the study of early Irish saints comprises, because it was written relatively soon after Columba's (Colmcille's) floruit.[26] But one senses shifting sand concerning the *Life of St. Columba* in the writings of Ó Riain when he quotes the most recent editors[27] of the *Life*, who state that Adamnán's real value "is less for the history of Columba than for his own ideas and for the circumstances of his own time" and then himself adds: "With a floruit in the late seventh century, Adamnán (*ob.* 704) might have been separated from Columba (*ob.* 597) by as many years again for all the real difference it would have made to the quality of his sources."[28] So what hope have we in identifying early Irish saints correctly in this day and age! The study of the surviving writings on saints, a science known as hagiography, is indeed treacherous terrain, especially for the amateur.

The Kilkenny church was obviously an important unit in the old extensive Catholic parish of Inishkeel. Dr. Maguire writes that it "was vastly more accessible and, we may fairly presume, vastly more frequented, than the parent church on the island." The old Inishkeel parish, being a very large[29] parish, paid the largest episcopal tribute of any of the parishes in the diocese and "The Bishop was evidently accustomed to visit this parish frequently, in ancient as in modern days, the outstanding point of difference being that, in the good old times, he was accompanied by a retinue of from fifty to two hundred attendants, all of whom were entitled to free and lavish entertainment at the expense of the parish."[30]

Dr. Maguire goes on to state that "Kilkenny ... was the chief centre of worship down to 1609, when it was forcibly annexed by the plundering Planters."[31] Dr. Pococke, having crossed the Gweebarra - you will remember, by curragh, with the horses swimming across - passed by here in 1752 and wrote: "From the Ferry I went westwards along the Strand, and passed under an old Church called Kilkenny, a chapel of Ease to Enniskeel."[32] This church continued to be used for Protestant service until the Glenties church was erected for that purpose in 1825.[33]

Within the old graveyard here at Kilkenny stands a memorial stone erected to the memory of the late Dr. Dermot Campbell, born 10 October 1942.

While holidaying abroad he disappeared when swimming offshore on 19 August 1980 and his body was never recovered. Dermot was immensely liked by the people of the Ardara area - a doyen of his profession, his greatest gift was that he was seen to be "the ordinary man's doctor" - and he will never be forgotton by those whose lives he touched. It is fitting that his memorial was erected at this spot by his wife Evelyn because he loved rambling - especially birdwatching - along the Gweebarra estuary. *Ar dheis Dé go raibh sé.*

As you continue along the coast road you will notice that your eyes are continually attracted by the expanse of the Gweebarra estuary on your right - the changing moods and colours, the seabirds, the indented coastline. That long hook of land, a rabbit's delight, snaking out into the estuary from this side is Roshin Point.[34] Further on is O'Boyle's (a surname we will meet frequently on our travels) island and beyond the glittering sands of Dooey is Seal Bay. The Gweebarra estuary has a resident community of common seals, numbering 120-40. The officers of the Wildlife Service keep a watchful eye on their well being. The common seal does not grow as big as the grey seal whose habitat is out under the cliffs of the coastline.[35]

With their human-shaped heads and doleful eyes seals are fascinating to watch. But I'm not the first person to discover this! Monk Gibbon, who was a frequent visitor to this area, writing in 1935, states: "I have seen the seals one very hot day in September. Only a mile from the house a steep pyramid of sand guards the narrow entrance to the Gweebarra estuary; through this the tide flows with such force that it is really dangerous for a boat at any time except extreme slack water. ...

"From this pyramid one looks up the estuary for five miles to the spot where the Gweebarra bridge spans the river. This is one of the finest views in the world, equal to the bay of Palermo, equal to that superb view from Virgil's tomb across the bay to Vesuvius and Sorrento. There is no city in the foreground here, no reminder of man at all except the white cottages dotted about the hillside irregularly. ... On the opposite side is a beach, so magnificently wide, so completely deserted, that the thought of crossing to it lingers in the mind like a pilgrimage long intended. I have never seen a human soul on this beach. ... The place is called Seal Bay. In very hot weather, we have been told, the seals come and lie out on the great beach on the far side, basking in the sunlight." Having crossed over he goes on: "I catch sight of a black head in the water and presently the seal splashes again about twenty yards up the channel, for the tide is partly out. ... Only then do I look round me carefully and discover a dozen or more companions lying on the different rocks about seventy yards out in the channel. ... They have dragged themselves out of the water and are lying on the lower ledges of the little islets and on the rocks bared by the tide, basking in the sun ... some are glossy black, others are pale brown, or yellow, or silver-grey, according to the time that they have been out of the water. I can hear them grunting, a deep gurgling 'wuffling' sound, and presently an old bull seal lifts his head and gives a tremendous roar, perhaps of challenge. ... There is a huge silver-grey seal on the point of rock nearest me; behind, a little above it, are four younger seals whose coats are a pale yellowy brown. Extraordinarily mild and melancholy eyes gaze at me across the intervening stretch of water from under the brown overhanging fur. When the fur dries and the sleek black glossiness of the head in the water is gone, the whole head takes on an almost human semblance because of these great wistful contemplative eyes. The seals might be fellow souls brooding on the mystery of infinity."[36]

We leave this idyllic setting and continue on to Maas, where a road goes off to the left to Glenties, but we stay to the right. The name Maas is derived from the Gaelic *más*: a thigh, here indicating a long, low or thigh-shaped hill. After a few hundred metres a very minor path goes off down to the right to the strand; this is a nice walk when the tide is out, especially in the initial stages where the "bent" - covered land - resounds to the staccatto sounds of disturbed wildlife. The little circular rocky island standing starkly before you out on the strand is called *Dún na Reált* - The Fort of the Star - surely a striking title. There is evidence of a built-up cashel on part of the perimeter of the little island. It is regarded as a "gentle" place (i.e. frequented by fairies) and people have been said to have disappeared into its hollows and never been seen again.

Passing over the little bridge, where at high tide the water threatens to engulf the road from both sides, we pass through Ballyeristin[37] and proceed up the hill and on to the straight road. Do you see that big house on the crest of the hill away up to the right? Well, it was up this lane and past this big house, Ardlougher House [*árd*: high; *luachair*: rushes, sedge; the height of the rushes], that the old road to Narin–Portnoo used to go. It continued down to the base of Ardlougher, where it is still visible sweeping down the side of the hill, skirted the strand (it is seen crossing the strand in Taylor and Skinner's map of 1777), continued over through Castlegoland, passing behind the late Charlie Gallagher's (of whom more later) house and Bernie McNelis's, went north of the Glebe House, and on towards Portnoo. Under the Grand Jury system, the equivalent of the present-day County Council until its abolition by the Local Government Act of 1898, there was a spate of road building and road improvements in this area in the second half of the 18th century and it was during this time that the new road through Clooney was built. On 24 March 1760[38] Richard Nesbitt and James Maxwell were appointed as road overseers in the Inishkeel (parish) area. In 1772 a new road was started from the Bellanagoal bridge (at Shovlin's thatched house at Beagh) to Narin; a new road to Rosbeg was under construction; £37.10 was paid to James Maxwell himself (he lived at Castlegoland) "for damage he sustained by a cut of new road drawn through his land".[39] This is the present-day road through Clogher and Clooney.

Halfway down the far side of Ardlougher Hill and facing out towards the Gweebarra is a shrub- and bracken-covered mound, the old ecclesiastical site known as Kilmacanny. There are a number of grave markers on the mound. One slab on the west side has a small oval perforation. Lying in a drain to the south-east of the mound is a small cross slab, 1.6 m. x .3 m. at the arms, and on one face is a simple cross in relief at the centre of a broad cross-shaped groove.[40] It is thought that in the past people were carrying this cross-incised slab away from the original mound, possibly going to use it for building purposes, and it being too heavy they abandoned it in the drain where it still lies.

Peter McHugh, who owns this land and who has been very helpful to me, told me that when he was young the land around the mound was ploughed up annually and that they would frequently unearth skeletons, which they immediately re-interred.

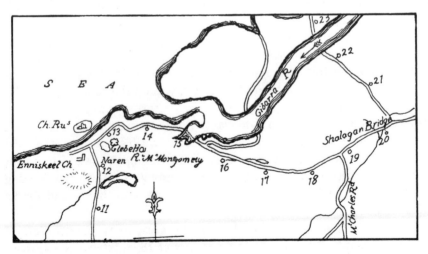

Detail from Taylor and Skinner's map of 1777,
showing the old route crossing the strand below Ardlougher

I find Kilmacanny a very interesting site, not least because we know so little about it. Are there any hints to its past history? William Harkin, writing in 1893, states: "near Ardlogher House, the residence of Patrick Gallagher, J. P., is a celebrated well with a flagstone at the bottom, on which there is said to be an inscription, probably Ogham, which has not been deciphered."[41] I have not found the well and consequently not the incribed stone; the well was probably covered in over the years. However it is unlikely that there was an Ogham-inscribed slab here, as Ogham is generally found more to the south and east of Ireland, in the broad region most affected by the Roman-inspired spread of Christanity (in 431 there was a small Christian mission to Ireland, inspired from Rome, that of Palladius and his followers[42]) rather than in the areas where the introduction of Christianity was British inspired (around the middle of the 5th century there was a second mission – Patrick's – to the north of Ireland and inspired from what is now the north of England[43]). After all "Ogham was a native stroke-writing ... using tally sticks and the Roman numeral system of incremental strokes, as a main inspiration, and had at least one inventor familiar with Latin grammatical theory."[44]

Possibly the clue to Kilmacanny is the stone with the hole through it. Stones with holes through them were very important in pagan Ireland.

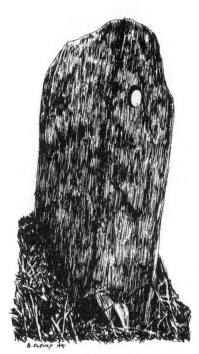

Kilmacanny holed stone

Bargains were made, contracts cemented or marriage engagements sealed while the contracting parties held hands or touched fingers through the hole in the stone. It is possible, with a lot of imagination, to see this site as being an important meeting place before the arrival of Christianity. One could visualise those early people who travelled along the Gweebarra and the west coast of Donegal by boat coming to this site on regular occasions and making their contracts between one another. Yet the small circumference of the hole and its situation out towards the edge of the stone would suggest that the perforation is of no importance; possibly it is just a geological fault. Isabel Crozier, a respected archaeologist who visited this site in 1938 and again in 1957, states that the holed stone is probably 8th or 9th century.[45] However, it is difficult to see how one could come to any definite conclusion about its dating.

Nevertheless it is interesting to mention a few of the traditions associated with stones which had larger holes through them. Describing a stone in Co. Antrim, in 1878, a fisherman said he knew of the practice of clothes being drawn through the aperture in a stone for curing sore limbs and in Co. Cork a man who lived near a perforated stone stated that "women used to draw clothes through the hole" when approaching their confinement, in order to secure a favourable result.[46]

But we stray. It is likely that Kilmacanny's niche is that of an early Columban settlement. Dr. Maguire thinks that the founder of this site was Mochonna, brother of St. Mura of Fahan (near Buncrana), but I would suggest that in *Cill Mo Cainnigh* (or, more correctly, *Cill Mo Chonna*) we are again dealing with a hypocoristic form of the name Colm (Columba, Colmcille) just as we were at nearby Kilkenny (*Cill Chainnigh*).

If you continue down the old road by the side of Kilmacanny, and pass Castlegoland strand, you have the large expanse of a rabbit warren on the seaward side. There are the remains of a small cemetery down close to the water's edge. In earlier days bodies were brought from far and near to be buried on nearby Inishkeel island. But because the island was only approachable at certain times of the month when the strand cleared after a spring tide, and because there would be other times, even if one tried to go out by boat, when the sea would be too rough, there were chosen sites around this whole area where bodies were buried when it was impossible to take the remains out to the sacred island. It is said that some of these burials were only temporary and that after some days or weeks the bodies were exhumed and brought out to the island and reburied. However, I am sure that many of these bodies were interred for eternity in these so-called temporary graveyards. This site down behind Castlegoland strand, in an area called

Meenagoland, is marked now by only a few barely discernible gravestones, the whole area having been covered up by sand over the years.

We continue on the main road, which passes through Clooney [*An Chluanaidh*; *cluain*: an insulated (i.e. water on two of its three sides) meadow[47]; the word *cluain* is present in 1,800 placenames in Ireland] and Clogher [*Clochar*: a stoney place, *cloch*: a stone; there are forty-five Cloghers in Ireland and the word forms a part of forty-two other placenames]. The little road going off to the left, past the thatched cottage, leads to Clooney wood and Loughfad; we will approach this area later from the Kilclooney church road. But now we turn right at the Garda barracks and go down briefly to Castlegoland [*Caiseal Gualann*; *caiseal*: a stone enclosure, derived from the Latin *castellum*; *gualann*: a shoulder, referring to a prominent hill which overlooks the coastal plain].

One person whom my generation associates with Castlegoland is the late Charlie Gallagher, who died in recent years.[48] I had a long chat with Charlie at his home on 5 August 1983. Charlie's great-grandfather was known as Proinnseas Mór. He is said to have come from Co. Tyrone and was the first member of the family to settle in Castlegoland: he built the present house. Proinnseas Mór had three sons, Patrick, William and Neil. The family farm was divided between the three brothers, two in Castlegoland proper and the other in nearby Ardlougher. Each of Proinnseas Mór's three sons had very large families of twelve to fourteen children and a school was built below Ardlougher Hill for the Gallagher children to be educated; the remains of the school are still visible. The children of the three brothers filled the little school on their own. Both German and French were taught to them in this school, and from the Ardlougher house came three Gallagher priests, Father James, who is buried in Rathmullan, and Father Frank and Father Hugh who are buried in Dungloe.

Charlie stated that there used to be a small castle in this area and that numerous English coins of the reign of King George had been found. There had formerly been a large deer-park in Castlegoland and he pointed out a few remaining pillars with high ditches over beside Loch Salt. These pillars had had gates on them. There were gates going into each of the separate deer-parks and the gates and ditches were used to keep the deer in. He pointed out the site of two "kitchen middens" (these are early habitation sites along the coast) near his home. He also mentioned that the large field extending away to the east had been called Gallantroman [*gallán*: a pillar stone, derived from the word *Gall* – it had formerly been believed that pillar stones had first been erected in Ireland by the Gauls; *tromán*: a diminutive of *tromm* – an elder tree or a place producing elder, a bore tree]. Possibly the correct name here is *Garraí an tromán* [*garraí*: a garden or park], but it is definitely pronounced Gallantroman. Charlie also pointed out two ruined dolmens on the hillside behind his house. He stated that there used to be an old[49] village called Claggan[50] on the hillside behind his house and that the people had been banished from this village and resettled in Clooney in Penal times.

Having had a peep through the keyhole at Castlegoland's intriguing, but now, sadly, lost history, we continue towards Narin. We have the plain of Clooney away to our right, with Clooney Lough and the golfcourse evident. With Boleymore[51] and Irishtown on our right we climb up into the townland of Narin where we have a panoramic view of Croey Head stretching out towards Arranmore island, with Roaninish island out on the horizon. We catch our first glimpse, just out from Narin strand, of historic Inishkeel island, forever associated with Conall Caol. An area of the sea, between Inishkeel and Croey Head, where you see the waves rolling in and then breaking up, is known to the fishermen, who avoid it, as *Boilg Chonaill*. This underwater shelf derives its name from the Gaelic word *boilg*, a bellows, and denotes an area of the sea where the waves break and spout up water.

What does the name Narin mean? Does it derive from *An Fhearthainn*: rain? This is the generally accepted view. There is a 17th century poem written by Nuala Ní Dhónaill[52] of which the 10th verse is written as:

Is aoibhinn aoibhinn Leitir Mhic a' Bhaird,
Oileán sáimh Innse Caoil,
Cill Túruis na ndumhchann bán,
Is sruth na trágha le n-a thaoibh.

The first line refers to Lettermacaward, an area we have already skirted, the second line to the island of Inishkeel, and the third and fourth lines to Kiltoorish which we have yet to meet on our travels. In an article in the *Donegal Annual* of 1970 one of our more learned Gaelic scholars, Niall Ó Dónaill, points out that in the original version the second line read "*Is Fearann sámh Inse Caoil*" rather than "*Oileán sáimh Innse Caoil*" [*Oileán*: an island; *fearann*: domain, farm, grounds]. In its topographical use *fearann* is applied to a particular portion of land or territory.[53] It often forms the first part of a placename in which the latter part is formed by a personal or family name, commemorating former possessors,[54] e.g. Farranmacbride in Glencolumbkille. Consequently one gets a sense of a *fearann* being part of a unit or belonging to a person or place, as in *Fearann sámh Inse Caoil*, the tranquil *fearann*[55] of Inishkeel.

We are discussing the word *fearann* because it is possible that it is the basis for the name Narin. Under what other guise does Narin seem to appear in 17th-century references? In 1608[56] we read of "Farehan" (suggesting *fearthainn*: rain); in 1620[57] we note "Farhni" and, alternatively, "Farni"; in 1642[58] it is listed as "Farine al' Arrine" and as "Farrhine al' Arrine"; in 1642[59] we read twice of a "quarter called Farhyn" (surely *fearann*). Niall Ó Dónaill seems in no doubt about the earlier version of the name Narin – "*Ar Fhearann Inse Caoil a bheirtear an Fheárthainn anois*[60] – *Fearann Inse Caoil* is now called Narin."

It is also of interest that in the Down Survey maps of 1659 the Narin area in general is mapped as church land and is named "Maghereymannagh" – *Machaire Manach* – the plain of the monks. This included the coastal plain and "The Sandy Hills and Mountaines of ye quarter of Maghereymannagh". Presumably *Fearann Inse Caoil* would roughly correspond to this same area of church land.

However I must point out that the learned Niall Ó Dónaill's comments were limited to an article in which he was revising the text of a 17th century Gaelic poem; his priority at the time of writing was not a close examination of the meaning of the placename Narin. So, on our behalf, I requested an in-depth analysis of the placename Narin from Dónall Mac Giolla Easpaig, an expert in placenames in the Ordnance Survey in Dublin. He agrees that there was an original initial *F-* and that the final *-n* of the definite article *an* subsequently became attached to the initial of the name. He continues: "If one was to ignore the rest of the evidence, Narin could be explained as being derived from a form such as *ar an Fhearann*. However, this evidence is crucial in reconstructing the original form. Neither the documentary evidence nor the present pronunciation of the name by native speakers is compatible with *fearann*. Both of these sources are fairly consistent in showing a 'h'[61] sound after the internal 'r'. In addition, the pronunciation clearly indicates a final slender '- nn'. Taking the evidence as a whole, we may confidently say that the original form of the name was *An Fhearthainn*. So much for the form, what of the meaning? *Fearthainn* is the more common word for 'rain' in Donegal Irish, but *báisteach* does occur. In origin, however, *fearthainn* is the verbal noun of the verb *fearaim* which had a broad spectrum of meaning in the early language: 'grant, supply, provide', 'give forth, pour', 'do, perform'. The placename, *An Fhearthainn*, therefore, probably did not mean 'rain' at all, but could have any of the attested, or indeed unattested, meanings of the verb *fearaim*. The name could as equally mean a 'grant (of land)', or a 'gushing forth' as in a stream. It is worth noting that we have a name with similar meaning to *An Fhearthainn* in Donegal. I am referring to Frosses, *Na Frasa*, which is the plural of the word *fras* meaning 'shower', an unlikely meaning in the context of placenames."

In 1864 we read that "Naran is a primitive little fishing village, pleasantly situated opposite the island of Inishkeel, on which the antiquary will find a couple of ruined churches. The hills which rise just behind the village should be ascended for the sake of the magnificent view, particularly in the direction of Ardara, where the coast-scenery of the cliffs is of the highest order. The whole of the promontory between Naran and Ardara, is worth exploring for the sake of the remains."[62]

It is encouraging for those of us who are interested in our heritage, when arriving into Narin, to find that the restaurant in the hostelry on the left, known as the "Narin Inn", is called "The Dolmen Restaurant". This refers to the large Kilclooney portal tomb which we will see later on our travels. It is pleasing to find that the name of the local drama group is "The Dallán Forgaill Players", a reference to the ancient St. Dallán Forgaill whom we will be discussing on the island of Inishkeel.

The area around Narin has its own interest for us. From 1896 we read: "Recently, while some visitors from Raphoe were inspecting the sandhills at Narin, a small village on the western coast, they uncovered a prehistoric grave of the usual cist type. ... Inside were found two very well preserved skeletons, one beneath the other. The upper measured 5' 3" in length, and the lower appeared somewhat smaller. ... There are, evidently, other graves in these hills, and a thorough examination of them might yield some good results. Among them, at the same time, were picked up ... a large number of flints, most of these being well chipped to arrow-heads and 'scraped' patterns. The skulls of the skeletons were removed, and, with all the other objects, are now in the possession of Mr. C. Porter, Raphoe."[63]

People lived among the sand dunes of Narin in very early times. We have already mentioned two of these early habitation sites (kitchen middens) at Castlegoland. Other similar sites which we will meet later on are at Loughros More – out behind Magheramore – and especially at Maghera. We will discuss sandhill settlements in more detail when we reach Maghera. In the meantime, back to the Narin sandhills. From 1914 we read: "A considerable quantity of flint was found here in the hollows of the sandhills. ... Many (of the flints) were nicely dressed, into knives, with handles, and these occurred in large quantities. ... Bones and teeth of the ox, pig, and sheep, and shells of oyster, cockle, limpet, and periwinkle were found, and furnished evidence as to the food of these people."[64]

From 1802 we come across a reference to lead mines at Narin and to the presence of lead ore "near Portnew, in Boylagh". The writer also mentions that lead ore was "rich at Mullentyboyle, in Glantice. It had been worked in the memory of some old people, by Sir Albert Conyngham, but was desisted from, owing to the influx into the pits of the Onea river, under whose level the pits happened to be."[65]

It's time we started down towards the strand, on our way out to Inishkeel, because I think the tide is on the turn! Just before we reach the beach, opposite Peter Shovlin's cafe and close to the rocks where a little cottage now stands, is a spot which is called Churchtown. On the Ordnance Survey maps we find the words "Church, site of" and "graveyard (disused)" marked on this headland overlooking Narin strand. The word Churchtown no longer figures in local nomenclature, and an older name still, "Maghernakilla", is completely forgotten. The building in question was a church of the Protestant faith and is referred to in church records as the "New Church of St. James, consecrated July 25th, 1724." The parish plate consisted of a communion plate bearing the date 1724, as well as a chalice, flagon and paten of silver – "The gift of Sir Henry Caldwell to ye Church of Iniskeel, September 1st 1724."[66]

Earlier, in 1622 (shortly after the Plantation), the Select Vestry of the Established Church decided, since the church on Inishkeel island was unfit for use, to transfer Divine Service to Kildowns (Kiltoorish). We read: "The ancient parish church being ruinated in former time built in an island into a great arm of the sea and, therefore, innaccesible by the water is fitting to be transferred to Kildowns in the midst of the said parish where there is already a Chapel of Ease."[67] Service continued at Kiltoorish until 1723 when the vestry again gave its "consent to remove Church to Mackrickiel" (*Machaire na Cille*), which is the Churchtown at Narin referred to above.

Right, on to the beach. And what a beach! Its hard to do it justice in words, but Monk Gibbon, writing in 1935, comes close: "There is something magnificently rhythmic about the sweep of this beach. I know of no other with such a triumphant curve. Looking across at the huge crescent of yellow sand, with the dunes crowned with pale green sea-rushes rising behind, earth and ocean seem to have come to some mutual and lovely agreement. There is no encroachment, only complete harmony. It is as though land flowed into sea, rather than sea into land. In only one other place that I have seen is there the same effect. Naxos,[68] with its orange and lemon groves on the site of that lost Greek city, flows out equally effortlessly into the blue waters of the Mediterranean."[69]

When you walk on to Narin strand (and hopefully we are going to prevent cars getting on to this beach from 1992) there is a stone sticking out of the sand and on it is written, "Keep the Beach Clean". In some years this stone is completely covered by sand and at other times part of the stone is exposed. The injunction was painted on the stone by the Rev. Canon Cormac

Lloyd a few decades ago. When I was a child the Barrett family gave donkey rides to children on the beach and we used to get on the donkey by standing up on the stone. It is known locally as the "riding stone", but what many people do not realise is that this is possibly an ancient and significant standing stone. It is marked on the revised Ordnance Survey map of 1847-50 as the "Maghernakilla Standing Stone". We noted earlier that "Maghernakilla" applied to Churchtown in an earlier age. It appears in the Inquisition of 1642 as *Magherykill al'*[70] *Sranadarragh* and as *Magheryoghill*. Maghernakilla is derived from *machaire*: a plain, and *cill*: a church; the plain of the church. It applies to the area from the old church site at Churchtown along through the Narin sandhills.

Isn't it sad that the top of this standing stone on Narin beach was shattered in 1990, having survived for countless years. The practice of allowing cars on to the beach was surely a factor in its being damaged.

With the passing centuries the sea has gradually eaten into the sandbanks at Narin. In former times the land would have extended out much further, closer to Inishkeel island, and tradition has it that in fairly recent times one could throw a stone across from the mainland on to the island. The Maghernakilla standing stone would probably have been firmly implanted on dry land and not on the beach, but gradually the sea encroached on it and it sank down into the wet sand.

It was likely that this stone was a termon stone, indicating a boundary of church land or monastic land, and it was presumably associated with Inishkeel island. In Ireland, as in other Christian countries, many of the churches had the right of sanctuary. Land around the church was marked by crosses or pillar stones; this land was regarded as belonging exclusively to the church. Criminals fleeing from justice, or fugitives from their enemies, were safe once they had taken refuge in the church itself or inside the boundary. The Gaelic word for these *termini* or boundaries is *tearmann*. Because of the role of these boundary stones through the ages the word *tearmann* is now taken to mean "shelter", "sanctuary" or "protection". We will mention the concept of sanctuary again in the Tullymore–Maas area (at Lackatermon portal tomb) and at the site of Shanaghan church in Loughros Point.

Now back to our *turas* to Inishkeel island and some of the folklore attached to it. We remember how the people of Doochary and Lettermacaward used to walk barefoot to the island, do the *turas*, and then walk back and either go to Mass or proceed to do the *turas* in Derryleconnell. Inhabitants of the Croaghs (*Na Cruatha*) also went on pilgrimage to Inishkeel. The following testimony[71] from Anna Nic a' Luain from *Cruach Thoibrid, Na*

Cruacha, from August 1948, gives us an insight into old ways and into Conall's pre-eminent position in the folklore of this general area: "The penance that people get from the clergy now is nothing compared to what it used to be; the old people used to say that a penance that used to be imposed was that you had to leave home in the bare feet, walk barefoot to do the Lough Derg pilgrimage and walk back home again. Another type of penance was to do the *turas* to Inishkeel, fasting, three Fridays in a row."

She continues, echoing the traditional version of Conall's arrival: "Conall had no sense when he was a young man. And he was spoiled; one day he struck his father over the head with a hammer. When he went to the priest, the penance he was given was that he would have to go out to an island and spend so long on the island that the birds of the air would nest in the palm of his hand and rear their young there. This was a very severe penance and Conall went off and walked along until he came to the island of Inishkeel, just off the coast. The old people say that he spent seven years there and lived on nothing but what he could get from the sea and the rocks. In the seventh year there was a very good summer and one day he was lying out in the middle of the island and he fell asleep; it is not known how long he slept, but when he awoke there was a nest in the palm of his hand and the little birds had hatched out in the nest. He knew then that he had done his penance and he did a *turas* around the island praying at certain places that he knew well by now, and in fact he spent the rest of his life on Inishkeel doing the *turas* regularly. There is not a year since then that you do not have hundreds of people walking across the island, doing the *turas* of St. Conall."

Again we read of Conall killing his father and of the birds nesting in his hand: "...the penance imposed on Conall, after the killing of his father, was to go to this island and remain there until a bird of the strand made a nest in his palm, and brought out her young there.

"Conall went in through humble obedience, although he had no hopes that he should ever again come out. There was no shelter on the island, and the first night Conall slept there he lay down with the skies for a roof. God put a deep slumber on him. [This continued for so many days that] the birds of the air thought he was dead, and one of them came and made her nest in his [out-stretched] palm. Conall awoke not till the young birds were fit to fly. Then Conall awoke, the birds took to wing, and Conall found the empty nest in his palm.

"He knew then that his sin was forgiven.

"Some time after this Conall made a *turas* on the island, and the people of Tirconaill walk that *turas* to this day."[72]

In view of the constant thread going through the legends associating Conall's arrival in this area with birds, I found it interesting that the bird theme has survived in the belief in Derryleconnell which holds that it is a good omen if birds are strongly in evidence while doing the *turas*.

I mentioned earlier that before the gradual erosion of land by the sea that Inishkeel was much closer to the mainland; but if we are to believe legend it was not possible to walk over to it: "At certain times now there is a strand out to Inishkeel island, but in days gone by there never was a strand. The mainland was close to the island, but the water never cleared out of the channel between the mainland and the island. One day Conall and another man wanted to get out to the island. The other man said to Conall:

'I'll jump it,' but he ended up in the channel.

"Then Conall said: 'With God's help, I'll jump it.'

"With that the channel dried up, and there has been a strand there ever since. The whole strand dried up because he had asked for God's help before he made any attempt to jump."[73]

But how would you get out to the island if you couldn't see it? Again folklore tells us what happened:

"At that time Inniskeel was under enchantment: at times it appeared, and at times disappeared. It was a druidic isle, and no one could reach it but a person who should succeed in casting a stone on it, thereby breaking the enchantment. On one occasion whilst the island was visible there were two men in company with Conall (on the mainland).

"'I will put in a stone, with God's help!' said the first man. He failed to get in the stone.

"'I will put in a stone, with God's help!' quoth the second man, but he likewise failed.

"Conall spoke next: 'With God's help, I will put in a stone!' he said. He succeeded (because with his first words he had invoked God's help). The water cleared off the island, and it was left just as it is to-day."[74]

Finally (the tide could have come in and gone out again by this time), we come ashore on Inishkeel island, the spiritual core of this book.

Notes

1   Cannon, *A Tour of Lettermacaward*, p. 3.
2   Waddington, T.A.J. *Guide to Donegal and the North-West of Ireland*, p. 47.
3   John O'Donovan, O.S. Letters J (1835) p. 110.
4   McParlan, *Statistical Survey of the County of Donegal* (1802), p. 27.

5 · From R. Ó Cochlain, "A Landlord Makes Improvements, 1786," in *D.A.* (1974) extracted from *Faulkner's Dublin Journal*, 1786.

6   *European Magazine* (1794); quoted in *J.R.S.A.I.*, vol. 115 (1985), p. 55.

7   *Faulkners Dublin Journal* (1786); quoted in *J.R.S.A.I.*, vol. 115 (1985), p.55.

8   Inquisitions (hereinafter Inq.), 7 Jos. I.

9   Dept. of Irish Folklore, U.C.D., ms. 336, pp. 1-18, as told by Donie Breslin of Leitir.

10   Mary Donatus, *Beasts and Birds in the Lives of the Early Irish Saints*, p. 199.

11   However apart from *Uaimh Naomh Brennain* we have other references to Brendan in this area. This is a *Dún Bhreannain* and, more importantly, in the 1608 Rawlinson Ms. A. 237 there is listed "the Chapple of Moynbrenan, the tiethes of this chaple belongeth to the Deane of Raffoe". In *D.A.* (1978), p. 369, P. Ó Gallchóir, using a reference from 1622, locates it as "the chapel of Litter Mc Ward, alias Munbranan, near the rivulet of Gibber" (the Gweebarra). My father had wondered whether the "Chapple of Moynbrenan" might be "the old ruin beside the Protestant church in Meenagowan (Lettermacaward)". Perhaps a Leitir scholar might investigate more fully and establish Brendan's reputation in this area.

12   A *Vita Brendani* and a *Navigatio Brendani*.

13   *Betha Colaim Chille - The Life of Colmcille -* was written by Manus O'Donnell, 21st Lord of Tír Chonaill. One of the most interesting and colourful figures of the Gaelic world in the 16th century, he became ruler of Tír Chonaill in 1537 and died in 1564. His career was set in the declining years of Gaelic Ireland, when the traditional ways of life were under constant pressure from the expanding English power. He was a fierce, tough soldier, but he was also a man of considerable intellectual and literary ability. He took a deep and active interest in the great *Life of Colmcille* with which his name is associated. It is a wonderful book, simply written with a fund of stories of the saint from his birth at Gartan to his death in Iona. One of the most remarkable is the story of the seven children of the King of India who came to visit the saint on Tory. The *Life* has preserved many old legends and has been described as a bridge between medieval Irish tradition and modern folklore (abridged from an article by J.G. Simms, *D.A.*, 1962).

14   *Vita Sancti Columbae*.

15   O'Donnell op. cit. p. 69.

16   Ibid. p. 167.

17   Cannon, *A Tour of Lettermacaward.*

18   Patrick MacGill, *The Rat-Pit*, pp. 6-9.

19   p. 277.

20   The *Annals of Ulster* (hereafter *A.U.*) record Cainnech's birth at 521 and 527, and his death at 599 and 600. These dates remind us that little is definite about our early saints.

21   *H.D.R.*, vol. I, p. 491.

22   *Martyrology of Donegal* (hereafter *M.O.D.*), p. 273.

23   *Folia Gadelica* (hereafter *F.G.*), pp. 20-35.

24 "The Dál Fiatach of eastern Down (perhaps the only 'fír-Ulaid'), the Dál nAraide of Antrim and their close relatives, the Uí Echach of western Down were heirs to the 'polity of Ulaid'." (*F.G.*, p. 26.)

25 "In origin, the ending -*oc* is a Britannic, not an Irish, hypocoristic suffix, from Celtic – *aco-*. (*F.G.*, p. 26.)

26 Period at which a person was alive.

27 A.O and M.O Anderson, *Adamnán's Life of Columba*.

28 *F.G.*, p. 30.

29 The present Catholic parish of Ardara was founded in 1829, being made up of parts of the old parishes of Inishkeel and Killybegs.

30 *H.D.R.*, vol. I, pp. 474-5.

31 Ibid. p. 491.

32 *Dr. Pococke's Irish Tour*, p. 67.

33 *H.D.R.*, vol. I, p. 491.

34 *Ros*: a promontory; -*in*: a diminutive. The names Roshin and Ranny (*Rinn*: a point, peninsula) are common all along this western coastline. The Rosses, *Na Rosa*, an extensive area north of the Gweebarra, is so called because of the large number of promontories that jut out into the sea along its coast. Gweebarra, *Gaoth Beara*, is derived from *gaoth*: an estuary and *beara*: genitive of *bior*, water, a stream. A similiar type of name is repeated further up the coast in the placename Gweedore: *Gaoth*, as above; *Dobhair*, an old Gaelic (and Cymric) word for water, corresponding to the Sanscrit *dabhra*, the sea. The words *bior* and *dobhar* are very ancient names for water; in this area they became in time proper names for two rivers, the *Abhainn Bheara* (see *Scathlan* 3, 1986) and the *Dobhar*. The word *dobhar* (water) is the basis for the name Dover in the southeast of England and for the river Dour at Aberdeen – we are told that the ancient population group the Tuatha Dé Dannan spent seven years in the north of Alba at "Dobar & Iardobar" (*Onom. Goed.*, p. 348). A third *goath* on the west coast of Donegal is noted in the annals – *Gaoth Luachrois* at Loughros, Ardara (*A.F.M.*, vol. III, p. 123).

35 The Gaelic word for a seal is *rón*; Plinny called seals *Marini Vituli* – literally the meat of the sea, an indication that people ate seals. We have an account from *c.* 1750 of people eating seals on Owey island off the north-west coast of Donegal: "They used kill great numbers of seals, the flesh of which they salted for winter; and were so fond of it, as to prefer it to any other kind of meat." (Joseph C. Walker, *Memoir of the Armour and Weapons of the Irish* (Dublin: 1758). They were also eaten as meat off the west coast of Scotland – Martin, writing in 1703, states that in Harris seals "are eat by the meaner people who say they are very nourishing" (*West Islands*, p. 36). At a rocky island off the coast of Harris we read in 1703 of a yearly fishing of seals, "where the parish minister has his choice of all the young seals, and that which he takes is called *Cullen Mory*, i.e. the Virgin Mary's Seal. So many as 320 have been killed at one time. The natives salt the fish with the ashes of burnt sea-ware. People of distinction eat the hams only." (Ibid. pp. 61-65). See Hardiman's ed. of O'Flaherty's *West Connaught*, p. 27, pp. 95-96.

36   *The Seals*, pp. 43-48.

37   The origin of this placename is open to interpretation. I have never seen a satisfactory explanation of it. In the 17th century it is written as "Bally gristeene" (1608) and as "Irishton al' Ballyeristine" (1642). My own view of its original form is that it may have been *Baile iar-ros tonn*. You have to try to project your mind back in time to make an attempt to interpret many placenames. My theory is that when earlier people were travelling down the Gweebarra river by small boat, the most westerly peninsulas jutting out into the estuary which they encountered before reaching the open sea were here in the vicinity of Ballyeristin. And it is exactly off Ballyeristin that the bar-mouth is situated; consequently one finds a lot of waves here. So my interpretation of Ballyeristin would be "the place (*baile*) of the western peninsulas (*iar-ros*) of the waves (*tonn*)". Stop off along the Gweebarra and have a look. An early coastal habitation site has recently (1991) come to light on Roshin Point, which we have just passed on the Gweebarra estuary, thus confirming that there was maritime traffic in and out of the Gweebarra from pre-historic times.

38   Grand Jury Presentments. In these records we also find, at April 1759, that William Barrett (it does not state where he was from) was convicted at the Lent Assizes for cow-stealing. On 24 March 1760, William Barrett, under sentence of death for cow-stealing, made his escape and was at large. We then read that William Barrett was transmitted to Derry gaol; and on 28 July 1760 he was transported to His Majesty's plantations in America. The modern-day court cases in the *Donegal Democrat* seem tame after reading this!

39   Meeting of Grand Jury, Lifford, 9 April 1772.

40   *A.S.D.*, p. 248.

41   *Scenery and Antiquities of North-West Donegal*, p. 80.

42   Ryan, *Ireland and Insular Art A.D. 500-1200*, p. 7.

43   Ibid.

44   Ibid. p. 8.

45   *D.A.* (1957), p. 68.

46   "On Holed and Perforated Stones in Ireland," *J.R.S.A.I.* (1896), pp. 158-169.

47   The exact meaning of *cluain* is a fertile piece of land, or a green arable spot, with bog or marsh on one side and water on the other. Its frequent occurence in our ecclesiastical names – e.g. Kilcloony – is explained by the inclination of the early hermits to select lonely and retired places for their own habitations. Later, in our discussion on St. Conall, we will come across *Cluain Chonaill* and *Cluain Dalláin*.

48   The other is Bernie McNelis, a true friend of the Narin and Portnoo Golf Club.

49   In the Inq of 25 May 1632 we read that "Edm. O'Bresslan and others meere Irishmen, held the half quarter of Cahsell gowtan ... and hath corne now groweinge upon the same".

50   *Claigeann*: a skull; the term is often applied to a prominent hill; in *The Donegal Highlands* Dr. McDevitt writes that "The glebe-house (Rev. J. Ovens) is hidden under the rocky head of Castlegoland hill." There were also hills called Claigin (Inq., 17 Car. I, 20 April 1642, Lifford) at Narin (near the Greenhouse Brae)

and at Rosbeg (behind Old Eden house).

51   *Buaile*: a milking or dairy place; *mór*: big; where cows were brought together morning and evening to be fed and milked.

52   Ó Muirgheasa, *Dhá Chéad de Cheoltaibh Uladh*, pp. 347-50. The poem is attributed to Nuala Ní Néill, but Niall Ó Dónaill ascribes it to Nuala Ní Dhónaill.

53   Joyce, vol. II, p. 380.

54   Ibid. pp. 380-81.

55   In the writings of Pádraig Ó Riain, Professor of Irish at U.C.C., we again get a sense of a *fearann* being a particular portion of land when he tells us, while discussing the cults of saints, that in "the Irish Life of Adamnán which, to judge by its language, may have been composed as early as the tenth century, Ireland, or at least its Northern half, is divided into the four *ferainn* (cult areas?) of Colm Cille, Patrick, Ciarán and Finnian". *J.C.H.A.S.*, vol. 82, part 2, p. 73.

56   Rawlinson Ms. A. 237.

57   Inq., 9. Jas. I., Lifford, 27 March.

58   Inq., 30 Car. I.

59   Inq., 32 Car. I.

60   *D.A.* (1970), p. 205.

61   Mac Giolla Easpaig also notes a 1614 reference to "Farhin".

62   John Murray, *Handbook for Travellers in Ireland*, p. 92.

63   *J.R.S.A.I.* (1896), pp. 382-83.

64   *J.R.S.A.I.* (1914), p. 196.

65   McParlan, *Statistical Survey of the County of Donegal*, pp. 24-25

66   Leslie, *Raphoe Clergy and Parishes*, p. 75.

67   Ibid.

68   I have been to Naxos and I can vouch for the beauty of that island, with its wealth of archaeological interest. The weather is a little more reliable than it is around Narin! (Rain? What rain?)

69   *The Seals*, pp. 60-61.

70   al': In the Inquisitions al' means "alias", indicating that a place was known by a number of names. In this instance Sranadarragh - *Srath na dá ráth* [*dá*: two; *rath*: an earthen enclosure or "fort"] - would suggest that there were two "forts" here in earlier times. (See reference to forts at Dunmore Head later.)

71   Collected by Seán Ó hEochaidh; translated into English by the author.

72   *Béaloideas, Iml. 1, Uimh. 111 (Meitheamh* 1928) pp. 255-56; the author Énrí Ó Muirgheasa adds: "I got this version from Brian MacPhillips, an aged man who lived near Ardara - hard by the Owenea Bridge. He told me the tale on the roadside, and as I had not writing materials by me it is not given word for word as he told it. This was about the year 1913. He said that *Gearán* was the name of St. Conall's mother, and as his own mother was a MacGearan or O'Gearan - I don't recollect which - [now anglicised Sharpe (!) in Co. Donegal] he was very proud of this. He is now dead." In the same publication (pp. 254-55) Énrí Ó Muirgheasa details another version of the tradition of Conall striking his father and adds: "I wrote down

this story in 1912 from Maurice O'Heekin of Crannóg Bhuidhe, near Ardara, Co. Donegal. He was a fine, intelligent story-teller, but is long since dead. His people came from Connacht about 1690, from Co. Sligo, where they were probably dispossessed after the Williamite wars. The ancestor who trekked from Co. Sligo and whose name was Nachor had a gun and a greyhound, and the remainder of his wordly possessions were tied up in a calf-skin. Maurice, the story-teller, could recount all his ancestors back to Nachor. See *Oidhche Airneail i dTír Chonaill* for a number of other stories taken down from this story-teller."

73   Dept. of Irish Folklore, ms. 948, pp. 27-33, Roise Brennan.

74   *Béaloideas, Iml.I, Uimh. III (Meitheamh* 1928), p. 255.

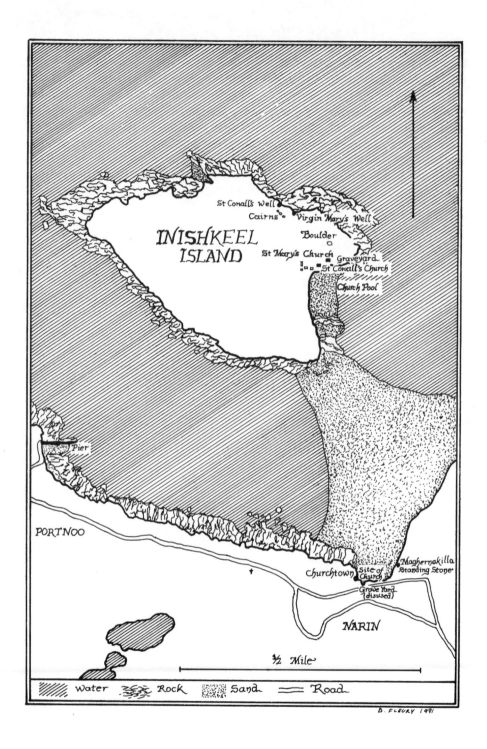

INISHKEEL ISLAND

St Conall's Well
Cairns
Virgin Mary's Well
Boulder
St Mary's Church
Graveyard
St Conall's Church
Church Pool

Pier

PORTNOO

Churchtown
Site of Church
Maghernakilla Standing Stone
Grave Yard (disused)

NARIN

½ Mile

Water   Rock   Sand   Road

B. FLEURY 1991

III

On Inishkeel Island

I'M NOT THE first person to fall under the spell of Inishkeel island - Isabel Crozier, in 1957, writes: "Inishkeel is the most loved place of all. ... On first setting foot in the island one is conscious of an atmosphere of sanctity and peace. It is treeless, and the effect of dazzling light on sand and sea, the strong colours and soft Atlantic air is entrancing."[1]

Having put your shoes back on again - surely you didn't wear them across the beach but preferred instead the feel of sand and, where the strand has not dried out yet, water on your feet - you go northwards through the rock outcrops and come on to a little sandy beach. Off this beach is the "Church Pool", a safe anchorage and marked (by an anchor) as such on MacKenzie's chart of 1775. Continuing along the highest part of the beach, bearing leftwards, you come to a little gate. The remains of a number of roofless buildings are visible. The tall building on the left was formerly the home of the Barrett[2] family. Richard Barrett, whose parents were James and Sarah, was the last householder on the island and left in 1904. His daughter Sarah and son John live near by on the mainland; regretably their brother Andy, the historian of the family, died recently (1990). John, with others, keeps livestock out on the island; his sons, George and Patrick, regularly got out to tend to the animals. They have always been very helpful to me and on one memorable occasion a few years ago, when we in the Donegal Historical Society visited the island on one of our Field Days, they were of particular assistance when the tide started to come in a little sooner than we had expected!

Up to the right are the remains of two churches - St. Conall's and St. Mary's. It is popularly believed that parts of the ruins of the two old churches date back to the days of St. Conall. This accounts for the fact that the more westerly structure is always referred to as "the church" and the other as "the monastery". Both of course are churches of relatively recent origin. Indeed we have evidence of the destruction of the possible original buildings here as early as the 7th century. The *Annals of the Four Masters* tell us that in the year 619 A.D. "Doir, son of Aedh Allainn, was slain by Failbhe Flann Fidhbhadh, as he (Failbhe) himself said:

"What advantage to me is the slaying of Doir, as I did not slay Dairene?

It is then one kills the chaffer, when he destroyes his young ones."

He was afterwards killed in revenge of Doir. His mother lamenting him, said:

"It was the mortal wounding of a noble, not the demolition of Inis-cail, for which the shouts of the enemies were exultingly raised around the head of Failbhe Flann Fidhbhadh."[3]

Aedh Allann was Monarch of Ireland from 605-612 A.D.; Failbhe Flann was king of Munster and died in 633 A.D.[4] What brought the latter as far north as this I don't know; it seems he was very unpopular[5] on his accession to the throne of Munster; possibly his later actions (e.g. killing Doir) maintained his unpopularity and he may have been seeking sanctuary on Inishkeel (if so, surely an indication that the island had already achieved fame by this early date) when his enemies arrived, killed him and laid waste the island.

Though there is much discussion in historical academia at the present day concerning the nature of early Christian buildings I think we are safe in assuming that the original settlement here probably consisted of stone "beehive" huts [clochans; *cloch*, a stone] and small oratories. Stone would have been abundant here and timber all but absent. Dr. H.G. Leask, writing in 1955, informs us that "these clochans and small oratories would have been built on the corbel principle, a structural method of great antiquity first practised in Ireland, so far as we can judge, by the Bronze Age builders of the great passage-graves of Newgrange, Dowth, etc."[6] The best surviving specimens of clochans that we have are on the Skellig islands, off the coast of Kerry. Dr. Leask continues: "In the typical clochan the corbel principle is well applied; in fact, the structure is composed entirely of corbelling from foundation to closing stone. Each course of stonework, laid without mortar and nearly horizontally, overhangs by a little the course below. As it rises the building gradually narrows until its apex can be closed by a single slab and the 'dome' then be finished by more stones to secure the 'closer' in position and complete the beehive outline. All the courses slope outwards slightly to direct the rain away from the interior. The normal clochan is circular or nearly so in plan – roughly oval."[7] As they are in the barely discernible remains at Kilclooney.

Dr. Leask continues: "The monastic centres of the early Irish church were very similar to those of the earliest monastic societies of Syria and Egypt.

That is to say, associations of monks, each dwelling under self-imposed discipline in his separate cell, grouped with others about one or more: the complex is called a *laura*."[8] The settlement on Inishkeel would initially have been a simple little refuge of hermits (a hermitage) who had come out here to live in isolation in their clochans, close to God and without distractions. Dr. Leask continues: "The more austere among holy men sought even greater isolation as hermits, and built their cells and oratories in relatively inaccessible and often inhospitable places: islands in sea or lake, headlands, even hilltops, remote valleys, 'deserts' (dysarts) in the marginal lands. A constant feature of these early hermitages and monasteries, small or large, was its enclosure – an encircling rampart of earth or stone. This was as necessary to a monastery as to a farmhouse of the times, and for the hermit it served, in addition, to shut out all but the heavens from his sight and thoughts."[9] You will remember that the remains of the church and graveyard, and presumable the position of the original building at Kilkenny, on the Gweebarra, are situated inside the enclosure of Cashelnavean.

The most complete monastic cashel remaining is that on the island of Inishmurray[10] off the Sligo coast. My late father and a small group of other enthusiasts were once ferried out to this island and given a conducted tour of it by the late Lord Mountbatten, who was very interested in its history. The substantial remains of an enclosure at the early monastic site on Rathlin O'Birne island off the coast of Glencolumbkille are also still visible.

On Inishkeel the first church we meet is the more westerly St. Conall's. The ruins[11] of this church, 15 m. x 5.15 m. internally, are built of rubble with ashlar quoins and grit-stone dressings and testify to a number of different building periods. The windows in the south wall are of 17th century character. Some of the repairs were carried out in fairly recent times – money was collected in the 1960s to help preserve these old buildings. It was these funds which helped to construct, among other things, the little altar which is up against the east wall of St. Conall's church. Earlier photographs do not show the flagstone with the cross incised on it, so it is likely that this flagstone was found when the place was being cleaned up in the '60s and was then placed, standing, on top of the altar when the latter was rebuilt in 1967 A large flagstone with a central hole in it, lying flat on the altar, was used in the *turas* in earlier times – a healing stone was ground around in it (of this, more anon).

Just immediately outside and east of the door of St. Conall's church is a very interesting flagstone, bearing a Crucifixion scene, lying flat in the grass. It is broken into two parts. It had lain hidden here until it was found, broken, lying under rubble and clay close to the "front" wall of St. Conall's church by the workmen repairing the church in 1963.[12] On it Christ is shown crucified against the background of a cross. His head is upright, suggesting that he is still alive – his head is usually tilted to one side if it is being suggested that he is dead. Possibly he is wearing a beard, but I don't think so. He is wearing a long tunic with sleeves, known as a *colobium*; the outer edge of the tunic on Christ's right lower body is not as well defined as on his left. A vertical groove with expanded ends extends almost the whole height of Christ's long garment, but its significance is not known. Christ's feet point outwards and appear to be covered with clog-shaped shoes. A possible vertical line a little below his feet may represent a *subpedaneum* or footstool. On Christ's left the end of the corss runs out, down towards the bottom of the slab, into first a triquetra design and then ends in a spiral design above the triquetra. The same designs were possibly repeated on the right, but only the terminal spiral is now visible. The triquetra is thought to represent the Trinity; there is a very fine triquetra knot on the Kilaghtee cross slab near Bruckless and we will discuss it later.

A feature of some Crucifixion scenes is the representation of Longinus, the centurion who pierced Christ in the side with a lance, and Stephaton who raised a pole with a sponge containing vinegar to the dying Christ. On

The recumbent Crucifixion flagstone

this slab to the right of Christ's lower tunic, is a figure with outstretched hands. No lance is visible, but judging by the angle of his arms and hands I think we can take it that this is Longinus thrusting his lance into Christ's right ribs.

On Christ's left only the feet of what I take to be Stephaton survive, though I think there is a suggestion of a pole extending from the inner broken edge of the slab towards Christ's left armpit. Beneath Christ's arm are creatures which seem to have a bird-like body with wings, but a human head, and which may represent angels. Christ's left hand – a big broad hand – is more clear than his right.

These two artefacts are not from Inishkeel. They are re-produced here merely to illustrate points made in the text. In the Tynan Crucifixion plaque (after J.R.S.A.I., vol. 112), below, Longinus and Stephaton are clearly shown, as are bird-like angels with exotic wings which are seen to support the head of Christ. The Cavan ("Queens") brooch (after Darwin Dolinka Korda), right, demonstrates elongated bird-forms flanking a head.

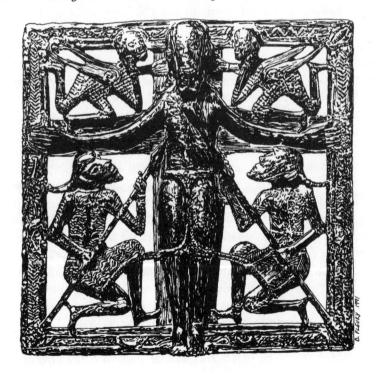

Above each of the arms of the cross there is a six-legged bird-like creature; the bird on Christ's right has a human head and presumably the bird on the left is meant to have one too; these creatures are thought to represent angels. It is possible that the numerous legs on each bird are a poor representation of wings. Further up towards the top of Christ's head, on both sides, and out at the end of the raised hood-moulding which runs along the top of the slab, are more birds – one "upside-down" bird on Christ's right and on his left two or three (three, I'd say) extending down from the end of the hood-moulding and behind the six-legged "bird". The shape of these four birds suggests that they represent swans.

Why are there birds clustered up around Christ's head? The symbolic use of the bird form in Christian belief is common, as in the representation of the Holy Spirit as a dove, of the angels as winged, the appearance of a soul released from the body as a bird, etc. Naturally they also appear in Christian art – examples of birds flanking Christ on the cross are very common; the cross is seen as the Tree of Life and the birds feed of this tree. Angels with multiple wings, represented by birds, are often seen on both sides of Christ's head – supporting his head, dare I say keeping it upright and therefore keeping Christ alive. Birds, very often elongated, flanking Christ's head, their ribbon-like bodies stretching down to his chin, are such an iconographic cliché that in trying to interpret works of art where there is uncertainty over the identity of the head or face, one can often presume that the head is meant to represent Christ because this particular head and bird motif is such a distinctive one. We will return to the theme of birds shortly when we discuss the "swan cross slab", which is east of St. Mary's church.

None of these decorated slabs can be looked at in isolation; it is only by comparing their characteristics with other slabs, plaques, manuscript pages, jewellery, etc., from other parts of Ireland, Britain and further abroad that they can be dated. In the case of this recumbent slab the points of interest, apart from the birds, are the probable lance and sponge bearers, the design of the cross and of Christ's tunic and the fact that Christ appears to be clean-shaven – representation of a bearded Christ crucified in a long tunic are often 8th century, a cleanshaven Christ argues for a date not before the 9th century;[13] the figure with the outstretched hands on Christ's right (Longinus?) wears a triangular cloak[14] like that of the figures of the east face of the upright ("swan") slab which we will describe later; and some aspects of the cross on which Christ is shown crucified are similar to the Carndonagh Cross[15] (and east face of the Carndonagh Stele).

In trying to interpret this Crucifixion scene I have relied on the British Archaeological Reports, British Series 152, of 1986. It is the only substantial written work on this stone. In it the slab is ascribed a 9th-century date. I would enter a note of caution concerning its dating, though as an amateur I must be careful of what I say. Nevertheless, it has occured to me that this slab is not "quite right" – the six-legged bird-angels look clumsy, the slab doesn't look as if it were ever meant to stand erect, which is what I would expect of a 9th century work (incidentally, there is nothing on the underside of the slab). The material is slatey, not a medium commonly used for early Christian (this term is now being replaced by "early Medieval") cross slabs – the same type of stone is used for other much later (18th century) grave slabs here on Inishkeel. Possibly this slab is indeed 9th century, but I have a feeling that when a complete corpus of early Christian stonework is compiled in the future that this recumbent Crucifixion slab may well be excluded.

We now go up and enter St. Mary's church. Consisting of nave and chancel it is built of rubble with grit-stone dressings. The fabric testifies to two distinct building periods, the nave being a medieval rebuilding on to an earlier 13th-century chancel.[16] This dating is echoed in an article by D.M. Waterman in 1964; he draws attention to "two fragmentary examples of Transitional architecture, a building style which is by no means common in the north-west of Ireland". The first example is this church (the second is Killaghtee church near Bruckless). He concludes that "the present nave is a later medieval addition to the chancel, which retains detail of early 13th century character". He refers to "at least ten triple-roll-moulded jambstones which can most readily be identified as forming part of the responds of an arch, and presumably of a chancel arch. If this identification is correct, then an early 13th century nave can be inferred." He continues: "the function of a number of other moulded dressings cannot be readily determined. These show a combination of rolls, sometimes of keeled profile, and hollows." He goes on to mention "two dressings with small bifid keeled arris rolls. The presence of such paired rolls is significant for the dating of the 13th century work in the church; this detail appears elsewhere in the west of Ireland only at Boyle Abbey in work of *c.*1205-18 and in three churches in the east of the country in work of *c.*1210-40. The work at Boyle is remarkably close, and a date of *c.*1220-30 for the Inishkeel church seems reasonable."[17]

The lovely moulded stones in this church which Mr. Waterman was dis cussing always catch the eye. Locals call them the "Gospel Books" because their appearance resembles books on a bookshelf.

Lying on the ground on your right just before you walk out the door of St. Mary's church is a little decorated grave slab bearing a Maltese cross.[18] Outside, just in front of the church, is a grave slab bearing a Latin cross.[19]

We now walk eastwards past the gable of St. Mary's church towards two items of interest which, for the sake of simplicity, I will call the "swan cross slab" and the "interlace cross shaft". On our way we would do well to remember that when Henry Wheeler visited this island in 1932 to photograph the swan cross slab there was part of another broken cross slab lying close to the wall of one of the churches. He writes: "There is, or was, a third, much smaller, fragment of a stone slab, near one of the ruined churches. It has a cross on both sides with swans on the arms of one of them. The swan motif may be connected with the Children of Lir, but this is only conjecture."[20] This fragment (about 1 foot square in size) of another cross slab has not been seen for many years; hopefully it, and other as yet undiscovered artefacts, will turn up in years to come if this site is properly investigated.

Now to the "swan cross slab". Françoise Henry, in 1940, writes: "In Donegal two very beautiful slabs, one at Drumhallagh, nearly opposite to Fahan, the other on the island of Inishkeel, near Portnoo, carry right into the eighth century a monumental shape and a style that goes back to the Carndonagh carvings. But the string interlacing, and the very different rounder, more mellow treatment, leave no place for doubt as to their later date. The Inishkeel slab is so weathered that its subjects are not too easy to identify. There are on one side two squat figures which seem to be made for St. Paul and St. Anthony."[21]

The "two squat figures" referred to here are on the bottom of the east face, so we will look at this side of the cross slab first. Peter Harbinson, in 1986, writes: "The east face is dominated by a cross filled out with single-strand interlace more closely meshed than that at Carndonagh or Fahan. Beneath the arms of the cross there are two figures with stylised triangular[22] robes, and standing where (?)Paul and Anthony can be seen on the Drumhallagh[23] pillar, but as they lack their attributes, they are best left unidentified. Beneath the cross there is a much-worn carving of two long-robed figures with heads bowed towards one another over a table. Henry's suggested identification of these two figures as saints Paul and Anthony is almost certainly correct, and finds support in the representation of the two saints on the Pictish stone at Nigg in Ross-shire, though the Nigg animals are lacking at Inishkeel."[24] Here we appear to have a representation of Paul and Anthony breaking bread over an altar. They were both Egyptian desert hermits and scenes from their lives were often shown on cross slabs and Irish High Crosses – they started making their appearance on the latter in the 9th century.[25] St. Anthony was the first hermit of the Egyptian desert and was seen in particular as a patron and model of monastic life.[26] The Paul and

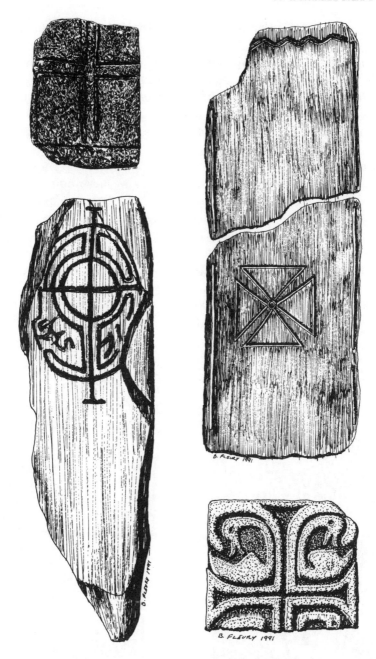

1. Cross-inscribed flagstone on the altar; 2. Grave slab bearing a Maltese cross; 3. Grave slab bearing a cross (Latin) in circle motif; 4. The now-missing fragment of a cross slab (after Henry).

Anthony scene on this slab is so weathered that it is difficult to make it out nowadays.

The west face is an interpreter's delight – or nightmare. The cross is shorter than on the east face, though its shape is fairly similar. However, in its outline the cross has no harsh, sharp angles – the whole profile of the cross is soft, with nicely rounded angles; because of this the four terminals of the cross are broader than on the east face, the bottom of the cross being actually fan-shaped.

Above each arm of the cross is a figure and a swan. The figures are wearing the same triangular-shaped cloaks as we have noted on the east face, and earlier on the recumbent slab outside St. Conall's church. What do the swans represent? Françoise Henry considered that "One cannot help thinking of the Children of Lir changed by a spell into swans whose story haunts all that north-west coast."[27] In fact these swans are here simply because all cross slabs represent the Crucifixion scene, even though Christ may not be present on the cross, as in this case, and, as we saw when dealing with the recumbent Crucifixion slab outside St. Conall's church earlier, birds are often placed close to Christ and to the cross, the Tree of Life. From 1988

Swan cross slab, Inishkeel. East (l) and west (r) faces.

we read: "In Early Christian and Byzantine art birds often acted as Christian symbols. Peacocks symbolised the Resurrection and immortality because their flesh was believed never to decay. They are often shown in pairs, as are doves, which may represent the soul, the Eucharist or the revelation of divine truths. Both appear in association with the Cross, with fountains or chalices and with the Tree of Life.

"Insular artists were evidently aware of this symbolism. Paired peacocks flank the head of the figure on folio 32ᵛ in the *Book of Kells*, where they act as a kind of heraldic emblem of Christ. Two birds likewise flank the head of Christ in a Crucifixion scene in a late eighth-century Insular manuscript from Würzburg. The placing of birds on the arms of crosses at Reask, County Kerry and Inishkeel, County Donegal, follows a long-standing tradition, for birds appear in a similar position, for example, on the fifth-century sarcophagus of Honorius in the Mausoleum of Galla Placidia at Ravenna."[28]

Our Inishkeel artist would have put swan-like birds on his cross slabs because he would have been familiar with them in this area – as long ago as the 12th century it was written that "Swans are very plentiful in the northern part of Ireland."[29]

Below the cross on this side is an interesting scene of two figures on a chariot, which has a wheel with very stylised spokes around a circular axle, being drawn by a horse. Chariot scenes with some similarity to this one appear on the bases of some of the Irish High Crosses – on the north base of the North Cross at Ahenny, Co. Tipperary, the east side of the pedestal of the Cross of the Scriptures at Clonmacnois, and on the Cross of Saints Patrick and Columba at Kells.[30] Another interesting chariot scene was that on the now perished Meigle slab in Perthshire, Scotland.[31] However in most of these other cases the chariot and horsemen are part of a bigger scene and the other elements in the picture help to interpret it; but in the case of Inishkeel there is not enough information to help us guess what the artist was depicting. It is probably a Gospel scene. Chariots would not have been in common usage, especially in this remote area, though there is a history of chariot use in Ireland. Chariots are said to have come into use in Ireland during the Iron Age.[32] Ancient Irish manuscripts are filled with descriptions of cavalcades containing chariots and of the epic heroes using them for military purposes. But we read also that "chariots were not only used in war; they were rather a method of transport for the upper classes, kings, nobles and, in the early medieval period, ecclesiastics also. Indeed it is recorded in the *Annals of Ulster* (1020) that a chariot was still used by the Abbot of Armagh."[33]

That chariots were not for humble folk is demonstrated by the anecdote

that when St. Brigit's druid father could no longer tolerate the girl's exces-
sive generosity to the poor he said to her, "Not for honour or reverence to
thee art thou carried in the chariot, but to take thee to sell thee."[34]

In recent years there has been some doubt expressed about whether there
are one or two figures on the Inishkeel chariot. Photographs taken in the
middle of this century clearly demonstrate two humans above a very high,
possibly eight-spoked wheel. Though only one horse is depicted it is probable that we are to assume that there are two. Referring to chariot scenes on
Irish High Crosses in which only one horse appears, Peter Harbison observes that though "The sculptor has depicted only one horse drawing the
'chariot' ... a second horse must be imagined as strutting inside the one
shown." He continues: "One feature reproduced on all the 'chariots' on the
High Cross bases is the large spoked wheel. ... When compared with the size
of the people in the vehicles, and also compared with the size of the animals
pulling them, the wheels seem to be inordinately large."[35] His words describe
the chariot scene on the Inishkeel slab very accurately and we must deduce
that the inspiration for this scene came from the Irish High Crosses. Since
the Kells High Cross is dated to "around the 9th century"[36] we can presume
that this places the Inishkeel cross slab at a slightly later period in the same
century.

As we were discussing chariots I thought you might be interested in this
excerpt from a book entitled *The Borrowed Bride,* by Dunkineely man
Patrick Sarsfield Cassidy in New York a century ago – in 1892. Describing a
cavalcade of the powerful local O'Boyle sept he writes:

Thus the chariot, thus the escort
Winding by Gweebarra bay;
Clanking swords and clattering horse-hoofs
Tell their progress on the way.
Far behind fades wild Tra-Enagh,
Sea strand of the screaming bird,
Where the myriad fowls of ocean
O'er the billows' roar are heard.

Now the silvery sands of Nairn
Take the impress of their feet;
Wind they past Kilclooney *Cromlach,*
With its own love-story sweet.
Turn they now towards the Glenties,
Through the mountains' deep defile,
Down the broad, green glen of hunting–

Faud-na-Sealga mile on mile,
'Til the *Dysard*, with its hospice,
Bids them halt and rest awhile.[37]

In the past there are those who saw pagan symbolism in some of these cross slabs. Referring to this particular one, my father, writing in 1970, voiced their theory: "There are those who see in the horse-drawn vehicle a representation of the sun-god in his chariot. The relative position of the figures would remind one strongly of the Trundholm sun disc (believed to be of Irish origin) found in Denmank in 1902. The presence of the swans lend colour to this theory. Our Bronze Age ancestors believed that the sun crossed the sky each day on a horse-drawn chariot and returned in the night by the underworld on the back of a swan. The prevalence of sun-worship in Ireland is well attested by the numerous solar symbols of Caiseal Aongusa, Dowth and Lough Crewe. It is not unusual to find sculptors of early Christian times mingle semi-pagan scenes with their ornaments. Perhaps they still had a longing for the art of earlier times, or else had a desire to placate the deity of the old faith as well as the God of the Christians."[38]

The bird-motif was much in evidence, too, in pagan times. Ravens and crows were associated with pagan Celtic religion, particularly with a trio of Irish goddesses, one of whom is frequently called Badb or "Crow" after the form she took, while another, the Mórrígan, was associated with ravens. These goddesses in their bird forms were prophetic of death or disaster on the battlefield.[39] In the Late Bronze Age and Early Iron Age, throughout Europe a certain well-defined scheme of design for bronze work and pottery prevailed in which the leading motifs were wheels, boats, the human figure, and birds – particularly swans. All these were associated with sun worship and the swan was the emblem of the northern sun-god.[40] A connection has been traced between bird-figures and the worship of thermal springs and the design of a swan's head has been found on votive offerings at many ancient watering places.[41]

Françoise Henry, in discussing the chariot scene at Ahenny, Co. Tipperary, states that it is a hunting scene and, while conceding that "these hunting pictures have pagan antecedents", adds that "in the hands of the Christian artist they have of course taken on a completely different significance."[42] She suggests that they represent an allegorical image of the spread of Christianity, quoting the writing of St. Columbanus: "From that moment when the Son of God deigned to become Man, and riding over the sea of nations on those two most fiery steeds of the Spirit of God – I mean the apostles Peter and Paul – disturbed many waters and increased with countless thousands of people the fleet of his chariots, himself the highest Charioteer of his own carriage, who is Christ, the true Father, the Herd of Israel, over the channels' surge, over the dolphins' backs, over the swelling flood, reached even unto us."[43]

Dating a decorated stone such as this "swan cross slab" on Inishkeel depends on comparing characteristics it may have with similar ones in other places. In some cases the design on a cross slab would have been created by someone who saw a similar pattern on a stone elsewhere; sometimes the inspiration came from portable Christian objects such as manuscripts, ivories and metalwork. Formerly cross slabs such as this were looked at in a purely Irish context and dated earlier, but nowadays their designs are being compared more and more with Hiberno-Saxon metalwork and dated later. Thus Françoise Henry, writing in 1940, attributed this cross slab to the 8th century, while in more recent times Robert Stevenson of Edinburgh, in a number of articles, suggests that the sculptures at Fahan, Carndonagh etc. (to which the Inishkeel slabs would be related) are characteristic of Celto-Scandinavian Cumbria and are probably 10th century.[44] Finally, Peter Harbison dates this cross slab to the 9th century and adds that "it ought to be pointed out that certain features of this slab find an echo in a portion of a cross-shaft from Lancaster which cannot be dated precisely, but which is

Interlace cross-shaft, Inishkeel

likely to belong to the 8th or 9th century. A somewhat remoter parallel is provided by the slab from Wensley in Yorkshire.[45]

Just east of the "swan cross slab" is the "interlace cross-shaft" – an upright shaft of a now-broken cross – at least the slight extension from its present south top suggests that arms originally projected to form a cross. The west face of the shaft is not decorated,[46] but the east face is decorated with a broad band interlace design – four reprinted patterns of an elaborate interlace knot.[47] Françoise Henry, in 1940, writes: "Again in the north of Ireland, on the little island of Inishkeel, near Portnoo, there is the wide, thin shaft of a cross carved on one side only with a very clear-cut ribbon interlacing – the remains obviously of a monument similar to the Carndonagh cross, but less elaborate."[48] She was of the opinion that this broad (rather than narrow) plaited ribbon interlace existed for only a short time in Irish art and that its origin must be in the East, where it appears mostly in textiles and paintings, and it was probably transmitted to Ireland through manuscripts. She dated the Carndonagh cross and the Inishkeel cross shaft to the 7th century. Nowadays, however, the trend is to give the Carndonagh cross a 9th[49] century or later[50] dating, so presumably the Inishkeel cross stem would also be approximately 9th century. Finally might I add that the whole subject of interlace design and its origins is a complex[51] one requiring much further study.

We will now proceed to do the *turas*; there is not much point in being out here on Inishkeel and leaving the island without having gone around the traditional "stations".

Notes

1   *D.A.*, p. 67.
2   John Barrett was Rector of Inishkeel 1802-44; he lived at the Glebe, at Clooney; we will refer to him later; he died in October 1844, aged eighty-seven years.
3   *Annals of the Four Masters* (hereafter *A.F.M.*), vol. I, pp. 242-43.
4   Ibid., p. 253. The *A.U.* inform us that he died in 636 A.D., that he was the ancestor of the powerful Munster sept of the MacCarthys and that he was from Femhin, commonly called Maigh Femhin, a plain in Co. Tipperary.
5   *A.F.M.*, vol. I, p. 252: The Book of Munster tells us
      "It is the same as to be without anything
      If Failbhe Flann be the king."
6   H.G. Leask, *Irish Churches and Monastic Buildings*, vol. I, pp. 17-18.
7   Ibid. p. 18.
8   Ibid. p. 11.

9   I have relied on the writings of Dr. Leask because he describes well the type of stone buildings which were probably the original structures here. In other places, where timber would have been at hand, the early churches would have been wooden (*dairthech*, literally oak-house, was the term used, as opposed to *damlaic*, a stone church). There is a fine article, "The study of early Irish churches," by Ann Hamlin in *Ireland and Europe*, pp. 117-26. In the same publication I would recommend "The layout of Irish early Christian monasteries," pp. 105-113, by Michael Herity.

10   See Patrick Heraughty, *Inishmurray, Ancient Monastic Island* (1982).

11   The east gable is almost at full height; it is lit by a narrow rectangular lintelled window with moulded jambs. The interior face of the south wall shows many signs of rebuilding. The three single-light windows in the south wall have similar moulded jambs; the more westerly window has a simple lancet head, the central window a trefoil head, and the original head of the east window has been replaced by a reused double-chamfered voussoir. (The windows are of 14th-century character.) The chamfered jambs of the pointed door at the west end of the south wall are weathered, and the splayed ingoings are without rear-arch. The west gable is featureless and only the east and west returns of the north wall survive. Some moulded fragments from the east church, St. Mary's, and the sill of a single-light window form part of the low, rectangular altar-like platform reconstructed at the east end of this church for the laying of St. Conall's memorial plaque in 1967. (Above abridged from *A.S.D.*, pp. 272-73.)

12   *D.A.* (1963), p. 252.

13   *British Archaeological Reports* (hereafter *B.A.R.*), British Series 152 (1986) p. 52.

14   Ibid. p. 65.

15   Ibid. Françoise Henry, *Irish Art in the Early Christian Period to AD 800*, p. 125: "another slab has been discovered on Inishkeel in 1963 by P. McGill who kindly sent me a photograph of it; it bears a Crucifixion with a cross of the same outline as the Carndonagh Cross."

16   *A.S.D.*, p. 272; it continues: "the south wall with east return and west half of the north wall survive almost to full height. Only the quoins of the south-east corner, with its three quarter round shaft rising to a corbel stone, remains; the north-east corner has fallen away. The east window has likewise fallen but the surviving fragments of moulded architrave which completely framed the window interior, indicate a splaying opening with plunging sill. Numerous other moulded dressings including two capitals, undoubtedly coeval in date, have been reused in the walling of the medieval nave, mostly in the upper courses of the south wall. Many can be readily identified as forming part of responds and an arch, and their profiles indicate an early 13th century date for the chancel. ... The south door has a pointed head, draw-bar socket and segmental rear-arch."

17   "Notes on Transitional Architectural Fragments in Co. Donegal," *U.J.A.*, vol. 27 (1964), pp. 133-36.

18   The top left corner is broken off and missing. The remainder is in two con-

joining parts. The slab is .96 m. x .85 m. x .03 m. A Maltese cross with a central circle decorates the slab.

19   "It is 1.8m x .27m to .56m x .06m. It is decorated by a simple Latin cross, with bar terminals to three arms, quartering four incomplete concentric circles." (*A.S.D.*, p. 273). Cross in circle motifs are very common on early Christian monuments in Ireland; a simple incised cross-in-circle motif is found on an upright cross slab on Rathlin O'Birne Island near Glencolumbkille; there is also an example at Conwal, near Letterkenny. Crosses in circles or in circular frames on grave slabs were in common use in Ireland as early as the 7th century. *J.R.S.A.I.*, vol. 118 (1988), p. 100).

20   H. Wheeler to P. McGill, 24 July 1953; see also *J.R.S.A.I.*, vol. 64, (1934), p. 262.

21   Henry, *Irish Art in the Early Christian Period to A.D. 800,* pp. 108-9.

22   As on the figure to the right of Christ's body on the recumbent slab which we have described earlier.

23   Where St. Garvan, supposed brother of St. Shanaghan of Loughros, is said to have had his foundation.

24   *B.A.R.* British Series 152 (1986) p. 64.

25   Ibid., p. 63.

26   *Irish Art in the Early Christian Period to A.D. 800,* pp. 148-49.

27   *Irish Art in the Early Christian Period,* p. 109.

28   *The Antiquaries Journal,* vol. LXVIII, part 1, p. 94.

29   Giraldus Cambrensis, *The Topography of Ireland,* 1185-1188 A.D., ed. by J. O'Meara, p. 26.

30   *B.A.R.,* British Series 152 (1986), p. 64.

31   G. Anderson *Scotland in Early Christian Times* (1881).

32   *J.R.S.A.I.,* vol. 113 (1983), p. 24.

33   Ibid.

34   Donatus, *Beasts and Birds in the Lives of the Early Irish Saints,* p. 46.

35   "The Old Irish 'Chariot'," *Antiquity,* vol. 45 (1971), pp. 171-77.

36   Ibid. p. 173.

37   pp. 186-87.

38   *H.P.A.,* p. 32.

39   *J.R.S.A.I.,* vol. 113 (1983), p. 24.

40   *J.R.S.A.I.* (1912), p. 8.

41   Ibid.

42   *Irish Art in the Early Christian Period to A.D. 800,* p. 151.

43   Ibid.

44   *J.R.S.A.I.* (1956), pp. 93-96; *J.R.S.A.I.* (1985), pp. 92-95.

45   *B.A.R.,* British Series 152 (1986), p. 65.

46   Though it has a recess 8 cm. in width and 2 cm. deep along each edge (*A.S.D.*, p. 274).

47   Alastair Rowan, *Buildings of North-West Ulster,* p. 456.

48   *Irish Art in the Early Christian Period,* p. 59.
49   *B.A.R.,* British Series 152 (1986), pp. 49-71.
50   *J.R.S.A.I.* (1985), R.K. Stevenson, pp. 92-95.
51   See R.K. Stevenson, "Aspects of Ambiguity in Crosses and Interlace," *U.J.A.,* vols. 44, 45 (1981-82), pp. 1-27.

IV

THE *TURAS* ON INISHKEEL ISLAND

"HERE IS A celebrated well, which, with the church, is dedicated to St. Conall, and yearly visited by a great concourse of pilgrims, on the 12th of May."[1] This observation on the Inishkeel *turas* comes from 1750. Nowadays the *turas* can be done any time between 22 May – locally accepted as St. Conall's feast-day – and 12 September. Most written works list 22 May as Conall's feast-day; our calendar was revised forward eleven days in 1583 (11 May becoming 22 May) and one is tempted to suggest that the reference of 1750 to people doing the *turas* on 12 May is a throw-back to a time when Conall's feast-day would have been 11 May.

From 1835 we read: "On this island the natives were in the habit of performing *turas*es, but lately it became a place of amusement and drinking, so that the R.C. clergy thought it proper to condemn the practice. ... During the *Turas* the senior of the house of O'Breslen (of which family St. Conall is said to have been a member and the Patron) attended with the Bell of the Saint called Bearnan Conaill.[2] He generally sat or stood or knelt at a Sacred Rocky place called Conall's Bed, and praying in Latin held forth the Bell to be kissed by Pilgrims for which office it was a part of the ceremony, that he should receive more or less from each of them"[3] – i.e. be paid by them.

Though the opposition of the clergy ended the carnival atmosphere of the big *turas* days, people continued to come to the island and do the traditional "rounds". How the *turas* was performed earlier in this century we can gather from these observations, made in August 1919:

"The pilgrims take off their shoes and stockings (if they are wearing any) as soon as they have reached the island.

"Then they walk barefoot to the holy spring, a trickle of water with a strong iron flavour, on the rocks on the north side of the island. Here they first wash their feet in one of the rock pools before approaching the spring, in front of which they kneel and pray, afterwards drinking a little from a limpet shell. The water is also bottled and taken away by some. After this the pilgrim comes up on to the grass above the the rocks and spring, where there are three heaps of stones. Round each of these he walks at least three times, and taking stones from the bottom places them on top; after walking round a heap of stones he kneels before it to pray.

"On leaving the three stone heaps the pilgrim goes east towards a large block of stone also partially covered by the stones contributed by pilgrims, and bearing among others a rounded oval black stone with four parallel white strata in it. Here again he walks round, puts one or more stones on the top and prays. He also takes the oval stone with the white strata, crosses himself with it, passes it round his body, and if he so desires, touches with it any afflicted part of his body.

"Next he climbs on the wall into the churchyard and walks three times round a ruined chapel on the north side of it, prays, and then moves down to the chapel of St. Conal itself. This chapel has the east, south and west walls still standing. The pilgrim walks around it from the east end, round by the south side and back, round the west end to the east again, bowing or curtseying while passing the doors on the south side, and also in some cases when passing in sight of the altar, while coming up by the ruined north wall. The chapel is circumambulated at least three times, the pilgrim then entering the chapel over the north wall and kneeling in front of the altar. The altar consists of a stone slab lying on the ground, once apparently raised on other stones beneath it like a dolmen. It has a round hole in the north end and four rounded stones lying on it which are regarded as healing stones. The pilgrim kneels in front of the altar and grinds round one of the healing stones in the round hole. He then takes each healing stone in turn, crosses himself with it, passes it round his waist from left to right, applies it in some cases to any particularly afflicted part of the body (one pilgrim was seen to touch her foot with it), crosses himself with it again and replaces it upon the altar.

"The pilgrim then leaves the chapel by the doorway on the south side, kneeling and praying in the doorway before leaving. One old woman – the same that touched her foot with the healing stone – was seen to scrape some grit off a stone of the doorway and apply it to her big toe.

"The pilgrims after leaving the chapel of St. Conal have completed the observance and return to the shore where they can put on their shoes again. While at the well and the altar they tear off bits of rag, sometimes apparently brought for the purpose, and leave bits sticking in the rocks near the spring and under or near the altar stone. Some drop pence through the round hole in the stone, and some leave rosaries, scapulars, hair-pins, hair-combs and similar articles by or under the altar stone. The object of the pilgrimage seems to be to obtain relief from some specific complaint, but it is said that the water of the holy spring has properties other than curative in that it has the power of driving away rats and similar vermin when sprinkled in the house."[4]

We will have a brief look at what folklore and literature tell us about the wells and stones used in the *turas* before we go on to record how the *turas* is done nowadays. The extract from 1919 referred to the pilgrims washing their feet in one of the rock pools before approaching the first well. This is the rock pool about which we heard earlier the story from the Doochary area, which said that if the water in this pool turned red when one was washing one's feet, then one of the "party" would be dead within a year. The Gaelic word used to describe this rock pool in folklore is *dabhach*; *tobar* is the generally accepted word for a well.

One comes across references[5] in local folklore to the recurring theme of people who were opposed to the *turas* throwing stones used as part of the *turas* into the sea, and of the stones being returned with the next big wave or being brought in overnight by the sea. Another theme that recurs is that of people who were not of the Catholic faith, but who had an ailment of one type or another, requesting local people who were known to do the *turas* to do it for them, in the hope that their illness would be cured. This leads to amusing stories, where the person doing the *turas* is so desperate to show its efficacy by obtaining relief for the person for whom he is doing it, that he continually appeals, while doing the rounds, to St. Conall to please, please grant alleviation of the sickness, or otherwise the credibility of the *turas* will be diminished in the eyes of others. One person who was under particular pressure to prove the efficacy of the *turas* finishes it by pleading to St. Conall: "*má rinne tú ariamh é, déan anois é* (if ever you did it, please do it now!)."[6]

Of particular interest is the reference from 1919 to the "rounded oval black stone with four parallel white strata in it" which was on top of a large block of stone that one still visits in the middle of the *turas*. The rounded stone however, is gone now. My local informant, Beatrice McHugh, tells me that the stone disappeared "about twenty years ago". She and other local people were doing the *turas* at Easter one year and they saw a group of young men larking about with the stone. Obviously this group of young people, who most likely were in high spirits, enjoying their Easter break, would not have been aware of the significance of the striped stone. This is the stone that used to be passed around the body three times. Folklore from the Doochary area confirms its use during the *turas* in times past, and Isabel

Crozier, writing in 1957, states: "a dark slated stone with curious bands of white quartz, barrel-shaped, and resting on a rock table, is also included in the pattern. Borlase wrote[7] of a similar stone at Cape St. Vincent in Portugal, which was passed round the body sun-ways for different ailments."[8]

The healing stones on the altar, referred to in 1919, have also disappeared. They too must have been there in 1957 because again Isabel Crozier states: "On the altar repose several rounded stones which form part of the ritual for the summer pilgrimages."[9]

The *turas* on Inishkeel island is still done with great devotion by a lot of local people. I have been to the great cathedrals of Notre Dame, Rheims and Santiago de Compostella and have heard the choirs in all of these places, but I find doing the *turas* on Inishkeel island on a summer's day, surrounded by the sounds of the sea, the squawking of the birds and with a carpet of early summer flowers underfoot an even more uplifting experience. Beatrice McHugh is a lovely, gentle, humourous lady in her nineties who lives near by on the mainland and who does the *turas* at every opportunity – when the tide permits. This is how Beatrice instructed me to do the Inishkeel *turas*:

"You first go to St. Conall's well on the far side of the island. This is a spot where the water drips down from above into a pool of water. You kneel here on the rocks at St. Conall's well and say an Act of Contrition, seven Our Fathers, Hail Marys and Glorias and then the Creed. You can step in under the dripping water if you wish and say another Our Father and three Hail Marys and sprinkle yourself with the water. Near the well there is the indentation in a rock which is supposed to have been left by St. Conall's arm when he was resting. Sometimes people lie on their backs on this rock, which is known as St. Conall's bed. Then kneeling at St. Conall's bed you say three Our Fathers, Hail Marys, Glorias and the Creed. You then climb up from the rocks on to the grass above and go to the three cairns of stones. You walk around each cairn of stones clockwise three times. While doing the three rounds of each cairn five Our Fathers, Hail Marys, Glorias and the Creed are said at each; while walking around each cairn you lift stones from the perimeter and throw them up on top of it.

"You then proceed to the Virgin Mary's well (also known as Priest Boyle's well) and, kneeling, say five Our Fathers, Hail Marys, Glorias and the Creed and sprinkle yourself with the water. The next stop on the journey is the large boulder behind [north of] the churchyard [this is the boulder on which the stone with the stripes used to be]; while walking to this large stone you pray for the suffering souls in Purgatory. You walk around this rock three times, again saying five Our Fathers, Hail Marys, Glorias and the Creed.

"The journey is then continued over the little wall stile [south of the big boulder] and down to the old churches. Seven decades of the rosary are then started. You walk around St. Mary's church in a clockwise direction three times, then around St. Conall's church, in a clockwise direction, until the seven decades of the rosary are completed.

"You then kneel in front of the altar inside St. Conall's church and pray for the Pope's and your own intentions. Then you kneel at the door, looking out from St. Conall's church and say three Our Fathers, Hail Marys, Glorias and the Creed, in honour of St. Conall and St. Dallán. A request can now be made of St. Conall and St. Dallán. If so desired, you can then make your way to the large flat rock on the left, which is known as St. Joseph's bed, and you can lie on this rock. This is generally done by people who suffer from back trouble."

Nowadays the *turasanna* at Derryleconnell, Inishkeel, Bruckless, etc. are confined to the the historic sites in these localities. One does not hear now of people walking barefoot from the Lettermacaward-Doochary area to Inishkeel. There are suggestions that in past times there used to be a much longer *turas*, extending from Inishkeel across the bays to Laconnell and even going all the way to Glencolumbkille. When we reach Glencolumbkille on our travels we will find that folklore from that area supports the concept of this long linear *turas* from Glencolumbkille to Inishkeel, and Professor Michael Herity, an authority on the Glencolumbkille area, also notes[10] it in his writings. Hitherto, I always doubted it myself. Rev. Dr. Maguire, in his

Beatrice on her
turas

History of the Diocese of Raphoe written in 1920, supports the concept of an Inishkeel-Laconnell *turas*: "We are also informed by unbroken tradition, confirmed by ineffaceable landmarks, that the Inniskeel *Turas* formerly embraced a long pilgrimage over 'Bothair', through a moor waste from Narin to Oitir Chonail,[11] on the Carn side of Loughross Mor, thence to Conall's Well[12] and thence to Conall's Cross,[13] and lastly across the Loughross Beag inlet to Conall's Flag."[14]

In addition to St. Conall's well and St. Conall's cross there are many other cross-inscribed slabs on the Loughros Point peninsula and I think it is possible that in later times these were all part of a *turas* confined to the Point itself; meantime back to the concept of the Inishkeel-Laconnell-Glencolumbkille *turas*. My father, writing in 1970, states:

"This, we were told, was the *turas* laid out by St. Conall himself. But from our wider knowledge we know that those early saints had no intention of founding 'stations' or pilgrimage sites. In his journeys, St. Conall was merely performing his ecclesiastical duties in the area alotted to his charge, or doing missionary work in the neighbouring *tuatha*[15]. The 'stations' came into being through the devotion of succeeding generations, who offered him their prayers, as intercessor, venerated the ground whereon he trod, the wells where he baptised, and the rocks where he prayed or rested in the course of his journeyings. The aforementioned sacred spots could have marked a portion of the route to Glencolumbkille..."[16]

Folklore gives us a glimpse of St. Conall on his travels across the inlets and peninsulas: "One day as Conall was passing through Barkillew[17], in the mountains behind Laconnell, possibly on his way back from Glencolumbkille, his enemies began to follow him. He quickened down towards the sea and went to cross the water at Loughros Beg. He went across where the second channel is and managed to escape the hunt. He was so exhausted from fleeing his enemies that he lay down on the sand. He fell asleep on the strand and the tide began to come in. As the incoming water approached the spot where Conall was lying the sand actually began to rise up. The strand beneath Conall continued to rise until it was above the level of the water. The incoming tide never touched Conall. This little island is visible for anybody to see, even until this day. No matter how big a tide there is, this island is never covered by the incoming water, in honour of the time that St. Conall lay on it."[18]

We now finish with the Inishkeel *turas* and our brief discussion about the longer pilgrimage to Laconnell and Glencolumbkille: we will discuss the latter subject again at Loughros Point. Let us now have a look at St. Conall's bell, and its history, which formed an integral part of the old *turas*.

Notes

1   Butler's Journey, quoted by McParlan in *Statistical Survey of the County of Donegal*, p. 112.

2   We will refer in detail to St. Conall's Bell in the next chapter.

3   O.S. Letters of Donegal; John O'Donovan, writing from Ardara; TD, pp. 114-15, 117-19, ms. pp. 202-4, 206-7.

4   By J.H. Hutton; reproduced in *Sacred Waters*, pp. 79-80.

5   Dept. of Irish Folklore, ms. 948, pp. 27-33.

6   Dept. of Irish Folklore, ms. 948, pp. 44-47, Seán Bán McMenamin, who states that St. Conall's feast-day was 22 May and that it always used to be a holiday (*lá saoire*) in the area long ago – presumably to allow the people to do the *turas*.

7   W.C. Borlase, *Dolmens of Ireland*, vol. III, p. 719.

8   *D.A.* (1957), p. 68.

9   Ibid.

10   Herity, *Gleanncholmcille*, p. 37.

11   Marked Connell's Bank on the O.S. maps; *oitir*: a bank or ridge in the sea.

12   On Loughros Point peninsula.

13   Also on Loughros Point peninsula.

14   At Laconnell.

15   *Tuath*: a territory, region; an old Gaelic word, it originally meant a population group capable of maintaining 3,000 (or fewer, down to 700) soldiers in emergency and by extension the land it occupied; ruled by a king.

16   *H.P.A.*, p. 16.

17   *Barr*: top; *coill*: a wood; *Barr Coilleadh*.

18   Dept. of Irish Folklore, ms. 1735, p. 52; Pádraig Ó Sibhleáin *as Iochtar Tíre*; the general Kilclooney–Narin area is often referred to as "Downstrands" – *Iochtar Tíre* [*íochtar*: lower, bottom, though it can also mean northern; *tír*: land, country].

V

St. Conall's Bell

WE MENTIONED EARLIER that prior to the Inishkeel *turas* being banned by the Roman Catholic clergy in 1850 – because of the "fair day" atmosphere of drinking and fighting – the senior of the house of O'Breslin (who were one of the *erenagh* families of Inishkeel) attended with the bell called the *Beárnán Chonaill* – so called [*beárnán*: a little gap] because it was gap toothed, eaten with rust and full of holes. The elder O'Breslin sat or stood or knelt at St. Conall's bed and praying in Latin held forth the bell to be kissed by the pilgrims. He could charge a fee for this honour – "that he should receive more or less from each of them" in John O'Donovan's words. Local tradition tells us that O'Breslin said to each pilgrim: "*Pinginn domhsa agus póg don Bheárnáin* – a penny to me and you can kiss the *Beárnán*." Naturally after the abolition of the "station" by the clergy the earning value of the bell to O'Breslin would have diminished and this may have been a factor in its sale to Major Nesbitt, a topic we will deal with shortly.

It was the tradition throughout Ireland in earlier centuries to enclose venerated relics of early saints in richly ornamented bejewelled cases or shrines; St. Conall's bell was no exception and it is the bronze shrine surrounding the bell, now in the British Museum in London, which is of most artistic interest.

However, first the bell. Cormac Bourke tells us that "Early Irish hand-bells fall into two distinct classes on the basis of the material used in their manufacture. The first group are made from sheet iron with riveted joints and an overall coating of bronze. The second group are made from cast bronze."[1] St. Conall's bell belongs to the first group. It is of simple "box" form made of sheet iron, riveted on one side and with remains of bronze plating, stands about 7" high, by 5.25" x 3.5" at the base; at the top it is 3.75" by 1.25". Because the bell had become worn and eaten, by the 12th century something had to be done to hold it together so a new bronze top was riveted on to the original bell. This bronze fitting is decorated with an ornate cross set in panels bearing different interlace motifs.

In the 15th century the decorated bronze shrine, in which to encase the bell for protection, was created. It is decorated with silver panels and a cabochon rock-crystal. The front of the shrine bears a Crucifixion scene surrounded by numerous panels representing various religious figures. In the panel beneath the Crucifixion is a circular setting which possibly used to contain a relic of St. Conall. On the back of the shrine is one undivided panel, on which appears three rows of figures, four in each row. There is black-letter inscription here and there on the margins of the shrine. The shrine-case has a loop attaching a carrying chain – the elder O'Breslin used to wear the bell and shrine by hanging the chain around his neck; he also brought the bell and shrine to the home of sick people and placed it around their necks.

What do we know of the history of St. Conall's bell? Firstly let us look at the possible origin of such bells in general. We have no proof of bells having been used before the introduction of Christanity.[2] It is thought that they were introduced to this country by the first missionaries: "Small bells ... were undoubtedly introduced with Christianity. ... Their use amongst the Christian clergy is supposed to have been coeval with their religion; and the missionaries, who were sent to convert the Pagan Irish, would not omit bringing with them an appendage of their profession which is still thought so necessary."[3] We find in the *Lives of St. Patrick*, preserved in the *Book of Armagh*, that Patrick is described as introducing bells through the country – "He carried with him across the Shannon, fifty bells, fifty patens, fifty chalices, Altar books of the law, books of the Gospel, and left them in new places."[4] Whether Patrick ever crossed the Shannon is another question altogether! Finally I would add that it has been suggested[5] that their origin lies in the little bells used by the Romans at their dining-tables to summon their servants.

Why was the bell in the possession of the O'Breslins? Because they were the erenagh [*airchinneach*: steward of church lands; from this word comes the surname McInerney: *Mac an Airchinnigh*] family of the Inishkeel religious foundation. In the appendix to the 1609 Inquisition we are told that "in the said barony of Tireheugh is alsoe the parishe of Eniskeele, containinge in all six ballibetaghes, of which there are fower quarters[6] of herenagh land, whereof there are three severall herenaghs, viz. O'Breslan, O'Keran and O'Moyny." The coarb [*comharba*: a co-heir or successor] and erenagh held prominent positions in the old Gaelic church organisation. In early

Shrine of St. Conall's bell (by kind permission of the British Museum)

*Artist's impression of the back of the shrine
(after British Museum photograph)*

centuries the coarb was the successor of the founder of the local church. He was the rector or parish priest. From the beginning the erenagh's role was to look after and develop the land around the religious institution, allowing the ordained clergy to contemplate higher matters – "in auncient times there weare divers landes given by temporall lords to saintes or holie men in the said com,[7] for celebratinge divine service and prayinge for their soules healthes, and that the said saintes or holy men, dedicatinge themselves onely to praier and the service of God, did, for their better ease, ordaine and constitute severall herenaghes to manure and occupie those landes, which were usually a whole sept, and the principall of the sept was named the herenagh."[8] After the 12th-century church reform many of the coarbships became laicised. The lay coarb and erenagh had a hereditary position and one local sept often controlled it for centuries.[9] We are told that the erenagh had "to provide from his revenue for the support of the clergy and the maintenance of religious services, churches and chapels. He was often the custodian of the shrine or bell of the local saint."[10]

In 1609 we saw mention of the erenagh families of "O'Breslan, O'Keran and O'Moyny". Dr. Maguire, in his *History of the Diocese of Raphoe*, states that in 1609 the English scribe wrote O'Keran in mistake for Maolcaorain[11] – Mulherns, a branch of the O'Moynys (Mooneys) – and contends that the O'Mooneys and the Mulherns were entitled to be called coarbs and could claim blood relationship with the founder of the original monastery. Another possibility is that O'Keran should have been written O'Geran, now anglicised Sharp.[12]

However, there is no doubt about the O'Breslins; they were certainly erenaghs of Inishkeel and therefore were probably in custody of St. Conall's bell for many centuries. They are among the very first people that we can identify as having occupied the territory between the Gweebarra and the Owenea rivers and it appears as if the first Breslin to be mentioned in the ancient historical sources actually lived in the Loughadoon–Summy area. Their centre of power later moved northwards and they were lords of Fanad[13] until about 1263 A.D. In the next century (from at least 1322) we find them brehons[14] in Fermanagh where they remained until the Plantation, and erenaghs[15] in one parish there too – Derryvullan – as well as erenaghs here in Inishkeel.[16] In 1420 Murrogh O'Breslin was parish priest of the large parish of Inishkeel[17] and Maolmuire O'Breslin, who visited Rome in 1443,[18] was at that time parish priest of Inishkeel.[19] By this time the influence of the powerful O'Boyle sept was increasing in this area and in later years they supplied many of the parish priests of Inishkeel.

Tradition tells us that from the era of St. Conall the O'Breslins were in possession of the bell; it was passed from one generation of the family to the next, remaining in the possession of the eldest son. It is said that whenever there was strife in the country the bell was hidden for safe keeping. Sometimes when unrest in the area lasted a long time the site where the bell had been hidden was forgotton: "When the Planters first came to the shores of the Gweebarra, O'Breslin took with him the bell and shrine and buried them safely in Magheramore. In the stress and strain of the times the spot was forgotten, and it was feared that the relic was irretrievably lost. But a number of the faithful pledged themselves to the task of recovering it, and day after day, in prayer and fasting repaired to Magheramore. Tradition avers that their faith and patience were at length rewarded. Like the lost and buried bell of Vermich[20] the *Beárnán* sent forth its musical note from its subterranean hiding and was recovered."[21]

Tradition tells us that later, during the Penal Times, anxiety for the safety of St. Conall's bell caused it to be mislaid again and it was lost for many years. Then one Sunday, as a young girl herded cattle in the wood of Garrowchuill [*Garbh Choill*: the rough wood], she heard a tinkling sound overhead and the long-lost relic fell to the ground at her feet. The news quickly spread that it had dropped from the sky. Investigation revealed, however, that it had fallen from a crevice in the fork of an overhanging tree where some careful hand had hidden it long before. It had fallen because one of the cattle had been scratching itself against the tree.

Folklore tells us that the O'Breslins used to bring the bell from place to place throughout the countryside to people who were ill. The sick person hung the bell around his or her neck and said certain prescribed prayers and very soon he or she would start on the road to recovery, if that was God's will. Local legend also attests that it was not in fact one of the O'Breslins themselves who finally sold the bell to Major Nesbitt of Woodhill House, Ardara.

This latter claim brings us to the next stage in the bell's history. By the 1830s the bell was in the posession of Major Nesbitt. It is said to have been sold to him by its elderly keeper, Connell MacMichael O'Breslin, who lived in Glengesh, Ardara, and who had fallen on hard times. In 1833, when Dr. Petrie exhibited drawings of it to the Royal Irish Academy, it was in the possession of Major Nesbitt.[22] John O'Donovan examined the bell in Woodhill House in 1835 and wrote: "I have just returned from Major Nesbitt's who received me with great urbanity and showed me all his collection. ... Beárnán Conaill is a beautiful and elaborately decorated relic. ... The Bell is enclosed in a case and rattles inside it, but it has not been opened these centuries back, perhaps not since the formation of the case." He then goes on to describe the shrine-case and finishes: "The Major has several other things, but nothing that Mr. Petrie has not in his collection excepting a meadog or knife, and a torque or golden collar."[23]

The drawings of the bell exhibited in 1833 by Petrie, and made[24] in Woodhill House, were later used to illustrate the bell in a book published in 1872; this publication gives us concrete information on the theft of the bell from Major Nesbitt, and its subsequent travels. Here is the account: "In 1833, when the late Dr. Petrie exhibited drawings of it to the Royal Irish Academy, it was in the possession of Major Nesbitt, of Wood Hill, Ardara. He bought it of a man called Breslin of the parish of Glencolumkille,[25] in the same county of Donegal, who was the hereditary keeper, the consideration paid being three young cows and an annuity. It is said that the cows died the next day, and that Breslin never prospered afterwards. The tradition in the county is that Breslin's ancestor was a servant to St. Conall of Inis Cael.

"Major Nesbitt died 3rd January, 1845, and the same night his house was plundered. I have been informed by the Rev. G.N. Tredenneck, of Keldoney, a nephew of the late Major, who was in the house at the time of the robbery, that, besides the bell, there were stolen, a most valuable portable altar, studded with precious stones, several gold torques, and ornaments of value,

*Front view of bell
(courtesy of the British
Museum)*

and many gold coins. Captain Richard Nesbitt, who succeeded to the property of his brother, offered a reward of £100 for discovery of the perpetrators of the robbery, but without effect, and it was afterwards found that the thief was a near relative, staying in the house at the same time, and that the articles having been conveyed to England and disposed of, the reward proved ineffectual. Though the young thief was well known, there were reasons for not prosecuting him for the felony, and he was allowed to leave the neighbourhood; since which time he has died in Birmingham. I have also been informed by Sir James Dombrain, a most intimate friend of the late Major, that he was at Wood Hill when the *Barnan of S. Conall*, as it was always called, was purchased of the last surviving member of the family of Breslin, who was then an old man. The Major requested Sir James to open the case, and he took out the bell but not without great difficulty. The relic was once offered to Sir James for £10, but he declined the purchase, and for many years it lay *perdue*.

"About 1858 Mr. Robert Moore, who exhibited it at Worcester,[26] bought the bell of a furniture dealer in Birmingham for £3. It had not been in the dealer's hands many days; it had been brought to him by a poor woman, who sold it to him for five shillings. A few days afterwards the woman returned to the dealer in company with her husband, and was desirous to get it back; but it had in the meantime passed into the safe keeping of Mr. Moore, who resolutely refused to part with it, although they offered him £50. After it was exhibited at Worcester the authorities of the British Museum negotiated with Mr. Moore for the purchase of it; but on declining his terms, it was afterwards sold for £80 to A.W. Franks, Esq., of London, in whose possession it now remains."[27]

Mr. Franks subsequently had the bell and shrine transferred to the Medieval and Later Antiquities section of the British Museum.

To this day the shrine for the bell of St. Conall is on permanent display in the British Museum, London. In 1983 I had the pleasure of examining the shrine at close quarters. Before going on a trip to London I wrote to the British Museum, asking to be allowed to view the shrine. On arrival at the museum I was brought down into the bowels of the building. I brought my daughter Eleanor, then aged eight, with me, because I was keenly aware that probably nobody from this area in my lifetime had had the chance to view the shrine closely and I wanted Eleanor to see it too. When the lift had descended to the lower floors of the museum and my daughter and I stepped out there was disquiet for a moment because they had only been expecting one visitor and were unhappy that I had brought an extra person, even someone as young as Eleanor. This was because they prefer an atmosphere of quiet and calm on account of the study and indexing which goes on in these lower floors of the museum. Nonetheless, the shrine was brought along and placed on the table in front of us. I examined the shrine for a short time and if there was disquiet earlier there was surely confusion now when I stated that this was not the shrine of the bell of St. Conall. I had brought along my copy of W. J. Doherty's wonderful book, *Inishowen and Tirconnaill*, in which there is a detailed description of the *Beárnán Chonaill*. As evidence of my claim that the shrine before me was not that of St. Conall I pointed out to the staff that the shrine did not look like the one represented in W.J. Doherty's book. It subsequently turned out that the shrine placed before me was that of the Beárnán Coulawn[28] – someone had made a simple mistake in the Gaelic names. The correct one was then found by the helpful staff and set before me and I can confirm to you that it is indeed a beautiful object. Next time you are in London and have time to spare, go and have a look at it in the Medieval and Later Antiquities section of the British Museum, where it is on permanent display.[29]

We now leave the subject of the bell and shrine and enter very perilous ground indeed – the question of who St. Conall really was. It is a question which many would regard as being unanswerable.

Notes

1   *J.R.S.A.I.* (1980), p. 54.
2   Petrie, *P.R.I.A.*, vol. 1 (1836-40).
3   Walker, *Historical Memories of the Irish Bards*, p. 127. Walker adds that "In *Laoi na Seilge*, an Irish poem, which was written at a very early period, *white books and bells* are mentioned as appendages of the priesthood."
4   Ellacombe, *The Church Bells of Devon*, p. 369.
5   F. Henry, *Irish Art in the Early Christian Period to A.D. 800*.
6   Here the land measurement of four quarters to the ballybetagh (an old Irish land measurement, *baile biatach*) is used, so these three families between them obviously owned a sixth of the old medieval parish of Inishkeel. Quarter: *ceathramhadh* from *ceathair*: four.
7   *Comitate*: country; *D.A.* (1960), p. 273.
8   Appendix in Inquisitions, Ultonia, vol. 2.
9   *D.A.* (1960), p. 273.
10   Ibid.
11   See *A.F.M.* 985 A.D., vol. 2, p. 719: "Maelciarain ua Maighne, successor of Colum-Cille was cruelly martyred"; see Colby, *Ordnance Survey of the County of Londonderry*, p. 38: "Maolciaran, the grandson of Maighne... The O'Maighnes were

hereditary *erenaghs* of Inishkeel and are still a numerous tribe. They usually write their name Mooney."

12　See p. 52, n. 72.

13　The early accounts of the Breslin family in the *A.U.* reflect the violent relationship which this powerful sept had with its neighbours – clans who had equal lust for power; and indeed treachery was not confined to the opposing camps:

1186 A.D: Conn ua Breislen, candle of hospitality and champion of the North of Ireland, was killed by a party of the Cenél-Eoghain.

1214 A.D: Donn ua Breislen was killed by his own council in treachery.

1251 A.D: Gilla-Crist ua Breslen, chief of Fanad and his kinsman were killed by Ceallach ua Baighill (O'Boyle) the dumb. (In the previous year Niall ua Cannannan [Cannon], king of Tír-Conaill, was killed).

1261 A.D: Conchobur ua Neill was ... killed ... by Donn ua Breslen, chief of Fanad.

1263 A.D: Donn ua Breslen was killed by Domhnall ua Domhnaill in Rath – both in the court of the bishop. (For 1263 the *A.U.* also have the interesting entry: "A hot Summer in this year.")

These brief references reveal a collage of many of the great Donegal families in conflict – the Breslins, Boyles, Cannons and O'Donnells (by now being supported by the MacSweeneys).

14　*A.U.*, 1440 A.D: "Domnall ua Breislen, namely, an eminent brehon and one who was to be ollam of the Fir-Manach, died."

15　*A.U.*, 1495 A.D: "Ua Breislen, namely, Eogan, son of Eogan, son of Pierce, son of Saerdalach, that is, the brehon of Mag Uidhir and herenagh of the Third of Daire-Maelain, died."

16　*D.A.* (1960), p. 281.

17　*H.D.R.*, vol. I, p. 498.

18　Ibid. p. 259.

19　Ibid. p. 498.

20　The reference to the Bell of Vermich refers to a tradition of a bell which was said to have been heard underground. There are numerous references in the literature to churches and towns being swallowed up by earthquakes and that the bells of the buried churches would continue to be heard to ring at certain times of the year.

21　P.J. McGill, *Irish Press*, 21 April 1954.

22　Ellacombe, *The Bhurch Bells of Devon*, p. 367.

23　O.S. Letters, pp. 117-18, 19 October.

24　Though used by Petrie, the drawings were actually made by George du Noyer, of the O.S., in Woodhill.

25　Breslin lived in Glengesh, which was part of the Parish of Glencolumbkille until the Ardara Parish was created in 1829; so we can deduce that the bell and shrine came into the possession of Major Nesbitt prior to 1829.

26　It was exhibited in Worcester in 1862 when the Archaeological Institute held their congress there; it was then in the possession of Robert Moore of Birmingham; it is fully described in the catalogue of the exhibition by Albert Wray.

27   Ellacombe, *The Church Bells of Devon*, p. 367.

28   Which, I learned later, had been found in a hollow tree at a place called Killcuilawn in the mountains of Co. Tipperary; named after St. Cuilleann.

29   The registration numbers of the bell and shrine are BM, MLA 1889, 9-2, 22 (Bell), 23 (Shrine). Monochrome photographs are available. Please give the registration numbers of the bell or shrine if you are ordering photographs. The views available are as follows:

Bell   PS 110962 – side view

         PS 110963 – side view

         AS 11-2 – front view

Shrine AS 17.55 – panel with saints

         AS 17.56 – crucifixion

I would recommend the latter.

VI

WHO WAS CONALL CAOL?

WHO WAS ST. CONALL? When I decided to write a book based on the sites of west Donegal associated with St. Conall I never thought I'd have such difficulty in ascertaining who he really was. The study of what has been written on saints – hagiography – is very difficult and not an area for an amateur like myself to become embroiled. The problem is that even though Conall is said to have died about the years 590[1] to 596[2] A.D. we come across no written references to him for many centuries afterwards. When these references to him do appear they are very short and mostly suggest that he was known as Conall Caolmaine, that his feast-day was 22 May, that he was associated with Inishkeel and that he was born of the Cenél Conaill – a term applied to the many septs who sprang from Conall Gulban [cenél: race, nation]. Conall's pedigree occurs in the following manuscripts:

(1) The 15th century *Book of Lecan*:[3]
Conall Mór Mac Maine Chail Caelmaine
(2) The 15th century *Mac Firbis Genealogies*:[4]
Conall Mac Maine Caoil no Caolmaine
(3) The 17th century *Trias Thaumaturga*:[5]
Conailus de Iniscaoil, filius Manu Coelii
(4) The 17th century *Martyrology of Donegal*: [6]
22 May: Conall, Abbot of Inis Caoil, in Cinél Conaill, and he is himself of the Cinél Conaill, according to the Naemhsheanchus.[7]

(5) In the early 10th century *Martyrology of Tallaght*[8] the entry regarding Conaill, Inse Cail, appears at 22 May.

(6) His name also occurs in the *Félire Oengusso* which is contained in the 15th century *Leabhar Breac*,[9] at 11 May. It reads: Féil Conaill Inse Cail, ó inis cail a n-iarthar Tíre Conaill.

Conall's supposed family[10] tree is given in the 17th century by Michael Ó Clérigh and his colleagues (the Four Masters) and I have represented it here beside that of St. Columba, since it suggests that they were related:

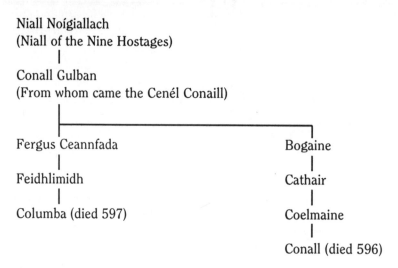

Niall Noígiallach
(Niall of the Nine Hostages)

Conall Gulban
(From whom came the Cenél Conaill)

Fergus Ceannfada   Bogaine

Feidhlimidh   Cathair

Columba (died 597)   Coelmaine

                                    Conall (died 596)

Niall Noígiallach was the first High King (*Ard-Rí*) of Ireland. The high-king-ship of Ireland was held for six hundred years, from about 404 to 1002, by the descendants of Niall Noígiallach and his brothers.[11] Columba's descent from this royal blood is not in doubt. It is the accounts[12] written about Columba within a hundred years of his death which make his pedigree so certain, a pedigree (three of his first cousins were monarchs of Ireland) which helped him become the most illustrious of the saints of Ireland. However we have no written works from an early date to support Conall's pedigree and it must therefore be questioned. A family tree recorded a thousand years after his supposed death, and with no earlier written records to support it, must be doubted.[13]

What else do we know of Conall from the written sources? He has long been associated with the *Cáin Domhnaigh*[14] which includes an epistle and a highly technical law tract on the observance of Sunday and the punishments for its violation. This document is included in, among others, *The Yellow Book of Lecan*,[15] and the Gaelic text itself declares that it was brought from Rome by Conall Mac Coelmaine. Pleasant as it would be to believe that this epistle had been brought back by Conall while on a pilgrimage to Rome[16] – it said that Conall wrote the epistle down in his own hand from an epistle which was sent down from Heaven to Conall while he was saying mass at the Altar of Peter in Rome[17] – it is now believed that Ireland probably received this epistle from the Frankish dominions where it was spreading in the 8th century, long after Conall's supposed lifespan.

The remaining written reference we have on Conall is from John Colgan's *Acta Sanctorum*,[18] published in 1645. He writes of "S. Conaldi cognomento coel seu Coely Abbatis de Inis-coel, in Tirconallia". Conall is only mentioned because of his association with Dallán Forgaill, though it must be pointed out that the *Acta Sanctorum* is incomplete – it ends in March. Mention is made of Dallán Forgaill because his feast-day is in January, whereas Colgan had not reached Conall's feast-day which is in May. We are told that they were close friends and were both buried in Inishkeel. The Dallán Forgaill national school, opened in 1933 (now closed) at Kilclooney, the Dallán Forgaill drama group in Narin, and the prayers at the end of the Inishkeel *turas* "to St. Conall and St. Dallán" remind us that Dallán still lives in the hearts of the people of this area. So I think it is only deserving that we have a look at what we have been told about him, from various sources – most of which was based on Colgan's original work. We start with the *Martyrology of Donegal*, 1630, which at 29 January states: "Dallán Forgaill, of Maighin, of the race of Colla Uais,[19] Monarch of Ireland. His name was Eochaidh, son of Colla, son of Erc. It was he that composed the celebrated panegyric on Colum Cille, which is called Amhra Choluim Chille, and another little Amhra on Seanán of Inis-Cathaigh. And he was interred at Inis-Caoil, a place sacred to Conall of Inis-Caoil."

Dallán Forgaill is said to have been the most important man of letters of his time in Ireland. *The Amhra*[20] *Choluim Chille* referred to above is of consuming interest to scholars, who have as yet not managed to interpret it completely. This is because the language used is that of the ancient *filidh*, the poets/satirists in the old Celtic order of things – "*The Amra Choluim-cille*, 'Eulogy of Colum-cille', is a composition of extraordinary obscurity, partly because of the antiquity of the language, but mainly by reason of its intentionally artificial character. It is indeed the most famous example of *bérla na filid*, that pseudo-rhetorical, arbitrarily reconstructed phraseology [21] and diction which was regarded as a distinct language, the use of which was the insignia and the prerogative of the *filid*.... There is, as yet, no satisfactory translation of the *Amra*...."[22]

We will complete our look, for now, at Dallán Forgaill, by reviewing the interpretations of earlier writers, all based on John Colgan's work of 1647. Dr. Maguire in 1920, writes: "It is now time to say something of St. Connell's famous friend, Dallan Forgail. 'Euchodius' is the Latin form given by Colgan for his original name. The better known appellation of Dallan is obviously derived from *dall*, blind; for at an early stage in his career he lost the use of his eyes. Notwithstanding this dismal fate, he became the most eminent man of letters in Ireland, at a time when the paths of scholarship were eagerly pursued by a host of able men. He was antiquary, philosopher, rhetorician, and poet, all in one. He was the literary chief, the file laureate of Erin in his day. A saint's life and a martyr's death crown the glory of his fame.

"He was born, as Colgan tells us, in Teallach Eathach, which we take to be Tullyhaw, in Cavan. Removed by only a few degrees of descent from Colla, King of Ireland, St. Maidoc, of the same lineage, was his cousin. From his mother, Forghella, he received the second name, Forgail, which we some-times find added in the old writers. Nothing that parental care could accom-plish, was left undone to perfect his education in sacred or secular subjects. From an early date he took to the antiquarian lore of his country, as a spe-cial study. It was in this department, so indispensable for an Irish scholar of the sixth century, that he first attained an eminent place. Nor unlikely, his re-search into ancient records had something to do with the difficulty of the style in which he wrote. It appeared archaic even to experts who lived cen-turies before Colgan wrote; and we are told by this author how, in the schools of Irish antiquities, it was usual to expound Dallan's compositions by adding long commentaries on these rare specimens of the old Celtic tongue."[23]

From an earlier date, 1873, we read: "Colgan, at p. 204 of his *Acta Sanctorum*, says that the merits of St. Connell are set forth in a beautiful panegyric[24] pronounced upon him by St. Dallan, who was his intimate friend and enthusiastic admirer. This St. Dallan was a very distinguished scholar and antiquarian. ... The learning and ability of St. Dallan are praised at great length by Colgan, who enumerates a good many of his works which he him-self has seen and read, but found very difficult to understand. These works, like others of the same class, have disappeared, unfortunately, since Colgan's time. Between St. Dallan and St. Connell there existed, as I have already re-marked, the closest friendship, and hence we find St. Dallan often on a visit with St. Connell at Inishkeel. This friendship grew at last into an intense af-fection, which made St. Dallan frequently pray that he might be buried in the same grave with St. Connell, to whom he mentioned the subject of this prayer, and accompanied it with a request that if he were the survivor he would take care to have his remains laid in the grave which he had prepared for himself at Inishkeel. On the occasion of one of these visits of St. Dallan to the island, a band of pirates broke into the monastery, and in their career of plunder seized St. Dallan, cut off his head, and flung it into the sea. St. Connell, who contrived to escape the fury of the pirates, when he came forth from his hiding place and heard the fate of his dear friend, fell upon his knees, and prayed with great fervour for a short time, when the head of St. Dallan rose out of the waters, advanced and replaced itself upon the trunk, and then St. Connell buried the body in the grave destined for himself, where the two saints now repose, under the walls of that monastery in which they had spent so many happy days together."[25]

I wish that the quest for Conall's origins could be left on this inspirational note, but this can't be done. The problem is, as I've pointed out earlier, that we are dealing with references written hundreds and hundreds of years after his suggested lifespan. Imagine if somebody set out to write about you in five hundred years time; how accurate would it be, even though nowadays there are many methods of storing information? However I do concede that in earlier society genealogy was very important and family trees were handed down orally from one generation to another.

To understand the revisionist way in which an attempt is made to unravel any details of our early saints, we must take a broad look at early Christianity in Ireland and the way in which it was spread in the following centuries. Though it is likely that there were early Christians in Munster – including St. Ciarán who is associated with the Kilcar area of Co. Donegal – before Palladius arrived in 431 A.D. with a small Christian mission, the introduction of Christianity throughout Ireland has been generally attributed to St. Patrick, whose mission arrived "around the middle of that century"[26] (5th). Every schoolchild knows that when he first came to Ireland he tended sheep for Miliucc, who is said to have had a daughter named Brónach, of whom we will hear more later. Though it is likely that Patrick's mission was confined to the area represented by present-day east Ulster, subsequent embellishment of his achievements would have us believe that he journeyed throughout the length and breadth of Ireland.

Patrick's mission was inspired by a form of church organisation in what is now the north of England.[27] In the beginning the Christian church in Ireland, as in the rest of western Europe, was episcopal – based on the ecclesiastical jurisdiction of a bishop – but gradually its character changed and the organisation became monastic. This is a very important point; as some of the great monastic centres – as Armagh had become by the 7th century – became more powerful they made claim to many outlying churches throughout the country and after taking control of these churches they then encouraged the cult and reputation of their own founder, often obliterating the memory of the holy man who had first set up the outlying church. Thus the cults of Patrick and Colmcille and other luminaries grew and grew over the centuries, at the expense of other less powerful earlier ecclesiastics.

Close to the area of Patrick's mission in east Ulster, and perhaps linked[28] with it, there was, at the same time, a very influential monastic centre at Nendrum (Mahee island) in Strangford Lough. I mention this place because it will be suggested later that the founder of this centre, an early ecclesiastic named Mochóe - also called Cóelán - is one and the same as Conall Caol of Inishkeel. Mochóe's death is recorded by the annalists at 496, 497 and 490[29] and his feast-day is given as 23 June. Traditionally we have been told that Conall Caol died *c.* 596, but if he is synonomous with Mochóe (Cóelán), who died *c.* 496, then this brings his possible lifespan back to a very early stage of Christianity in Ireland. We are told that Mochóe was first converted by St. Patrick - "Now while Patrick was (going) along his way, he saw a tender youth herding swine. Mochaoi was his name (*'Mochae a ainm'*). Patrick preached to him and baptized him, and tonsured him [*romberr:* clipped the beard], and gave him a gospel (*soiscéal*) and a credence table (*menistir*). And he gave him, also, at another time, a crozier ... and Mochae promised a shaven pig every year to Patrick, and this is still offered."[30] Brónach, daughter of Miliucc, Patrick's old master, is said to be the mother of Mochóe (Cóelán).

We will for now leave the subject of Mochóe (Cóelán) and east Ulster - we will return to it later - and come back to Inishkeel and examine the place-name *Inis Caoil* and the local family tree assigned to Conall Mac Caolmaine, though bearing in mind that it is unlikely to reveal Conall's true identity to us. We would do well to remember Ó Riain's words of caution: "saints' pedigrees are generally far more useful pointers to the spread of their cults than to their places of origin, which had already been mostly forgotten by the end of the seventh century".[31]

The Gaelic for Inishkeel is *Inis Caoil* [*inis*: an island, *caol*: narrow, slender]. *Inis Caoil*, however, does not translate as "the narrow island" - an examination of the early source material (genealogies, martyrologies, etc.) reveals that the second part of the name cannot be explained as an adjective as it does not change in form in the genitive case. The second element must therefore be explained as the genitive singular of the noun *caol* with the meaning "slender, narrow person, place or thing". [32]

In the source material variations of the word "*caol*" appear - in particular "*cael*", "*coel*" and "*cail*". Later we will find these words appearing in association with saints other than Conall of *Inis Caoil*, possibly suggesting a connection.

A random sample of Conall's genealogies recorded at the start of this chapter is:

Conall Mac Maine Caol no Caolmaine

Conall Mór Mac Maine Chail Caelmaine

Conall m. Maine Cail ar slicht Cathair m. Bogaine

m. Conaill Gulban

and the quatrain:

Conall mór mac Maine Chaoil,
Caolmaine mac do Chathaoir;
Cathaoir, ba coimseach ngoile,
an sechtmadh mac Boghaine.

As demonstrated in Conall's supposed family tree earlier in the chapter these genealogies suggest that Conall was a son (m. = *mac*, son of) of a Maine or Caolmaine, who was a son of Cathaoir who in turn was a son of Bogaine. The latter, Enda Bogaine, was an undoubtedly real figure in history, a son of Conall Gulban (*obs.* 464) and the man who gave his name to the sept called the Cenél mBogaine whose kings ruled much of south-west Donegal for over five centuries. The Cenél mBogaine were a branch of the Cenél Conaill – named after Conall Gulban – and thus we often find Conall Caol being assigned to the Cenél Conaill in the genealogies.

The name Cathair also appears regularly in the genealogies written in the 17th century by that prince of scribes, Cú Choigriche Ó'Cléirigh,[33] one of the Four Masters. The latter informs us that Cathair was a son of Enda Bógaine and states that Caelmaine, Conall Caol's alleged father, was a son of this Cathair.[34] However I have my reservations about the name Caelmaine. It only occurs in the genealogies in relation to Conall Caol, though that is understandable enough (as father of a famous son), but it appears in such a variety of forms – Maine Chail, Maine caoil, Caelmaine, Maine Caoil – that I suspect it is bogus. There is no doubt that through the ages the word "caol" was associated with St. Conall, just as it was with the island of *Inis Caoil*, but of the name "Caolmaine" I have misgivings. I must remind you again that the genealogies of saints written down hundreds of years after their lifespan must be suspect and are the result of centuries of oral history finally being written and then rewritten, transcribed, added to, adapted to political ends, rewritten after plagues had decimated monastic communities and then being copied and recopied by scribes who themselves were not slow to use their imagination in trying to explain obscure facts.

A close examination of what the genealogists wrote suggests that Caolmaine is possibly a bogus name made up from Maine Chaoil/Maine caoll/Maine Chail. Thus we could have "Conall son of Maine Caol" or "Conall son of Maine of Caol" – the latter meaning either "Conall from Caol" or more probably "Maine of Caol".

"Maine" was a very common name in ancient Ireland; it crops up in the genealogies so frequently that it is unlikely to help us in our search. Possibly the most illustrious Maine was he who was brother of the progenitor of the Cenél Conaill, Conall Gulban, and who gave his name to an area in

Westmeath [*Tír Maine*, better known as *Teffia* (*Tethbe*)] – a county where there are traces of a St. Conall cult to be found. We will refer to this county later.

Before going any further I think we should see if investigating the name "Conall" throws any light on our enquiries. If nothing else at least it has been demonstrated from the genealogies that "Conall" is the proper spelling of this Christian name! There are a number of other variations in use.

The first thing to point out is that the geographical area to which the cult of Conall Caol is generally associated – present-day west Donegal – forms part of *Tír Chonaill* and was peopled by the Cenél Conaill. It is my opinion that the name Conall, subsequently given to the ecclesiastic who is said to have introduced Christianity among the Cenél Conaill who inhabited the territory bordering *Inis Caoil*, would have been influenced by an inclination among the Cenél Conaill to honour their great progenitor, also named Conall (Conall Gulban). In other words, there are shades here of an ancestral cum Christian cult.

We will concentrate for now on the name "Conall" to see if it will shed any light on our quest. Was it a common name? Yes, it occurs frequently in early historical references. Conall Cernach, Conall Cremthainne and Conall Corc are just a few of the more illustrious earlier Conalls.

The name Conall crops up frequently in the table[35] of kings of the ancient Dalriada kingdom of east Ulster and Scotland. In 640[36] we find a Conall Cáel in his first year in joint sovereignty (with Ceallach) as High King (*Ard-Rí*) of Ireland – surely this should warn us that trying to come to a concrete conclusion about "our own" Conall Caol, or any other early figure in history, is fraught with danger. This King Conall Cáel (*obs.* 645) was of the Cenél Conaill of *Tír Chonaill,* so you can imagine the problems it caused the scribes over the years in trying not to mix up the genealogies of King Conall Cáel and St. Conall Cáel!

In addition the plain of present-day Co. Louth was known as Conaille – sometimes this can be confused with the personal name Conall. But at last we do come across a "Conall" which might help our search – at Clondallan, now the parish of Clonallon, in the diocese of Dromore, Co. Down. We are told: "This church was first presided over by St. Conall, who succeeded St. Carbreus, as Bishop of Coleraine, about the year 570."[37]

That this Conall did become bishop of Coleraine is verified by Adamnán, who, writing *c.* 680 A.D., refers to *"Conallus, episcopus Culerathin"*.[38] However for now our main interest in Clondallan is that in its proper form, *Cluain Dalláin*, it also bears a reference to Dallán Forgaill. Have we, here in Co. Down, a connection between Conall and Dallán, said to be buried together in Inishkeel? Yes, possibly, but it doesn't necessarily mean that they ended up in Inishkeel or even that Conall of *Cluain Dalláin* and Conall of *Inis Caoil* were the same person. We might well be dealing with two different Conall cults.

The feast-day of this Conall of *Cluain Dalláin* is 2 April; the *Martyrology of Donegal* tells us that he was "Conall, son of Aedh[39] of Cluain (i.e. of *Cluain Dalláin*), near Snamh Each, i.e., the harbour near unto the Cael in Ui-Eathach of Uladh. He was of the race of Irial, son of Conall Cearnach."[40] "Cael" is the Narrow Water, near Warrenpoint in Co. Down; "Ui-Eathach of Uladh" is the present barony of Iveagh, Co. Down, in which Warrenpoint and Clonallon are located. Dr. Reeves, writing in 1847, informs us that the barony originally derived its name from a Mic Eachach Cobha (i.e. son of Eochaidh Cobha), a member of an ancient family – the Uí Eachach – of the race of Ir, and that his descendents included Mic Caolbaidh (*obs.* A.D. 358) and Mac Conaill (*temp.* S. Patricci).[41]

Pádraig Ó Riain in his *Corpus* includes Conall of Clonallon as a member of the Sil Iareil Mic Conuill as follows:

"Conall mac Aeda na ndail

as e congaibh Cluain Dallain"

and gives him a Dál nAraide[42] genealogy: "Conall m. Aeda m. Saráin m. Maine m. Fothaid m. Conaill m. Echdach [or alternatively Caelbaidh in some sources[43]] m. Cruind Ba Drui.

"Is é congaib Cluain Dallain i nDál Echach i fail Chuain Snama Ech."[44]

In this brief examination of the genealogy of Conall Mac Aeda and the area which encompasses the ecclesiastical site with which he was associated – *Cluain Dalláin* – there crop up enough names of place and people, such as "the Cael", "Mic Caolbaidh", "Caelbaidh" and "Maine" to suggest that here we might be dealing with the same cult as that of Conall Mac Caolmaine of *Inis Caoil*. And just as the latter was given a Cenél mBógaine royal pedigree in *Tír Chonaill*, so Conall of *Cluain Dalláin*'s Dál nAraide genealogy is perceived as being a royal one – from *Clonallon Parish: Its Annals and Antiquities* we read: "St. Conall, who flourished in the century after St. Patrick's death and called by Marianus Gorman 'The Great', is generally credited with building the first Christian church in Clonallon. ... He was, moreover, of princely pedigree, being sixth in descent from Caolbha, the 123rd Monarch of Ireland and the 47th King of Ulaidh."[45]

In my opinion the royal pedigree given to Conall of *Cluain Dalláin* is just too neat to be true. The tribes referred to in relation to him – the Uí Eachach, Sil Iareil Mic Conuill, the Dál nAraide – were all groups who lived in the ancient kingdom of *Ulaid*, in the north-east of Ireland. The south-eastern limit of this kingdom was the mouth of the Boyne (*Inbher Colpa*). If you examine the Dál nAraide genealogy given just now to Conall of *Cluain Dalláin* (m. Aeda m. Saráin m. Maine m. Fothaid m. Conaill, etc.) you will see that it almost minutely mirrors the right-hand list[46] (read upwards) of the kings of the *Ulaid* which is illustrated below:[47]

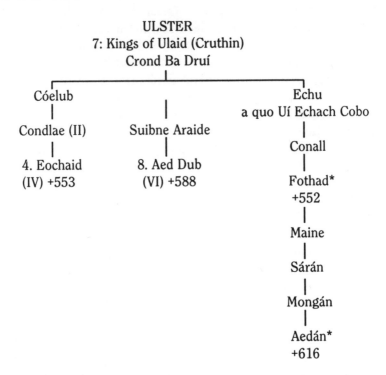

ULSTER
7: Kings of Ulaid (Cruthin)
Crond Ba Druí

Cóelub — Condlae (II) — 4. Eochaid (IV) +553

Suibne Araide — 8. Aed Dub (VI) +588

Echu
a quo Uí Echach Cobo — Conall — Fothad* +552 — Maine — Sárán — Mongán — Aedán* +616

I suspect the genealogy of Conall of *Cluain Dalláin*. However that is not to say that Conall of *Cluain Dalláin* was not a real and important figure in the early church in east Ulster – the early sources indicate that he was.

Church of Ireland services are still held in Clonallon parish church, on the outskirts of Warrenpoint, Co. Down. The cult of Conall has now disappeared from the area, but Dallán is still remembered in local nomenclature – in Warrenpoint we have Dallan Road, Dallan Hill, Dallan View and Dallan Avenue. Interestingly enough we have possible evidence of the spread of Conall's cult into north Co. Down in that Waringstown was "antiently called Clan-Connell" (? *Cluain Chonaill*).[48]

Trying to come to concrete conclusions about the cults of the early saints may be a wholly impossible task; we are flirting with shadows. Of one thing we can be relatively confident, and that is that it is likely that early

Christianity reached the Cenél Conaill of what is now west Donegal via the sea route from east Co. Down. For that reason we will dwell further here on the east coast of Ulster.

It was hinted at earlier, and will be suggested later, that Conall Caol of *Inis Caoil* and an early (*obs. c.* 496) ecclesiastic named Cóelán, associated with Nendrum, in east Co. Down, may be one and the same. Possibly Cóelán derived his name because he originally hailed from the Caol area of south Co. Down. Near Dundrum Bay on the east Down coast was (in the 1306 Taxation Roll[49]) a church called Kilschaelyn, presumably associated with the cult of Cóelán (Cáelán). North of Kilschaelyn, towards Strangford Lough, was Rathcolpe, now the village of Raholp. This was the church of Tassach (Assicus), who is also associated with Rathlin O'Birne island off the coast of Glencolumbkille in south-west Donegal. Cóelán is associated with Aughnish island in the estuary of the Swilly at Ramelton in north Donegal. We have established by now that early Christian hermits, travelling by boat, often sought the solitude of off-shore islands, and with Cóelán associated with Aughnish and Assicus associated with Rathlin O'Birne I think it likely that *Inis Caoil*, off the coast of Donegal and situated between Aughnish and Rathlin O'Birne, was also chosen as the site of an early hermitage by those

East Ulster

bringing Christianity from east Ulster and that the name *Inis Caoil* probably harks back to the cult of the ecclesiastic which was introduced there - that of Cóelán (Cóel-án, Cáel-án) of Nendrum. It is of interest that in the genealogies (*Corpus*) we read of a member of St. Patrick's "team" called *Cael gilla* [*Cael*, Patrick's "boy"], who would equate with the "tender youth" Móchóe (Cóelán) noted earlier being baptised by Patrick. We have already mentioned John Colgan referring in 1645 to "*S. Conaldi cognomento coel seu Coely*" i.e. "St. Conall, also known as Coel or Coely".

North of Dundrum Bay is the barony of Lecale (*Leth Cathail*). The cult of Cóelán is present here too - he is given an Eoganachta pedigree - at a place named Kilclief (*Caelan Cilli Clethi*[50]), which is a townland and a parish. The ancient name for Dundrum Bay is *Tráig Dromma.*[51] It is worth noting here that Colgan also refers to Conall of *Cluain Dalláin* as "*Conallum Droma*"[52] - possibly this would suggest an association with Dromore (*Druim* – *mór*), also in Co. Down, but alternatively the suffix "*Droma*" may come from *Tráig Dromma*. An area along the shoreline of Dundrum Bay was known as *Achad Cáel* (*Cáil*).[53] These names might suggest that the cult of Cáel-án/Cáel/? Conall was venerated along much of the west and south Co. Down coastline.

We now leave Co. Down and travel southwards. East of Kells, Co. Meath, is the village of Crossakeel (*Crosa Caoil/Cáil*),[54] possibly a cult site of Cóelán. Just south of Crossakeel is Killalon and attractive as it would be to translate this as *Cill Dalláin*, suggesting a Cóelán/Dallán linked cult here, the proper ancient translation of Killalon is *Caille Fhallamhain*.[55] On the north side of Kells was the cult site of Caelbadh of *Cill-Caelbadh*.

In east Co. Meath, near Slane, and just north of the river Boyne, is Dowth, now the centre of much archaeological activity. The early ecclesiastic associated with Dowth - ancient name *Dubaid* - is Senchán. This is said to be the Senchán associated with the cult of Conall Caol in west Donegal - at Shanaghan, near Ardara and at Shanaghan, Bruckless. We will refer again to him at Shanaghan, Ardara.

In the genealogical list of an early tribe from the Slane area - the Sil nAedha Slaine - we read of "*Senach epscop* [bishop], *Garbhan epscop, ocus Aedhan epscop, Caelan, Corpmac et Fiachraigh. As e an Caelan o ta tochar cula Caelain; as i a clann fine achni Martraige* ...."[56] You will have noted the presence of a Cáelán, whom we are told gave his name to *cula Cáeláin* which is in Co. Meath.[57] I am not certain that this Cáeleán was an ecclesiastic but it is of interest that in making mention of the *Martraige* with whom Cáelán was associated Hogan writes of the "*Comarba*[58] *Finnein, Coluimcille agus na Martraige*[59]."[60] This, to my mind, suggests that the cults of St. Finian (usually associated with Movilla [*Mag Bíle*], Co. Down], St.

Colmcille and St. Cáelán were celebrated in this area. This preamble on a Sil nAedha Slaine genealogy might be bringing us up a cul-de-sac (*cula Cáeláin!*) but what drew my eye to it, apart from the name Caelan, was the name Corpmac (Cormac). And this is why: while discussing an ecclesiastic named Cormac of Trim (Co. Meath), John Colgan, writing in 1645, lists a number of Cormacs, among them a "*S. Cormacus Presbyter de Achadh-finnigh iuxta fluvius Dothra*"[61] i.e. a St. Cormac who lived near the Dodder river in Leinster. What is so intriguing is that he then tells us that this cleric was buried in *Inis Caoil*! Why an ecclesiastic from so far away would be buried in *Inis Caoil* is certainly an intriguing question.

Another cleric, mo-Chritoc, also known as Criotán,[62] is associated with *Achadh Finnigh* on the banks of the Dodder.[63] Possibly Cormac/mo-Chritoc/Criotán were the one person – they share 11 May as their feast-day (a date assigned to Conall of *Inis Caoil* in some of the martyrologies). In Nendrum, Co. Down – which we associate with Cóelán – a bishop Critán (feast-day 17 May) died in 638 A.D. One wonders if the scribes might not have mixed up Cormac of Trim (*Ath Truim*) with Critán, Abbot (*Comarba*) of Nendrum, over the years. In Gaelic "*Cormac Atha Truim*" and "*Comarba nAondroma*" could easily have been interchanged in transmission, especially when written in Old Irish.[64] Might an abbot of Nendrum be buried in *Inis Caoil*? If so it would certainly cement the Nendrum – *Inis Caoil* connection.

We now move westwards into Co. Westmeath. One reason for doing so is that – if you can remember that far back! – it was noted earlier in this chapter that the *Martyrology of Donegal* states that Dallán Forgaill was "*ó Mhaighin*" i.e. from Maighin. John Colgan informs us in the year 1645 that Maighin is in what is now Co. Westmeath. This is the modern parish of Mayne – *parráiste Mhaighne* – situated between the parish of Rathgarve and the river Inny, not far from Castlepollard. This parish, or rather its ancient church, is noticed in the *Tripartite Life of St. Patrick*: "Patrick attempted to set up at *Ath Maigne* in Asal ... *Maigen* near it to the south belonged to Patrick. One of his people, the son of Díocholl, founded it, but by deceit it now belongs to Columcille."[66] This latter statement reflects the rivalry between the Patrician and Columban communities in making claims to control over outlying churches.

West of Mayne in the parish of Street (barony of Moygoish) is the townland of Clonconnell, translated as *Cluain Chonaill*. That this is a reference to an ecclesiastic named Conall is undoubted because in *Field Namebook 14* it is referred to as "*Fearann na mBráthar*, land of the Friars".[67] In the parish of Templeoran, also in the barony of Moygoish, is the townland of Killdallan, translated *Cill Dallán*.[68] There seems little doubt that the cults of

Conall and Dallán travelled together in this area; one wonders if the great cult of Colmcille was the vehicle by which these lesser cults travelled.

Within Co. Westmeath we find traces of the cults of a number of saints who have associations with southwest Donegal. The principal church of Aed mac Bricc – who is identified with *Sliabh Liag* near Glencolumbkille – was situated at Killare (*Cill Áir*), Co. Westmeath, and he was also associated with Rathugh (*Ráth Aedo*) in the same county. In the parish next to Killare, Conra, there was a *Tobar Maodhóig*,[69] suggesting a vestige of the cult of Maedoc, said to be closely related to Dallán Forgaill.

In the north of Co. Westmeath, on an island – *Inis Uachtair* – in Lough Sheelin stands the ruins of a church associated with St. Carthach, the same saint who gave his name to Kilcar (*Cill Cartha*) in south-west Donegal.

One wonders if the cults of Aed mac Bricc, Maedoc and Carthach came to Donegal via the great cult of Colmcille.

Before starting northwards I would mention that in east Co. Galway a St. Conall was venerated at Kilconnel, *Cill Chonaill*, east of Ballinasloe. Possibly this site, in *Uí-Maine*, was dedicated to "our" St. Conall, though Colgan attributes it to Conall of *Cluain Dalláin*.[70]

Our reason for having come to Westmeath was that Dallán Forgaill was "from Maighin". We must understand that here we are being told that he was associated with the ecclesiastical foundation at Maighin, not that he was born in Maighin. John Colgan is emphatic about his place of birth; he tells us that it was anciently called *Masraige agus Cathrige Sleacht*, modern (1645) name *Teallach Eathach*.[71] The former are very old names, the word "*Cathraige*" deriving from the Cathraige, a "tribe of Firbolgs",[72] "*Aon de forslintib Erenn*".[73] *Masraige Maige Slecht* ("*i mBreifni Connacht*") and *Teallach Eathach* equate with the modern barony of Tullyhaw in the north of Co. Cavan. Within the barony of Tullyhaw is the parish of Kildallan, *Cill Dalláin*. The Christian name "*Dallán*" is still viable here, four or five young men in the parish bearing the name. Within the parish of Kildallan is the town of Ballyconnell. No, it sounded too easy! I am assured by my Cavan friends that the name Ballyconnell is not attributed to a St. Conall but to Conall Cernach who fought a battle at the river here. Dallán Forgaill's alleged close relative, St. Maedoc, is said to have been born on a nearby island.

We now return to Co. Donegal; as we proceed we can reflect that we have established that the cults of Dallán and Conall Caol were associated with *Inis Caoil* and that Dallán and a St. Conall were inter-linked in south Co. Down and in Westmeath. Though it seems too much of a coincidence that Dallán was associated with both Conall of *Inis Caoil* and Conall of *Cluain*

Dalláin there are no grounds for concluding that *Inis Caoil* and *Cluain Dalláin* were branches of the one Conall cult.

How do we explain this phenomenon of the same saints being venerated in completely different places, and yet in most of these places the saint is claimed as being local, appears to have local origins, is said to be buried in the area, and so on? Some light is shed on this by a short examination of earlier writings on saints and by a quick glance at the method of spread of devotion to a saint (cults and *wanderkults*). We referred briefly to this latter topic earlier at Kilkenny, on the Gweebarra.

As I've suggested before, one has to be very wary of much of what has been written about our early saints, not just that written in the middle ages, but even the earlier works. As Kenney says: "the ecclesiastics of the reorganised Celtic Church in Ireland after the Great Plague[74] and the Pascal Controversy[75] had but a hazy notion of the early history of Irish Christianity."[76] Allied to that the use of hypocorisms – pet names – had died out by the beginning of the 7th century. So, earlier saints' many names were not recognised by later writers and they thought they were dealing with numerous saints instead of one. *Do-, da-, mo-* (=my) were often put before a name, *-occ* and *-óg* (little or dear) and *-án* (also a diminutive) after a name. For example, St. Maedoc of Ferns, Co. Wexford, is a famous early church figure, but he was known by different names thoughout the country; the founder of Ferns had been a Bishop Aed (Aodh); in various places Aed changed to Aidan (Aed-án) Maedóc (Mo-Aodh-occ), Moedhóg (Mo-Aodh-óg), even Mogue in Ferns itself and in Co. Cavan and Co. Leitrim "where his memory is still held in the highest veneration".[77] No wonder the later writers often failed to recognize that they were dealing with the cult of the same saint in different guises in different places. I didn't pick Maedoc of Ferns randomly as an example – he and Dallán Forgaill are said to have been brothers' sons.

Earlier I have quoted the genealogy of various saints, including those of Conall of *Cluain Dalláin* and Conall Mac Caolmaine of Inishkeel. Experts in this field dismiss these pedigrees. P. Ó Riain states that "J.V. Kelleher speaks of the general corpus of saints' genealogies as a text composed with one purpose only, 'to conceal forever the fact that some of the notable early clerics had been unpalatably plebeian'."[78] O'Riain, while agreeing that in seeking the origins of a saint the pedigree must indeed be viewed as a fabrication, is of the opinion that the purpose of the fiction was not to conceal the saint's real origins but "to legitimize the localization, or several localizations which had overtaken the saint's cult. Thus, as many as seven or eight different pedigrees may survive for an originally single saint whose cult had undergone segmentation. Findbarr is a case in point."[79]

Professor Ó Riain, an acknowledged Irish expert in the study of early saints, has made an intensive study of the cult of St. Finnbarr of Cork.[80] The origins of this cult rest with Finnian of Movilla (*Mag Bíle*), Co. Down – whose cult St. Conall is also associated with, hence my discussing it here. Finnian was a renowned teacher and we are told that Colmcille while still "a youth, went to the aged man, the venerable bishop Finnio, his master". In later years, as the cult of Colmcille spread throughout the country the cult of Finnian went with it, because he was known, having been his teacher, to have been associated with Colmcille. There was a multiplying effect; as the cult of Finnian of Co. Down spread, with it went that of other early saints associated with his "home" area of north-east Ulster, e.g. Cóelán. As Finnian's cult wandered, the adoptive churches in different areas localised and personalised his cult, so that it appeared as if this holy man had actually lived in and had been associated with the particular church in that area – he was given a more local name, his "relics"[81] and his "burial tomb"[82] gradually appeared in each area, etc., etc. So even though we can presume that Finnian himself, who died in 579, never left north-east Ulster, his cult later divided into many different "saints" throughout Ireland, e.g. Finbarr of Cork. His cult went under many guises – "saints" called Finnian, Finnio, Vinniavus, Findbarrus, Barrfhind, Barron, Bairre. Referring elsewhere to Findbarr of Cork, Ó Riain concludes: "Thus, a probably originally single saint Findbarr eventually acquired six or more different statements of his descent, each more or less in line with the location of one of the several churches of which he was patron. Implicit in each such statement was a total claim to the saint, who was thus provided with the six or more separate and false identities by which he is known."[83]

As the might of the Colmcille cult spread, bringing with it the cult of Colmcille's master, Finnian, the cult of others associated with Finnian and east Ulster travelled on the back of Finnian's cult. Among the saints associated with Finnian's pseudonyms, Finbarr and Bairrfhinn, in the Irish Calender of saints are:

Conall Mac Aeda of Coleraine.

Conall Mac Aeda of a church near Carlingford (*Cluain Dalláin*).

Mochóe of Nendrum.

A Cáelchú in the diocese of Cork.

A Cáelchú in the diocese of Clogher.

Cóelán or Mochóe of Aughnish, near Ramelton.

Conall of Inishkeel.[84]

With the revisionist view being that the old tribal pedigree given to a saint should be viewed as just a local attempt to take over and give body to the *wanderkult* of a saint, most emphasis is nowadays placed on the collated Irish Calendar of Saints in trying to elucidate the origins and associations of early saints. Study of the several copies of the Calendar is best left to the professional scholars. However, as an amateur I found it interesting that in the freely available *Martyrology of Donegal* the name Brónach appears at 2 April, the feast-day of Conall of *Cluain Dalláin*. This might suggest that Conall of *Cluain Dalláin* was in the Patrician fold, at least politically, since Brónach is said to be a daughter of Miliucc, of St. Patrick fame and, very interestingly, is said to be the mother[85] of Cóelán of Nendrum.

In north Donegal we have evidence of the cults of Cóelán and Dallán Forgaill in close proximity. John Colgan, in 1645, speaks of the churches of *Disert Dalláin* and *Tulach Dalláin* and locates the latter in the diocese of Raphoe.[86] In the estuary of the river Swilly, three miles from Ramelton, is Aughnish island where there was an ecclesiastical foundation, now gone, dedicated to Cóelán.[87] Down the Swilly and west of the Saltpans is Clondallan (*Cluain Dalláin*) townland.[88] This would appear to confirm that the cults of Cóelán and Dallán travelled together in this part of Donegal.

Very Rev. John J. Silke, Catholic Diocesan Archivist for the diocese of Raphoe, is an expert on the study of early saints. In discussing the importance of waterways in spreading the early faith he states: "The practice was for monks seeking solitude to leave large ecclesiastical establishments, first for islets in nearby lakes and rivers; then when their solitude there was disrupted for islands off the coast; and finally to put to sea in search of even remoter islands."[89] He suggests that given Cóelán's early date (died 596) Christianity may have spread from north-east Ulster along the sea route and into Donegal's long winding bays. He continues: "If, as seems plain, Nendrum's influence reached out to Donegal, the idea of monasticism may have been introduced fairly early among the Cenél Conaill. ... Places like Aughnish, Rathlin O'Birne and Inishkeel were such as were sought out by ascetics. There may indeed be a suspicion that Conall Caol, the saint of Inishkeel, and Cáelán are one and the same."[90]

If we have trouble claiming Conall as our own the problem is made greater by the fact that devotion to him also travelled south and westwards. There is a foundation at Drumconnell, south of Boyle, Co. Roscommon, attributed to Conall. Further south we read that he is the patron saint of Dromcliffe, Co. Clare, a parish variously described as "the parish of St. Conald in the diocese of Killaloe,"[91] and as the "ecclesia Sancti Conaldi".[92] In addition, we are told that in the will of Ceallachan, king of Cashel, whose floruit was in the middle of the 10th century, the king bequeathed "to Connal's church on the Fergus,

a bell".[93] At the head of a broad valley that extends north from Dingle harbour in Co. Kerry is an enclosure which includes a burial ground and a large
cross not unlike St. Conall's cross on Loughros Point, Ardara. This enclosure is located in an area called Reenconnall (*Rinn Chonaill*).[94] Could we
possibly have here the most southerly extension of the cult of St. Conall?

I have stated earlier that professional hagiographers use the collated Irish
Calendar of Saints in seeking associations between the cults of various
saints. For the simple observations that I will be making we will confine ourselves to those who share their feast-days with Conall of *Inis Caoil* and with
Cóelán of Nendrum in the *Martyrology of Donegal*. The thinking behind this
exercise is that over the centuries the lists were continually written and
rewritten and if a scribe while at a particular saint's feast-day knew of an association between that saint and another then he added the name of the
latter to that date – described by Ó Riain as "the practice of inserting names
in a list."[95] He adds: "Thus, over a long period of transmission the saints entered for a particular festival, or, as is often the case, an immediate succession of festivals, form something in the way of an inter-related group."[96]

The feast-day of Conall, abbot of *Inis Caoil*, is 22 May. Others who share
this day are "The Sons of Eochaidh" and "The Seven Sons of Ednius of
Maighin". When we remember that Dallán Forgaill was also known as
Eochaidh and that he was "of Maighin", this suggests a strong inter-relation-
ship between Conall and the followers of Dallán. Another who shared this
feast-day was Ronan Finn who is associated with Magheralin (*Lann Rónáin
Find*) townland and parish in the barony of Iveagh Lower, Co. Down.

The feast-day of Cóelán of Nendrum is 23 June. Among others sharing this
day are "The Children of Senchán" and "The Children of Senán". Senchán,
who is celebrated at Dowth, Co. Meath, is associated with the cult of Conall
Caol in west Donegal – at Shanaghan, Ardara and Shanaghan, Bruckless.
The cult of Senán was widespread – among the places he was venerated was
at *Achad Cóel* ("*Senan Achaid Cael*")[97] on the shores of Dundrum Bay, Co.
Down.

So, as we finish, what do I think is the origin of the cult of Conall Caol?
Well, I think it hinges on the word "*caol*". From the early source material I
would place most reliance on the *Martyrology of Tallaght* and the *Félire
Oengusso* which speak of "Conaill Inse Cail" and "Féil Conaill Inse Cail" respectively. We have noted earlier that the words *caol/cael/cáil* are inter-
changable. No less an authority than John Colgan observes this and enlarges
on it: "I notice the word Caol, Cail, or Coel (for it is written [spelled] in different ways by former writers) which means 'thin', and by usage had passed
over into the literal name. It may have two derived diminutives peculiar to

men, like Caolan, Cailan or Coelan and Cailten or Coelten, all meaning the same thing."[98]

It is my opinion, for what it is worth, that Christianity was introduced to *Inis Caoil* by missionaries, travelling by boat, who were inspired by Cóelán of Nendrum. Possibly the latter originally hailed from the *Caol* or *Achad Cáil* areas of south Co. Down. We have noted already that Cóelán was venerated on a little island in north Donegal and that Tassach, also associated with east Co. Down, was celebrated on the island of Rathlin O'Birne off the coast of south-west Donegal. Whether the cult of Cóelán arrived in *Inis Caoil* in the form of Cóelán or Cóel/Cáel or Conall Caol is a question, but I would estimate that it arrived as Cóelán and that, since the largest early population group which the missionaries had to convert were the Cenél Conaill, the cult gradually took on the name of Conall. It may have taken a few generations to do so, but it seems too much of a coincidence to find such an eminent saint as Conall among the Cenél Conaill, and the attraction of a combined ancestral (Conall Gulban) and Christian (Conall Caol) cult must have appealed. Much the same situation obtained among the Cenél Eogain, it seems, judging by the cult of Eogan of *Ard Srátha* (Ardstraw, near Strabane, in Co. Tyrone).

I would think that it was the might of the Colmcille cult – after all, he was of the Cenél Conaill too – which helped spread the name of Conall outside of *Tír Chonaill*. Conall was associated with Dallán – let us not forget that Colgan told us that Dallán wrote a work in praise of Conall – and Dallán was certainly associated with Colmcille. Possibly it was through the latter that Conall also became attached to the cult of Finnian of Co. Down.

As regards the Cenél mBógaine pedigree given to Conall of Inishkeel, this could be explained by the fact that the early hermit(s) on Inishkeel would have been succeeded in later years by members of the local Cenél mBógaine, who were a branch of the Cenél Conaill – in Ó Riain's words "the form taken by the saint's pedigree often reflects that of the family which provided successors in the abbacy of his church."[99]

However, who am I to say that a Conall – from among either the Cenél Conaill or from a remnant of one of the other local tribes – was not among the early converts and that it is he whom we honour?

Indeed if we were to disregard all that I have been saying about the genealogies of the saints not being reliable and were to try finally to explain the "Maine" in Conall's name (Conall mac Maine Caoil) and give it a local flavour, then it might be thus: the O'Breslin family, associated with the area between the Gweebarra and the Owenea rivers since the time of our earliest historical records, were one of the erenagh families of *Inis Caoil*.[100] They were the most powerful political force in the Inishkeel area in the early days of Christianity, and it is possible that the first Inishkeel abbot of local extraction was one of their number. If not they may later have claimed that he was. Another erenagh family of *Inis Caoil* were the O'Mooneys: "The O'Maighnes were hereditary *erenachs* of Inishkeel and are still a numerous tribe. They usually write their name Mooney." We have already note one of the ua Maighne sept holding a very prominent clerical position – "Maelciarain Ua Maighne, *comarba Colaim Chille*, was cruelly matyred..." in 985 A.D.[101] It would appear that in the name Conall *mac Maine*, descent from the ua Maighne sept is being claimed. There was probably great rivalry between the O'Breslins and themselves. It does not surprise one that with a member of their sept having held such a powerful position as *Comarba Colaim Chille* (Superior of all the Columban churches) that the Ua Maighne sept – particularly those members who became clerical scribes – rightly or wrongly subsequently claimed the other great Cenél Conaill saint – Conall of *Inis Caoil* – as one of their number. It could also be interpreted as an attempt to ensure that his cult was included within the Columban fold.

In conclusion it must be said that though our facts concerning him may be few and far between there is nothing shadowy about the imprint that the founding figure known to us as Conall has left on much of present-day south-west Donegal.

There is no doubt that in the early stages of Christianity in the north-west the ecclesiastical foundation on Inishkeel was an important pivot, its influence reaching into much of south-west Donegal. It is likely that the founder was an inspirational figure whose charisma fuelled the faith of later generations of ecclesiastics on the island. That belief in him in the form of Conall of Inishkeel has been harboured by people down through the ages and, carefully and lovingly handed down to us, is far more important and relevant that a mere biography of the man.

I was recently in conversation with an old friend of my father's about St. Conall and he stated that he hoped that in my assessment I would give "Conall Naofa" (St. Conall) *cothrom na Féinne* (adjudicate on him fairly) because it was St. Conall "who had introduced books and writing to west Donegal". Hopefully Conall's stature in our society will remain undiminished.

Earlier in this chapter it was mentioned that the *Cáin Domhnaigh* is said to have been brought from Rome to this country by Conall Mac Caolmaine. The text states: "This is the enactment of the law of Sunday which Conall Mac Coelmaine brought from the east, who had gone on a pilgrimage to Rome; and he had prayed there his three prayers, and they had all been granted him. These are his three prayers: He over whom shall go the clay of the island in which he is buried, his soul shall not approach the pain of hell; and foreign hordes shall not visit his church except once; and whenever every other tower of Ara Mór is lowest, then it is that his own church and his tower shall be highest."[102] Generation after generation of people in south-west Donegal must have believed that Conall's first prayer had been granted him, because they continued to be buried beside him under the clay of his island, century after century. Whether Inishkeel was visited by more than the foreign horde who cut off Dallán's head I do not know. But it is to his third prayer that I wish to draw attention; "his own church and his tower" are not now highest – the site here is neglected and the buildings are in disarray. Over a hundred years ago, in 1873, a writer commented: "The venerable ruin, and the old graveyard in which it stands, are sadly neglected. This is a shame and a pity. Let us hope that some effort will soon be made to save the ruin from utter destruction, and the old graveyard from being, what it is now, a preserve for sheep and cattle."[103]

Have we made any progress in preserving our heritage since then?

Notes

1   M. Archdall, *Monasticon Hibernicum,* vol. 1, p. 100.

2   *Irish Ecclesiastical Record,* September 1887.

3   Fo. 58B; ci. 2; fo. 36 (in the Royal Irish Academy).

4   p. 700 (in the Royal Irish Academy).

5   p. 480: written by Inishowen-born friar John Colgan about 1647.

6   Written in 1630 by Donegal monk Michael Ó Clérigh; a list of the feast-days of the saints of Ireland.

7   The *Naoimhsheanchus,* a poetical history of the saints of Ireland; possibly dated to early in the 10th century.

8   A list of the saints under each day of the year; originally possibly early 10th century, it appeared in the 12th century *Book of Leinster.*

9   Fo. 34A (in the Royal Irish Academy).

10   "Conall m Maine caoil m Cathaoir m Boghuine m Conaill gulban. O Inis Caoil a ttuiscert Chineil Conuill, 22 Maij". (*Gonoalogiao Rogum ot Sanctorum Hiborniao*).

Ó Riain in his *Corpus* (p. 76) gives his genealogy as "Conall m. Maine Cail ar slicht (Cathair m.) Bogaine m. Conaill Gulban" and (p. 82) as

"Conal mór mac Maine Chaoil,

Caolmaine mac do Chathaoir;

Cathaoir, ba coimseach ngoile,

an sechtmadh mac Boghaine".

11 Kenney, p. 323.

12 Though note that some unease is now detectable regarding Adamnán's *Life of St. Columba.*

13 It is difficult to accept, too, because though Conall is given a date of death (596) close to Columba's (597) he is allegedly a generation later than Columba. This can happen; an uncle can often be younger than his nephew. However, Rev. T. O'Donnell, OFM, a past President of the Donegal Historical Society, obviously had doubts about tying the two men together in earlier years because in 1971 (*D.A.*, p. 67) he states that Conall "flourished about the years 590-627".

14 *Cáin*: a law, rule; *Domhnach*; Sunday. This rule enjoins, under severe penalties, that every class shall abstain from all kinds of work on Sunday and that none shall travel on that day; wherever one happens to be on Saturday evening, there he shall remain until Monday morning. Though there were some exceptions, such as bringing a physician to a sick person, relieving a woman in labour, saving a house from fire, etc., a priest was forbidden to travel on Sunday or Sunday night, indeed from vesper time on Saturday night till Monday morning, unless to attend a sick person likely to die before the following morning.

15 T.C.D., class H. 2, 16, col. 217.

16 See *Ériu*, vol. 2, (1905), pp. 189-212 for a full account of the *Cáin Domhnaigh.*

17 "One of the most remarkable of Christian myths is that of the letter of Christ which fell from Heaven. It has been current from the 6th century to the present day, and – at one time or another – in all Christian lands from Abyssinia to Iceland and from Ireland to Russia." (Kenney, p. 476.)

18 pp. 203-5.

19 Ó Riain gives his Colla Uais genealogies as follows:
   (a) Dallan m. Colla are slicht Echach m. Colla Uais.
   (b) Eochaidh m. Aililla, i. Dallan Forgaill, ar slicht Colla Uais.
   (c) Eochaidh mac Colla os cech druing,
       dar chomainm Dallan Forguill,
       mic Eirc mic Muiredaig min
       mic Colla Uais gan fairbrigh. (*Corpus*, pp. 64, 77, 92.)

20 *Amhra*: An elegy, eulogy; see O'Kelleher and Schoepperle, *Betha Colaim Chille*, pp. 358-59.

21 e.g. "Ní dísceoil duae Néill
        Ní uachtat oenmaige mór mairg, mór deilm díolaing
        Ris re asneid Colum cen bith cen chill
        Co. india dui sceo Nera?"

"The mount of Niall (i.e. Ireland) is not silent, the great sorrow is not the cry of a single plain, the great cry hard to bear when it is told that Colum is without life, without a church. How shall a fool tell of him, or even Nera [traditionally a great scholar]?"

The resources of this poetic language were then rhythm, alliteration, inversion and parallelism; there is no sign of rhyme or of division into stanzas. (Dylan, *Early Irish*

Society, p. 28.)

22   Kenney, p. 427.

23   *H.D.R.*, vol. I, p. 272.

24   Unfortunately it no longer exists.

25   Archdall, *Monasticon Hibernicum*, p. 196.

26   Ryan, *Ireland and Insular Art*, p. 7. (The traditional dating is that Patrick laboured here from 432 to 461.)

27   Ryan *op. cit.*, p. 7.

28   *D.A.* (1987), p. 4.

29   E.S. Towill, *U.J.A.*, vol. 27, (1964), p. 105.

30   Stokes, *Tripartite Life of St. Patrick*; quoted in *U.J.A.* (1964), p. 117.

31   *Peritia*, vol. 1, (1982), p. 158.

32   My thanks, again, to Dónall Mac Giolla Easpaig.

33   We should be proud that this man who did so much to gather together a vast store of information on the history of our country spent some part of 1631-32 living within a few hundred yards of the present-day village of Ardara. Inquisitions taken at Lifford on 25 May 1632 informs us that "COOCHOGERY O'CLERY, a meere Irishman, and not of the English or British descent or Sirname, held the half quarter of land of Coobeg and Dowghill, in the proporcon of Monargane, barronie of Boylagh and Banagh, and co' Donnegall, from WIL' FARRELL esq. assignee to the earle of Annandell, from hollantide 1631, until may 1632." (Coobeg = ?*Coill Beag*, Dowghill = Doohill, *Dubh Choill*, near Ardara). However "being a meere Irishman" he was dispossessed. We are informed that "Shortly after this period he removed, with other families of Tirconnell, to Ballcroy, in the south of Erris barony, County Mayo, under the guidance of Rory O'Donnell, the son of Colonel Manus O'Donnell, who was slain at Benburb in 1646, and who was a son of the celebrated Niall Garbh O'Donnell who died in the Tower of London in the year 1626. He carried with him his books, which were his chief treasure." (*Analecta Hibernica*, p. xii.)

34   The O'Clery Book of Genealogies, *Analecta Hibernica*, no. 18, p. 3.

35   At the end of Reeves' ed. of Adamnán's *Life of St. Columba*.

36   *A.F.M.*, vol. I, p. 257.

37   Reeves, *Ecclesiastical Antiquities of Down, Connor and Dromore*, p. 114.

38   Reeves' ed. of Adamnán's *Life of St. Columba*, p. 97 (Cap 50); see also O'Kelleher and Schoepperle ed. of O'Donnell's *Betha Colaim Chille*, item 144, p. 147: "Another time a holy bishop that was called Conall prepared a feast for Columcille."

39   Among Dallán Forgaill's extant works is an ode to Aodh, the son of Duach the black, king of Orgian. (See Hardiman's *Irish Minstrelsy*, pp. 357-60.) This is just an incidental point.

40   pp. 92-93.

41   *Ecclesiastical Antiquities of Down, Connor and Dromore*, p. 349.

42   An ancient tribe who held lands in south Co. Antrim and north Co. Down.

43   *Book of Ballymote, Book of Lecan* and the *Leabhar Breac*.

44   p. 104
45   Padraic Keenan, *Clonallan Parish: Its Annals and Antiquities,* p. 3.
46   Which I have cut short.
47   Taken from F.J. Byrne, *Irish Kings and High-Kings,* p. 287.
48   Smith and Harris, *The Ancient and Present State of the County of Down,* p. 104.
49   Towill, op. cit., p. 114.
50   Ó Riain, *Corpus,* p. 40.
51   *O.G.,* p. 644.
52   *Trias Thaumaturga,* p. 281, n. 11.
53   *O.G.,* p. 644.
54   Rev. P. Walsh, *The Placenames of Westmeath,* p. 317.
55   Ibid. pp. 316-17.
56   *Analecta Hibernica,* no. 18, pp. 58-59.
57   *O.G.,* p. 318.
58   A religious position.
59   From which derives Martryl townland and parish four miles north-west of Navan, Co. Meath.
60   *O.G.,* p. 536.
61   *Acta Sanctorum,* p. 360.
62   *M.O.D.,* pp. 124-25.
63   *O.G.,* p. 355.
64   My thanks to Arthur Spears for this suggestion.
65   *Acta Sanctorum,* p. 205.
66   Rev. P. Walsh, *The Placenames of Westmeath,* p. 52; (see also *Vita Tripartita,* p. 78, and *Trias Thaumaturga,* p. 129).
67   Walsh, op. cit.
68   Ibid. p. 326.
69   Ibid. p. 23.
70   *Trias Thaumaturga,* p. 281, n. 11.
71   *Acta Sanctorum,* p. 203.
72   *O.G.,* p. 171.
73   Ibid.
74   Of 664-65 A.D., which decimated the monastic population.
75   Of the 7th and early 8th century; the northern churches in Ireland wished to adhere to the Jewish calendar – a lunar calendar with a mean year of 354 days; the British and southern Irish churches adopted the Julian (Roman) calendar of 365 days; the controversy, involving disagreements and expulsions, lasted well over a century.
76   Kenny, p. 478.
77   *A.D.M.,* vol. I, p. 247.
78   *Peritia,* vol. I, (1982), p. 157; Kelleher, *Studia Hibernica* 3 (1963), p. 119.
79   *Peritia,* vol. I, (1982), p. 157.

80   *J.C.H.A.S.*, vol. LLXXXII, no. 236 (1977), pp 63-82.

81   "...relics were essential to the progress of Christianity from as early as the fourth century" (Ó Riain, op. cit.).

82   "The tomb always remained the mainspring of the cult's progress, but its prestige was so great that once a cult had become a *wanderkult*, the burial place of the saint tended to multiply." (Ó Riain, op. cit.)

83   *Corpus*, p. XIV.

84   *J.C.H.A.S.*, vol. LXXXII (1977), pp. 79-82.

85   "Brónach ingen Milchon m. Buain, 'ca mbaé Patric i ndaire, mathair Mochae Noen-dromma oc Loch Cuan...," etc. (*Corpus*, p. 179).

86   *Acta Sanctorum*, p. 205.

87   *O.G.*, p. 393.

88   Very Rev. Dr. J.J. Silke, *Donegal Democrat*, 17 June 1988.

89   *D.A.* (1987), p. 14.

90   Ibid.

91   D.F. Gleeson, *Molua* (1958), pp. 46-47.

92   Ibid.

93   Ibid.

94   Judith Cuppage, *Archaeological Survey of the Dingle Peninsula* (1986), p. 345. My thanks to Professor Michael Herity for drawing this to my attention.

95   *J.C.H.A.S.*, vol. LXXXLL (1977), p. 68.

96   Ibid.

97   *Corpus*, p. 15.

98   *Trias Thaumaturga*, p. 379a, n. 7B; in *Vita Sancti Columbae*, p. 60, n. a.

99   *Corpus*, p. XV.

100 See p. 82.

101 See p. 89 n. 11. In this area at the present day we would translate Mooney as Ó Maonaigh. Woulfe (*Sloinnte Gaedheal is Gall*, 1923) translates Ó Maine (des of Maine) as "Many", "Meaney" but adds that "its angl. forms can hardly be distinguished from those of Ó Maonaigh" (Mooneys). However our interest need not be in the anglicised forms, only in the possible mac Maine/ua Maighne/O'Maighne connection.

102 *Ériu*, vol. 2 (1905), p. 203.

103 Archdall, *Monasticon Hibernicum*, p. 197.

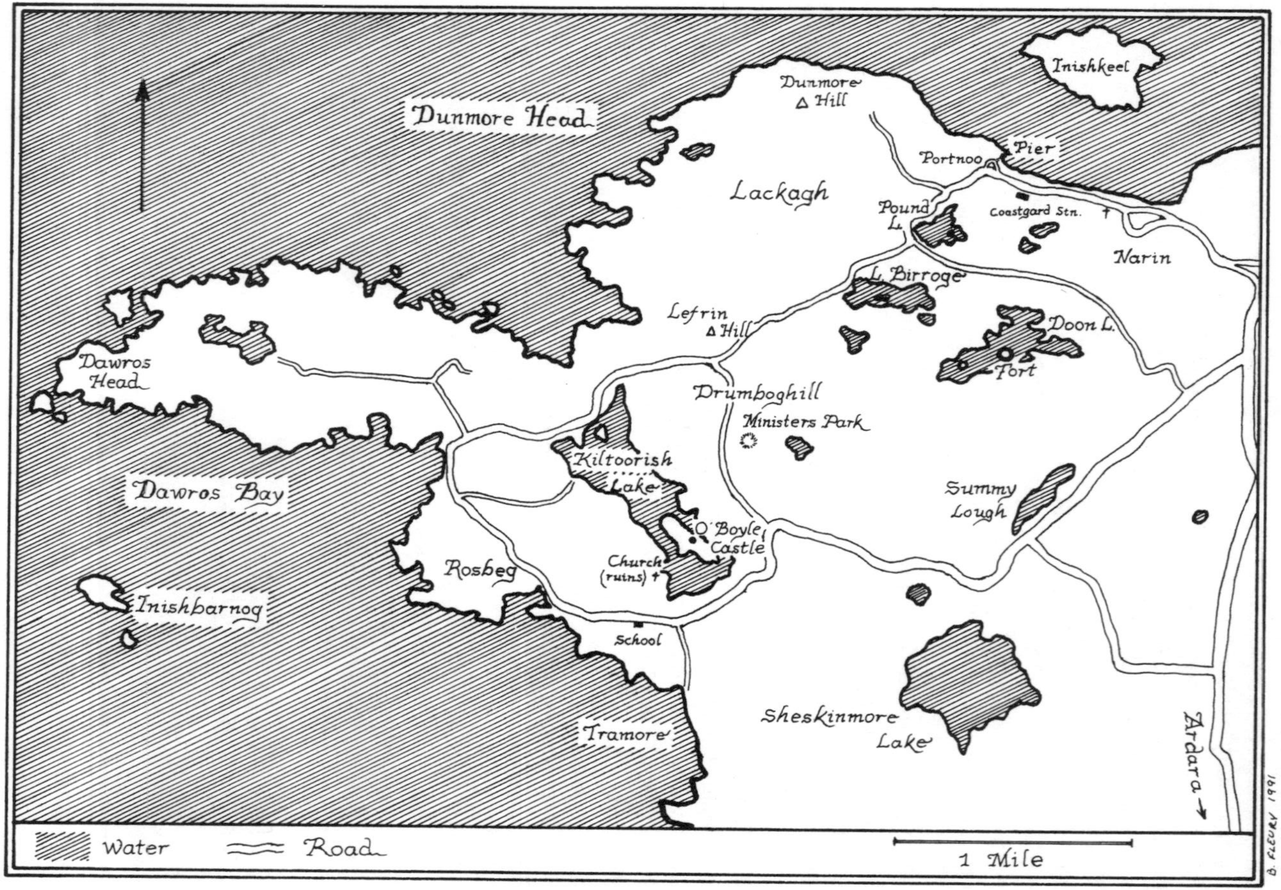

B. FLEURY 1991

Ardara →

1 Mile

Inishkeel

Narin

Portnoo Pier

coastguard Stn.

Pound L.

L. Birroge

Doon L.

Fort

Summy Lough

Sheskinmore Lake

Dunmore △ Hill

Lackagh

Lefrin △ Hill

Drumboghill

Ministers Park

Boyle's Castle

Kiltoorish Lake

Church (ruins) †

School

Tramore

Dunmore Head

Rosbeg

Dawros Bay

Dawros Head

Inishbarnog

Water

═══ Road

VII

PORTNOO TO ROSBEG

Portnoo to Lackagh

L EAVING THE SACRED island of Inishkeel we set off towards Portnoo, Rosbeg and the Dawros peninsula. As we go along the top of the hill, on our right we have a beautiful view of Narin strand, Inishkeel island, the Rosses off to the north, and on the horizon out at sea is Roaninish island [*roan*: a seal; *inis*: an island; Seal island]. On our left we pass St. Conall's Church (Church of Ireland), the few homes of the Barretts who used to live on the island, the dwelling of Beatrice McHugh who so reverently does the *turas* and we pass the ruins of the old coastguard station up on the hill. This coastguard station was destroyed by a Company of the Old I.R.A. on 16 May 1921. Down to our right we have Portnoo pier, the building of which was started on 13 April 1905. Many people think that the name "Portnoo" - Portnoo is part of Lackagh townland, it is not a townland in itself - only dates from the erection of the pier in 1905. This does not seem to be the case; it appears to be an old name. Portnoo is usually translated as *Port Nua*, [*nua*: new, (the) New Port]. However I think this translation must be questioned. *Úr* would be the Gaelic word most commonly used in Donegal to translate "new", not *nua*, though there are instances of *nua* being used in placenames.[1]

In a list of placenames written down in Lifford on 20 April 1642 the name "Portnokeene" appears. There is no great reason[2] to doubt that it is our present-day Portnoo, because listed beside it are "Lackagh al' Lackagh", "Donnmore" and other names which I can place in this area.[3] I would translate Portnokeene as *Port na nDumhchann* [*dumhach*: a sand dune], the port of the sand dunes. Alternatively it might translate as *Port na nDumhcha Chaoin*, the port of the smooth sand dunes, but the former seems more natural, and very appropriate.

Placenames are generally of great antiquity. We have evidence from all the

historical artefacts – soon to be described – from this area that it was populated from an early age. It is likely that in early times when man was travelling along this west coast in curraghs that it was the flash of the white
sandhills – which would have been much higher then than now – here at
Narin which alerted him to turn his boat into this safe port, the existence of
which would have been known to all those early boatmen – the port at the
sandhills.

If the tides haven't allowed you to get to Inishkeel and find solace there,
then you can always rest your weary soul here at Portnoo, because it is a secluded and peaceful spot:

A voyage dreary,
And coasting weary,
Bring me to anchor
In sweet Portnoo.
Above that harbour
There is an arbour,
From storm's wild ardour
A refuge true;
I love to rest there,
With friendship blest there,
By friends caressed there,
With sorrows few,
'Tis a beacon seeming,
With heav'ns light gleaming,
For ever beaming
Above Portnoo.[4]

We have the following delightful description of Portnoo from the year
1900. "Portnoo is a small seaside place in the parish of Inishkeel, Co.
Donegal. A grand sea rolls in from the broad Atlantic, and a fine yellow
sandy shore stretches away in the distance. Large quantities of fish are taken
there, and the number of porpoises, rolling over like huge barrels in the
waves close to the shore, testifies to the shoals of herring and mackerel that
abound in these waters."[5]

Since writers with much greater descriptive powers than I possess have
passed this way in earlier years, I won't attempt to replace their splendid
cameos with poorer efforts of my own. So we will continue with Lloyd
Praeger's wonderful description of this area, especially its geology, flora and
fauna:

"South of the long narrow estuary of the Gweebarra River we come at
once to the wild Dawros promontory (*Damh ros*, headland of the oxen), not

lofty, but full of little heathery hills and lakes, with a sandy or cliffy shore –
a particularly attractive area, as is borne out by the existence of hotels at
Narin, Portnoo and Dawros, all near its ocean-washed extremity. I shall take
Portnoo as exemplifying what the visitor will find in this region. Facing
north, with a hill to westward, it is sheltered from the direct ocean blasts,
and wind-torn trees can grow here and there. You look out across
Gweebarra Bay to a high promontory ending in Crohy Head and its old
watchtower, beyond which lies Arranmore with the high stack of Illanaran
off its seaward end. West of that all is ocean. Below the scattered line of
houses of Portnoo, green fields, white with Pignut instead of Dailies, slope
steeply to a rocky shore, but to the right this gives way to a great beach of
yellow sand, which at low tide connects with Inishkeel, where you will find
the relics of a bygone ecclesiastical settlement, with two early churches, and
some incised crosses of primitive type. Down by the little harbour you
cannot but be struck by the great variety of rocks, and the evidence they
bear of intense crushing and twisting. There are slates, highly contorted,
with veins of yellowish granite injected into them, and black crystalline limestone, which you will know by its smooth surface and little undercut pool-
hollows with drainage channels like miniature canons leading from them –
effects of the eating away of this soluble rock by rain and spray. Above the
grassy slope of Portnoo, the scene changes abruptly, for everywhere there is
rock and heather and lakelet, stretching southward to Loughros More Bay
(*Lochros mor*, lake of the great wood or promontory).[6] Eastwards, this
country stretches away to Glenties; westwards it ends close by in a wild line
of great cliffs, which decrease as one goes towards Dawros Head. The heath-
land is dotted with granite boulders instead of bushes, and Juniper replace
the familiar Gorse. This is a late place, and in early June it is still spring; the
slope of the sea full of Primroses, Wild Hyacinths and even Wood Anemones;
and in the little lakes the Water Lobelia and American Pipewort are yet
hardly stirring.

"You see about Portnoo few of the birds which are associated with the
inland country-side – Rooks, Jackdaws, Sparrows, and so on. Instead there
are more attractive species characteristic of the moorland – Yellow-hammers,
Stonechats, Wheatears, Linnets, Reed-Sparrows; on the lakes are plenty of
Teal and Coot, Water-hens and Dabchicks; and 'sauntering hither on listless
wings', are the Gulls. Red-beaked Choughs are everywhere, playing in the air
and calling to each other. From the sea-rocks you watch Gannets fishing,
Divers of different kinds, Shell-Duck, and all the Puffin fraternity; and Great
Grey Seals watch you with their brown dog-like eyes."[7]

On our left we pass the now sadly-neglected Portnoo Hotel. It was the scene of many nights of merriment and music over the years – which reminds me of an excerpt from the year 1911:

"I was talking with a fiddler the other evening in a house where there was a dance, up by Portnoo. I happened to mention the name of another fiddler I had heard playing a night or two before in Ardara. 'Him, is it?' put in my friend. 'Why, he's no fiddler at all. He's only an old stroller. He doesn't know the differs between "Kyrie Eleison" and "The Devil's Dreams"!' He became very indignant. I interrupted once or twice, trying to turn the conversation but all to no purpose; he still went on. Finally to quiet him, I asked him could he play 'The Sally Gardens'. He stopped to think for a while, fondling the strings of his instrument lovingly with his rough hands; then he said that he didn't know the tune by that name, but that if I'd lilt or whistle the first few bars of it, it might come to him. I whistled them. 'Oh,' says he, 'that's "The Maids of Mourne Shore". That's the name we give it in these parts.' He played the tune for me quite beautifully. Then there was a call from the man of the house for 'The Fairy Reel,' and the dancers took the floor again. The fiddlers in Donegal are 'all sorts,' as they say – farmers, blacksmiths, fisher boys, who play for the love of the thing, and strollers (usually blind men) who wander about from house to house and from fair to fair playing for money. When they are playing I notice they catch the bow in a curious way with their thumbs between the horsehair and the stick. At a dance it is no uncommon thing to see a 'bench' of seven or eight of them. They join in the applause at the end of each item, rasping their bows together on the strings and stamping vigorously with their feet."[8]

We now leave the musicians of Portnoo and continue in the direction of Rosbeg. On our right, between us and the sea, we have an area called Lackagh [*Leacach*: a derivative form of *leac*, a flagstone, and indicating an area strewn with flat stones], extending up into Lackaghmore and rising into Dunmore Hill [*dún*: a fort or enclosure; *mór*: big]. One would conclude that this area was known for its plentiful large stones and stone enclosures. This would be correct – from 1845 we read: "From Doonmore Hill, which rises to the north-west of Lackagh, and upon which there are two forts, ten old forts can be seen. It is probably the grand signal station, so that a signal made there would alarm the rest." Though there are numerous clusters of large stones on Dunmore hill at the present day none of them could be identified as being the definite remains of one of the two forts. Our writer from 1845 continues: "The views from eminences in this neighbourhood are of the oldest kind. From Lackagh Hill, above Portnoo, there is a magnificent ocean scene. Immediately in the foreground is a great sweeping strand, while exactly under, the green island of Iniskeel softens the scene, and upon it the

eye will linger, resting a while for relief from the almost painful effort necessary in contemplating such a varied and extensive prospect."[9]

Lackagh is indeed an historic area. A Bronze-Age sword has been found in
Lackagh in the past and it is now in the National Museum, Dublin - ref. no.
N.M.I. 1941: 331.[10] Older maps show a souterrain in the Lackagh area. The
site was thought to have been lost, but its spacious interior has come to light
again recently. A souterrain was usually marked on maps as a "cave". The
late Charlie Gallagher of Castlegoland, whom we mentioned earlier, told me
that caves at Lackaghmore above Portnoo had formerly been occupied by
people at times of strife and impending invasions. We will never now find
out the real story of this interesting facet of the history of Lackagh.
However, we leave Lackagh with a very definite, undoubted event - a reference to the O'Boyle family, the powerful local sept whom we will discuss
when we get to Kiltoorish, and who are mentioned in the *Annals of the Four
Masters* in the year 1530: "Conor Oge O'Boyle, Tanist of Boylagh, was slain
by the sons of O'Boyle (Niall, the son of Turlough), on the Leacach, on the
6th of January."[11]

Majestic Loughadoon and its surroundings

We pass Lough Pound on our left (an island in this lough which appears to
have been artificially constructed by stone may have been a crannóg) and
turn left over a minor road to view the majestic fort of Loughadoon [*loch*: a

*Lackagh bronze sword
(after George Eogan)*

lake; *dún*: the primary meaning of the word *dún* is "strong" or "firm" - *dún*: *firmus, fortis*. As a noun it signifies a citadel, a fortified royal residence. It is found in many languages - Welsh: *din*; Anglo-Saxon: *tūn*; old high German: *zun*[12]]. Many words were used in Ireland to signify an enclosure where people lived - *caiseal, rath, lios*. However a *dún* was generally the residence of the king or chief.

After continuing along this little road, going in the direction of Kilclooney, and having passed the site of the former public dump - thankfully relocated - we turn off to the right and go up to the house of Francie McHugh. The lake on which "Doon Fort",[13] also known as "O'Boyle Fort", stands is some distance behind Francie McHugh's house. Francie has a few boats on the lake and he hires these out at a minimal rate to people wishing to row across to the fort. He keeps a visitors' book in the house and you should call in first before venturing down to the lake. Francie's home might be quiet now, because his family are all reared, but it wasn't always so. Major Adams, who used to spend long vacations in Woodhill House, Ardara, and whom I remember very well from my childhood, writing in the *Donegal Annual* of 1953/54 about Loughadoon states: "On arrival at the loch we found a large and cheerful family where I had obtained the boat on my previous visit, but a bigger boy acted as oarsman and guide on this occasion."[14]

On approaching by boat the first view you receive of the fort, having

Loughadoon

rounded a headland, suggests that it is floating in the water, a sight you will always remember. Some feel that it looks menacing because of the manner in which it rises out of the waters of the lake. This large stone structure takes up almost the entire area of the island in the middle of the lake; indeed it appears that in earlier times it rose straight out of the water and there was no land visible outside the walls. Lord George Hill, writing in 1845, states: "At the present time, the water of the lake does not actually wash the wall all round, though before the lake was drained off a little (about forty years ago), the fort, in its more perfect state, appeared *standing up out of the water*: but even still it presents a most imposing appearance."[15]

Doon Fort is often compared to a similar structure situated on top of a hill in north Donegal – the Grianan of Aileach. Alistair Rowan, in his book *The Buildings of North-West Ulster*, in discussing buildings of early Christian origin in this area, states: "Of buildings in this period little or nothing remains visible except for two remarkable STONE FORTS: the Grianan of Aileach and Doon Fort. Both are splendid monuments, splendid in scale, in situation, and in evocative power, and they lift Ulster architecture to an unaccustomed level of importance. Eminently primitive in appearance, both consist of a great circular cashel built of dry stone walls with a single entrance, with mural passages and stairs within the enclosure that give access to the wall heads."[16]

One part of the wall of the cashel is collapsed at the present time, and hopefully will soon be repaired, but prior to the mid-1950s the cashel was in a much worse state of decay. Lloyd Praeger, writing in 1937, states: "all that is now standing[17] – about half the circumference of the wall – is original work, beautifully dry-built of the local slatey rock, and densely covered with a shaggy coat of grey lichen."[18] Some restoration was carried out by Bord Fáilte on the fort in 1955 at a cost of £750. A number of cabins[19] that had been built and used by poteen makers in former times were cleared from the inside, and the stones used to make a landing stage for small boats.

Doon Fort is not circular as in most cases, but is oval in shape. The oval-shaped area of grass inside, measuring some 36.6 m. x 25.8 m., is enclosed by a massive stone fortification averaging 4 m. wide at the base and 4.8 m. in height externally. The wall is battered, similar to the Grianan of Aileach, leading to a narrowing of the wall as it rises. Access to the top of the wall is gained by four sets of short flights of steps. A parapet runs along the external side of the top of the wall. The entrance to the cashel is fairly narrow, 1.8 m. wide, and may originally have been roofed.[20] There are two creep-passages within the walls of the fort which you can enter and creep along.[21]

When was this structure built and why? In a stimulating article in the

Donegal Annual of 1989 Professor Eitienne Rynne of University College Galway argues that these large monuments such as the Grianan of Aileach and "O'Boyle's Fort" on Lough Doon, which are clearly related and can be confidently dated to the Pagan Celtic Early Iron Age, that is to within probably a couple of centuries on either side of the birth of Christ, were built for ceremonial purposes and not as defensive military sites.

He states that there are four main reasons why a monument would be built, namely for burial, habitation, military or ceremonial purposes, and adds that the stepped and terraced walls of these large structures are much more suitable for looking inwards than for looking outwards. One should regard these monuments as amphitheatres rather than as defensive stockades.[22] It is a stimulating argument and we must remember that he is addressing the question of why these large structures such as Doon Fort and the Grianan of Aileach were originally constructed; he is not questioning the fact that they were used for a variety of purposes later on.

However I will adhere to the traditional belief – that this structure on Loughadoon was built as a defensive fortification. It has no terracing on the inside wall; apart from where the stairs are, the wall rises up sheer. However, it is its location, built on a lake hidden away here among the hills which are dotted with other lakes, which suggests that its role was defensive. We know that this area has been inhabited from early times – we have already mentioned the bronze sword found in nearby Lackagh and we will soon discuss the Late Bronze Age gold lunula found here in Drumboghill, close to Loughadoon – and it is likely that this fort was built as a hiding place in times of strife or attack. One can imagine the women and children and livestock being brought to this hidden place at times of threat while the men kept a wary eye, elsewhere, on invaders and enemies and possibly engaged them in battle, content that their families were safe on Loughadoon.

Over the centuries Loughadoon would have been used for a variety of purposes. Evidence of habitation is given by the finding of a portion of a rotary quern[23] – used for grinding cereals – while the green interior of the fort was being used for other purposes – setting potatoes – in 1959. People were obviously interred in the interior of Loughadoon because Mr. Adams, in discussing Loughadoon in 1954, states: "The guide told us that his father was setting part of the inside of the fort with potatoes two or three years ago and came upon what, from the boy's description, was undoubtedly a cist grave."[24] Loughadoon is also known as "O'Boyle's Fort"; doubtless it was used by this very powerful sept for centuries during the years of their great influence from 1300 to 1600. One of their principal residences was at nearby Kiltoorish. William Harkin, writing about Loughadoon in 1893, states: "On an island in this lough is a building called Bawawn,[25] supposed to have been a cow-fortress belonging to the O'Boyles."[26]

Though it may have had various uses over the centuries, there is no doubting the antiquity of this great structure. Rev. Pádraig Ó Gallachóir, discussing Loughadoon in the *Donegal Annual* of 1970, states: "Its early history is wrapped in silence, so that it must have been known by another name in the long ago. Was this fortified islet the ancient Oilean Lermogha in Loch Senmogha in Tir Ainmire mentioned by Hogan, in his *Onomasticon Goedelicum* (p.18)? Would it then have been a stronghold of the old Tuath Senmogha before the days of the Cenel Conaill? Probably we shall never know."[27]

I have always thought that this suggestion made by Rev. Fr. Ó Gallachóir of a possible extant ancient name for Loughadoon was romantic and intriguing, but that we could never come to a conclusion about it. Now I think that possibly we can. There is a second reference similar to the one he quotes and it speaks of *"Lermagh, a quo oilen Lermagha for Loch Sencha i tir Ainmirech mir Tuathail; Breslen a chedainm Lermagha."*[28] The key to both references is *"Tír Ainmirech"* once you understand that this is the ancient name for the territory which lay between the Owenea river and the Gweebarra.[29] Can you think of any other island in a lake within this confined

Loughadoon

area which would have been important enough that its name would have been preserved through the ages? In my opinion *Oilean Lermogha* was the name for the early fortified island in Loughadoon, the latter being formerly known as *Loch Senmogha*. The lake derived its ancient name in association with the early population group who lived in this area and who were called the Tuath Senmogha.[30]

Now matters become even more interesting. You will notice that in the second reference the lake is not called *Loch Senmogha* but is termed *Loch Sencha*. In a list of placenames from 1642[31] the placename Synagh appears. It is written as Synagh ( ), the empty bracken possibly indicating that it had been intended to include an alternative name within it. In the list Synagh is placed between Tullyard and Dawros. In a note made before his death my father had equated Synagh with Summy, writing "Synagh – might be Shannagh: Summy". There is no other placename in that particular list which could possibly correspond to the modern name Summy. The townland of Summy is situated beside Loughadoon and indeed may originally have included the Loughadoon area. I think it likely that the "Sencha" of *Loch Sencha* equates with "Synagh" (? = Summy).

Summy is represented in an alternative list[32] of placenames dated 1608 and is written "Summagh". That most difficult of modern placenames to in-

Loughadoon

terpret, Summy ("Summagh"), might be explained as a badly corrupted version of the ancient name *Seanmagh* (the old plain[33]), associated with the Tuath Senmogha [*magh=mogh*, so *Senmagha/Senmogha* and *Lermagha/Lermogha* are interchangeable]. This suggestion is supported by the other 17th-century forms in which the placename is written – "Shamagh" (1620) and "Samagh" (1642, 1659 and 1684). It is written "Sannogh" in 1654. Sencha/Synagh/Sannogh appears to have been an alternative placename used and might represent *Seanachaidh*, the old field, often written Shanagh or Shanagh.[34] That the word *sean* (*sen*), "ancient" or "old", occurs in the topographical names in this area should not surprise us. This general area was inhabited from a very early age – shortly we will come to discuss a gold lunula which was found in this area and which dates to about 1,600 B.C. I think it likely that the population group called the Tuath Senmogha obtained their name simply because they were known – in the early oral history of man – to have been resident in and associated with an area which had been populated by man from very early times – the *Senmogha*.

I believe these are valid conclusions and if so it is particularly exciting to have confirmed the ancient names for Loughadoon and its fortified island – *Loch Senmagha* and *Oilean Lermagha*.

One other point of interest. The first name of Lermagh, who gave the island its name, was Breislen ("*Breislen a chedainm*"). This is the very earliest reference that exists to the Breslin name. The Breslins were of Cenél Conaill stock and probably took control of this area – most likely from the Tuath Senmogha – in the 5th century A.D. The very name Breislen "Lermagha" [*ler*: great number, multitude; *magh*: a plain] would seem to support the view that the Breslins held sway over much of this area. The genealogies give the official role of progenitor of the Breslin sept to Lermagh's son Conaing ("a *quo muinter Breislen*").[35] If your surname is Breslin you should make a point of visiting the fortified island of Loughadoon because in doing so you are setting foot on the ground which has the oldest association on this earth with the (O) Breslin sept, the island of Breislen Lermagha.

Whatever the history of the fortification in Loughadoon we must endeavour to preserve it for future generations. A portion of the wall has been collapsed now for years and surely in this age of increased awareness of our heritage this is totally unacceptable. Hopefully repairs will be carried out. As we make our departure from Loughadoon I would mention that there are slight remains, consisting of collapsed walling, of a second cashel on another small island to the west in Loughadoon. It is heavily vegetated.

We now leave Loughadoon and retrace our steps towards the Portnoo-

Rosbeg road. On Lough Birroge, which we passed earlier on our way to
Loughadoon, and which is on our left as we reach the Portnoo–Rosbeg road,
are the remains of another cashel. An island close to the southern shore of
the lake is almost completely enclosed by a cashel wall. Most of the wall has
collapsed but a short stretch to the south-west survives. This cashel used to
be connected with the mainland by a causeway of small flagstones. Where
the wall of the cashel does survive, 26 to 33 courses of stone are intact and
display a clear curving batter as on Doon Fort.[36] Lord George Hill, passing
by in 1846, and trying to explain the name Lough Birroge states: "It is ...
called Lough Birroge, or Burrog. The legend is that *Burrog* means 'Young
Bridget;' that she was the sister of Fin McCool, and resided in this little
island."[37] Local folklore[38] tells us that a witch lived in Lough Birroge and
that her sister, another witch, lived in Loughadoon.

The road descends, with Lefrin hill on the right, and we come to a little by-
road going off to the left at the foot of Lefrin hill. If we follow this little by-
road we pass a group of derelict cottages; this is the old village of
Drumboghill and it is now a silent place. Past the cottages, over on the left
at a spot known as "The Minister's Park" are the remains of another cashel.
My father, writing in 1958, states: "'The Minister's Park' is a verdant plateau
with the fort occupying its highest point. Very little of the original structure
now remains, but the stones, which once formed part of this imposing
building, can be seen in the mighty fences which surround the field. Enough
is left, however, to enable us to measure its ground dimensions. ... In one or
two places one can notice that the foundation consisted of two concentric
walls with a space between. In all probability this space ultimately became a
creep passage as in the neighbouring fort at Loughadoon.

"Some five or six feet from the north-west boundary of the inner space one
notices a few long, loose stones. On removing these, one is gazing down into
a subterranean passage, 5.5 feet deep and 3.5 feet wide. The sides are stone-
built and the roof is of thick flags. To the north of this opening the roof
would seem to have collapsed; a short distance from the southern end it is
blocked with rubble."[39]

It is now only a shoft stretch of underground passage, but in former times
the north-west end of the passage may have continued under the enclosing
wall. The term for an underground passage such as this is a "souterrain",
and we have already mentioned that there used to be one at Lackagh.
Souterrains are artificial underground structures built to allow access and
they are usually associated with sites of habitation. Where it has been possible to date souterrains, they have been found to have been constructed between the 6th and the 12th centuries. It is thought that they were originally

used as hiding places in times of strife, and they may have been used for storing and preserving food in a cold place in times of peace.

In a few places here at "The Minister's Park" one can notice the remains of an outer fortification about 32" out from the remains of the cashel. So the whole plateau would seem to have been protected by another fortification built on the hillfort principle.

We have now encountered three stone enclosures – at Loughadoon, Lough Birroge and here at "The Minister's Park" – within a small area, supporting our view that we are in the midst of a most historic locality. This supposition is strengthened by our next topic for discussion – a beautiful gold lunula (collar) found here in Drumboghill at the beginning of this century and now in the National Museum.

The Gold Lunula

The gold lunula was found by a man named Craig while paring a bog at a spot called the *Coiscéim Chung* in Drumboghill. Thinking it was part of a coffin plate he threw it under a hedge where it lay for a year or more.[40] Eventually it came into the possession of a local shopkeeper who disposed of it to the Rev. R.H. Sewell, of Liverpool; he brought it out of the country, but

Drumboghill lunula

it was later acquired by the Royal Irish Academy as treasure trove and is now in the National Museum in Dublin.

Lunulae are regarded as being a distinctive Irish ornament, dating from the Early Bronze Age.[41] "The most characteristically Irish of the Early Bronze Age gold ornaments is the lunula, a crescentic collar made from thin sheet gold. While a few are completely unornamented, normally there is a finely incised pattern of triangles, lozenges and chevrons near the points of the crescent and along the edges of the broad part of the plate. This ornamentation is so fine that it is visible only on close examination. When being worn the lunula evidently relied for effect on its sheer expanse of glittering metal."[42] "The Drumboghill lunula is engraved at the sides with oblongs, the lower of which consist of alternate plain and shaded bands, the lowest being edged on each side with shaded dog-tooth ornament. The inner and outer curves of the lunula are incised with a continuous cross-hatched band."[43]

A study has compared the ornamentation on some of the Irish lunulae to motifs on Beaker[44] pottery and considers Beaker influence on the collars to have occurred between 1700 and 1600 B.C.. The same study lists eighty-one lunulae as having been found in Ireland. "In addition, twenty-two lunulae are known which are not of Irish provenance, eleven in Britain, nine in northwest France and one each in Luxembourg and Germany. Since an Irish origin for the type as a whole is hardly disputable, these latter may be exports, or some may have been made by travelling Irish craftsmen."[45] The occurrence of these lunulae, of Irish origin, on the continent, such as the one at Hanover in Germany, gives an idea of the trade routes from Ireland approximately 1500 years before the time of Christ. And when we set off to Germany nowadays, courtesy of Lufthansa or Aer Lingus, we still have the temerity to think of ourselves as intrepid travellers!

We now leave Drumboghill, without going into the thorny question of where the gold was mined which was cold worked (casting of gold had not yet begun) into lunulae around the 17th century B.C., and rejoin the Portnoo–Rosbeg road.

Around Dawros
We pass Ballyhillagh – "The ruins near the old fishing port of Ballyhillagh might repay investigation. Through long heather one can trace round the rectangular remains, as well as a long souterrain-like structure with one exit in the face of an escarpment"[46] – and continue towards Eden, Dawros and Rosbeg.

The presence of an area called "Eden" on this peninsula is indeed interesting. Initially I thought it was a post-Plantation English name, but in fact the placename Eden comes from the Gaelic word *éadan*: a forehead, and indicates a hill-brow, which correctly reflects the topographical character of this area. On our right is the original Old Eden House and on our left is New Eden House which was built around the turn of the century. The families Hamilton and, later, Johnson are those associated with the more recent history of the area.

Lord George Hill, passing through this area in 1846, was impressed: "The tourist will feel much enjoyment in driving through the extraordinary district on the coast in the vicinity of Eden, the residence of G. Hamilton, Esq. The undulations of the land seem interminable, and the face of the country is rugged and broken beyond conception, yet the pasturage seems of the finest kind, and of immense extent; the luxuriant green, contrasting most agreeably with the wild rocks, and contributing to compensate amply for their extreme roughness."[47]

Mr. McParlan, writing in 1802, testifies to the courage of the Hamiltons. Referring to the whale fishing carried out by the Nesbitt family, which we will be discussing in detail later, he states: "Great numbers of those [whales] come on this coast; Mr. Nisbett generally killed two, three and sometimes four in one season, about 20 years ago; one of the whales however, angry at this invasion of their empire of the ocean, gave Mr. Nesbitt's boat a whisk of its tail, and shattered it in pieces; two men were lost; the activity and good swimming of Mr. James Hamilton of Eden saved many lives, and among them Mr. Nesbitt's, who was the last picked out of the waves. This accident put an end to his whale fishing."[48] This incident is thought to have occurred about the year 1785.

William Harkin, writing in 1893, states: "Eden House[49] [is] the charming residence of Major Johnston. The gallant Major is the possessor of a very interesting museum, consisting of coins of the time of Edward Bruce, of Edward II, Henry VIII and Elizabeth, and ones of Philip and Mary, all of which were found on the sandhills[50] adjacent. A pair of candlesticks which stood the siege of Derry, and a most extraordinary relic of the ascendancy days, completes the rare collection. The latter is a badge or clasp of brass, with the picture of Enniskillen Castle raised thereon, surrounded with orange lilies and purple rockets. Some trophies of the chase are also to be seen, notably the head of a wild goat shot by Major Johnston on Slievetooey. Mosville,[51] the residence of Colonel Hamilton, is in this district also, and is a very handsome seaside residence."[52]

Major Johnston of Eden House was killed by active members of the Old I.R.A. on 28 August 1920. On that night there was a general raid to obtain arms carried out all over Ireland by the I.R.A. Some members of a local company of the Old I.R.A. entered the house looking for guns and there was a shooting incident, said to have been accidental. A source, now deceased, who had knowledge of the happenings of that fateful night, stated that the shooting of Major Johnston was not intended and that his death was greatly regretted by the members of the Old I.R.A. who took part in the raid.

The names Dawros and Rosbeg derive from the Gaelic word *ros*, a peninsula, which we have already discussed when we passed along the Gweebarra estuary. [Dawros: *damh*: an ox, a stag; *damh ros*: the peninsula of the oxen. Rosbeg: *beag* little, small; the little peninsula.] Before proceeding through Rosbeg village and coastline with its panoramic sea views extending out to Tormore, I would like to mention a survey that was carried out in this area in 1821. This survey was organised by the North West of Ireland Agricultural Society. They sent out a questionnaire to various areas and the answers from this parish were supplied by Rev. John Barrett, who was Church of Ireland rector of the parish of Inishkeel from 1802-44. Curiously, the actual questions in the survey have been lost, but we are in possession of the answers. We can only guess at the questions from the answers supplied by the Rev. Barrett. His material gives us a valuable insight into living conditions in the year 1821 in this area; it refers to the old parish of Inishkeel, consisting of 151 townlands, which took in a very large area prior to the formation of the Ardara parish in 1829.

He states: "In the farms bordering on the Shores, the usual succession of crops is, first, potatoes, followed by barley, then oats or flax. In our very sandy district, rye is sown which answers well; wheat would grow in many places, but there are no flour mills within 30 miles, and the prevalence of illicit distillation induces the farmer to prefer the sowing of barley. Barley and oats are the only descriptions of grain in the parish. From the universal practice of illicit distillation, grain sells much higher in this parish than in many other parts of Ireland. Provisions are generally dearer here than in other parts of Ireland; the cause I conceive to be an over abundant population, bad husbandry, small farms and the great consumption of grain in illicit distillation. Were it not for the importation of provisions from the province of Connaught, this parish would very frequently be in danger of starving.

"The entire of this parish is interspersed with moors and bogs and I know of no inhabitant one mile distant from fuel. The sum paid for permission to cut a dark of turf, that is, as much as three men cut in a day, varies from one shilling and eight pence (1s 8d) to two shillings and six pence (2s 6d). The landlord receives no rent for bog.

"There are neither woods, orchards, nurseries or plantations in this Parish, and I know from experience they would all thrive; I planted a few pear, apple and plum trees which produce most abundantly. In former times it is evident that this country abounded in woods; even the trails seem covered with underwood. My respected friend and neighbour, Major Nesbitt of Woodhill in Killybegs parish, has planted an extensive orchard, a number of shrubs and forest trees of all kinds and they all thrive most admirably.

"In spring it is almost impossible to procure labourers, all being employed in the planting of their own potatoes. To give general employment I would recommend the establishment of manufactures, of which the parish is almost totally destitute. Premiums might be advantageously offered for the apprenticing of children to trades. The usual custom at present is, when there are six sons, the father divides the already too scanty farm into six parts, and thus creates six families of beggars, instead of apprenticing five of his sons to trades and giving his farm to one.

"An able manservant's wages average about £5 per annum. A maid servant's about £2 10s per annum. Labour is uniformly performed by the day; the usual price 6d per day and food. I give to my labourers 10d a day without food.

"In the districts bordering on the sea shore, sea weeds is almost the only manure used, from its producing a greater weight of potatoes on a given surface than any other manure known here. As to lime, it is never used as manure here; why I cannot tell.

"I never saw oxen used in husbandry in the County of Donegal except by myself. I always have two – they answer very well. They plough and harrow and bring home my turf. I never shoe them.

"In this parish spade tillage is almost exclusively used, from the small size of the farms and the consequent inability to purchase ploughs.

"A small breed of black Cattle is usually raised in this Parish; also a small breed of sheep well adapted to soil and Climate. Horses are little used for Agricultural purposes, except for the carrying of sea and other manures. They are of a small kind, produced between the Irish and the Scotch. The swine are not large but well shaped; and probably better adapted to the scanty fare of the poor farmers of this District. I do not think that any improvements have been made in the breeds of horses, black Cattle, or Sheep in this parish for the last 20 years. In pigs I have perceived a substitution of the short-legged for the long-legged Irish breed.

"I live very near the sea shore. The shore abounds in creeks, but, lying on the Great Atlantic none safe. Dawros is an excellent harbour; the Church Pool [Inishkeel] is extremely safe in the summer months, but not during winter. There are two ferries between this parish and Lettermacaward for people only, the cattle must swim.

"Some years since, a silver mine was discovered in the Townland of Glenaboghill in this Parish; an English miner pronounced it to be very rich; it has since been worked. The quarry is about five miles from the sea. Mr. Hamilton of Brownhall is the Proprietor.

"Very little limestone is raised, as the inhabitants don't raise it as manure, and all convenient to the shore prefer the digging of shells of Cockles, mussels, and oysters, from the superior facility of burning them, to be used in buildings, the lime produced is of a whiteness superior to that from limestone, but requires less sand to constitute mortar.

"There are many sulphurous and steel springs in this parish, but the only celebrated one is in the Townland of Dawros, near to the shore. It is of a strong sulphurous quality and has much benefited the few who used it in schophulous complaints.

"From what I have already stated, it is evident that the situation of the inhabitants as to domestic comforts is very bad. Few, very few, are the means of earning money in this parish; but when by servitude at home or in Scotland, whither many go annually, a small sum of money is earned, it is expended on the purchase of a farm from some of those who annually emigrate to America. They then marry and entail misery as a large family. The general conditions of farm houses is bad, that of cottages wretched; the want of cleanliness is the obvious defect.

"There is a strong and general inclination for education in all classes, but the object is often defeated by the poverty of the parents, obliging them to keep their children at home for agricultural purposes, and thus they frequently forget what they have learned. The expenses of each of the classes is the same – for Arithmetic, reading and writing about 3s 6d per quarter; for reading and spelling only, 2s 6d per quarter. There are ten schools in the Parish. The only town is Glenties; the principal villages are Narin and Cloghboy. I know of no other consisting of twenty houses contiguous.

"There are only a few small boats. My table is usually supplied with fish taken by a curragh, a species of boat composed of wicker work and covered with a horse's skin. Cod and pollock [are the usual fish]. If the weather be not very fine, no boat will venture from the shore. When the sea is extremely calm, they will go four leagues from the land, aware that were a wind off land to arise, America is the nearest shore. Not more than 30 people are employed [in fishing] and even that small number are only employed in the summer months when the weather is calm. No fish are cured for distant markets and there is no market to which fresh fish could be sent. I learn that herring have been, of late years, frequently on this coast, but were not taken for want of nets."

I'm sure you will agree with me that Rev. Barrett's answers, which I have rearranged into one continuous narrative, give a remarkable insight into the lifestyle, severely restricted by poverty, of the people of west Donegal at the beginning of the 19th century. Though poor in material wealth, we now travel on to the historically rich area of Kiltoorish.

Notes

1   Quiggin, *A Dialect of Donegal*; Dónall Mac Giolla Easpaig, whose advice we sought earlier at Narin, is happy to accept *Portnoo* as a derivation of *Port Nua*.

2   But there is a minor one. Earlier, at Narin, we read that McParlan noted the presence of lead ore "near Portnoo, in Boylagh". He also states that lead ore "is to be seen on the high mountain called Portnockan, parish of Inishkeel, Boylagh". "Portnockan" surely equates with "Portnokeene"; was a history of lead or copper mining a factor in the make-up of the name Portnoo? The Gaelic for lead or copper is *umha*; Portnoo: *Port an umha*. Placenames!

3   E.g. Aighrosse – Aghros Hill; Clagine – at the Greenhouse Brae; Mollaghalla – near Lough Pound; Tober – Toberaslackan at the foot of Narin hill.

4   McDevitt, *The Most Rev. James McDevitt, D.D., Bishop of Raphoe, a memoir*, p. 51.

5   *J.R.S.A.I.*, Part II, (1900), p. 148.

6   This is an incorrect translation of Loughros More.

7   Praeger, *The Way That I Went*, pp. 39-40.

8   Campbell, *Mearing Stones*, pp. 34-35.

9   Hill, *Useful Hints to Donegal Tourists*, p. 36.

10   From Eogan, *Catalogue of Irish Bronze Swords*, we read: "No. 137. The tang has been cast on. It has a very slight flanges, and one rivet-hole at which the two low ridges which run up the web converge. The terminal end is missing. Ricasso present. The plain blade is a pointed oval in cross-section. Bibl: Morris, 'Some Features of Bronze Swords,' *CLAJ*, 6, p. 320."

11   *A.F.M.*, vol. v, p. 1397.

12   Joyce, vol. I, p. 277.

13   A meaningless anglicisation, since the word "doon" (*dún*) signifies much the same as the word "fort".

14   pp. 491-98.

15   *Useful Hints to Donegal Tourists*, p. 36.

16   Rowan, *The Buildings of North-West Ulster*, p. 23.

17   A photograph in Raftery, *Prehistoric Ireland*, p. 28, shows various parts of the walls of the cashel in a collapsed condition. Raftery suggests that the site represents a compromise between a land cashel and a crannóg. A similar photograph in the *D.A.* (1951) also shows collapse of the walls in a number of places.

18   Praeger, *The Way That I Went*, p. 40.

19   In *J.R.S.A.I.*, vol. 117 (1987), a sketch of Doon Fort drawn just before the turn of the century is shown. It depicts "the low walls of a structure, 16 x 8 feet, built against the low walls of the north-west fort wall".

20   *A.S.D.*, p. 136.

21   On the south-south-west side of the entrance an opening gives access at ground level to a wall-passage. A flight of steps at the south-south-west end of this passage rises to an opening in the top of the wall. On the north-north-east side of the entrance an opening above ground level enters a second wall passage, narrower and lower than the first. The north-north-east end of this passage turns at right angles forming a low creep which enters from the base of the interior of the cashel wall face. (*A.S.D.*)

22   *D.A.* (1989), pp. 54-56.

23   We will discuss querns in more detail at the site of the crannóg at Crannogeboy, Loughros Point.

24   *D.A.* (1953-54), p. 494.

25   The term bawn is the anglicised form of the Irish *badhun*, an enclosure or fortress for cows. The word occurs in the form *bó-dhún* in the *Annals of Lough Cé* at the years 1199 and 1200 (Joyce, vol. I, p. 308).

26   *North-West Donegal*, p. 79; Harkin was from Creeslough.

27   p. 249

28   The O'Clery Book of Genealogies, *Analecta Hibernica*, no. 18, p. 3.

29   Ibid. p. 27: "*Tir Ainmire at-beror frisin mbloidh tire o Ghaoth bera co h-abhainn Fiadha.*"

30   *Book of Ballymote* 51B.

31   Inq., Ultonia 30 Car. I.

32   Rawlinson MS. A. 237, reproduced in *Analecta Hibernica*, no. 3 (1931).

33   The word *mag(h)* can be translated as "a plain", "an open stretch of land, usually uncultivated, which may include minor elevations or depression". The *Seanmagh* may originally have included most of the present-day Dawros–Kilclooney area when it was occupied by the Tuath Senmogha. It is of interest that in a restricted sense a *mag(h)* can mean a field or green attached to a "fort". (*Dictionary of the Irish Language*, R.I.A.).

34   Joyce, vol. III, pp. 551, 553.

35   O'Clery, op. cit, p. 3.

36   *A.S.D.*, p. 136.

37   *Useful Hints to Donegal Tourists*, p. 36. Hill goes on to state that there were extensive slate quarries on the shore of Lough Birroge; the slates were of a heavy, thick description and he felt that they were "providentially adapted to a stormy region; as from their weight, wind had scarcely the power of displacing them".

38   It is said that the Loughadoon witch drove her cow to pasture every day and turned it into stone at night. One evening as the cow was returning from grazing it was accidentally struck by a fisherman. Both were turned to stone. It is claimed that

the Loughadoon witch died as a result and that her sister in Lough Birroge, who was engaged in building herself a new residence, heard the piercing death cries and dropped dead herself. The stone she was lifting at the time is said to be still visible. In Loughadoon it is said that the cow can now and again be heard lowing in the depths of the lake in search of its mistress.

39   *D.A.* (1958), p. 74.

40   *H.P.A.*, p. 2.

41   From *c.* 2200 B.C. to *c.* 1200 B.C.

42   Kelly, *Early Ireland*, p. 180.

43   Armstrong, *Catalogue of Irish Gold Ornaments*, p. 57; its registration no. in the catalogue is 6: 1909. See also Coffey, *P.R.I.A.*, vol. 27, p. 253.

44   "The Beaker Folk, as they were called, are often hailed nowadays as the heralds of the metal age in these latitudes, although there is as yet no cogent evidence to show that they were responsible for the first metal working in Ireland. They made a very distinctive kind of Beaker-shaped pottery bearing characteristic decoration, with the help of which we can trace their presence from Ireland to Hungary and from Scandinavia to Sicily. As itinerant metal-workers, they have been likened to modern gypsies. Where they originated no one yet knows, but most of the Beaker groups who arrived in England and who eventually made their way to Ireland came from the Middle Rhine." (*J.R.S.A.I.*, vol. 103 (1973), p. 95.)

45   Kelly, op. cit., p. 180.

46   *H.P.A.*, p. 10.

47   *Useful Hints to Donegal Tourists*, p. 36.

48   *Statistical Survey of the County of Donegal*, p. 73.

49   i.e. New Eden House.

50   This is probably a reference to the sandhills of Magheramore near by, which was the site of a great fair for many centuries, hence the presence of coins; we will discuss this fair later.

51   Mosville is synonomous with the original Dawros Bay Hotel, later Fricks Hotel, which no longer functions as a hotel. The present hotel in Dawros, owned by the Molloy family, was formerly known as Cliff View. The original Dawros Bay Hotel is referred to in *Waddington's Guide* "...perched near the extreme point of a rugged, jutting headland is Dawros Bay Hotel. The hotel, which was formerly the mansion of Lt. Col. Hamilton, was built by his father, Judge Hamilton, Recorder of Cork. The hotel is beautifully furnished, and maintains a generous table."

52   *Scenery and Antiquities of North-Western Donegal*, p. 80

VIII

KILTOORISH AND THE O'BOYLES

WE DRIVE THROUGH Rosbeg and arrive in the townland of Kiltoorish. The former Kiltoorish school is on your right. This school, erected in 1890, was closed in 1973 and is now used as a community centre. The earliest school building in this area is believed to have been a thatched structure and stood at a spot called Loughside, not far from the gates of the present "Kiltoorish Hall" (which was formerly known as "Loughside"). Protestants and Catholics attended this school.

Interpreting the meaning of the name Kiltoorish is not easy. In the first instance we might translate it as *Cill Turais*, the church of the *turas* - a *turas*, such as we have already described at Derryleconnell and Inishkeel island, in which one visits certain sites and says prescribed prayers at each site. It has been suggested that Kiltoorish formed part of the long *turas* done from Inishkeel island, which we have already referred to, in which one would walk from Inishkeel island over "Bothair" to Kiltoorish and then across Loughros More Bay and Loughros Beg Bay to Laconnell and on into Glencolumbkille. Supporters of this interpretation of the meaning of Kiltoorish could take comfort from the fact that it is marked on Laurie and Whittles' erratic 1798 map as "Killturviskeel" - *Cill Turais Caoil*, "The church of the *turas* of (Conall) Caol".

Possibly the placename started off as *Cill Damhros*, the church of Dawros, and may have been corrupted to *Cill Turais* in later years because the church here was involved in the long linear *turas* to Laconnell and Glencolumbkille. We have already noted at Churchtown, near Narin strand, that Kiltoorish was referred to as "Kildowns" (? = Killdawros) in 1622. In 1620 it is written "Killowas". In the Down Survey of 1659 it is mapped as "Kilturvis" and is church land. The name is written as Killowras al' Dawrosse in 1642.[1] It appears that both *Cill Turais* and *Cill Damhros* were in use as names here, the former surviving into the present day.

Close to the western shore of Kiltoorish Lough are the remains of an old church; we will describe it shortly. This is not the site of the original cill in this area. The earlier ecclesiastical foundation was situated at a spot known locally as *Lus na hAirne*[2] [*lus*: a herb or a plant; *airne*: the sloe; *Lus na hAirne*: sloe plant or sloe bush. The well-known Killarney in Co. Kerry translates as *Cill Airneadh*, the church of the sloes]. It consists of a holy well and a grave-plot shrouded in blackthorn bushes. It is evident that the little well was well-cared for at one time, but it has been neglected for many a day. Here and there under the bushes one can discern stones standing about 1' or 1.5' feet above the level of the ground, evidently the markers of grave plots. In the early part of this century many people had great faith in the efficacy of this well for the cure of toothache and head complaints. Water from it was often carried long distances. Mr. and Mrs. John Craig (R.I.P.) who lived near by could tell of many cures effected here.[3]

Lus na hAirne is situated up in the hills on the west face of Kiltoorish Lough, further north than the ruins of the old church on the lakeside. This old building, on the western shore of the lake, was a chapel of ease to Inishkeel; when dealing with Churchtown, at Narin, earlier, I mentioned that in 1622 parish services were removed from Inishkeel island to this church. In 1724 services were transferred to the new church of St. James at Narin.

In discussing the old church at Kiltoorish, my father, writing in 1970, states: "Most of the wall structure of the old church remained intact until a few years ago when the eastern gable, with its altar, little stone cross,[4] and ornamented window, was pushed out and demolished by a tree growing on the inside. The little graveyard surrounding it has tombstones bearing dates from 1600 to 1819, and it was used until comparatively recent times by a few families, Catholic and Protestant. Kiltoorish and Kilkenny were chapels of ease to the main church on Inishkeel. The writer ventures the opinion that they were built between 1400 and 1500 A.D. On account of their accessability these churches gradually superseded the mother church on the island."[5]

"Immediately below the heights of Eden, is the remarkable lake of Kiltoorish, from which rises a large and beautifully verdant island – the shores of the lake being equally green. On this island are the remains of the O'Boyle's castle."[6] With this reference from 1846 we broach the subject of the O'Boyle sept, associated with Kiltoorish for many years. The pedigree of the O'Boyles, like that of other great Donegal families such as the Ó Canannans, O'Donnells and Ó Gallachóirs, goes back into the mists of early history. In the 4th century A.D. a war-like group from north Connacht overran most of north-west Ireland. They were lead by eight sons of Niall of the Nine Hostages[7] one of whom was Conall Gulban.[8] (The element Gulban in Conall's name is the same as that in the name of the Sligo mountain, Ben Bulben, which in ancient times was called Ben Gulban.) When Conall Gulban and his brothers had conquered the north-west corner of Ulster, they partitioned it among themselves.

At that time and probably from a much earlier period Ireland had been subdivided into a number of territorial divisions know as *Tricha Céts*, each containing thirty *Baile Biataighs* or townlands. Conall's share of the conquered territory comprised, according to the *Book of Fenagh* and other sources, the *Tricha Cét Easa Ruaidh*, the *Tricha Cét Bógaine* and the *Tricha Cét Luighdheach*, extending from the Erne to Loch Swilly. These formed Conall's own immediate principality which was the nucleus of later *Tír Chonaill*. They were afterwards possessed by his posterity, the Cenél nAedha Easa Ruaidh, the Cenél mBógaine and the Cenél Luighdheach, who were collectively known as the Cenél Conaill.[9] Conall's son Enda Bógaine was the progenitor of the Cenél mBógaine whose kings ruled the territory from the Eany to the Dobhar for over five centuries. From Ainmire mac Melghe mac Enda Bógaine sprang the Cenél nAinmirech and the Muintir Breislen who occupied *Tír Ainmirech* between the Owenea and Gweebarra. The last mention of the Cenél mBógaine in the annals was in 1035 A.D. when their king Flaithbeartach Ó Murchadha was slain "with many people". From then on they fade into obscurity. Not till much later do we hear of other ruling familes, the O'Boyles and the MacSweeneys, in *Tír Bógaine* (Boylagh and Banagh).[10]

One of Conall's great grandsons, Ainmire mac Sétna, became High King of Ireland and so did Ainmire's son Aedh. The latter gave his name to *Tír Aedha* and to the Cenél nAedha Easa Ruaidh which included the O'Cannons, the Ó Maeldoraidhs and the Ó Gallachóirs (Gallaghers).

From Lughaidh, brother of Ainmire, sprang the Cenél Luighdheach, which included the O'Donnells, the O'Boyles, the O'Dohertys, etc. As the power of the O'Cannons and Ó Maeldoraidhs began to wane the O'Donnells – known as Clann Dalach, after one of their number, Dalach, who was lord of the Cenél Conaill from 868 A.D. to 896 A.D – began to rise in influence and became in time the royal family of *Tír Chonaill*. They are still looked upon as the royalty of *Tír Chonaill*.

The territory of the Cenél Luighdheach was to the north of the territory of the Cenél mBógaine and extended from the Dobhar to the Swilly. Before the O'Boyles came to the Kiltoorish area they ruled the three northern *tuaths* of Rosguill, Clochaneely and Tory.

In the 13th century the O'Boyles – who derived their name from Baighell (ó Baighell, i.e. descendant of Baighell – O'Boyle) who lived nine generations after the time of Conall Gulban – controlled all west Donegal, from Mulroy in the north to the Eske in the south. They were loyal allies of the O'Donnells over the next four, crucial centuries. In the year 1247 A.D. we are told that in a battle "O'Donnell was slain on the spot, as well as the Cammhuinealach (Wry-necked) O'Boyle,[11] the head Chieftain of the Three Tuathas".[12]

Gradually the sway of the O'Boyle sept became more confined – "the coming of the MacSweeney *gallóglaigh* involved the loss of much of their territory in the north-west of the present county, till they were left with Boylagh, from Eske to Gweedore. The entrance of a Connacht branch of the MacSweeneys in the early fifteenth century to control Banagh left the O'Boyles finally confined to a partitioned chiefdom – Boylagh Uachtarach: from Eske to Inver and Boylagh Iochtarach: from Loghross to Gweebara."[13]

The three great O'Boyle residencies of this "partitioned chiefdom" were the castles at Ballyweel [*Baile Uí Bhaoill*, Boyle's Town] near Donegal town, Crannogeboy at Loughros Point near Ardara, and here at Kiltoorish. The *crannóg* at Crannogeboy – distinct from the O'Boyle castle which also stood at Crannogeboy – and Doon Fort (O'Boyle's Fort) here at Drumboghill were other structures (boltholes perhaps?) used by the family. The few metres[14] of the wall of the castle which survive on the island here on Kiltoorish lake are now all that remain of their three castles.

The history of the O'Boyle sept shows all the courage, tragedy, enthronements and infighting which one would expect in perusing the records of any great tribe. We will look at a few examples from the annals. Again, as in our earlier footnote on the O'Breslin family, you will note that the history of the O'Boyles is intertwined with the other great tribes of *Tír Chonaill* and *Tír Eoghain*.

Our first reference, from the *Annals of Ulster*, should engender in us a healthy respect for any person who claims membership of the O'Boyle sept! It reads:

1160 A.D. "Ua Canannain, king of Cenel-Conaill, was killed by the Cenel-Conaill themselves, – namely, a house was burned by Ua Baighill upon him."

In 1197 a great battle was fought "where two hundred of them (the Irish) were killed, around their king", including "the sons of Ua Baighill and other nobles".

1203 A.D. "Domnall Carrach Ua Dochartaigh, king of Tir-Conaill was killed by Muinnter-Baighill after pillaging many churches and territories."

1223 A.D. "Tadhg O'Baighill (namely, son of Ceallach), splendour of the North of Ireland, died."

(In 1249 A.D. the *Annals* inform us that "Niall Ua Canannain took the kingship of Tir-Conaill this year" and add the interesting postscript, "Great crop on trees this year.")

1259 A.D. "Sigraidh O'Baighill was killed by his own kinsmen." (Later, at Loughros Point, we will have mention of a Shewgrie O'Boyle, presumably the same person as this Sigraidh: *Sygray O'Broychill, subregulus trium Tuoha* – of the three Territories.)

From the *Annals of the Four Masters* we note a few later entries:

1517 A.D. "Donagh, the son of Turlough O'Boyle, a man who, for his means, was the best gentleman, and who had carried on the most war, and performed most dangerous exploits, of all of who had come of his own tribe, set out with the crew of a boat for Torach; but a wind drove them westwards through the sea, and no tidings of them was ever since heard."

1530 A.D. "The daughter of O'Boyle, i.e. Rose daughter of Turlough, son of Niall Roe, a charitable and truly hospitable woman, died."

1532 A.D. "Mary, the daughter of MacSweeney Fanad, and wife of O'Boyle, died suddenly, after having been thrown from her horse, at the door of her own mansion, on the 21st April."

1536 A.D. "The first person who went out to watch for the army [of O'Donnell] was O'Boyle (Niall, the son of Turlough), who supposed that his enemies would soon come up to him, and that he would be able to wreak his vengeance upon them. But the people of Hugh Boy, the son of O'Donnell, went at the same time, without giving notice to O'Boyle, or his people, to guard another pass. Both parties met, and neither of them recognising the other, they proceeded to strike at each other. Fiercely and resolutely did O'Boyle fight in this skirmish against his enemies (as he thought), and he unsparingly cut off great numbers of (the opposite) host; but as he was slaughtering them in this manner, they formed a huge circle around him, so that he at last met his death from his own true and faithful friends, on the second of the Calends of August ... . The death of the person being the here slain, i.e. Niall, the son of Turlough, was a cause of great grief to the poor and indigent, and to the literati and the kerns."

Following which, in 1540 A.D., Donnell,[15] the son of Niall O'Boyle, was styled O'Boyle.

The allegiance of the O'Boyles to the O'Donnells in their continued fight against the English was unwavering. In *Beatha Aodha Ruaidh Ui Dhomhnaill*,[16] [*The Life of Hugh Roe O'Donnell, Prince of Tirconnell (1586-1602)*] we are told how the legendary chieftain, having escaped from prison in 1591 but suffering from frostbite, had "returned to Ballyshannon and remained there. He called in physicians to examine his feet, but they could not cure him until his two great toes were cut off in the end, and he was not quite recovered for a whole year. However, he did not omit during that time to do what was necessary to unite the people, to destroy and slay thieves, and to avenge his wrongs on his enemies. He was on his sick-bed, as we have said, from the beginning of spring to April. When he saw the great cold of the spring season departing and the summer weather approaching it seemed to him a long time to be on his sick-bed without leaving the castle where he was, for his physicians did not permit him, and what he did, contrary to their prohibition, was to send messengers to the Cinel Conaill (such of them as were obedient to his parents), and to assemble and collect them to the east of the well known mountain, i.e. Bearnas More of Tir Hugh. He resolved to go himself to the meeting, and those that were to the west of the mountain which we have mentioned assembled to him. O'Boyle came, Tadhg Oge, son of Tadhg, son of Turlough, a famous chief of the Cinel Conaill."

So it is no surprise to find after the defeat of the Gaelic chieftains in the battle of Kinsale in early January 1602, the subsequent departure of Aodh Rua O'Donnell to Spain and the later "Flight of the Earls", that the O'Boyles continued to carry the flag against the English. Tadhg Oge, mentioned above, was the last inaugurated chieftain of the O'Boyles. He died at Drumark, near the old O'Boyle stronghold of Ballyweel (*Báile Uí Bhaoill*) and was buried at the friary at Donegal town in May, 1607. He was succeeded by his son, Turlough Rua of Kiltoorish. Let us continue in the words of Fr. Pádraig Ó Gallachóir, doyen of the Co. Donegal Historical Society: "Turlogh Roe ... became the most outstanding of the Tirconaill leaders in the war of 1641. One suspects, but without any evidence, that he was educated abroad, because the important position he later holds in the Supreme Council of the Confederation would hardly be his because of birth alone. This remarkable man was early recognised by both the Irish and English as the principal leader of influence in Tirconaill, after the Flight of the Earls, which took place in the September after his father's death, and the consequent unofficial recognition of Turlogh Roe as chief of his name.

"Kiltoorish in Drumboghill townland, near Portnoo, was the seat of Turlogh Roe. Here too in Drumboghill was the old O'Boyle bastille on Lough an Dúin ... with many another reminder like Lough Birroge and Crannogeboy, of the centuries-old sway here of the *Baollaigh beadaidhe*.

"A grant of 2,000 acres in Kilmacrenan Barony transplanted Turlogh Roe, with others of the old Irish nobility, in 1611. On his new property around Creeslough and Dunfanaghy he 'built a good bawn and a house of lime and stone, in which he and his family' were living in 1619. His wife was a Maguire[17] of Fermanagh and the site of his house can be identified today by the old remains in the townland of Faugher, near Dunfanaghy. By 1622 Turlogh had evidently regained the ancestral property at Kiltoorish, where he apparently returned. In that year his new house at Faugher is rented to an English family and he has English tenants in others of his houses there along with Irish on those same lands.

"His return to Kiltoorish did not pass unnoticed by the Gael or Gall. O'Boyle's house became a hospitable refuge for the outlaw from the stranger's stern rule, a shelter for the bard and a port of call for the exile from Spain. Kiltoorish became an important enough spot for a spy ..."[18]

This English spy acted as a butler in Turlough Rua's household. The following reports,[19] based on his observations, written in Dublin on 28 August 1628 tell us that "Tirlogh Roe O'Boyle ... had entertained Tirlogh McGawre [Maguire; remember Turlough Rua's wife was a Maguire] who had just come from Spain in harvest time 1626. This man brought letters to O'Boyle from Spain, but from whom he [the spy] knows not. There was a report, however, that the Spaniards would come into the Kingdom before long and that their landing place would be Killybegs. Conogher oge O'Boyle, a great bishop and priest, recently come out of Spain, and who commands all the priests in the country, generally lives with Tirlogh Roe. When serving the two Tirloghs and the Bishop with drink – for he was butler in the house – examinate heard Tirlogh Roe often say that he expected Irish captains to come with the Spanish soldiers."

The reports continue: "When in March 1627 five ships, reported to be pirates, came into Killybegs, Tirlogh Roe sent them sheep and got two swords from them. All the servants of the household are armed and ready to join the Spaniards. Tirlogh is chiefly advised by one Cormick McGougherie. He has also recently entertained Owen O'Boolarth, a poor man of great ability and a good linguist, who might be useful to the King. The Bishop has recently gone to Spain, presumably to get accurate information on the intentions of that country."

From 11 October 1628 we read this intriguing, and ultimately chilling, report: "Tirlogh Roe O'Boyle received last spring year in his house at Kiltourish in the County Donegal Tirlogh McArdell, a proclaimed rebel, who had been prosecuted by Lord Blayney and driven out of the County Monaghan. This rebel used to ride with Tirlogh's wife and break in colts, and stayed with O'Boyle for three months, after which he went to stay with O'Boyle's mother-in-law, Eveline Nyne Gwyre [Maguire]. Afterwards he tried to go and live with O'Boyle's brother in Scotland, but the brother would not take him in. He returned to Ireland and was taken and executed by Lord Blayney."

Ten days afterwards, 21 October 1628, Sir William Steward wrote to the Lord Deputy informing him that he "has sent Tirlogh Roe O'Boyle to gaol at Lifford" and added menacingly "Tirlogh has something on his mind which might be got out of him". But Turlough Rua survives and is unheard of again until the Rebellion of 1641.

In the 1641 wars Turlough Rua was early in the field and Boylagh was quickly secured by the Gael – we find Turlough Rua, his son Turlough Óg, and his brother, Tadhg Óg, active around Donegal town on the outbreak of hostilities.[20] In 1642 Tadgh Óg was taken prisoner and confined in Brook's Castle in Donegal town, and we hear no more of him. But the last is not heard of Turlough Rua and his son.

Owen Roe O'Neill was one of the inspirational leaders of the insurgence of the 1640s. However, because of a tradition of animosity between the Tyrone O'Neills and some of the Tír Chonaill clans, not all of the latter supported Owen Roe; they sided with the other allied leader, Ormonde. Turlough Rua O'Boyle and his son, however, were steadfastly behind Owen Roe. Rev. Fr. Ó Gallachóir continues: "Turlogh Rua with Bishop Heber Mac Mahon and Henry O'Neill are the Ulster representatives on the pro-Nuncio Supreme Council of the Confederation in 1647-8, when most of the rest of the Tirconaill leaders are with the Ormondites. Turlogh is prominent on the side of Owen Roe for the rest of the war and is one of Owen's trusted emissaries on many an occasion, as when, for instance, Bishop Heber and Turlogh negotiated for him the agreement with Ormonde in October 1649."[21]

After the death of Owen Roe we find Turlough's name and that of the Archbishop of Armagh signed to a letter introducing the son of Owen Roe (Colonel Henry O'Neill) to the Duke of Ormond, leader of the Royalists, who were also opposed to Cromwell.[22]

Bishop Heber MacMahon was now appointed general of the Ulster Army in place of Owen Roe. The final battle in the struggle was fought at Schariffhollis, near New Mills, Letterkenny, in July 1650. The Irish suffered a disastrous defeat, and amongst the many killed was Turlogh Óg O'Boyle, son of Turlogh Rua. Surrender and failure were words unknown to the chieftain of Boylagh. Within a short time we find him at a meeting of his brother officers at Belturbet, Co. Cavan, making further plans for the continuance of the war. More than a year later, in December 1651, his was the first name signed to an appeal to the Catholics of Leinster requesting their assistance in making one more attempt to free Ireland from the Cromwellian yoke. There is no mention of a reply.[23]

We hear of him once more in the Civil Survey of 1654 where it is stated that he was deprived of all his lands in the Barony of Kilmacrennan. How he spent the remainder of his days, and where he died we know not, but we can be almost certain that his death took place amongst his beloved kinsmen[24], and in the neighbourhood of their ancestral home.[25]

Notes

1   Inq., 20th April.

2   *H.P.A.*, p. 26.

3   Ibid.

4   Described in the *J.R.S.A.I.*, vol. 6 (6th series), vol. XLVI consec. series of 1916 by Henry Crawford as follows: "A pillar stone or erect slab 2 feet 4" high. On it a simple line cross of Latin form, with a small diamond shaped centre. Each extremity bifurcates into a pair of spirals."

5   *H.P.A.*, p. 26.

6   Hill, *Useful Hints to Donegal Tourists*, p. 36.

7   *D.A.* (1978), p. 368.

8   High King of Ireland from 379-405 A.D; you will remember that St. Columba was descended from him and that Conall Caol's genealogy claimed descent from him.

9   James Hogan, *The Tricha Cét and Related Land Measures*, pp. 201-4; *Lebor na Cert*, ed. Myles Dillon, pp. 66-69.

10   The O'Clery Book of Genealogies, *Analecta Hibernica* no. 18, pp. 3, 16, 27.

11   Gilla Ua Baighill (see *A.U.*, 1247 A.D.)

12   *A.F.M.*, vol. III, p. 323.

13   Ó Gallachóir, *Essays*, p. 82; Cf. N. Ó Dónaill, *D.A.*, vol. 1, pp. 96, 245-48; *Leabhar Chlainne Suibhne* (ed. Father P. Walsh), p. xxxviii.

14   "...only c. 6m. of the W. wall of the castle survives, 2m. thick and 3.5m. high. It is in a parlous condition and has a mural stairs, 1.3m. wide and 1.5m. high, rising from S. to N. The S. Section, set back to *c*.92 cms thick above the stairs, preserves the remains of a simple rectangular window. The grass-covered lower courses of a number of walls survive to the W... . In 1847 Fagan recorded that 'to its eastern end stood a round tower, the base of which is still traceable and which together with two gables of the castle, stood within memory about 40 ft. high. The castle and courtyard is supposed to have stood 150 ft. by 150 ft... much of the walls were without cement...' One gable fell in 1793, the other In 1844, and its tower fell around the time of the latter date. There were formerly three cannon on the island but two were lost in an attempt to bring them across the lake in the 18th century, the third lay within a few yards of the castle in 1847 (Fagan Bk. 22, 24-31)." This footnote is abridged from the *A.S.D.*, p. 371. We will refer to the third cannon in the section on the Spanish Armada.

15   Donnell died on 4 August 1549.

16 By Lughaidh Ó Cléirigh, ed. Rev. Denis Murphy, p. 39.

17 A family whose exploits dominate vol. III of the *A.U.*

18 Ó Gallachóir, *Essays*, pp. 82-83.

19 They appear in the Calendar of State Papers of Ireland, 1625-32, pp. 382-83, 393, 396.

20 Ó Gallachóir, *Essays*, p. 83.

21 Ibid. pp. 103-4.

22 *H.P.A.*, p. 58.

23 Ibid.

24 In 1659 a Teague Óg O'Boyle, perhaps his brother, was the resident claimant for Maas. At the same period there was a Turlogh Ballagh O'Boyle in possession of the Five Quarters of Loughros. He had fifty-seven Irish tenants and lived at Crannogeboy. We do not know the site of Turlogh Ballagh's residence, but it may have been within the "Bawne" so well known as "O'Boyle's Castle".

25 *H.P.A.*, p. 58.

IX

KILTOORISH AND THE ARMADA

No tengo mas que dar te.

OFF TO THE right, at Kiltoorish, is a large beach, appropriately called Tramore [*trá*: a beach; *mór*: big], washed by mighty breakers rolling into the bay from the wild Atlantic. Into this bay in 1588 – the great Spanish Armada having been routed by a number of factors in the English Channel in late July and early August – came the *Duquesa Santa Ana*. She was a 900-ton Andalusian vessel.

The *Duquesa* had been named in honour of the wife of the Duke of Medina Sidonia who was Andalusian. Thirty-eight-year-old Don Alonzo Perez de Guzman, 7th duke of Medina Sidonia, was the commander of the whole Armada. We are told that "at the age of twenty-two, after an engagement lasting six years and by special dispensation from the Pope, he married Dōna Ana de Silva Mendoza, then aged ten and a half. The marriage was consummated that very night; as Medina Sidonia's biographer explains, 'The Duchess's judgement and discretion more than made up for any disadvantage that her age might have had for the marriage.'"[1]

The *Duquesa* had earlier been at anchor in Blacksod Bay off the coast of Mayo. While it was at anchorage another Armada ship called the *Rata Encoronada* went aground. The *Rata* was a characteristic Mediterranean merchantman – a huge, pot-bellied tub, which had been converted into a warship, but which was almost incapable of sailing into the wind.[2] Her captain was Don Alonzo Martinez de Leiva, second-in-command of the whole Armada. Of all the lords, knights and great captains of the Armada, he was the best loved and the most admired. He was always referred to as *"El Buen Alonzo de Leiva"*, or "Don Alonzo himself". We are told that the Commander of the Armada, the Duke of Medina Sidonia, would consult "all the generals and Alonzo de Leiva". He was the King's favourite and the idol of the nobility and the people alike.[3] He held the distinguished titles of Knight of Santiago and Commander of Alcuescar.

Off the Mayo coast Don Alonzo and his crew of 700-800 men and their valuables transferred to the *Duquesa Santa Ana*. Hulks such as the *Duquesa* were the direct descendants of that medieval vessel, the *nao*: transport ships of enormous capacity, but slow and unwieldy to manoeuvre.[4]

Captain Don Pedro Mares of the *Duquesa* originally commanded a total force of 357 men according to the Lisbon[5] muster but this number had probably been reduced by war and disease until it was something within the region of 300. Now a further 700-800 men from the *Rata Encoronada* were brought aboard the *Duquesa* before she sailed from Blacksod Bay. Don Alonzo de Leiva, the senior ranking officer, assumed command.

The *Duquesa* had been damaged, how badly is not known, and makeshift repairs had been made. Fears were expressed that they would not survive the strong gales if they tried to make their way back to Spain. They decided to sail for Scotland which was thought to be sympathetic to Spain, so they headed north.[6] Rolling badly she hardly made any progress in two days and we are told that "one of the great ships which lay before Torane was driven back with a contrary wind but afterwards put to sea again".[7]

Out in the open sea, the *Duquesa* met repeatedly shifting winds. They ran northwards; the *Duquesa* cleared Rathlin O'Birne island off the coast of Glencolumbkille and negotiated the awesome seas of Tormore, but it seems probable that at the time she was being blown hard by the west wind towards the shore. At some point the crew decided that the only way to save their ship from being wrecked by what clearly was a strong wind freshening to a gale was to seek what shelter they could find and anchor. They were at the mouth of Loughros More Bay, between Slievetooey on the southern side and Dawros Head on the northern.

Somewhere in this bay they dropped anchor and came to a halt, rolling heavily in the growing seas. They were anchored in some seventy feet of water, on a sandy and rocky bottom, possibly between Dawros and Loughros Point. This was a very unsafe anchorage. *The Sailing Directions* says quite bluntly of Loughros More Bay that there are no secure anchorages easy of access; the bottom was sand over rock, in other words a shallowish skim of sand lying on a rocky underbed – the poorest holding for any anchor. The gale worsened and broke the anchor cable[8] (in all probability it shifted the anchor as well; the *Duquesa*, like many other Armada ships, had left most of her big anchors in the mud at Calais), and thus helpless before wind and sea, drifted deeper into the bay towards the mainland. She struck the sandy bottom of Loughros More beside a rocky spur south-east of Rosbeg. If you walk down to the Tramore beach and then head west on to the shoulder of rocky headland that juts out in a sharp finger into the bay, this is the spot where she went aground.[9]

The seas were running heavily, washing over the *Duquesa*, but she was holding her own and not yet beginning to break up. When low tide came the men began to go overboard into the cold and still turbulent Atlantic waters. Don Alonzo had been injured at the time of the grounding of the ship and he had to be carried ashore. With Don Alonzo hurt and in some pain, the company began to gather on the rocks and sand as the men gradually struggled ashore. Among them were some of Spain's finest young noblemen, carrying their jewel boxes under their arms. Sixty sons and nephews of the most noble families in Spain had sailed with Don Alonzo de Leiva;[10] they had deemed it a point of honour to serve under no one but him, such was the esteem in which he was held.

At that time, September 1588, the castle on Kiltoorish Lough was in a ruinous condition. The Spanish party crossed the sand dunes to the north and waded out to the island in Kiltoorish Lough. They then began to fortify themselves around the ruined castle on the island. They had brought a number of cannon from the ship and presumably mounted these around the ruins of the castle. Food and other provisions were brought from the ship, as were supplies of clothing, weapons, ammunition and other necessities. Gradually the camp assumed a soldierly appearance. We have mentioned

Duquesa Santa Ana, *an artist's impression (after Sténuit's engraving)*

earlier, when discussing the O'Boyle clan, that the MacSweeneys had started eating into O'Boyle territory in the early 15th century. It appears that the area around Rosbeg was MacSweeney country at the time of the grounding of the *Duquesa*. Relations with the MacSweeneys were opened by the Spanish; the local sept was that of MacSweeney *na dTuath* (Doe). Don Alonzo sent an Irish cleric who had been aboard the *Rata* to see MacSweeney further up the coast. The cleric was well treated and assured that the Spaniards would receive as much help as MacSweeney could give.

The area around Dawros was by no means depopulated in the later 16th century and it is certain that many eyes had seen the *Duquesa* being wrecked and afterwards all her men coming ashore. Gradually reports began to reach the English authorities by way of spies. Alarm began to spread among the English as reports came in daily, confirming the strength of the Spanish force and the fact that they were being given help by MacSweeney. Donegal had long been the underbelly of English power in Ireland and panic swept through the English ranks at the prospect of Spanish and Irish massing together. However, the real situation was very different. Don Alonzo de Leiva, injured, clearly had not the slightest intention of creating trouble or of joining with the Irish. His thoughts were pre-occupied with getting out of Ireland as fast as he could and of somehow sailing home to Spain. De Leiva stayed at Kiltoorish for nine days, during which time daily trips by the Spaniards to the wreck of the *Duquesa* stripped her of everything of value except the bigger guns, and probably MacSweeney got those. Then a message came from the south that three Spanish ships lay at anchor in the harbour of Killybegs, less than twenty miles across the mountains. But in fact, of the three ships that had approached Killybegs, one had been lost outside the harbour and a second one inside it, while the third one was in need of repair; this third vessel was the Neapolitan galleass *Girona*. However, De Leiva, thinking that there were three ships in Killybegs, decided at once to leave the fortified camp at Kiltoorish and head south. He was placed on a litter carried by four men and the Spaniards left the island and started towards Killybegs, leaving behind on Kiltoorish the cannon[11] which they had

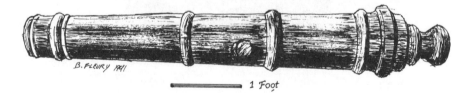

The Kiltoorish Island cannon

taken off the *Duquesa*.

The thousand-strong party headed south-east along the coast from Rosbeg to Ardara, then probably no more than a collection of huts. From there they turned directly south and climbed over the hills and approached Killybegs. An unpleasant surprise now awaited the Spanish – the report had been of three Spanish ships, but only one, the *Girona*, remained afloat. This was a severe blow. One ship could not carry an extra thousand men together with its own complement and those from the two smaller ships wrecked around the harbour. The *Girona* carried about 102 sailors, 196 soldiers and 244 rowers. Almost exactly half the rowers were impressed convicts (the remainder of the rowers, surprisingly enough, included 68 volunteers; one can only hope that they had not been disappointed in their choice of careers!) Eventually around 1,300 men packed into the *Girona*, leaving some 200 behind. Just before dawn on 26 October 1588, repaired and ready for sea, she lifted her anchor and slipped out of Killybegs, under the command of Don Alonzo de Leiva, who though injured at Rosbeg, had assumed control because of his position as second-in-command of the entire Armada. On the night of 28 October she struck a reef at *Port na Spáinigh*[12] near Lacada Point on the Antrim coast, and of the entire ship's complement of 1,350 there were only nine survivors.

This was the hand that fate dealt to Don Alonzo de Leiva and his admiring group of young noblemen, who had already survived two shipwrecks – that of the *Rata Encoronada* off the Mayo coast and the *Duquesa Santa Ana* at Rosbeg. Great was the lamentation in their native country when news trickled back to Spain of the loss of so many of their young chivalry. Many hearts were broken; one thinks particularly of the lady who gave her nobleman a small gold ring, possibly at their last meeting before he left to join the Armada. Over the years, as his body withered away in the deep waters off the Antrim coast, this ring slipped from his finger and fell on to the ocean floor. In 1967, together with many other objects, it was recovered by divers. It is a small gold ring with one terminal in the form of a hand holding a heart, the other a buckle; it is inscribed *"No tengo mas que dar te"* – "I have nothing more to give thee."[13]

Notes

1   Robert Sténuit, *Treasures of the Armada*, p. 30.
2   Ibid. p. 113.
3   Ibid. p. 43.

4   Ibid. p. 117.

5   The Armada had initially sailed from Lisbon.

6   Most of what follows on the Armada is taken from Niall Fallon's excellent book *The Armada in Ireland*. Rather than give separate notification of each reference from this book which I will use, this note is to be taken as a general appreciation.

7   Comerford to Byngham, 27 September 1588, quoted in *Treasures of the Armada*, p. 117.

8   "There fell a great storm which broke in sunder all their cables" – so reported an actual member of the crew, an eyewitness to all the events, James Machary, a native of Co. Tipperary who was later interrogated by the English authorities.

9   It is claimed in the area in modern times that the outline of the ship can be made out after the sand has been shifted by a particularly heavy storm. This is possible. Only those parts of the ship which are encased in sand could have survived over the years; any timber exposed to the water would have been gradually eaten away by the seaworm *Terrado navallis* ("the gribble").

10   Sténuit, *Treasures of the Armada*, p. 45.

11   Only one cannon was present on the island in later years. The cannon, of the falcon type (quite a number of cannon types are named after birds) and made of cast iron, lay on the island on Kiltoorish Lough until it was, unfortunately, removed in August 1969. In the 16th century most cannon were made of bronze or wrought-iron; guns made of cast-iron, on the other hand, were almost an innovation at the time of the Armada. Only six cast-iron guns have been recorded on Armada wreck-sites; only one is connected with an Irish wreck and this is the one which lay here at Kiltoorish. The other five are preserved in the Shetland Museum in Lerwick and came from *El Gran Grifon* (Laurence Flanagan, *Ireland's Armada Legacy*, p. 68). The Kiltoorish cannon is described as "quite a plain piece, 2.35m long with a bore of some 15mm" (Flanagan p. 68). A falcon is a cannon whose diameter at the bore is 5", weight 750 lbs., length 7', load 2.25 lbs., shot 2.5" diameter and 2.5 lbs. weight. In 1969 the cannon was removed by car and trailer to a private house in the North of Ireland. Hopefully, someday, if a heritage centre were to be built in this general area, it might be returned to its rightful surroundings.

12   See map in Sténuit, *Treasures of the Armada*, p. 135.

13   My method of ending the Armada piece is inspired by Sténuit, *Treasures of the Armada*.

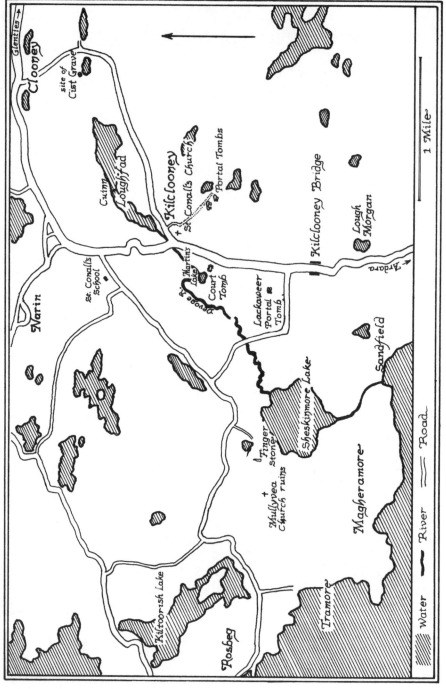

G. FLEURY 1991

Glenties →

Clooney

site of
Cist Grave

Loughfad

Cairn

Kilclooney

St Conall's Church

Portal Tombs

Kilclooney Bridge

Narin

St Conall's
School

R. Martin's
Lake

Court
Tomb

R. Drobose

Lackaweer
Portal
Tomb

Lough
Morgan

Ardara →

Sandfield

Finger
Stones

Sheskinmore Lake

Mullyvea
Church ruins

Magheramore

Kilfoorish Lake

Rosbeg

Tramore

Water   River   Road

1 Mile

X

FROM KILTOORISH DOWN TO KILCLOONEY AND LOUGHFAD

WITH ALL OUR talk of things past let us not forget the present-day amenities offered in this area by way of Tramore with its beautiful strand and caravan park, and the fishing in Kiltoorish and nearby lakes. In fact there was another amenity here in the recent past that does not exist now – did you know that there used to be a nine-hole golf course here? In *The Land of Lakes* we read: "There is a good nine-hole golf course, which is reached by rowing across Kiltooris Lough". The author then goes on to describe the lake fishing in the area, starting with Kiltoorish: "This lough is nearly a mile long, and the fishing on it, especially from the middle of April until the middle of June, is quite beyond the average. In the early spring one seldom fastens with a fish of less than 5 oz. or 6 oz. And a decent basket on a decent day will consist of, say, ten brace of fish weighing from 10 lbs. to 12 lbs. The trout in Kiltooris run up to 3 lbs. or more in weight, and one's basket generally includes a fish or two well over a pound, and now and again a beautiful basket of nearly all big fish will be had. The trout in this lough are very game fish. There are hotel boats on Kiltooris, and also on Lough Fad, Summy Lough, Clooney Lough, Doon Lough, Pound Lough and Lough Birroge, all of which hold plenty of trout, and some of them, notably Summy, hold big fish. The best killing patterns are Hare's Ear, March Brown, and Claret and Partridge. The charge for man and boat per day is 5s."[1]

We now continue eastwards from Kiltoorish in the direction of the Ardara–Kilclooney road. Away over to our right are the plain and sand dunes of Magheramore, which we will refer to in more detail on the road from Kilclooney to Ardara. Just on this side of the plain of Magheramore are the ruins of an old church at Mullyvea. This little church is more accessible from the road we are now travelling along than it is from the Ardara–Kilclooney road. At one period the building was used as a school.[2] It is likely that mass was celebrated at this church during Penal times when celebration of the Catholic rites was prohibited. Standing on top of a hill near by is an impressive standing stone, a finger-stone – long and narrow. It may have been erected as a directional signpost to people travelling across the plain to the little church where mass was to be said unknown to the authorities. According to a strong local tradition mass was celebrated there up to the middle of the last century. Francie McHugh, the Loughadoon boatman whom we have met earlier on our travels, states that his grandfather, Dan Boyle of Mullyvea, was caretaker of the little church and that Fr. McGarvey (whom we will meet later when we visit Loughros Point) often said mass there. This corresponds with tradition in the neighbouring townland of Sandfield where older people used to talk of Fr. McGarvey riding across the Sandfield *léana* [*léana*: grassy land with a wet, spongy bottom] on his way to say mass.[3] Mr. McHugh tells the story of a man named Gallagher from Cleengort who got up on a Sunday morning during the Penal days and prayed to God to direct him to where he could hear mass. One place he visited, in vain, was Kilmacanny, along the shore of the Gweebarra estuary,

*The directional finger-stone over-
looking the plain of Magheramore*

which we have visited earlier. Then he turned his footsteps to Mullyvea. Meantime in the mass house the priest was ready, but the candles would not light. Twice he sent a messenger to the top of the neighbouring hill to see if there was anyone coming towards the church. The messenger reported in the negative. Still the candles refused to light. A third time the messenger went to the hilltop and this time reported a man in the distance. Once he arrived at the church the candles lighted as usual and mass was celebrated without further delay.

Fr. McGarvey was involved in another incident from this area which demonstrates that forces other than supernatural could be invoked to come to his aid. And possibly not to his pleasing! Here is the account, exactly as told to me: "One Sunday Fr. McGarvey was coming across the Sandfield *léana* on his red mare to say mass at Mullyvea. When the wee mare jumped the river she lay down. Though the priest coaxed and coaxed her she wouldn't get up. Then Fr. McGarvey spotted the mass clerk who was up on Mullyvea watching out for him. He 'winded' to the clerk to come down and told him to go for 'Mickey Dibbs'. The latter, named Mickey Boyle, but known as 'Mickey Dibbs' because of his habit of exclaiming 'Ah Dibbs' when trouble reared its head, was not Fr. McGarvey's favourite person. He was well known in the locality because of the cures he had effected for sick people and his alternative practices and beliefs had often brought him into conflict with the religious establishment. 'Fr. McGarvey's wee mare lay down and won't get up and he wants you down to help, the mass people are all waiting,' exclaimed the clerk. 'Ah Dibbs,' said Mickey, 'why would I go down? Sure didn't he call me off the altar' [i.e. criticised him from the pulpit]. However Mickey relented and picking up a turf-coal out of the fire in his tongs he set off down to the *léana*.

"Mickey sauntered around the mare a few times but didn't attempt to get her up. Then he walked up to the priest and further discomfited him by asking him to open his coat and cutting out a wee square out of the lining of the priest's coat. He followed this by picking nine hairs out of the mare's tail. Placing the hairs on the piece of cloth he then put the latter on the hot coal and held it with the tongs under the mare's nose. When she smelled her own hair burning up she got like a shot! Mickey went off home, satisfied."

It was Francie McHugh, again, who related this story to me. A close relation of Francie had, as a young girl, attended the great fair of Magheramore, which we will hear more of shortly, in the last few years before it died out. She remembered old women at the fair whose income came from serving syrup-covered bread to the throngs. Each woman kept a fire going and on it she had various pots of hot syrup. She would spread the syrup on the bread with a goose feather, one of which rested in each pot of hot syrup on the fire. Francie's source remembered men, taking a break from the drinking and carousing, approaching the women for more bread and syrup and exclaiming: "Rub your feather again, ma'am!"

Just a few hundred yards before we reach the Kilclooney–Ardara road, in a field[4] into the left there are the remains of a small portal tomb. This is a diminutive example of a dolmen, consisting of two sidestones and an inset backstone. A single inset portal-stone is in position at the east. A slab, laid horizontally, covers the chamber. Traces of a round mound, reaching a maximum height of 1 m., surround the tomb.[5] This portal tomb is in the townland of Kilclooney More, but this particular area is known as Lackaweer, generally translated as *Leac Mhuire*, the Virgin Mary's flagstone, explained by the fact that earlier generations would not have understood the origins of the portal tomb, but were aware of its mystique, and, accordingly, assigned to it a Christian function. However, I think the placename Lackaweer has an even more interesting origin, being derived from *Leacamhaer* [*leac*: a flagstone and *maer*: a steward or keeper]. The word *maer*[6] harks back to very early times when the *maer* was the appointed keeper or guardian of cattle, land and sacred relics belonging to the local chieftain. The office was hereditary; certain lands were held in fee by families who acted as guardians of the local chieftain's valuables. Lacaweer translates as "the stewart's flagstone".

We now turn towards the Kilclooney–Loughfad area where we have the remains of a court cairn, two portal tombs and a cist burial site; before we examine these man-made monuments in detail, we will have a brief look at the society which erected them and how this society evolved.

Geologists estimate that the oldest rock so far dated has an age of 3,500 million years, and that the earth must have had a rocky crust stretching back still farther in time. In Ireland our oldest rock, near Rosslare in Wexford, has an age of 2,400 million years. Man only made his first appearance in Ireland about 9,000 years ago. At this time (7000 B.C.) Ireland had been resmothered in trees and these Mesolithic (Middle Stone-Age) people were hunters and fishers and were restricted to roaming along the shores of lakes and rivers and along the coast because they did not have the tools to clear their way into the large forests.

A later people to come to Ireland, who started clearing away the forests with their polished stone axes and who began farming, are known as the Neolithic people. These Neolithic farmers were the people who built the great megalithic tombs such as the court cairns and portal tombs (dolmens). The Neolithic way of life, with its domestic animals, its cultivated crops, its pottery and its polished stone implements, began in the Middle East, and had reached south-east Europe before 5000 B.C. These people utilised agriculture and stock-raising as a means of controlling their food supply.

However, evidence for agriculture is slight. Emphasis was on cattle-grazing rather than on cereal-farming, and the woodland clearances were designed to give grazing areas rather than tillage plots. It was the polished stone axe, suitably mounted on a wooden handle, that enabled these farmers to establish a degree of mastery over their environment which had not been achieved by their Mesolithic predecessors. Frank Mitchell, whose excellent book *Reading the Irish Landscape* I have relied upon heavily here,[7] writes that "successful Neolithic communities tended to expand in size. As they did so, two things became apparent, first that at certain times of the year there was a considerable amount of spare adult labour, and second that if this was to be employed in an organised fashion, qualities of leadership had to be still further developed."

He continues: "Like all primitive folk these Neolithic people will have seen their surroundings as peopled, not only by the living community, but also by potentially beneficial deities who had to be propitiated, by hostile demons who had to be avoided or exorcised, and by the spirits of the former members of the community. The first farmers to reach Ireland obviously believed in the continuity of community after death, and after cremating the body, they would deposit the burned bones in a communal tomb. This belief and practice were common to all the early farming communities along the western seaboard of Europe from Spain to Scandinavia, and must have had its origin further to the east, probably on the shores of the Mediterranean."[8]

There are some who would question the theory that the megalithic tombs

Lackaweer portal tomb

were built by a settled agricultural people who had free time available. Possibly they were built for an almost opposite reason – that they were erected as reassuring structures at a time of stress in the face of economic difficulties. At such times were they built to demarcate a particular group's territory? Were they orientated in a particular way towards the direction from which the group reckoned they had originally come? Did these people carry the bones of their deceased elders with them on their travels and inter them under megalithic structures at their chosen area of settlement as a re-assuring presence?

We associate the practise of collective inhumation and cremation in graves of rough unhewn stone, known as megalithic tombs, with the Neolithic age. The varieties of megalithic tombs we have in this area are the court tomb and the portal tomb – one court tomb and three portal tombs (dolmens) here at Kilclooney (including the small dolmen at Lackaweer). As the Neolithic Age merged into the Earlier Bronze Age – in about the 3rd millenium B.C. – changes were taking place in society and among them was a change in the burial customs; many of the dead were now being buried in individual graves, known as pits or cists, rather than the earlier custom of putting the ashes or bones – often disarticulated bones – of numbers of people under the great megalithic tombs. A cist grave has been excavated here at Loughfad, and we have already mentioned cist graves at the Narin sandhills and within Doon Fort. Cist graves, of course, contain skeletons since they are not associated with cremation.

As you drive from Ardara to Kilclooney, a few hundred yards on the Ardara side of the Kilclooney Roman Catholic church, just when you are on the brow of the hill, there is a house on your right and an iron gate on your left. Visible in the field inside this gate are the remains of a court tomb. This field is owned by Conal Shovlin and he has taken great care over the years to ensure that no further damage is done to the remains of this tomb.

Court tombs are generally considered to have been the earliest[9] megalithic structures erected in Ireland. About 330 of them have been identified, all of them, except for about half a dozen, lying in the northern third of Ireland. Their distribution is a scattered one, and suggests that they are the tombs of a rather spread-out ranching[10] community. The essential features of a court tomb are a ceremonial[11] courtyard set in front of a gallery divided into two, or more rarely into three or four burial chambers. The remains of more than 30 individuals in one chamber have been recorded.[12] The gallery would have been covered by a long cairn of stones (hence court tombs usually being re-ferred to as court cairns) and the court is normally placed at the east end. There are a lot of variations of this type of tomb which I will not go into here. The huge cairn of stones which would have covered the gallery and almost all of the stones that would have constituted the court have been removed over the centuries from the Kilclooney court tomb.[13]

Portal tombs appear to be closely related to the court tomb. They have hitherto often been referred to as portal dolmens or just dolmens.[14] There are 163[15] portal tombs in Ireland and, as in the case of the court cairns, the majority are in the northern half of the country.

Both portal and court tombs have quite similar altitude patterns[16] – they both show a distinct lowland bias. Almost 70% of portal tombs and 60% of court tombs lie below the 400-foot contour.[17] Important in the distribution pattern of both portal and court tombs is their proximity to coasts and rivers. The coastal pattern is most marked in the west where many of the tombs are closer to the sea than elsewhere.[18]

The standard portal[19] tomb is based on a tripod design with tall portals and lower backstone supporting a massive roofstone poised with its heavier end above the entrance.[20] The long cairns and lateral chambers which occur at a number of portal tomb sites are important elements linking the portal tombs with the court tomb series.[21] At Kilclooney the portal tombs stand in the middle of a cairn. So, in other words, while the galleries of court tombs are

My father, Patrick J. McGill, at the Kilclooney court tomb

known to have been covered with a cairn of stones there is evidence in some cases that the portal tombs did not originally stand silhouetted against the skyline as we see them now; they too were possibly incorporated in a cairn, as was the case with the two Kilclooney portal tombs. Dr. MacDevitt, writing in the relatively recent past (1865) states that "Both are enclosed by a stone circle."[22]

One approaches the two Kilclooney portal tombs by parking outside the Catholic church, walking a few metres along the Loughfad road and then taking a little road off to the right beside the houses. Please be careful to close any gates on the way up and down as there are cattle grazing in the area.

The larger Kilclooney portal tomb is marked "Dermot and Gráinne's Bed" (as are many of the dolmens of Ireland) on the Ordnance Survey map. At this site there are two portal tombs, standing about 9 m. apart, incorporated

The larger Kilclooney portal tomb.
I have chosen this view because it shows the neighbouring houses. It is my opinion that monuments such as this should be viewed as part of a living, changing landscape in which their place is ensured and should not always be portrayed in splendid isolation.

in the base of a cairn some 25 m. long. The larger tomb, towards the north, is set askew to the long axis of the cairn, with its entrance about 5 m. inside the end of the cairn. The portals are each about 1.7 m. high and between them is a sill 5 m. high. The great roof-stone, 4.2 m. long, rests in a sloping position, above the portals and on a pad stone on top of the back stone.[23] Five sherds of a Neolithic pot have been found on the surface of the ground inside the larger tomb.[24] The second tomb is similar in design but is much smaller and faces into the body of the cairn. The capstone of this tomb was displaced some seventy years ago by, it is said, a band of fighting tinkers who were camping in the laneway close to the site. The smaller tomb is unusual in having a lintel in position above the portals. Single corbels rest against the sidestones.

It has been suggested in the past[25] that on the capstone of the larger portal tomb are possibly two cupmarks, little round holes in the stone which some would allege hark back to the time of sun worship and veneration of the solar sytem. However, at the present day I don't think one can say with any certainty that there are cupmarks present.

As we have already noted, court tombs (court cairns) and portal tombs (dolmens) are associated with the culture of the first farming community, which started to appear in Ireland about 3500 B.C. Just east of Kilclooney, at Loughfad, are the remains of a cist grave, a type of burial which we associate with the Earlier Bronze Age (*c.* 2000 B.C. - 1200 B.C.) when, "Instead of

The smaller portal tomb

being laid to rest in the old family vaults that were the Stone Age megalithic tombs, many of the dead were now being buried in individual graves by themselves, at first more by inhumation and later, increasingly, by cremation."[26] The cist grave at Loughfad is typical of the way in which the Earlier Bronze Age people buried their dead. The body was usually placed in a crouched position in a simple box or cist of stone slabs, or a "stone coffin" as it was sometimes called in the past.[27] Often these cist graves had surface markings – sometimes they were covered by a mound of earth or a cairn of stones. These cist or box-like structures set into the ground are in stark contrast to the great stone tombs such as the court cairns and portal tombs, which were erected to house the dead by the earlier Neolithic people. Cremation is much less common than in the tombs of the Neolithic people and only one or two people would be buried in a single grave.

A mound at the south-west end of Killayenna Lough in Loughfad was excavated in 1937; the excavations were directed by my father who was acting on behalf of the National Museum.[28] For years the mound had been undisturbed, because for generations back this site was regarded as one of the "gentle" (i.e. associated with the fairies or "little people") spots in the district. The mound was said to have contained a hoard of Danish gold which was under the guardianship of a mysterious red-haired female, who is said to have made her appearance more than once in the past when anyone dared to infringe upon her charge. She was last seen over 150 years ago when the then owner of the land, disregarding "fireside tales", set about levelling the mound. He had just removed one stone when he felt an uncanny sensation coming over him and on looking up, saw there on the summit of the cairn the mysterious woman of tradition, her red hair flowing in the wind and her eyes blazing fire. She spoke not a word. The man disturbing her sanctuary beat a hasty retreat and kept a respectable distance from its precinct ever after.

But the lure of buried gold led to the mound being breached again in 1937, and because of this it was decided to excavate the site officially.[29] A cist, covered by cap-stones and containing two chambers or compartments was found. Each compartment contained an individual disarticulated skeleton, with the head to the west in each case. The skeletons were sent to Dr. R.G. Inkster of the School of Anatomy at Trinity College Dublin. One skeleton was of a male about 5' 8.5"; the second individual was of a height between 5' 3" and 5' 5", but it was impossible to make out what the sex of this second person was. This smaller second skeleton showed evidence of disuse – atrophy in the forearm-bones of the left side; the forearm bones were small and underused, probably as a result of some accident or disease.

Account No.   B65105
MRS G HACKETT-JONES
"TRINITY HOUSE"
11 CAMBRIDGE ROAD
GREAT SHELFORD
CAMBS
CB2 5JE

heffers:

W. Heffer & Sons Ltd. Booksellers
20 Trinity Street, Cambridge,
England CB2 3NG
Telephone: (0223) 358351
VAT Reg. No. 213 4152 13

Order No.

Till Reference   2 2   Time 12:26   Invoice No. 752476

                                                 Date 30/ 7/93

			£	p
DEPT3 COLLECTED ORDERS	1a	19.99	19.99	
				19.99

TOTAL £

RECEIPT	0 RATED	VATABLE	VAT
53396	19.99	0.00	0.00

Please keep this invoice to check against your monthly statement.
Payment is due in the month following receipt of the books
VAT is not charged on books as they are zero rated

H13

The shape and markings of the ankle bones in both skeletons indicated a considerable range of movement in all directions – probably the result of walking on rough or sloping ground. Dr. Inkster also concluded that the smaller person had suffered from an adenoid condition, while the teeth were considerably worn and showed clear evidence of gum infection amounting to severe pyorrhoea. The age of this individual was between thirty and forty years. (I'm sure you will agree that it is amazing the conclusions that can be drawn from an examination of 3,000-year-old skeletons!)

Two tiny skulls and other small bones discovered in the south-east sector of the mound along with pieces of flannel and fragments of wood bearing traces of nails would have been puzzling were it not that the Rev. Dr. Molloy, then Parish Priest of Glenties, had heard some days before that that portion of the mound had been used about eighty years previously for the burial of unbaptised infants. These small skulls were only 11 to 14" down from the surface. Unbaptised children were often buried in little graveyards used for that purpose, known as *cillíns*, and were also frequently buried in what were unquestionably pagan grave-mounds, as in the case of the Loughfad mound.

Nowadays there is little to be seen at the site on the shore of Killayenna Lough; after the mound had been excavated the large stones incorporated in the mound were scattered and the spot reclaimed for cultivation. However there is still plenty to see in this area; Clooney Wood with its beautiful walks should be visited; and a hike along the edge of Loughfad Lake (there are two lakes in this area, Killayenna and Loughfad) is rewarding. This long lake [*An Loch Fhada*; *fada*: long] is completely bisected in the middle by a man-made path of large stones, a passage known locally as "the Cuing". This is a very interesting word; it derives, Joyce says, from "*cong, conga* or *cunga* – a narrow neck, a strait where a river or lake contracts, the stream by which one lake empties itself into another very near it. It appears to be connected with *cuing*, which is the common word for the yoke borne by horses that are harnessed to a chariot or carriage. This term belongs chiefly to the north-west of Ireland; it is common in Donegal, where indeed it is a living word among the old natives who speak Irish."[30] The Gaelic word *cúing* means "narrow". There are other instances of the word in the topography of the general Kilclooney area; a spot in Loughfad is called *Abar Chuing*, [*abar*: a marshy piece of land], a term which was also applied to an area[31] in Kilclooney More. You will recall that the golden lunula was found in Drumboghill at a spot called the *Coiscéim Chung* [*coiscéim*: a step, a footstep]. So the word *cuing* appears to have been in general use in this area to signify a pathway through a morass or across a shallow sheet of water.

On our way back from Loughfad[32] towards the Kilclooney Roman Catholic church we pass the old Dallán Forgaill national school on our left; this school opened in 1937 and closed in June 1987; it had been preceded by earlier schools, among them a thatched building which stood at the site of the old Post Office in Kilclooney. The new St. Conall's national school, which opened in September 1987, now serves this area. It is nice to see the names Dallán Forgaill and Conall persisting in the social fabric of the community.

Now, what's the name of the Roman Catholic church here at Kilclooney? Yes, you've guessed it – St. Conall's! This church was preceded by the church of Ss. Peter and Paul which was solemnly opened on 29 June 1865[33] and it wasn't before time. A correspondent of the Dublin *Catholic Telegraph* writing from Co. Donegal about June 1857 refers to the parish of Ardara "where a congregation of 2,000 people assemble every Sunday to hear Mass in the open air, exposed to the inclemency of the weather, without any protection from the storm when it comes, and there must kneel on the damp dirty ground during the celebration of the Holy Sacrifice, which is offered in a miserable shed made of loose stones covered with earthen sods, with not sufficient shelter from the rain which often comes flowing down through the wretched covering upon the very altar where the priest is offering the most Holy Sacrifice."

This excerpt is taken to refer to the Kilclooney area, because by 1857 there was a Catholic church in Ardara village. The reference is probably to the *scálán* (an open-ended hut where mass was celebrated) which stood close to the present priest's house in Kilclooney in former times.

The *scálán* may have disappeared, but, interestingly, the bare outline of the earliest ecclesiastical foundation in the Kilclooney area is still discernible. The site of the original *Cill Chluainigh* is in a quiet, remote area, being situated on a small plateau on the left bank of the Duvoge river, about half a mile west of Kilclooney church and adjacent to the ruins of Martin's tuck-mill. Martin's Lough is located close by to the south-south-east. Barely visible at the southwest end are the foundations of two oval-shaped structures, which may have been early Christian oratories. The level space extending northwards from these is regarded as the cemetery.[34] One of the oval structures was known to the older generation as *Leaba na hAltóra*[35] – "the bed of the altar". There are traces of an embankment surrounding the site.

As we take our leave and start towards Ardara I would like briefly to mention the emblem of one of the success stories of this area, the Narin and Portnoo Golf Club. This progressive club, aware of the richness of our historical heritage in this area, chose a club emblem which depicts in one upper corner the larger portal tomb at Kilclooney, in the other upper corner the mighty stone enclosure at Loughadoon, and lower down are depicted the golden lunula from Drumboghill and the green wave-washed island of Inishkeel.

Notes

1   Edgar S. Shrubsole, *The Land of Lakes* (4th ed.), p. 28.

2   *H.P.A.*, p. 26.

3   Ibid.

4   This field used to belong to the late Charlie Gallagher of Castlegoland, whom we have mentioned earlier, but is now owned by Connell Boyle of Dooey.

5   *D.A.* (1968), p. 297.

6   Joyce, vol. II, pp. 113-14.

7   *Reading the Irish Landscape*, pp. 1, 78, 97, 102, 104.

8   Ibid. p. 106.

9   A rough guide to earlier held views is that the court tombs were dated to about 3000 B.C. and that portal tombs were a later (*c.* 2000 B.C.) simpler derivation of the court tomb. But in more recent years, with the aid of radiocarbon dating, the dates are being revised backwards and recent research has revealed court tombs dating to *c.* 3900 – 3400 B.C. and portal tombs to over 3000 B.C. Whether the two types of tomb were being used simultaneouly by population groups with different backgrounds is open to question. In conclusion, "The argument for seeing portal-tombs as being contemporary with the later stages of court cairn construction, and therefore with the Late Neolithic, ought to be deleted from the record, leaving the way open for a much earlier beginning for the portal-tombs in Ireland." (Harbison, *Pre-Christian Ireland*, p. 56.)

10   Mitchell, *Reading the Irish Landscape*, p. 108.

11   Peter Harbison states, in relation to court tombs, that "the reasonable hypothesis has also been put forward that court cairns were not primarily places for burials, but were 'temples' where the ritual involved would have taken place in the forecourt" and that pottery-laden layers of earth "may have been gathered up from earlier remains on the site and deposited in the galleries or laid down before they were built, in order to create a sympathetic magic to ensure good harvests". He continues: "It is certainly noteworthy that court cairns are never grouped together as cemeteries, and in their isolation they may have served as the focal cult centre for a scattered population, as the parish church does for the rural community of the Irish countryside today." (*Pre-Christian Ireland*, pp. 50-51.)

12   Mitchell, *Reading the Irish Landscape*, p. 108.

13   The monument consists of a massive gallery aligned east-west with two court-stones, 1.2 m. high, ajoining it at the north-east. The gallery is 6 m. long and up to 2.4 m. wide but lacks any segmentation. The massive entrance jambs and the back-

stone are all 1.8 m. high and the sidestones somewhat lower. A displaced lintel rests across the gallery while two tiers of corbels lie above its southern side. A second displaced lintel, 3 m. in maximum dimension, lies in front of the entrance jambs. The structure is incorporated in a low long mound of indefinite outline. (*A.S.D.*, p. 22.)

14   The word dolmen comes from two Breton words meaning "stone-table". The preferred term nowadays is a "portal tomb".

15   Michael J. O'Kelly, *Early Ireland,* p. 92.

16   *J.R.S.A.I.*, vol. 113 (1983), p. 84.

17   Ibid.

18   Ibid. p. 87.

19   Ibid.

20   The tomb entrance, which often tends to be orientated roughly eastwards, is marked by a pair of tall portal stones set inside the line of the side slabs. The chamber, straight-sided and often narrowing towards the rear, is usually covered by a single capstone of enormous size, poised high over the entrance, resting on the portal stones at the front and sloping downward towards the rear where it rests on the back-stone of the chamber, or, in a number of cases, on a lesser capstone which is supported on the chamber orthostats. The entrance through the portals may be closed by a doorstone but occasionally a low sill stone is placed there instead.

21   Seán Ó Nualláin, *J.R.S.A.I.*, vol. 113, p. 89.

22   *The Donegal Highlands,* p. 148.

23   *A.S.D.*, p. 32.

24   *D.A.* (1968), p. 297-98.

25   *D.A.* (1957), p. 66; Borlase, *The Dolmens of Ireland,* merely states: "I noticed two indentations, possibly cups."

26   *J.R.S.A.I.*, vol. 103 (1973), p. 94.

27   Kelly, *Early Ireland,* p. 189.

28   James Moore gave ready permission to excavate and he and his family showed many kindnesses while work was in progress. My father was assisted by Rev. Dr. Molloy and Mr. Hannon of the McDevitt Institute, Glenties, and by Garda Sgt. Coleman of Glenties who took photographs.

29   See *U.J.A.*, vol. 12 (6th series), vol. LXXII consec. series, (1942), pp. 122-126.

30   Joyce, vol. II, p. 409.

31   East of the late Joe (Geordie) Boyle's.

32   Part of Clogher and Loughfad was originally church land. In the Down Survey of 1659 the "3 Balliboes of Clogher and Loghfada" are mapped as church land. In the Inquisition lists we read (1620) of "10 part 'quarter' ter de Loghfadda in 32 ptes divisas" and (1642) of "10/32pt 'quarter' ter de Loughfadda al' Shracashell"; these were the temporal lands, so presumably 22/32 of Loughfad was church land. I wonder where was the cashel in this area? (Shracashell: *Srath Caisil*).

33   *H.D.R.*, vol. 1, p. 268.

34   *H.P.A.*, p. 28.

35   Ibid.

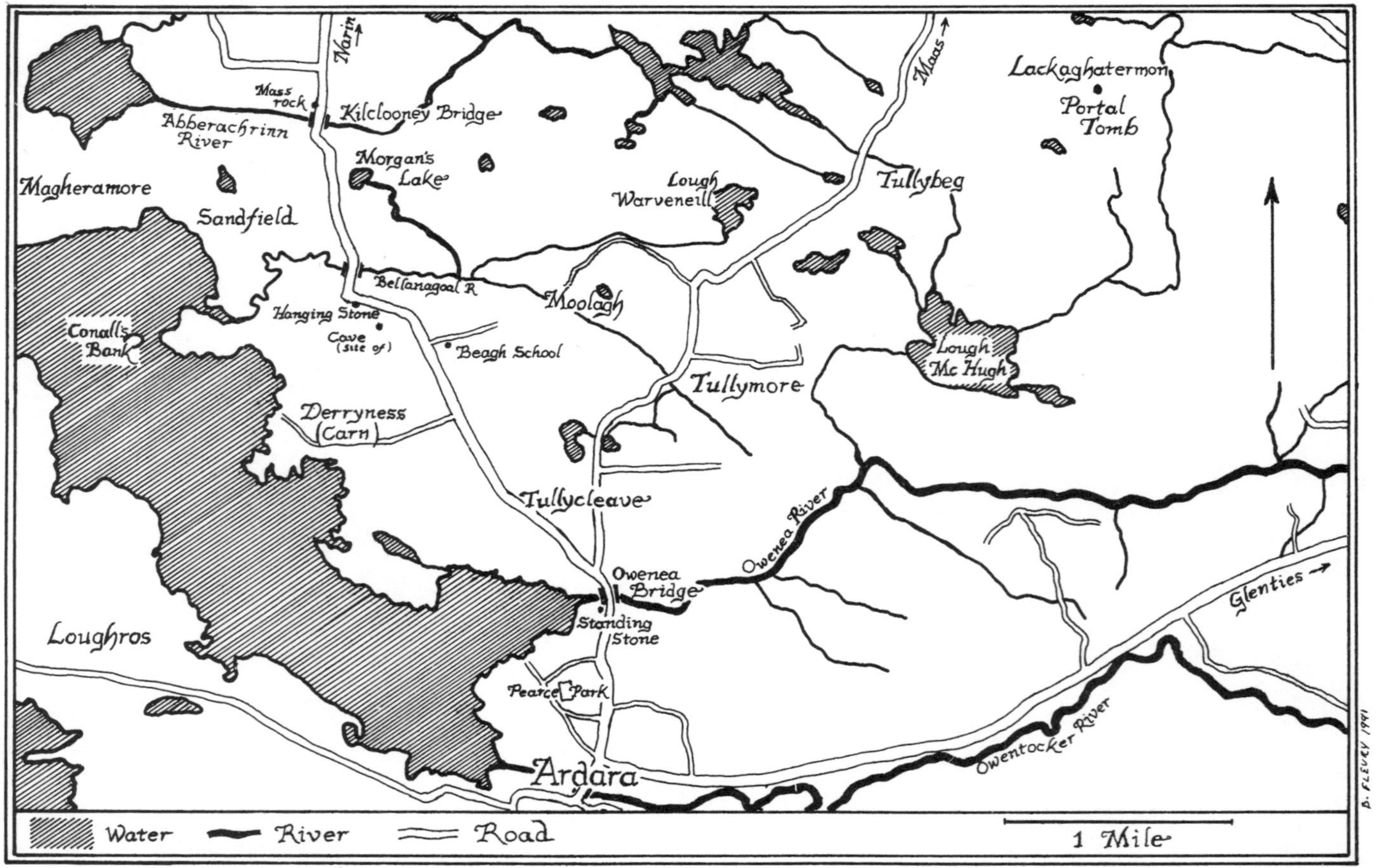

B. FLEURY 1941

Lackaghatermon
Portal Tomb

Tullybeg

Lough
Mc Hugh

Glenties

Owentocker River

Owenea River

Moos

Lough
Warveneill

Tullymore

Tullycleave

Owenea
Bridge

Standing
Stone

Ardara

Kilclooney Bridge

Morgan's
Lake

Mooagh

Bellanagool R.

Beagh School

Pearce Park

Martin

Abberachrinn
River

Sandfield

Moss
rock

Hanging Stone

Cove
(site of)

Derryness
(Carn)

Maghteramore

Conall's
Bank

Loughros

Water ~~~ River ═══ Road

1 Mile

XI

KILCLOONEY TO ARDARA

The Fair of Magheramore

PROCEEDING TOWARDS ARDARA, and passing the exit road from Rosbeg and Kiltoorish along which we have journeyed earlier, we note on our right a huge flat plain, with a sandy soil underneath, stretching out towards the Atlantic and ending in high sand dunes over behind the Tramore beach at Rosbeg. The area around these dunes off to the west was used as an early habitation site, just as were the sand dunes of Dooey, Narin, and Maghera (which we will be visiting later on). As recently as 1989 John Con McLoone of Rosbeg gave me a bronze stick pin, 7.7 cm. in length and with a square head reminiscent of a die, which had been found by one of his children in earlier years in these sand dunes. I arranged that John Con present the bronze pin to Ms. Paula Harvey, the then curator of the new County Museum in Letterkenny.

The flat area and the sand dunes, between us and the Atlantic, is called Magheramore [*machaire*: a derivative of *mágh*: a plain, a flat area; *mór*: big] and within it is the wildlife reserve of Sheskinmore [*seisceann*: a marsh, a boggy place; *mór*: big; *An tSeascainn Mhór*: a large marshy area (and ideal for wildlife)].

The plain of Magheramore will always have its place in history because of the great fair or *aonach* held there from ancient times. Following the Plantation of Ulster a royal patent was granted on 13 November 1620 to Sir John Murray, Earl of Annandale, for the holding of a fair at Magheramore on the 1st November and two days following. Why was an out-of-the-way place like Magheramore chosen as the site for a fair in the 1600s? It was probably because Magheramore was the site of a much earlier *aonach* or assembly, possibly dating back to early Celtic times.[1]

The English word "fair" only partially translates *aonach* (or *oenach*). "The Oenach once had pagan rites, holy fires, sacrifices, sometimes of men; it was a parliament and a conference, new laws were discussed and promulgated; there were games, athletics, horse races, musical competitions, mercantile transactions, sometimes spread over a couple of weeks."[2] Each tribal district could establish an *aonach,* and some *aontaí,* such as that at Tara, were of national importance. In time Christianity became incorporated into the *aonach,* and the clergy often brought along sacred relics to show to the populace, but in many places the pagan ramifications of the *aonach* continued; the irregular marriages, commemorating the marriage of the sun god Lug with Erin, continued at the *aonach* of Tailltiu in Co. Clare until about 1770.[3]

The *aonach* was often sited at a place where there was a burial mound or ring-fort, or a large standing stone – a megalith. One reason why ancient *aontaí* were held at places where there were megaliths was because standing stones were associated with fertility and cattle were often driven between the standing stones in an old fertility rite. There is no obvious ancient monument standing on Magheramore, but east-north-east of Sheskinmore Lough is an arc of stone wall; the chord of the arc would measure 30 m.;[4] the remains of the wall are made up of a double line of closely set stones, the wall ending in its east extremity in a large erratic boulder. It is not known what this structure was or what its use was, but prehistoric monuments are often located in areas of rough grazing and blanket bog such as this.

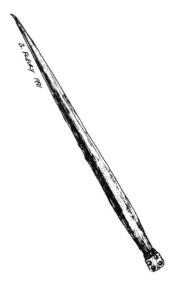

Bronze pin, Sandfield

From the many objects such as flints, bronze pins, etc., found over the years, we know that the sandhills here were sites of habitation from early times. In addition, as evidence of the early use of Magheramore, traces of iron smelting have been found in hollows in the plain. Where you find metallurgy, such as iron working, you will generally find trade, and where you find trade you will find a fair. Further evidence of mercantile activity in this area prior to the granting of the royal patent in 1620 turned up in August 1959 when a cut halfpenny of the reign of Henry III was found in the sandhills here at Magheramore. This halfpenny was struck at the ecclesiastical mint at Canterbury about the years 1260-70. It is now in the Ulster Museum in Belfast.

Interestingly, a connection has been established by sociologists between pedlars and fairs. Pedlars represent traders or merchants in their primitive form. In the Donegal of not so long ago there was a clear relationship between pedlars and tinsmiths. These tinsmiths may have been the survivors of the early traders in iron, who would have moved from Magheramore to the next great fair and so on.

After the granting of the patent in 1620 (regranted in 1629) to hold a fair at Magheramore on November 1 and for two days following, it appears that the date of the fair was afterwards brought forward to the first week in October[5] so as to accord with the farming economy in the district. The har-

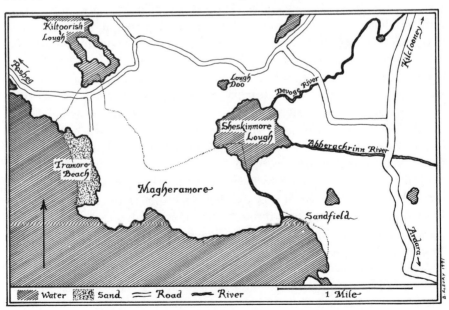

Magheramore

vest was now saved and gathered in. Sheep and cattle were being brought down from the mountains and surplus animals were in prime condition for marketing. The likelihood of more favourable weather at this time was another important consideration.

These old fairs lasted several days, and were organised in a recognised sequence. Goods and livestock came first, followed by sports, competitions and horse-racing and not infrequently ending in clan fights and bloodshed. The violence in the latter days of the great fairs belied the aims and sanctity of the original *aonach* when the laws[6] zealously guarded the inviolable peace of the *aonach* from disturbance.[7] Since there were no houses rows of booths and tents were set up for the period, so that the site of the fair might be described as a temporary town.[8] As well as the usual farm animals there was also on offer almost every household requirement – "the weaver was there with his frieze, his drugget and his linen; the spinner with her hanks of woollen yarn and her skeins of flax; the cooper with his churns, his noggins and his firkins; the nailer, the blanket-maker, the iron-workers and, of course, the tinsmiths."[9] There were hawkers, showmen and itinerant musicians, as well as beggars from all over the country, and one had never far to seek for the vendors of poteen.

These old-time fairs attained the height of their popularity towards the end of the 18th century and in the early years of the 19th. The removal of commercial restrictions by England in 1786 left an unlimited outlet for agricultural produce, and the enhanced demand consequent on the Napoleonic Wars, which ended with Waterloo in 1815, caused a marked increase in the price of everything people had to sell. Money was earned easily and spent readily. After the sales the drinking booths did a roaring trade. Many old Irish fairs suffered a serious setback as a result of the peace of 1815. Prices of agricultural produce came tumbling down, and all classes suffered as a result. The glamour of past greatness continued to attract crowds to Magheramore for some years after, but now the attendance was largely drawn from neighbouring parishes only. There was the additional drawback that, of the many new roads built in the area in the past century, not one served Magheramore, which was still dependent on its ancient bridle-paths. The fair continued to be held through the 1830s and the early 1840s, but it did not survive the Famine. About this time it was transferred to Ardara, carrying with it its time-honoured name. From that day on the fair of 1 October in Ardara was known as "The Fair of Magheramore".[10] Unfortunately, the fair days in Ardara, traditionally held on the first day of each month, are now also a thing of the past.

The passing years have not completely obliterated the memory of the old fairs at Magheramore. Dancing competitions took place towards the close of the fair. People took great pride in the art of dancing; in her book *Country and Town in Ireland under the Georges*, Constantia Maxwell says, "The Irish peasants learned to dance from dancing masters of their own class who went from cabin to cabin accompanied by a piper or a blind fiddler." Arthur Young, an Englishman, writing in 1776, makes special reference to dancing in Ireland and states: "It is an absolute system of education." Such proficiency in the art naturally led to keen competitions, and these formed one of the main attractions at the fair of Magheramore. There was keen rivalry between dancing partners from this side of the Gweebarra and those from the Rosses area. The story is told that on one occasion the qualifiers from this side of the Gweebarra were the son and daughter of a widowed beggar-woman; the girl danced with great grace and agility, but her brother's performance was of a somewhat lower standard. In desperation the locals sought an alternative male partner to accompany the girl before the grand final against the Rosses dancers. They could find only one man who could match the intricate turns and twists of the girl and this dancer was none other than James E. Nesbitt, son and heir of George Nesbitt of Woodhill, Ardara, a local landlord from a family we will be hearing much about later on. Like others of their class the Nesbitts were present at Magheramore. It was the one occasion in the year when the ascendancy mingled with the common crowds.[11] Realising the situation, James Nesbitt had come forward and offered to dance for the honour of the parish and the barony. His offer was accepted with rejoicing. The dance commenced, and there wasn't a sound to be heard on that wide field but the music of the fiddlers and the tapping of the dancers. The perfect timing and poetry of music displayed by Mr. Nesbitt and his partner had never before been equalled in Magheramore. Judges and gathering acclaimed them as winners – the landlord's son and the beggar-woman's graceful daughter.[12]

There was a less romantic side to these old-world fairs, and Magheramore was no exception. Those were the days of heavy drinking and hard fighting. The man who returned from a fair without having struck a blow could hardly look a cat straight in the eye for weeks after. Generosity at the tavern counter was regarded as an outstanding virtue, while he who was adept in a stick-fight was a local hero. Both of these qualifications counted for much with stern old fathers when asked to consent to their daughter's marriage; "a decent man and a fearless fighter" was a welcome addition to any family.

Quarrels were started on the most trivial of pretexts, but the faction fights which took place between one family, parish, barony and another usually resulted from feuds centuries old, perhaps even dating from tribal times. The weapons of combat were usually blackthorn sticks and ash-plants which had been kept in the smoke over the kitchen fire for months before use, and treated to periodic dressings of oil or grease to make them "tough" and pliable. The stick-fighter trained diligently under the eye of an experienced exponent. With so much preparation it will be readily understood that it took little provocation to get the big fight going. At many of these old fairs women also took part in the fray. Once the fighting had begun the priests and magistrates were unable to stop it; sometimes as many as five or six hundred people would be engaged.

The O'Boyles and the O'Gallaghers were the great contending factions at the fair of Magheramore. This senseless feud, the origin of which is unknown, continued for generations, if not for centuries. Men, healthy and strong, were maimed for life or sent to an early grave from the effects of blows received in these battles. Seldom was there any medical attention for the casualties, the main concern being to get them to some remote spot out of the way of the authorities. The man who had inflicted serious injuries went "on his banishment", and unless his victim fully recovered he never again returned to the district.

All this belongs to the past. However, to those who grew up at the beginning of this century, as my father did, faction fighting was still a reality. The O'Boyles and the O'Gallaghers of today have, thankfully, completely forgotten that there ever existed a feud between their ancestors.

The tradition of fighting at fairs is aptly summed up in this old verse:[13]
And at these fairs he ne'er was seen,
Without a cudgel and a *skean*;[14]
A cudgel of hard thorn or oak,
With which he many craniums broke;
With *skean* he'd stab and charge about,
And often let the blood come out.
To think that these lines were describing the *hero* in the poem!

We now pass from man and his quarrelsome ways to the next subject of our travels, the wildlife sanctuary at Sheskinmore, hopefully remembering that the original *aonach* was a dignified occasion, a dignity thankfully retained by the occupants of the wildlife sanctuary here.

Sheskinmore Wildlife Sanctuary

Sheskinmore is one of Ireland's most important wildlife reserves. It was established as a wildfowl sanctuary in the early 1980s. Its status as a unique place in Ireland is due to the wildfowl which frequent the area and to the different species of plants which grow here. There are at least sixteen different species of orchid growing in or around Sheskinmore Lake. The Dense-flowered orchid [*Neotinea maculata*, in Gaelic *Magairlín glas*] grows here, the only place outside the Burren area of Co. Clare where this species of orchid is found. There is a plant, *Najas flexilis* [the Slender naiad, in Gaelic *Síofróg uisce* (*uisce*: water)] growing in Sheskinmore Lake which is protected under the Wildlife Act because of the danger of its extinction. A type of waterweed, it needs 24" of water to grow and because of this Sheskinmore Lake cannot be drained at any time for fear of disturbing the plant and its habitat.

Also present, rooted in the lake bed but with their flowering shoots rising clear of the water, are two particularly attractive and interesting plants. These are Pipewort [*Eriocaulon aquaticum*, in Gaelic *Píbín uisce*), a colonist from America and only found in a few west coast lakes, and Water lobelia [*Lobelia dortmanna*, in Gaelic *Plúr an locháin*] with its delicate pale-blue flowers. Clear of the lake the Marsh helleborine [*Epipactis palustris*, in Gaelic *Cuaichín corraigh*], a quite rare type of orchid, grows in profusion here, accompanied by the Fragrant orchid [*Gymnadenia conopsea*, in Gaelic *Lus taghla*]. Both these species flower in June and July, being preceded by the marsh orchids which give a fine display a little earlier. Away from the marsh and over in the sand dunes pride of place must go to the vivid red pyramidal orchid [*Anacamptis pyramidalis*, in Gaelic *Magairlín na stuaice*], which is in bloom in July.

Prior to the Wildlife Service declaring this area a wildfowl sanctuary the Irish Wildbird Conservancy, a volunteer body, had established a nature reserve at Sheskinmore. It is only with the consent of the local landowners that these bodies have made strides and we must be thankful that their co-operation and their progressive vision regarding the value of Sheskinmore to the whole community has guaranteed its survival. Ireland is well endowed with sand dunes, but complete systems with dunes, machair grassland, marsh and lagoon are not so common. Few dune systems of any size are now without a road bisecting them, a caravan park and an erosion problem. Thanks to the landowners here this is one of the few.

Sheskinmore Lake was formerly a great fishing lake, but various drainage works in the 1940s and '50s greatly reduced the water level. There are two rivers flowing into it, bringing acidic water down from the mountains. Sand is blown into the lake from the surrounding sand dunes; 15% of sand is made up of calcium carbonate derived from decaying shells, giving sand a ph of 8; this neutralises the acidic water from the mountains, making it more alkaline, which encourages rare plants to grow here, plants which one wouldn't expect to find in this area.

As early as 1904 Philip Geen, an enthusiastic fisherman, observed the multiplicity of influences at work on the water in this area. He writes: "I had a splendid basket of brown trout in Loughs Derryduff and Sheskinmore and the little stream that connects them. When captured, the fish were of three different over-all colours. Those taken in the rocky upstream beds were quite the usual colours, while what we took from the centre peaty pools were dark, and down in the lower reaches, where golden sand blown in from the sea-shore formed the bed, the fish were as if a golden varnish had been put over their ordinary colours."[15]

The names of the two rivers – the Duvoge and the Abberachrinn – which flow into Sheskinmore Lough, support the view that the water would be dark and peaty before being exposed to the influence of sand. The Duvoge, a common name for a small river in Ireland, stems from *dubh*: black, and means 'little black river', while the Abberachrinn comes from *abar*: a mire, a boggy or marshy piece of land; *a chrinn*: of the trees (*crann*: a tree), indicating that its course is through marshy bogland which was formed by decaying prehistoric woodland.

Sheskinmore is a favourite hunting site for Merlin. Merlin is the smallest falcon in Europe, and breeds in the forest plantations around Ardara. Peregrine Falcons also frequent Sheskinmore, as do Hen Harriers in wintertime. Each year the Red-throated Diver breeds in one of the small mountain lakes near Portnoo. This is the only area in Ireland where this bird breeds: people around Portnoo refer to them as "Mooney's ducks". During the breeding season each year they can be seen bringing food from the sea to their nesting site.

The Chough also breeds near Ardara, in the mountain and sea cliffs. This is a black bird something like a Jackdaw but with red beak and legs. It is now a very rare bird throughout Britain because of the farming methods employed there. More Chough come into Sheskinmore in September and October – they tend to flock together at that time of year – than in any other part of Ireland and the British Isles. They are very sociable birds and do not cause any damage. Locally they are called the "Warren crow".

For many years a King Eider has been seen and photographed off Dunmore Head, Portnoo. A King Eider has been sighted at just seven locations in this country. European or Common Eider are, however, numerous around Donegal. These ducks breed mostly on the off-shore islands around Donegal and Sligo but are not found elsewhere in Ireland.

Each winter a flock of 20-40 Long-tailed Ducks are seen at Portnoo. This is one of the largest flocks in the country. They are usually found between Inishkeel island and the mainland. Because of their beautiful plumage they are also known as the sea pheasant. They can be seen easily from the public road, diving for food. They usually arrive in late November and leave in March or April.

Every autumn hundreds of wild geese come to these western areas to winter and these include Greenland White-fronted, Barnacle and Brent. The Greylag and Pink-footed Goose are rare visitors. All these birds are now fully protected under the law and cannot be hunted. The Greenland White-fronted Geese feed around Sheskinmore and the surrounding farms during the day and they go out to the mountain lakes at night time. They generally come to the area around the first week of October and leave about mid-April. The Wildlife Service keeps a close eye on them and each year they put leg rings and neck bands on a certain number and watch their breeding and migratory patterns over succeeding years. They breed in Greenland, but only about 7%-8% reproduce each year. Many are shot while flying over Iceland, so between their low breeding rate and their being shot they are a threatened species. Bog cotton [Common Bog Cotton, Hare's-tail Cottongrass, *Eriophorum vaginatum*, in Gaelic *Ceannbhán Gaelach*; a plant common in acid peatland] is the natural food of the Greenland White-fronted Geese; they pull it up and eat the roots. The Barnacle Geese live and feed on the offshore islands; they only come to Sheskinmore if the weather is bad. The Greenland White-fronted Geese never go out to the islands.

A few years ago we had a resident pair of Buzzards in the mountains close to Ardara, after an absence of many years. These birds live mostly on rabbits and carrion. Their feeding habits put them at risk of being poisoned; these ones probably ate poisoned carrion because they are no longer with us.

The coastline from Maghamore to Ardara

Hopefully this generation is beginning to appreciate how rich a heritage of wildlife we have in this area. Possibly we are only now regaining the esteem which our early ancestors had for wildlife, demonstrated by a story in the *Life of Colmcille*, compiled by Manus O'Donnell in 1532, which gives an account of a heron (or as we would call it locally, a crane) visiting Colmcille on the island of Iona in the 6th century. Colmcille, speaking to one of his fellow monks, says: "Go to the shore of this island, and thou shalt see a noble guest coming towards thee, to wit, an Irish crane that cometh from Erin to soujourn with me. She shall be weary and fordone, and her strength shall fail her sore by reason of the length of the journey and the voyage, and of the space she shall have flown." Colmcille goes on to request the monk to look after the crane when it arrives and to feed and care for it during its stay on the island. The crane stayed with Colmcille on Iona for three days and during that time it would not be parted from him. After three days the crane rose up and turned her face towards Erin. Colmcille wept bitterly, "and it doth appear further therefrom that not only did Colmcille love the human folk of his native land, but that he loved also the feathered things and winged creatures, and all her dumb living things."[16]

Giraldus Cambrensis, writing even earlier – about 1188 A.D. – testifies to the large crane (heron) population in Ireland at that time and gives an interesting theory to explain why we usually see the crane standing on one foot: "Cranes are so numerous that in one flock alone you will often see a hundred or about that number. These birds, by a natural instinct, take their turns by night in watching the common safety, standing on one leg only, while in the other featherless claw they hold a stone. They do this so that if they should go to sleep, they will be wakened again immediately by the fall of the stone and continue their watch."[17]

A poem written by Francis Harvey, resident in Donegal town, and a frequent visitor to this area, continues our theme and expresses better than any words that I could use the mood and atmosphere of this domain of the wild and free out here beside the Atlantic Ocean. And it is not without humour.

Heron
was assembled out of bits and scraps, not made.
Like one of those early flying machines held together
with glue and twine.
His undercarriage is an afterthought sticking out
behind.
He is all wings and no fuselage and probably hollow
inside.

Finn could have blown him off the palm of his hand.

He creaks into flight. The wind buffets him, gives him
a bumpy ride; it seems he must somehow end up
in a twisted heap of canvas and struts on the
mountainside.
But no: he tacks into weathers with a prow that rises
and falls in the swell.
The ghost of the pterodactyl haunts him in every cell.

He alights: furls his wings like a wet umbrella, settles,
rapt and murderous,
drying out in the wind and sun on the edge of a tarn
or hunched over a pool in the burn pretending he's
a blind one-legged beggarman or a mystic communing
with God.
Too late, too late for the fish or frog when it realises
he's not an old cod!

Heron invented slow motion long before the movies
came but
allows himself the lightning of his pickaxe for the killing
game.
Heron's the icon of the silences beyond the last tongues
of land where the islands float and quiver like mirages
in the light.
He's the hermit who daily petrifies himself in the reeds
of the penitential lake,

the logo of the lonely places past the last sheep and the
last house,
the El Greco or Modigliani doodle in a remote corner of
the evening sky where
the newsprint of distant waders swims before the eye,
Heron's that sudden outlandish screech you hear at
midnight
In the water meadows as he changes into the wrong gear.

Before we leave Sheskinmore I would like to express my gratitude to our
local Wildlife Officer, John Hennigan, who guided me through the dens and

pitfalls of writing about wildlife, a subject about which I knew little before I met him. His dedication, and that of his colleagues in the Wildlife Service, is enormous. Their influence on the preservation of our landscape is increasing all the time. Recently the Wildlife Officer in the Ballybofey area, John Byrne, reported seven archaeological sites, many of them megalithic tombs, which had not been recorded before. These men are out in all weathers and the rest of us, who are, sadly, only occasionally conscious of the many threats to our landscape and environment, owe them a great debt.

A departing note of caution. It is that extra quality of wilderness that makes Sheskinmore so special; it is its seclusion which makes it so acceptable to geese in winter and to breeding waders in summer. Birds such as geese need space and seclusion. In summer the diversity of breeding waders – e.g. Lapwing, Snipe, the tiny Dunlin which nest in open damp vegetation – is rare for a single site in Ireland. In addition the rare plant communities need continuity of care. All this would be impossible if people tramped over the terrain here unsupervised. For the time being we should leave Sheskinmore to the landowners and the experts, secure in the knowledge that formal visiting arrangements and vantage points will be initiated when it is thought wise.

Sandfield to Ardara.

The bridge over the Abberachrinn river, on the Narin–Ardara road, is called the Kilclooney bridge. The general area around this bridge is called Morganstown. Who this Morgan was, who also gave his name to a lake on your left, nobody knows, but I have reason to believe that in Morganstown we may be dealing with an older placename than one would think. In the Inquisitions of 1642, down here in the Portnoo–Maas area, we come across a place with the Scandinavian-looking name of Srajworadan, which of course isn't Scandinavian at all but is, I think, a corrupt anglicisation of the Gaelic *Srath Mhoradain* [*srath*: a holm, a field along a river], Moradain's or Morgan's Holm. I don't think this is too far-fetched a suggestion.

Continuing, we find ourselves in the townland of Sandfield. To our right the terrain, though still relatively flat, becomes more uneven as we leave Magheramore behind, and this is reflected in the Gaelic name for Sandfield (which is just a modern name), *Cor Mhachaire* [*cor*: a turn, a twist; in topographical terms it is interpreted as a round hill; *Cor Mhachaire*: the plain of the little round hills, the undulating plain]. One could be tempted, erroneously, bearing in mind the wealth of water-fowl in the general area, to interpret this placename as *Corr Mhachaire*, from *corr*: a heron (crane). Tradition tells us that the fair of Magheramore spilled over into Sandfield.

Just before Shovlin's (a common surname in this area) perfectly-preserved thatched house on the right we pass over another bridge. The name of the river here, the Bellanagoal, deserves comment. One could, for interest's sake, interpret the last syllable as the Gaelic word *gual*. *Gual* is nowadays cognate with the English word "coal", but it is really a throwback to the manufacture of charcoal in earlier times. The making of charcoal was understood and practised at a very early period in Ireland.[18] The spots where charcoal used to be manufactured in times of old are still discernible in various parts of the country. Places of this kind often retain names containing the word *gual*. We have already noted, when discussing the origin of the Abberachrinn river, that this area was wooded in ancient times and indeed we are told that the triangle of country between Ardara, Glenties and Narin was tree-covered as recently as the 16th century.[19] So there is no doubt that raw material was in plentiful supply for making charcoal.

However, interesting as this may be, we are on the wrong track. And "track" is the operative word. For centuries, before this road was built, the track used by people on the Rosbeg and Mullyvea–Ardara route ran along the coast, away down to the right. The terrain was wet. People had to cross the Murvagh,[20] which was liable to flooding, had to negotiate the mouth of the Bellanagoal river and then had to cross either a river emptying into or draining Sheskinmore Lough. A fork of land between two rivers is often termed a *gabhal* – we will discuss this word later.[21] It appears that the name Bellanagoal should be interpreted as *Béal Atha na Gabhail*, the entrance (mouth) to the ford of the fork of land – the fork of land yet to be crossed was presumably that which lay between the Bellanagoal river and the rivers associated with Sheskinmore Lough.

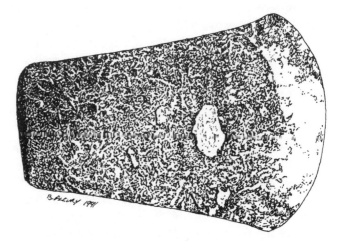

Sandfield bronze axe-head

Confirmation that this area was inhabited from very early times came with the discovery of a very well-preserved bronze axe-head here at Sandfield by the late Packie Shovlin of Meenaleck, Sandfield.

We cross over the river, round the corner, pass the Hanging Stone and proceed up the hill to Beagh – though of course we are already in the town-land of Beagh since we crossed the bridge; streams often delineate between townlands.

Beagh, *An Bheitheach*, derives from *beith*, a birch tree, and the termina-tion *-ach*: abounding in; birchland. Because Ireland formerly abounded in woods vast numbers of placenames are formed from words signifying woods and trees of various kinds, but as in so many places the landscape here is now bare of trees.

At the beginning of the stretch of level road leading on towards Ardara you will notice a low thatched building on your left at the top of the hill, with a road going off to the left beside it. This was the old Beagh school. It was the first school building to be erected in this area and is now used as a farm building. In the early decades of the last century it was erected by local people and roofed with fir. They collected £1 locally to provide it with a door and two small windows. They then went to the Murvagh to cut materials for thatching the school without asking the permission of the owner. He brought them to court, where a Rosbeg gentleman, an old acquaintance of the plaintiff, presided on the bench. The Beagh men were fined £1 and they had to start collecting again for the door and the windows.

One of the first teachers in this school was a man named Furey from Kilraine. He was partial to mutton and came to hear that a man named Micky Mór (Big Micky) who lived in an isolated cottage in the area had a habit of stealing fat sheep which he carved up and salted in tubs. At every opportunity Furey made his way to the cottage, and surreptitously selected a few choice pieces. Micky had so much that he never missed them but Furey foolishly gave his secret away; before long he had to leave the district hur-riedly.

Dan Sweeney was principal of this school for many years and taught down to the early part of this century. Matt Sweeney succeeded his father and re-tired in 1942. In a submission to the Irish Folklore Commission[22] in 1937 Matt Sweeney enlarges on Micky Mór, the local personality we have just re-ferred to. He states that James Kennedy, a local man on whose lands the re-mains of Micky Mór's house stood, had pointed out the shell of the old house to him. Only a few stones were standing at that time; it had measured about 18' in length and 14' in width and the fireplace was situated in the centre of the floor. Micky Mór had lived between the years 1800 and 1850.

He was of gigantic stature, 6' 5" in height and of enormous strength. We heard earlier of his penchant for stealing sheep and salting the meat. On one occasion, when his larder was getting low, he killed and carried to his cabin, a distance of four miles, a two-year-old heifer belonging to Captain Porter of Portnoo. Micky spent most of his time hunting and fishing and when game was scarce he did not hesitate to carry off his neighbours' fowl and sheep, but such was the fear that he instilled in the people of the locality that he was never brought to book for his misdeeds. He died about the year 1850 and it was said that for years afterwards his spirit wandered among the scenes of his earthly escapades, and daring indeed was the person who attempted to traverse the precincts of his old cabin after midnight.

Quite close to where Micky Mór used to live there was an *uaigh*: a cave or souterrain. We have already discussed souterrains and I have indicated that they were generally marked on the Ordnance Survey maps as caves. There is a "cave" marked here at Beagh on the 1847 Ordnance Survey map. Matt Sweeney refers to it in 1937 and states that it measured 8' x 4.5". He says that his informant, James Kennedy, stated that it used to be used as a hiding place in times of danger and in support of his contention had pointed out a hill near by which was used as a lookout station. The souterrain had been closed up in the early 1930s because a heifer belonging to the landowner had become wedged in it. This led to part of it being demolished and the remainder being closed in. My father visited this site in 1953 and states that Dinny Gallagher's uncle remembered when the souterrain was intact; you had to crawl through the entrance, but once inside you could stand up. My father also noted in 1953 that the site of an old fort could be traced on the hill behind James "Tailor" Kennedy's house.

The surnames Sweeney[23] and Gallagher are still strong in the Beagh area. We first hear of the clann *Mac Suibhne* (MacSweeneys, Sweeneys) in this country in the 13th century when they arrived in the Fanad area of Donegal from Scotland and drove out the O'Breslins[24] who had ruled Fanad in the 12th and first half of the 13th century. We have noted earlier how their increasing power gradually led to their making great inroads into traditional O'Boyle territory – in the 14th century some of them settled in Doe, near Creeslough in north-west Donegal, dislodging the O'Boyles, while others settled in north Connacht. Early in the 15th century a branch of these Connacht MacSweeneys settled in *Tír Bógaine* and Rahan, near Dunkineely, became their chief residence. So they had power bases north and south.

Every schoolchild has been taught that the MacSweeneys came as galloglasses[25] – mercenary soldiers – from Scotland to support the O'Donnells and we have traditionally been told that they were of Norse origin. But now their descent has been traced[26] to the ancient O'Neills, kings of Aileach. When this branch of the O'Neills moved to Scotland their name was changed, when surnames became obligatory, and the descendants of *Suibhne* (O'Neill)[27] became *Mac Suibhne*. They lived at Castle Sween in Knapdale, a part of Argyll, where they fostered O'Donnells, intermarried, and arrived in this country after the defeat of the Balliol faction at Bannockburn[28] and naturally threw in their lot here with the O'Donnells. We will shortly deal with a major battle that the MacSweeneys fought just up the road from here, at Carn, in 1588.

Of the pedigree of the Gallaghers (Ó Gallachóir) there is no dissent – they are of the Cenél nAinmirech, descended from Ainmire,[29] great-grandson of Conall Gulban. An ancient people, whose influence spread further than you might think in more recent years! From 1950 we read this interesting aside: "Senor Manuel Gallagher, 65-year-old Foreign Minister for Peru, has arrived in Washington for a Hemisphere Conference of Latin-American Statesmen. Speaking Peruvian (*sic*), Senor Gallagher told the Irish News Agency through an interpreter: 'My grandfather was a scientist and he came from Ireland. He came to Peru from County Donegal on the Charles Darwin expedition of the last century. He liked Peru so much that he stayed there and sent home to Ireland for his sweetheart who became my grandmother.' Senor Gallagher was born in Lima, capital of Peru, and he is the son of Patricia and Petranilla Gallagher."[30]

As we continue towards Ardara, over to our right, close to the sea, is an area known as Carn. The word Carn forms the whole or the beginning of the names of about 300 townlands in Ireland. The reason for its frequent occurrence is that it was usual in this country, as in many others, to pile a great heap of stones, usually called a *carn*[31] over the grave(s) of any person(s) of note. Carn in this instance, however, is not a townland. Derryness [*Doirinis*: *doir*: oak wood; *inis*: island; the island of the oak wood] is the proper townland name for this area, though it is known as Carn locally. Since there are no early references to Carn as a placename here, where did the name come from? Well, I think the clue is in the major recorded historical event which occurred here at Derryness in 1588 – a battle between the MacSweeneys. This general period saw a lot of internecine war between the MacSweeneys. In 1547 we are told that "Mac Sweeny Baghaineach (Niall Oge) was slain on the 3rd of September by the sons of his own brother";[32] in 1586 we read that "MacSweeny Banagh (Brian Oge, the son of Mulmurry) was slain on the 18th of May, by Niall Meirgeach, son of Mulmurry, son of Hugh (MacSweeny)."[33] It was this latter killing which led to the battle of Derryness in 1588. This is how the *Annals of the Four Masters* describe events: "Mac

Sweeny Banagh (Niall Meirgeach, the son of Mulmurry, son of Hugh, son of Niall) was slain on Doirinis, on St. Bridget's Day, by Donough, the son of Mulmurry Meirgeach, son of Niall. That event happened thus: after Brian Oge had been slain by Niall Meirgeach, as we have already stated, Donough, with his followers, were, moreover, banished into Connaught by Niall, and he remained for some time with the English, and for some time after that along with O'Neill. [At last] he made an incursion from a far distance against Niall, what Niall did not expect, for he thought that Donough would not come into the country while he [Niall] should live in it. Donough, after having passed three nights in the wilds and recesses of the country, received intelligence that Mac Sweeny was in the Lower Third of Boylagh,³⁴ and he sent spies to reconnoitre him; and the spies brought news to Donough that he would come up [i.e. southwards] across the strand on the day following: he [Donough] was prepared with all his forces to oppose him. They met at Doirinis, before mentioned, where a fierce battle was fought between them, in which Mac Sweeny was slain, together with a great number of his followers, and of the Clann-Sweeny of Munster. Mac Sweeny was beheaded, and his head was sent to Dublin. Donough was then styled Mac Sweeny."³⁵

It is likely that there were great cairns of stones erected over the graves of the fallen, stones which would have been removed for building purposes over the years, with the result that there is nowadays no trace of a *carn*.

The memory of this great battle lived on in the folklore of the people here. My father, writing in 1970, states: "The course of this battle along the shore of Derryness (opposite the island of that name) and up to 'War Hill' where the final engagement took place, is still a subject of conversation in the local village of Carn."³⁶ I would think that my father was particularly referring to the Melly family, who had a store of local knowledge.

Out in the bay, just off the coast of Carn, is a sandbank which we have referred to earlier in our travels – Conall's Bank (*Oitir Chonaill*). This is a reminder to us of the route which, folklore tells us, St. Conall of Inishkeel is said to have taken as he journeyed along the coastline from Inishkeel in the direction of Laconnell and Glencolumbkille.

More recent folklore tells us of a legendary blacksmith called Lochlann (it's not often I come across my own name in history!) O'Byrne;³⁷ he had a forge here in Carn and a large boulder served as one of the gables of the building. His fame spread far and wide and many stories are told of efforts made by competitors to try to steal the secret of his superior craftmanship. Though a blacksmith, his touch was so fine and delicate that it is said he used to make razors for Captain Hamilton of Eden, near Rosbeg.

I would not think of leaving the Carn area without remembering my good friend, John D. Stewart, who died in recent years. John D. was a man of letters and a great raconteur who lived in Belfast, and started coming to Ardara with his family in the mid-1960s. His literary output included a book on Gibralter and a number of dramatic plays. He frequently wrote of Ardara in his newspaper column, and many visitors over the years have attested that it was John D.'s writing about the area that inspired them to come to Ardara, and then, having come once, they continued to come back year after year.

John D. was a great lover of nature and especially of wildlife. He believed in humanism. In memory of "Stu" I will not use any of his own written works but instead will quote a few very brief lines written by the Czech poet, Ondra Lysohorsky, who also died in recent years and whose works were suppressed in Czechoslovakia. I think John would have liked him. A liberal humanist, he celebrated nature in contrast with the brutality of man, depicting his own caged condition in an endless series of symbols:

The last flock of birds has
passed by overhead,
I feel as lonely as if a
thousand friends had forsaken
me,
left me behind in my cage.[38]

I sincerely hope that John D. is now travelling with the flocks of wild birds which he loved so much – this was the afterlife he desired.

Leaving Carn we continue towards the Owenea bridge, passing through Tullycleave [*Tulaigh Chléibh*, hill of the breast, i.e. a breast-shaped hill. Tulach, Tully, etc. are derivatives of the root word *tul*, a hill or hillock; *tul* can also mean forehead, or front, indicating a prominence – such as a hill. *Cléibh* derives from *cliabh*, a basket, and is often used to denote the human chest, complete with ribs – reminiscent of the shape of a basket].

Over to our left we have Tullymore [*mór*: big] and Tullybeg [*beag*: small], these "Tullys" indicating the drumlin-like hillocks in the landscape here. From a height these hillocks look like green breast-shaped islands in a sea of moorland. There are 822 townlands with the word "*tullach*" in them in Ireland, of which over 54% are concentrated in Ulster. Interestingly, the word *tul* also indicates a "little hill" in the native language of Sardinia, giving rise to a suggestion in the past that the ancient people who built the great court tombs in the northern half of Ireland may have had their origin in Sardinia "where not only the court cairns, but the general landscape of limestone and granite are curiously alike to the Ulster countryside."[39] I would doubt this suggested link.

Well down in Tullymore, at a place named Moolagh – which is reached most easily via the little road that goes by the old Beagh school – a bronze sword was found in 1892. It was in a poorly preserved state and is said to have formed part of a hoard. It was found by a man named James Boyle in the bog near his home at Moolagh. It is now in the National Museum, ref. no. N.M. 1. 1900-46.[40] Naturally I wondered what else was in the "hoard" but in fact the only other item found with the sword was a spear-head.[41]

Because the terrain here is soft I envisaged that the name Moolagh derived from *múch*; smoke, used in a secondary sense to mean "suffocate or smother" and then applied to a morass "from some fanciful notion that in such a place men or beasts are liable to be suffocated".[42] However local pronunciation is *Maolach* [*maol*: bare, a bare hill; *maolach*: a place abounding in hillocks]. Nearby Meenarillagh translates as *Mín a' ghriollach*, the latter part being the genitive plural of *griollach*: puddle, quagmire.

A wooden container filled with butter was found in bogland in Tullybeg in 1969. The body of the vessel was carved from a single, roughly square piece of wood. The vessel was provided with two lugs and a hazel rod was bound round its middle. It was sent to the National Museum.[43]

Containers filled with butter are a fairly common find during turf-cutting. The art of making and preserving butter was known in Ireland from the earliest ages.[44] In later times it was customary to sink butter deep down in bogs, closed up in casks, to give it flavour. Among the various articles of food used by the Irish about 1650 was "butter made rancid by keeping in a bog"[45] and

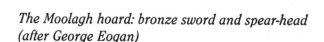

The Moolagh hoard: bronze sword and spear-head
(after George Eogan)

the well-known lampoon, the *Irish Hudibras*, printed in 1689, describes and Irish feast, which, among other things, had:

And butter to eat with their hog

Was seven years buried in a bog.

Bog butter, when recovered, is generally found to have been changed by the action of bog water into a partially-hardened greyish cheese-like substance.[46] A similar method of preserving butter has been noted in the Assam district of India; the butter is firmly pressed, is not salted, is put into an unglazed earthenware vase which is closed with a well-fitted cover, which is itself pasted with flour and water to exclude the air, and the whole is then buried in a dry bank of earth where it remains for about six months; when mature it is used by the people in their rice.[47]

Just before reaching the Owenea bridge there is a road going off to the left down towards Maas and the Gweebarra. The whole area west of this line between the Owenea bridge and Maas, extending out to the Atlantic, has been designated as an Area of Special Scientific Interest[48] because of the wealth of flora and fauna that is present here.

East of the Owenea bridge–Maas line is blanket bog, its recent history being dominated by its being worked for turf by Bord na Móna, a semi-state body. Now the hum of turf-cutting machines has gone and the pared-down landscape is quiet. There are indications that the solitude of this area was appreciated even in the far off era when Christianity was first introduced here. A few miles up along the Owenea river, best approached from the Glenties–Ardara road, is Glenconwell [*Gleann Congbhail*; *gleann*: a glen; *congbhail*: a habitation, usually applied to an ecclesiastical establishment]. A shrub-covered mound in Glenconwell known as Parkanancory [*páirc*: a field or enclosure; *ancoire*: a hermit, an anchorite, the Gaelic word *ancoire* being borrowed through the Latin from the Greek *anachórétés*] may mark the site of the original religious foundation. The anchorites were an order of ascetics who lived a thoroughly solitary life.

In the bogland near Lough MacHugh, between Glenconwell and Maas (and Letterilly), stands the remains of a portal tomb, in an area known as Lackaghatermon.[49] The first half of this placename obviously refers to the portal tomb itself, being derived from the word *leac*, a flagstone; the final element "-termon", *tearmann*, a refuge, sanctuary, we have discussed before – at Narin strand. If there was an early Christian foundation in this area, centered in Glenconwell, it is difficult to escape the conclusion that this portal tomb at Lackaghatermon, which would have pre-dated the coming of Christianity by over 2,000 years, was adopted as a boundary stone to the ecclesiastical lands and that anyone reaching this megalithic tomb would then be safe from pursuit and would be given sanctuary.

There is further evidence of ecclesiastic activity in this area. The part of the townland of Old Letterilly[50] which ran along the Owenea bridge–Maas road was formerly known as "Dronagh". This may well be just the remnant of a longer old placename. Joyce, in explaining a place named *Latnadronagh* in Cavan, writes: "*Leacht-na-dtruaghanach*, monument of the ascetics or hermits. The Irish ascetics often, in self-humiliation, called themselves *truaghan*, which means a wretched creature, from *truagh*, misery."[51]

Of further interest is that "Tollimore" and "Tollibeg" are included as church lands in the Down Survey maps of 1659, as is also the nearby "balliboe of Logh Derryduffe".

We now cross the bridge over the Owenea [*Abhainn Fhia*; *abhainn*: a river; *fiadh*: a wild deer or wild stag, though originally *fiadh* meant any wild animal and can also mean simply "a wild" (land). In modern Gaelic the older form of genitive, *fhiadh*, is not used, *fhia* is, thus *an Abhainn Fhia*].

One of our most impressive landmarks, a large standing stone, is situated immediately behind the cold ruined building which is on your right just after crossing the Owenea bridge. When I was a child this building was a shop and was owned by "Wee Joe". Dr. Pococke, whom we have not encountered

The Owenea standing stone

now for a long time, passed by here in 1752 and mentions the standing stone: "We then came to Locrasmore bay, and to a bridge over the river Oneck, where there is a stone set up on end nine feet high, four broad and three thick, they call it Fin McCoues shoulder stone, with which he used to divert himself by throwing it like a Quoit."[52] Local tradition alleges that Finn Mac Cumhal threw this stone from a mountainous area near Ardara called *Cró-na-Cléire* and that it landed here.

This impressive standing stone is 2.95 m. in height and is four-sided. The Gaelic word *gallán* is often used in Ireland to indicate one of these huge blocks of stone, which evidently owe their upright position not to accident but to the design and labour of an ancient people. Many theories have been promulgated relative to their origin. In some cases they mark the site of ancient burials – the erection of pillar stones as sepulchral monuments is often recorded in ancient Irish authorities; some served as boundary marks, while others pointed out the line of ancient roadways; it is also thought that pillars of stone were set up to mark the sites of notable events, and it is clear that certain standing stones were invested with sacred character – idol stones.

Because of the proximity of this standing stone to the Owenea river, and bearing in mind that rivers were often used as boundaries in the time before bridges were built, it is likely that this large stone was erected as a boundary stone at some time in the distant past. By crossing the Owenea we have moved from the ancient territory of *Tír Ainmirech* into *Tír Bógaine*. The chieftains after whom these territorial units were named lived in the early 5th century A.D. but I think it likely that this standing stone marked a boundary among the old tribes who inhabited this area even before 400 A.D.

The Owenea river is the foremost salmon fishing river in the area and it has been so for a long time. Thomas Addi, writing in 1730, states: "I also inquired into the value of Oye Nea fishing and Lochris fishing and am credibly informed by the salters and packers and other that they caught four tun of salmon this year at six tierces to the tunn, each tun being worth twelve pounds sterling in reason and sometimes eighteen pounds.[53] ... I observe that there is a broad strand and the current of the river runs much nearer to Mr. Murray's land than it is to Mr. Cunyngham's land. This is where they fish with boats, but where the box is fixed is above the strand, and the box is directly in the middle of the river."[54]

That the Owenea is at its best for the angler when in flood is also well established. Dr. MacDevitt, writing in 1865, states: "The angler in the river [Owenea] will have sport, if he is on at the time of a spate, but as it rises and falls very quickly, it will be hardly worth his while to go there on a chance."[55]

Edgar Shrubsole in *The Land of Lakes* reaffirms this view in his description of the Owenea. He writes: "Under favourable conditions the Owenea provides good sport with salmon from May to September, but it is absolutely necessary that a push of water should prevail, otherwise the fishing is indifferent, even if it is not a total failure. ... There are several really good pools on it, notably Boyles and Bryans. They can all be fished from the bank; wading is of little, if any, advantage. The salmon range in size from 6lbs. to 20 lbs. The early run fish will average 15 lbs., and the main runs consist principally of six and seven pounders. The best months for salmon are June and July; the next best month being September."[56]

Philip Geen wasn't so lucky with fishing conditions in the Owenea when he came here at the beginning of the century: "I was unfortunate in having quite low water during my week's stay, and so only tried the salmon twice. I saw large numbers jumping in most of the pools, particularly in Johnny Boyle's, Holly Bush, Whin Gardens, McGill's, and Brines Pools, but they were not in a taking mood, so I turned my attention to the trout, of which I got good baskets. Had I been a fortnight later my chances would have been good, as then the river rose and kept to a good fishing height for three weeks, during which period Mr. Lakin Warwick and three others got a hundred salmon between them."[57] Not bad!

I have enjoyed recounting the names of some of the pools on the Owenea because I have fished them myself and I thought that mention of them might give pleasure to others who have fond memories of fishing them and who might not now be capable of doing so for one reason or another.

Coming up the hill towards Ardara off towards the right, down amongst the fields, is the Pearse Memorial Park, the local Gaelic football pitch, which was officially opened on 13 June 1939. Many's an evening I spent playing football in this park when I was a young lad. We had a very good under-age team in Ardara at that time and we won all before us. I never pass this way without thinking of one of our team, Sean Campbell, who was killed in an accident in England when he was only eighteen years of age. We buried another of our gang, Rory O'Donnell, in Ardara this Christmas past.

Notes

1   I cannot *prove* that there was an ancient *aonach* held here; another fair which was granted in 1620 was at Dunkineely and it is possible that Magheramore and Dunkineely were chosen as sites for fairs because of their proximity respectively to the power bases of the O'Boyles at Kiltoorish and the MacSweenys at Rahan, Dunkineely, but I doubt this.

2   *J.R.S.A.I.*, vol. 44, part 1 (1919), p. 3.

3   Ibid. p. 2.

4   *A.S.D.*, p. 325.

5   *H.P.A.*, p. 66.

6   These laws also prevented encroachment on the "green" (*faithche*) where sports were held, provided for its clearing before sports, for its enclosures, and for the stands and platforms for the spectators.

7   *J.R.S.A.I.*, vol. 44, part 1 (1919), p. 2.

8   Possibly Magheramore had been more than just a "temporary" town; Denis Verschoyle, resident in South Africa, writing to my father in 1960, states: "I have a copy of one of O'Donovan's Ms. maps of Donegal drawn prior to the Ordnance Survey *c.* 1834 and Magheramore is shown as a town with a street but a pencil ring around it, possibly indicating demolition before the Ordnance Map was drawn. On another map of 1801 of which I have a copy, Magheramore is shown as a town in the same type as Ardara, Dunkineely etc."

9   *H.P.A.*, p. 67.

10   The above has been abridged from my father's book, *H.P.A*, pp. 68-69; most of the content of the remaining paragraphs on the old fair also come from my father, who, born in 1897, heard these stories about the fair of Magheramore from the older generation around Aighe.

11   According to my father's informants.

12   P.J. McGill, *Peoples Press*, 7, 14, 21 October 1950.

13   From *Hesper-nesographia, Canto.* iv., quoted in Walker's *Historical Memories of the Irish Bards*, p. 43.

14   i.e. *scian*, the Gaelic for dagger.

15   *Fishing in Ireland*, p. 101.

16   pp. 268-71.

17   *The Topography of Ireland*, ed. John J. O'Meara, p. 21.

18   Joyce, vol. II, p. 204.

19   See p. 20.

20   A coastal plain, liable to flooding by the sea. Possibly derived from *muir*, the sea, and *báigh*, drown. The placename occurs in an interesting reference to one of the O'Boyle sept in the *A.U.* at the year 1490 A.D:
"Toirdelbach, son of Toirdelbach Ua Buighill, namely, tanist of Muintir-Buighill, was killed by a fall, in racing upon the ridge of Murbach [spelt *Murbaigh* in Gaelic] on Ash-Wednesday of this year." However Joyce points to a different origin for the second syllable of the word; he writes (vol. I, p. 466): "The word occurs as a general term in Cormac's Glossary (*voce* 'tond'), where the seawaves are said to '*shave* the grass from off the *murbhach*.' In the Book of Rights it is spelled *Murmhagh*, which points to the etymology: *muir*, the sea, and *magh*, a plain – *murmhagh*, sea plain."

Murvagh golf course near Donegal town is now our best-known example of this placename.

21   At Edergole.

22 Now the Dept. of Irish Folklore, Belfield; ms. 336, pp. 175-81, Matt Sweeney, 5 April 1937.

23 Just earlier, at Sheskinmore, I quoted the poem "Heron". In the publication in which it appears – *The Orange Dove of Fiji* (Poems for the World Wide Fund for Nature) – is a poem entitled "The Eagle" by Matthew Sweeney. Matthew, whose parents live here at Beagh, is a great-grandson of Dan Sweeney, whom we noted just now as having taught in Beagh school down to the beginning of this century. Matthew has had four books of poetry and a children's storybook published. Another son of Beagh, Pádriag Mac Suibhne, is a noted Gaelic poet.

24 At Inishkeel island we noted that one branch of the O'Breslins retreated from Fanad to Inishkeel where they became erenaghs.

25 From the Gaelic word *gallóglach* [*gall*: a foreigner; *óglach*: a youth, a soldier; *gall-óglach*: a foreign soldier].

26 *D.A.* (1990), pp. 61-62.

27 Ibid. p. 62

28 Ibid.

29 "The Age of Christ, 566. After Ainmire, son of Sedna, was three years in the soverignty of Ireland, he was slain by Fearghus, son of nellin." (*A.F.M.*, vol. I, pp. 204-5). The death of this monarch is entered twice in the *A.U.*, first under 568, which is the true year, and again under 575, which is clearly a mistake.

30 *D.A.*, p. 238.

31 Occurs frequently in archaeological writings as the English word "cairn".

32 *A.F.M.*, vol. v, pp. 1150-51.

33 Ibid. pp. 1857-58.

34 i.e. the Rosses.

35 *A.F.M.*, vol. v, pp. 1864-67.

36 *H.P.A.*, p. 39.

37 Dept. of Irish Folklore, ms. 336, pp. 175-81, Matt Sweeney, 5 April 1937. My father used also tell of this famous blacksmith.

38 From "Birds of Passage," from the collection *In the Eye of the Storm* (1976).

39 G.B. Adams, *Bulletin of the Ulster Place Name Society*, vol. IV, part 1 (1956), quoted in *D.A.* (1957), p. 70.

40 It is mentioned in George Eogan's *Catalogue of Irish Bronze Swords*, No. 139: "Poorly preserved. The tang and part of the butt are missing. The blade is a pointed oval in cross-section and the edges are bevelled."

41 See E.C.R. Armstrong, "Some Irish Bronze Age Finds," *P.R.I.A.*, 36C (1921-24), p. 146; Fig. 8:1.

42 Joyce, vol. II, p. 392.

43 See National Museum, *Archaeological Acquisitions in the year 1969*, p. 28.

44 Joyce, vol. II, p. 207.

45 Sir William Perry, quoted in *J.R.S.A.I.*, vol. 2 (5th series), vol. XXII consec. series (1892), p. 356.

46 Joyce, vol. II, p. 208.

47   *J.R.S.A.I.* (1892), pp. 356-57.

48   There have been recent comments that this term is not "people-friendly" and that it should be replaced. After all, without the co-operation of the local populace little progress will be made in preserving the flora and fauna.

49   What is interesting about this portal tomb is that it is incorporated in a small stone enclosure, thus confirming the view expressed earlier at Kilclooney that at least some dolmens did not originally stand in splendid isolation as we see them now but were enclosed in a cairn of earth and stones, or were, at least, surrounded by an arrangement of stones.

50   Is Croaghkinny, a hill in the north of Litterilly, a further reference to Cainnech (? Colmcille) – *Cruach Cainnigh?*

51   Joyce, vol. III, p. 463.

52   *Dr. Pococke's Irish Tour,* pp. 67-68. The stone stands on the land of Frank McNelis of Tullymore, who is taking good care that no harm comes to it.

53   He continues: "The four tun amounting at that rate to forty-eight pounds sterling; the expenses of making a box 10/-; £7 for a boat, nets and men in a year; six shillings for each tierce and 4s 6d for salt to cure tierce of salmon and twopence per tierce for salting and packing; so that the charge on the aforesaid tun of salmon as near as I can learn is £20 6s 0d and there remains a profit to the tenant this year £27 14s 0d. And as Mr. Cunyngham's land is on one side of the river and Mr. Murray's land on the other side, the fishing is half to Mr. Murray and half to Mr. Cunyngham so that half the said profit this year is £13 12 0d."

54   Now in the Public Record Office, Belfast, ref. No. D2860/25/3: reprinted in the *D.A.* (1977), pp. 24-25.

55   *The Donegal Highlands,* pp. 144-45.

56   p. 21.

57   *Fishing in Ireland,* p. 100-1.

XII

ARDARA: PART 1

BEFORE ENTERING THE village of Ardara we will go over the Glenties road a few hundred yards to where there is a height with an earthen enclosure on it and from which Ardara derives its name – *Ard an Rátha*: the height of the earthen enclosure or ringfort. Up behind the national school, the site consists of a platform, 3.5 m. in height, surrounded by a low earthen bank. The sides of the platform are steep, dropping to a flat-bottomed ditch from 2.8 m. to 5.5 m. in width. There is an outer bank which survives up to .7 m. in height.[1] There is a number of gaps on the sides of the platform and inner bank but these appear to be of recent origin. The internal diameter of the ringfort is 27.7 m. north-south and 28.2 m. east-west.

Ringforts are so called because they are generally circular – though they can be penannular enclosures. They usually have an inner bank and an outer ditch and an entrance on to a fairly level internal area which is usually higher than the surrounding field level.[2] Ringforts have been given various titles – e.g. Danish forts – over the years, and many of us have been uncer-

Ardara Fort

tain of their original use. They are, in fact, single-family defended farm settlements of the early Christian period from approximately 500 A.D to 1000 A.D.[3] The ringforts which have been radiocarbon dated seem mainly to lie between the 4th and 8th centuries A.D.[4] Some ringforts continued in use up until the 17th century.[5]

In recent years much emphasis has been placed on making us understand that these structures were just the homesteads of one family and were not strong forts. However, they did have a defensive role too – some ringforts are surrounded by up to three banks. In a recent study of 134 ringforts at the royal site of Cruachain in Connacht it was found that 60% or less of the area of a ringfort was available for habitation.[6] The study concluded that "considerations other than the provision of occupation space were at work in the design of ringforts, with a minimum of 40% of the construction normally being given over to the structures of outer ditches and banks",[7] and that among these considerations were the constraints imposed by defence and prestige.

Yet, that was at a royal residence; ringforts in other areas, such as here, might not have been so impressive. What this area, like many others, probably did have in common with Cruachain was that there was originally a very large number of ringforts here. The Ordnance Survey map of 1847-50 shows the remains of eight enclosures in the general Gortnacart–Monargan area of Ardara – along the Owentocker river valley, just below this eminence. It is thought that when ringforts were in use they were visible from one to the other and it is likely that this was the case in this area as well. In regions where there was plenty of stone available – such as at Lackagh and Dunmore Head, near Portnoo – there was built a stone wall rather than an earthen bank and the structure became a cashel. It has already been suggested that the numerous enclosures in the Portnoo–Narin area were visible from Dunmore Head – the "grand signal-station".

Frank Mitchell in his wonderful book *Reading the Irish Landscape* gives us his view of the role of the *rath* or ringfort: "Raths are sometimes called ring-forts, but they are not forts, if we mean by that a strong-point capable of resisting siege for some time. Raths almost never have a well (for supplying water) and the bank and ditch would have offered little difficulty to a determined attack. But they could offer short term protection to livestock, and they were intervisible. I picture that all the raths of a vicinity would belong to the same clan. If cattle-raiders from other groups came into the locality, each clansman would drive his stock into his own rath, and then hurry off to assist in the defence of whatever rath was first attacked, and if possible drive off the raiders. Modern strategists would call it defence in depth; it was almost inevitable that the first rath to be attacked would be pillaged, but then the counter-attack would come and it would have a good chance of success."[8] It is possible that this *rath* overlooking Ardara was, among other things, the lookout point and signal station for the occupants of the river valley below, or possibly cattle and other stock were brought up from the other enclosures along the valley to this higher point when danger threatened.

Six miles east of Ardara is Glenties village, and though the temptation is great to "take a run over" – especially because of the presence in it of St. Connell's church and St. Connell's museum and heritage centre (opened in 1986, situated on the Ardara approach to the village, run by a very enthusiastic voluntary committee, open from June to September each year, and not to be missed), the annual Patrick MacGill Summer School held in August each year and the presence in the Roman Catholic church in nearby Edininfagh of a stained-glass representation of St. Connell – I have resisted the temptation because the area is well served by a book entitled *Glenties and Inniskeel* published in 1986 by Liam Briody.

Kilraine, between Glenties and Ardara, boasts a very large ringfort – internal diameter 37 m. – and there is a cross slab which is finely decorated on one side – though becoming quite weather-beaten – in the old graveyard here. Kilraine (*Cill Rignach*) is associated with the female St. Rignach. In Ó Riain's *Corpus* she is given a Cenél Maine pedigree and is said to have been venerated at Kilrainy townland and parish on the bounds of counties Kildare and Meath (*"Rignach i Cill Rignaige i Fothartaib Airbrech"*) and at Templerainy townland in the parish of Kilbride near Arklow, Co. Wicklow (*"Rignach i Cill Rignaige i nUib Enechglais"*). I would not care to surmise how her cult came to this area. One presumes that it was introduced with that of her "sister" saint, St. Cróine (Crón), celebrated at *Teampall Cróine*, near Dungloe – *"Cumman & Cron & Rignach tri ingena Aeda"* (Cenél Maine pedigree). St. Crón (Cróine) was venerated at Urglin townland and parish, Co. Carlow (*"Irchuilenn, in Fotharta Fea"*).

Closer to Ardara, just a few metres from the roadside in a field between the homes of Pat and Joe Lough, are the bare remains of a court tomb,[9] the only one in the Ardara area apart from the one at Kilclooney already described. Also here in Doochill [*dubh*: black; *coill*: a wood; *Dubhchoill*: the black or dark wood], on the other side of the Owentocker, just where the river forks, is a large mound on a hill which is an old burial ground thought to have been used for unbaptised children at one stage. There is also a mass-rock in the Doochill area. We have already noted that the great 17th century scribe Cú Choigriche Ó Cléirigh lived for a time in this locality.

Some earlier travellers have been unstinting in their praise of the approaches to Ardara and the village itself, if not too complimentary about surrounding areas and the work ethic of the Irish. Waddington's *Guide to Donegal* states: "From Glenties the drive to Ardara is along one of the glens. ... The road is a good one, and the country on each side possesses a soft pastoral beauty, which contrasts agreeably with the more mountainous aspects to which we have been accustomed. Ardara – the Hill of the Fort – takes its name from a very conspicuous earthen fort or rath near the town. It is beautifully situated at the head of Loughrosmore Bay, six miles from Glenties. The district is rich in natural attractiveness and historical interest."[10]

A traveller writing in 1887 states: "Ardara (the accent is on the last syllable) where we found ourselves at ten next morning is a very pretty place. At what exact point the district called the Rosses is supposed to end I know not; but after Glenties its peculiarities cease. It becomes fertile and green. Its desolation changes into cultivation, not of a very high type – first-class farming is unknown in Ireland, where if Nature does little, man does less. A patch of oats, a field of potatoes, a turf ridge for a fence, and a fallen tree or an old ladder balanced on two heaps of stones to serve for a gate, this is what one continually finds. Irish ingenuity uses anything for any purpose, just as it comes to hand; and Irish laziness generally leaves it there. To expect the luxuriant pastures, hay-meadows, harvest-fields, and above all, the neatly-kept hedgerows of England, or the highly-cultivated straths of Scotland, would be idle. Yet there are little oases here and there, and Ardara seemed to be one of them."

She continues: "Ardara – which is very picturesque in itself, and close on the borders of a most picturesque country – would, if it had a first rate hotel, be such a centre of travelling, that it might command its own custom. How many shops Ardara boasts I will not undertake to say. But I can answer for one good baker, of whom we purchased a capital loaf, divided into slices, which the said baker proposed to cut with a *hammy* knife – a pot of marmalade, and a spoon to eat it with, which gleamed like silver, price, one penny. Our driver assured us we should find 'plenty of wather' in the mountain streams, and we had several travelling cups. So thus luxuriously provided against all emergencies, we started afresh; in the best of spirits and the brightest of sunshine."[11]

Our next observer is not too enamoured by the village or its accommodation for travellers, but does concede to the scenic beauty of the surrounding area. From 1864 we read: "Ardara – *Hotel*: Mullaney's, – a stupid little town, with nothing whatever of interest save its extremely pretty situation, at the

Ardara

wooded base of steeply escarped hills. A pedestrian who is not particular about his accommodation will find it a very good starting point from whence to explore the grand beauties of the coast round by Loughros, Tormore, and Glen. From the peculiarity of the situation of Ardara all the roads that lead out of it ... are carried through so many gaps in the hills, the finest of them being that which goes through the pass of Glengesh, one of the wildest and steepest glens in the district."[12]

We finish extolling the beauty of this region with a later excerpt, from 1948, which echoes sentiments which were expressed earlier about the landscape here: "Loughros Bay at whose sandy head Ardara stands, has another attractive coast-line, dominated by the lumpy heights of the Slievetooies to the south. After the grandeurs of the North-west you will probably be tempted to dawdle a little hereabouts, for the country round the town has a suavity that you have not experienced for some time; there is something almost English in the softness of the river valleys and the sweetness of the meadows, with their fine full hedgerows and abundant trees."[13]

I seem to be portraying Ardara as having been a kind of paradise, especially in the last century; it was not. But though times were hard this did not prevent the locals from enjoying life and in some cases living to a ripe old age. From 1892 we read an interesting account of the lifestyle and living conditions of one old man: "When in Ardara, two years ago, I met a very active old man who showed me the earthen fort, or rath, from which the town is named. He was able to get over the ditches as nimbly as I could, and seemed to be possessed of an excellent constitution. In answer to my inquiries, he informed me his name was John Breslin, that he was a linen weaver by trade, and had worked for 60 years on the same loom, and was then 86 years old. The loom itself bore evidence of the truth of his statement, as the seat was almost worn through by friction, and brightly polished from constant use. His dwelling, which I visited, consisted of one apartment, about 16 feet by 12; his loom and bed occupied one side of it, and opposite was the door and window; underneath the latter was a table, and two chairs, the total remaining furniture of the house. A hole in the roof without any chimney brace allowed an exit for the smoke. He never had toothache or any other ache, he never lost a tooth, and bids fair to reach the hundred. He is married to his second wife, a woman 20 years his junior, has no family, is still living as I write (May, 1892), and has now attained 88 years. He writes to London and Dublin for orders for his towels, and seems to have formed a connexion who buys all he produces. I attribute this man's good health and entire freedom from pain and ache to his good consitution, his active life, and to the conditions under which he lives. His house is situated on very high ground, underneath the old Rath, and the large opening in the unceiled roof ventilates the place so perfectly that he breathes a perfectly pure atmosphere, both day and night. The house is about three miles distant from the ocean."[14]

This man had a great reputation as a linen weaver, and was locally known as "John the Towel". After his death his house became an outhouse belonging to the late Patrick Brennan of the Hillhead, and stood adjacent to his dwelling – where Joseph Brennan and his family now live.

As we begin our descent of the steep hill which forms the first part of Ardara village we have the Diamond visible down below; behind that is the green hump of Drumbarron,[15] and the concave-shaped, peaked mountain on the skyline is "The Cuntaman" [*Ceann na mBeann; ceann*: a head; *beann*: the genitive plural of *binn*, a mountain peak – the apex of the peaks]; to the naked eye the tip of this mountain is the highest point of the large mountain range which dominates Ardara from the south.

As we descend the hill we are reminded again of Inishkeel island and its legendary saint, Conall, because on our right is St. Connall's, a Church of Ireland building which dates from 1833. An earlier church had stood here, on a site given by George Nesbitt of Woodhill, and was consecrated on 11 June 1820. The present church consists of a harled three-bay hall with bellcote and porch and a short stone chancel which was added in 1908.[16] It cost £600 to build this church in 1833, and the money was gifted by the late Board of First Fruits.[17]

Just below, again on our right, is the Methodist church, built in 1832. A writer in that year states: "With Mr. Armstrong, the missionary, I waited on Major Nesbitt of Woodhill, to obtain from him a grant of ground on which to erect a Wesleyan Church. This gentleman, bearing testimony to the good effect of our society, most graciously assented to our request."[18] Before this church was built the Wesleyan Methodists had assembled in a schoolhouse on the Back Road in Ardara. This building served as a school during the day and as a church from 1813 until the new church was built in 1832. Matthew Stewart was the first to preach Wesleyanism in Ardara. In 1786 he came under the influence of John Wesley, while serving as a dragoon in the town of Athlone. Shortly afterwards he received the following letter from Wesley: "Go to that part of the country, the Barony of Boylagh and see what you can do. When you have spent the enclosed £5 and are in need of more, apply to your affectionate friend, John Wesley."

Arriving in Ardara some time later, Mr. Stewart put up at the local inn. A stranger in those days aroused interest, not least amongst the local clergy. When they found out that he was neither a commercial traveller nor a revenue man but a Methodist, whose business it was to preach the gospel, they told him that they were quite capable of looking after their respective flocks and that he was not wanted.

Undaunted, and the following day being a fair, Mr. Stewart took his stand on the Diamond and preached. Opposition was offered but two leading townsmen arranged themselves on the preacher's side and stood by him. He was taken home by them that day and he continued preaching in the area for some time, as well as starting up the classes for which Methodism became so well known.

You will have noted that the sites on which both churches here on the Front Street were erected were granted by members of the Nesbitt family. This is appropriate – it was under the patronage of the Nesbitt family, who first came to Woodhill in 1669, that the village grew. Prior to their coming the settlement here probably consisted of a few huts at the river-crossing, with possibly other dwellings situated along the river-bank to the west.

We know not how many centuries have passed since the beginnings of the town of Ardara took shape by the ford, but early in its existence it made claim to the dignity of age by appropriating the ancient name of the rath-crowned hill sheltering it to the north-east. The names *Ardtragh al' Ardra* and *Ardrae* appear in 1642, but these could be considered fairly recent references relative to the probable age of the initial settlement. History is silent on its early days and tradition has preserved but a few misty glimpses. The *seanchaí* (oral storyteller, from *sean*: old, ancient), who is seldom worried by chronology, paints a picture of those rough and ready times when unpopular travellers were subjected to a sound ducking in the pool below the ford. He shows us two or three little groups of cabins along the far[19] bank of the river, a field of waving corn on the site of the present Diamond, and an abbey standing in the Murlinn field.[20]

The original crossing site of the river may not, of course, have been where the present bridge stands. There are indications that the earlier Ardara may have been further down along the river – a tradition existed of habitation right on the water's edge, extending from behind the Nesbitt Arms Hotel and Frankie Brennan's – a place where people lived in recent memory, known to the inhabitants as Monte Carlo – to down below John Gallagher's, where there were a lot of houses earlier in this century.[21] Since people generally travelled close to the coast in ancient times the original track may have been closer to the sea and the settlement may then have gradually extended up along the idyllic valley of the Owentocker [appropriately named, from *abhainn*: a river; *socair*:[22] even, level, calm, tranquil; *Abhainn tSocair*: the quietly flowing river].

When Joshua set up twelve stones as a memorial of crossing the river Jordan it was possibly an early example of marking a fording place. In pre-historic ages most of the rivers were wider and shallower. They, therefore, lent themselves to fording. Roman fords were submerged portions of the constructed road, even more strongly constituted to resist the erosive effect of the water. In the early days of civilisation and commerce the river crossing was often a recognised place of exchange and trade. A settlement at the bridge-head naturally followed and the sighting of many of the world's mercantile centres points obviously to such an origin. History has been made on bridges; a bridge by virtue of its position is a natural rendezvous. Travellers, traders, warriors, wayfarers, envoys, pilgrims, lovers, dreamers and idlers – all meet at the bridge. Careers, histories, romances may start there; lives may end there. Violent death has come on the bridge in more ways than one – in earlier times fords were a recognised place for combat and some bridges have developed a special reputation for suicide attempts.[23]

Sally McHugh of the Front Street, who is a fount of information and who exchanged many items of interest with the late Packy McGrath, her erstwhile and very knowledgeable neighbour, assures me that the first bridge was built in Ardara in 1723, and repaired in 1929-30. We know there was a bridge in Ardara in 1752 because Dr. Pococke states: "We then went over the Ardragh on a bridge and soon had Locrasbeg bay to the west."[24]

We have arrived down at the bridge rather sooner than I had anticipated, via our reference to the village being developed under the ownership of the Nesbitt family. We will return later to the Front Street and the Back Road (above that is Ardconnell), but for now we will discuss another subject origi-nally associated with the Nesbitts – the fair day in Ardara. On the 16 May 1760, letters patent were granted to George Nesbitt, of Woodhill, authorising him to hold four yearly fairs – on 15 May, 1 August, 1 November and 22 December – and a weekly market (every Tuesday) "in or at the town of Ardara, and to have and receive all the usual customs, tolls, etc."[25] A Court of Pye Powder was to be held during the said fairs and markets – this court was set up to administer justice for all injuries done during the fair, but ex-tended no farther, and was framed to promote and protect the trade of the place where the fair was held "by deciding disputes as speedily as dust can fall from the feet, or before the litigating parties could have time to wipe the dust off their feet".[26]

It was only with the ending of the great fair at Magheramore in the mid-1800s that the fairs at Ardara began to prosper, and the main autumn fair was brought forward from 1 November to 1 October and thereafter referred to as the "Fair of Magheramore". That this change had not taken place by

1837 we can deduce from this extract from that year: "The village consists of 85 houses; it has a constabulary police station, and has a fair on the 1st November; petty sessions are held at irregular intervals."[27] That the numbers of houses and population of the village was increasing rapidly in these pre-Famine years we can glean from the following observations made in 1844-45: "Houses 102. Population in 1831: 456, 1841: 603. The church (the Church of Ireland) has an attendance of 300: the Roman Catholic chapel is the sole care of one officiate, and has an attendance of 1,000: a school-house[28] used as a Wesleyan place of worship, is attended by 40."[29] We are told that in 1840 "the National Board salaried a school at Ardara with £10, and one at Cronabais with £2; and granted £67 10s towards the building and fitting up of a girl's school at Ardara."[30]

Staying with this girls' school for a minute, but going back to our theme of the fair day, we read of the disruption caused in the school by a fair day in Ardara in 1855 – much to the annoyance of the schools' inspector:

"The day of my inspection happened, unfortunately, to have been the fair day of Ardara (1st August) and the attendance was in consequence, nearly fifty per cent below the average of the year: on rolls 29 + 36: present 9 + 10."[31]

During the last century and for most of this century the fair at Ardara played a large part in the social life of the people. Unfortunately over the last twenty years or so the fair has become a thing of the past, although a traditional-style "fair" has now been revived and is held around the first weekend in July each year.

The official Fair Green was located at the Hillhead, but animals were also displayed throughout the village and a lot of sideshow action took place on the Diamond. Older Ardara people will remember various characters performing on the Diamond on fair days – singers, people preaching the gospel, con-men, etc, etc. Joseph Campbell, in his book *Mearing Stones*, a wonderful book which I will refer to frequently, gives a vivid description of a wandering singer performing on the Diamond *circa* 1909: "A ballad-singer has come into Ardara. It is late afternoon. He stands in the middle of the Diamond – a sunburnt, dusty figure, a typical Ishmael and stroller of the roads. The women have come to their doors to hear him, and a benchful of police, for lack of something better to do, are laughing at him from the barrack front. The ballad he is singing is about Bonaparte and the Poor Old Woman. ... He howls out the verses in disjointed, unmusical bursts. He acts with head and arms, and at places where he has worked up to a particular frenzy he takes a run and gives a buck-jump in the air, blissfully unconscious, I suppose, that he is imitating the manner in which the *ballistea*, or ancient dancing-songs, were sung by the Romans. At the end of each verse he breaks into a curious chanted refrain ... and then there are more sidlings and buck-jumps. Some of the women throw him money, which he acknowledges by lifting his hat grandiosely. Others of them pass remarks, quite the reverse of complimentary, about his voice and ragged appearance ... 'Look at him with the seat out of his trousers, and he lepping like a good one,' says one woman. Another woman comes out of a shop with a crying child in her arms, and shouts at him: 'Will you go away, then? You're wakening the childer.' The ducks quack, the dogs howl, the poor ballad-singer roars louder than ever. I listen for a while, amused and interested. Then I get tired of it and pass on toward Brackey Bridge."[32]

A few years earlier, in 1904, we get a view of a fair day where raising funds for the newly-erected Catholic church was high on the agenda:

"You really should have been present at the fair held on the second[33] and third days of August, 1904, as then, in addition to the monster crowds, and their usual inbringings, every person of real importance was there, some of them presiding at stalls for the sale of the best that loving fingers could produce to aid in paying off the debt incurred in building the imposing Catholic Church in which they worship. Possibly the first thing to strike you would be the miscellaneous gathering of every possible kind of commodity, but, sooner or later, you must be impressed with the fact that the majority of the men are fine, strapping fellows, with an air of I-don't-care-for-anybody in their attitudes, movements, speech, and twinkling eyes. It might be, of course, that your attention would first be attracted by the charms of pretty feminine faces. There will be quite a gathering of ladies, whose charms do not end with their face. The proud poise of their heads, their suppleness of form, and the flowing lines of their figures enable them to wear with matchless grace the poorest garment, and with their luminous, grey eyes, shaded by long dark lashes, and their modesty, they form perfect pictures."[34]

One of the shops doing business on that August day in Ardara in 1904 had been opened just a few months earlier. Con Kennedy and Etta Connolly had the distinction of being the first couple to be married in the new Catholic church, in late 1903, and they opened a general drapery and boots business premises on the fair day, 2 March 1904. Their total taking from the first day's trading was 5s 7d (five shillings and seven pence).[35] The two eldest children of their marriage, Rev. Dean John Kennedy (now retired) and Mick Kennedy, born in 1904 and 1905 respectively, are both alive and well. Mick Kennedy, who lives with his wife Margaret on the Front Street, is the grand old man of the Ardara woollen and tweed industry. Mick assumed control of his father's business in 1928 and built it into a household name. As you descend the hill into Ardara village the factory-shop of Kennedy of Ardara is on your left.

Ardara, long known as the Capital of the Donegal Highlands, is especially noted for its tweed and woollen industries and there are many prominent family firms apart from Kennedy's. Further down the hill, again on the left, we have the fine-fronted shop of Cornelius Bonner and Son Ltd.[36] and further down again, on the left, at the site of the old police barracks, we have John Joe Campbell's shop. Across from John Joe's we have Willie McNelis's. Willie has been weaving tweed on his loom within the actual shop over the years and it has given many visitors great pleasure to see tweed being produced on the premises. Across the bridge and over the other side of Ardara is the late Colm Heron's shop – Colm died in recent years. This family business was started by Colm's late father, Joseph Heron, affectionately known as "Big Joe". In the 1930s "Big Joe" became interested in the manufacture of Donegal hand woven tweeds, and in the next decade he built his own factory and employed approximately twenty-five spinners and twenty-one hand weavers. In 1946 he started the handknit industry, which is being carried on in the present day by Colm's wife.[37] At the west end of Ardara village, on our right, we have Triona Design, again dealing in tweeds, and out the Killybegs road we have the formidable business of John Molloy (Ardara) Ltd., with their impressive factory-shop located along the road. The Molloy family have been involved in the tweed industry since the first years of this century. Near by is Ardara knitwear company, Ardara Aran, run by Michael Mac Geehan. Further up the Killybegs road, at Cashel, is the factory shop of *Garn Teoranta*.

Back in Ardara village we must call into the shop run by John McGill. He, too, deals in woollen produce, but the main attraction of his premises over the years has been that he supplies fishermen, both local and visiting, with their fishing licences and tackle. This latter branch of business he took upon himself after the death of "The Saddler" (Patrick Gildea) who had supplied fishermen for many decades. You can leave John's shop with a full array of fishing tackle and woollen socks to keep your feet warm on the riverside. John still runs the business, and his son Bosco is also involved.

Because of Ardara's traditionally premier role in the production of tweed in Donegal we will have a brief look at the history of woollens in general and then in this area in particular. In this field I am a novice, so I have borrowed largely from my father's writings.[38] For the scholar in this field I would recommend Judith Hoad's excellent book, *This is Donegal Tweed*, published in 1987.

Spinning and weaving are as old as civilisation; ancient Irish literature contains many references to fancy cloaks and coloured garments. The art of dyeing has been known from early times – for example, you will remember the numerous shells of the small, white dog-whelk [*Mucella (Purpura) lapillus l*][39] which we discussed earlier at Dooey and which were used to produce a purple dye. Earlier in this century a hoard of bronze objects of the Bronze Age was found at Airthear Maige, Co. Antrim.[40] The hoard was wrapped in a woollen cloak which had been preserved from total destruction by the antiseptic action of the bog. The design was herring-bone, the warp white and the weft dark-coloured, and the whole presenting an appearance hardly different from the herring-bone pattern of the present day.

In later times, in the middle ages, the popularity of Irish cloth on the Continent caused considerable unease to the woollen trade in England. By selling at lower prices cloth of a superior quality the Irish had already captured the principal markets of western Europe. By an act passed in October of 1668 the British woollen manufacturers appeared to have won the day, because this act forbade the Irish to send out any woollen goods to any place except England, from which they were virtually excluded by prohibitive tariffs. Sheep rearing was by then one of the chief agricultural pursuits – in 1672 it was estimated that there were four million sheep in Ireland.[41] Since export was prohibited, the disposal of a large quantity of wool presented a difficulty; the result was that the smuggling of Irish wool to the Continent became rife. Wool smuggling kept the woollen industry alive in Ireland, for without it the Irish farmer would have turned away from rearing sheep, and the whole industry would have died a certain death. But the smuggler preserved its existence for almost a hundred years, and when Free Trade permitted a resumption of work there was a plentiful supply of wool in the country.

The older generations had many tales of adventures associated with the illegal trafficking of wool. A small creek called Pollaniska [*poll*: a deep hole; *uisce*: water; presumably a spot where there was a good depth of water that allowed boats in] on the west coast of Slievetooey figures prominently in these stories. French wine was one of the items exchanged in payment for wool. My father, writing in 1970, states: "The nooks in which kegs of wine were placed and the flags on which rolls of tobacco were laid are still known to residents of neighbouring townlands."[42] Men carried these goods in creels on their backs to Ardara, Killybegs and even to Donegal town.

Nevertheless, during the time of the trade restrictions it appears that the Irish lost the art of making the finer materials and had forgotten also the method of dyeing. England with her modern machinery could sell woollens in Ireland at a price too low for the Irish to compete and though the Irish woollen industry struggled on, its heyday had passed and it existed only as the ghost of its former greatness.[43] By the beginning of the 19th century the woollen industry in Ireland had been reduced principally to a domestic industry carried on to provide the immediate wants of the peasantry, a situation which did not encourage any large-scale development. At this time the tweed was rough in design and plain in colour, as the local workers were uneducated in the use of the different vegetable dyes.

In about 1870[44] Neil McNelis started business in Ardara as a grocer and hotel[45] keeper. Foreseeing the potential of the homespun industry, he set out to secure markets and met with a fair amount of success. Institutions were his biggest purchasers; his principal difficulty was the lack of variety in the material he had to offer. The bulk of the production was white with an occasional silver grey, made by mixing black sheep's wool with white. With the exception of indigo, used solely for home wear, it would seem that the art of dyeing had been completely lost. The fact that "bawneen" – from the Gaelic word *bán*: white – is the only Gaelic word used in Donegal to designate homespun would indicate that our cloth had for centuries been made from virgin wool.

The art of dyeing was re-introduced to this area through the efforts of a most philanthropic lady, Mrs. Ernest Hart, whose husband was at one time president of the British Medical Association. In 1884 Dr. Hart and his wife came to Donegal to investigate conditions in the poverty-stricken congested areas. The potential of spinning and weaving as a livelihood for these poor people attracted their attention. They were convinced that development of cottage industries was the way forward and as a result of their endeavours the Donegal Industries Fund was set up.[46]

NEIL   McNELIS

Hand-Spun and Hand-Woven Tweed
Manufacturer

COTTAGE INDUSTRY | All Tweeds Made From
ARDARA, Co. DONEGAL.   Pure Native Wool

A reminder of a pivotal figure in the Ardara tweed revival

They came to the conclusion that if Donegal homespun had the colouring of Harris Tweed it would readily become a marketable commodity, and they selected a local man[47] to go to Harris to study the methods of dyeing in use there. The Gillespie Brothers of Newtownards, Co. Down, were employed by Messrs. Kennedy of Glenties to make looms which they auctioned outside the Nesbitt Arms Hotel on fair days and which fetched a price of £7 or £8 without attachments.[48]

Dr. Hart died about this time, but the work was continued by his wife who sacrificed most of her personal fortune in the enterprise. In addition, a British Parliament Select Committee grant of £1,000 to the Donegal Industries Fund in 1887 resulted in the establishment of a warehouse – Donegal House – in Wigmore Street, London W1. It became a centre of attraction for home and foreign visitors and the contacts made proved very useful in later years.

In 1893 an improvement scheme, supported by the Congested Districts Board – which had been set up in 1891 and which included the role of the earlier Industries Fund in its portfolio – was started in the Ardara area. This scheme provided for the inspection of the cloth, the stamping of superior pieces and the erection of a market for the storage and sale of the tweed. It wasn't long before Donegal homespun was attracting attention at international exhibitions and finding a market in many parts of the world. However, at home the market was not yet built and webs of tweed continued to be sold on the street like cattle or sheep on the fair days at Ardara.

The rolls of tweed were brought into Ardara on the day before the fair and inspected to see that they were of a certain required quality before being sold on the following day.[49] These "yarn markets" were a great event, attended by many people and there are numerous references, both photographic[50] and literary, to them. Here is a description from 1899: "If one could take a bird's-eye view of this country, at an early hour in the morning, on the last day of any month, he could not fail to notice the number of persons, single or in groups, men and women, who are moving along these roads from every direction towards Ardara. Each wayfarer carries on his or her back a large and heavy bundle wrapped in a white cloth, and slung in a rope generally made of twisted rushes. Some of these travellers have risen in the middle of the night, and have, perhaps, walked these wild roads for hours under a storm of sleet or snow. When they arrive in Ardara the nature of their business is soon made clear. The white bundles contain each a big roll of homespun cloth, and they are bringing them to the Depot of the Congested Districts Board to be examined by the Inspector.

"The morning after the inspection, the first day of every month, the rolls of cloth are handed back to the owners, and if they have not been stamped, the nature of the faults and the proper remedy for them, which are recorded in the Inspection-book, are pointed out. Patterns of new and saleable designs are also distributed to all who desire them. Then the Fair begins. The rolls of cloth are laid down on the footway, on both sides of the road; a great deal is brought in which was not finished in time for inspection; buyers are present from the neighbouring towns of Donegal, Killybegs, and Glenties, and there are several in Ardara itself. There is the usual bargaining and haggling; and Ardara, thronged with the mountain-folk, becomes for a time a Gaelic-speaking town. In two or three hours everything is disposed of, and generally at good prices; for now that certain defects in workmanship have been overcome, this beautiful and unique fabric, stained with the soft, unfading colours produced by the people from common plants and mosses, is in great demand."[51]

When the Congested Districts Board acquired the Tredennick, formerly the Nesbitt, estate which included the village of Ardara, they set about building proper indoor facilities and a market house known as "The Mart"[52] was erected at Ardara. It was officially opened by Cardinal O'Donnell in 1912. The building fulfilled all the requirements of that visualised by the Board as far back as 1893. It was used for measuring and inspecting, for storage and selling.

The tweed industry continued to go through many ups and downs, especially just before World War I because of the importations into the country of large quantities of machine-spun yarns, though the war itself, from 1914-18, gave a temporary but very lucrative boost to the local trade. This boom ended with a crash in the early days of June 1922. In the previous twelve months approximately £70,000 was paid to cottage producers for tweed sold in the Ardara Mart alone; in addition large quantities were being exported by McNelis & Company, Molloy & Company, etc. However, the money earned had been spent quickly and after 1922 many families found themselves worse off than they had been.

This situation remained more or less unchanged until the second year of World War II when the scarcity of clothing materials brought about a resumption of work on an unprecedented scale. Unfortunately the industry dwindled very quickly after the war and there was a complete closedown in December 1947.[53] Weaving was resumed in the "Mart" in February of the following year. In more recent years the tweed and homespun industry has continued to have its ups and downs, but the presence of so many far-seeing people in the industry in Ardara at the present time bodes very well for the future of this traditional Donegal industry.

As we leave the subject of tweed and weaving I would mention that whereas women have traditionally been associated with the carding and spinning of wool, the actual weaving is seen as the domain of the male. It was not always so and weaving was not always held in such high regard as a trade! The early *Annals of Clonmacnoise* remark of a man named John that he "was the sonne of a woman that could weave, which of all trades is of greatest reproach amongst the Irishrye, especially the sons and husbands of such trades-women, and therefore Shane More was nicknamed the weaving-woman's sonne."[54]

We have earlier had reference to "Mullaney's Hotel" and to the fact that Neil McNelis, one of the pioneers of the tweed revival in Ardara, was a hotel-keeper. Their premises were one and the same – the present-day Nesbitt Arms Hotel. It is ironic that for all the power which the Nesbitt family held in this area for generations, the only structure left which bears their name was never inhabited by any of the family. How it got its name is said to be thus: the owner of the building on this site, before it was purchased by the late Neil McNelis in about 1870, was said to have been Tom Molloney. Originally the site held three or four small low houses. Molloney built up the two-windowed little house on the side of the present hotel nearest Sharpe's (formerly F.X. Cannon's) to a higher level, but did not then roof it. When Major Nesbitt enquired why he had not completed the building, Molloney replied that he had gone as far as his means permitted him, adding that he would complete the building as soon as he had the money. Major Nesbitt is said to have replied that he would give him the finance to complete the building if he named the hotel "The Nesbitt Arms Hotel" after his family, who had long and worthy connections with the area. Mr. Molloney was delighted to agree.

This story has been given to us by local tradition and I'd say it is factual enough, though the original owner may have been Charlie Molloney and not Tom. We can prove an association between Tom Molloney and Major Nesbitt at the end of 1836 because the *Ballyshannon Herald* newspaper of 6 January 1837 tells us that at Donegal Quarter Sessions "Thomas Malony, Ardara (Reformer) claimed a lease by Mr. Nesbitt and was registered[55] (as a voter)." The same newspaper[56] tells us that a spirit licence[57] was granted to Charles Molloney, of Ardara, at Donegal Quarter Sessions on 28 December 1838. Less than ten years later the *Ballyshannon Herald* of 18 June 1847 informs us of the death of Charles Molloney: "On the seventh instant, Mr. Charles Molloney, innkeeper, in the 34th year of his life, died." So it would appear that Charles Molloney, who died in 1847, was the owner of the inn which became the Nesbitt Arms Hotel prior to Major Nesbitt's death in 1845, and it is likely that Tom Molloney was a brother of Charles' and succeeded him. *Griffith's Valuations* of 1857 confirm Tom Molloney as the then occupant of the site of the present hotel.

With that safely established now is as good a time as any to take a jaunt out the Wood Road to discuss the history of the Nesbitt family. We will then return to the Nesbitt Arms Hotel and continue our tour of the village.

Notes

1   *A.S.D.*, p. 155.
2   Prof. Michael Herity, *J.R.S.A.I.*, vol. 117 (1987), p. 125.
3   *A.S.D.*, p. 155.
4   Mitchell, *Reading the Irish Landscape*, p. 154.
5   Ibid.
6   Prof. Michael Herity, op. cit., pp. 125-41.
7   Ibid.
8   pp. 156-57.
9   At the north-east end are four stones representing the inner arc of a court. Running west from this are the remains of a gallery 5.5m. long, divided by ill-matched jambs into two chambers. The structure is incorporated in an irregular mound.
10   p. 47.
11   Dinah Mary Craik, *An Unknown Country*, pp. 159-60.
12   John Murray, *Handbook for Travellers in Ireland*, p. 93.
13   Michael Floyd, *The Face of Ireland*, p. 81.
14   Seaton F. Milligan, "Some Recent Cases of Remarkable Longevity," *J.R.S.A.I.*, vol. 2 (5th series), (1892), p. 234. When the writer was in Ardara in 1890 there was a much older man living in the area; he refers to him: "A man named Owen Byrne of Meenarylagh, three miles distant from Ardara, county Donegal, died on 8th April, 1892, at the reputed age of 105 years. My informant, a merchant residing in Ardara, gave me the following particulars: He said – 'I knew Owen, and attended his funeral; he was known to be the oldest man in the county, and used to tell stories of the old times. My father who is living, aged 92 years, was acquainted all his life with deceased, and stated, in support of his age, that when he was a growing boy, Owen was a young man courting the girls. He was a farmer, had his teeth up to the last, could see fairly well, and smoked and took a little stimulant all his life. He lived with his grandchildren, one of whom is 40 and another 42 years of age, his own children being dead.'"
15   Drumbarron: a variation of *Drumbaragh* [*Druim berrthach*: shorn or bare ridge; *bearradh*: shaving; *bearrthadh*: shaved] (Joyce, vol. III, p. 316).
16   Alistair Rowan, *Buildings of North-West Ulster*, p. 109.

17 *The Parliamentary Gazetter of Ireland* (1846), vol. I, p. 49.

18 This and the remainder on Methodism comes from a small publication, *Methodism in Ardara*, written by Oliver Lochart in 1982 to celebrate the 150th anniversary of the building of the church; Ollie is one of our most knowledgeable local historians.

19 The Drumbarron side.

20 *H.P.A.*, p. 1.

21 However, the maps accompanying *Griffith's Valuations* of 1857 show few small houses down along the river. They may only have been built in the half century after that.

22 *Socair* can mean level open land [*socair:* easy, in opposition to *docair:* difficult]; stand on the bridge in Ardara and look upriver.

23 F.W. Robins, *The Story of the Bridge*, foreword by Michael Floyd.

24 *Dr. Pococke's Irish Tour*, p. 68.

25 Copied from the Deed of Conveyance of Ardara Town Property Trust (1918), and reproduced in the *D.A.* (1960), p. 230. I will refer late, in the chapter on the Nesbitts, to a story about these fair day customs (taxes) and tolls.

26 Deed of Conveyance of Ardara Town Property Trust, 1918.

27 Samuel Lewis, *A Topographical Dictionary of Ireland*, vol. 1, p. 42.

28 In 1834 we are told that the Wesleyan Sunday School was attended by 29 boys and 38 girls; and 4 daily schools - one of which was aided with £24 from the Wesleyan Missionary Society, and another with £11 1s 6d from Robinson's Fund - had on their books 229 boys and 99 girls.

29 *The Parliamentary Gazetter of Ireland* (1846), vol. I, p. 49.

30 Ibid.

31 *D.A.* (1956), p. 103.

32 *Mearing Stones*, pp. 22-23.

33 1 August must have fallen on a Sunday.

34 Geen, *Fishing in Ireland*, pp. 107-8.

35 *Dearcadh* - Ardara parish magazine (1989).

36 Who is one of the area's two biggest employers, the other being John Molloy (Ardara) Ltd. Their contribution to the local economy should not be underestimated.

37 *Dearcadh* (1985), p. 13.

38 "The Irish Wollen Industry, from Earliest Times to Donegal Homespun," *D.A.* (1949), pp. 168-77; *H.P.A.*, pp. 80-86. I would also recommend Pádraig S. Mac a'Ghioll's article in *Dearcadh* (1990), pp. 30-32. The reports of the Congested Districts Board and of the Gaeltacht Commission are other valuable sources of information.

39 *J.R.S.A.I.*, vol. 91, part 1 (1961), p. 61.

40 *D.A.*, vol. 1, no. 3 (1949), p. 168.

41 Ibid. p. 172.

42 *H.P.A.*, p. 82.

43 *D.A.*, op. cit., p. 173.

44 *H.P.A.*, p. 82.
45 The Nesbitt Arms.
46 Pádraig S. Mac a'Ghoill, *Dearcadh* (1990), p. 31.
47 Dan Tighe, the Glen, Glenties.
48 *Dearcadh* (1990), p. 31.
49 Ardara on the 1st of each month and Carrick on the 14th were the big yarn markets.
50 See especially the photographs of W.L. Micks of the Congested Districts Board, now in the National Museum.
51 Stephen Gwynn, *Highways and Byways in Donegal and Antrim,* pp. 79-80.
52 This is the building now occupied by Triona Design.
53 The "unprecedented scale" of work and the final closedown are reflected in the amount of wool carded during those years. Because the usual rate of carding of wool by the people in their homes was far outstripped by the demand for tweed the Ardara Parish Council commenced carding operations in the "Mart" on 29 March 1943 and continued until 16 May 1946. A government department took over and carried on until Christmas 1947 when it closed down completely and weavers, carders and spinners were all thrown idle. The amount of wool carded over those years was:

Year ending April 1944:	100,879 lbs.
Year ending April 1945:	115,702 lbs.
Year ending April 1946:	117,233 lbs.
Year ending 15 May 1947:	4,282 lbs.

Nowadays the carding of wool can be seen on the Diamond in Ardara during the Traditional Fair, held over the first weekend of July, when there is an annual open-air exhibition of tweed-making – from the raw materials to the finished product. The cards in use for many years have been iron cards, but the earliest cards known were made by mounting flower heads of the teasel plant on a frame provided with a handle. Teasel is a plant something like a thistle. St. Blaise is regarded as the patron of wool carders; it is said that during his martyrdom his flesh was systematically torn by combs used by wool carders.
54 Quoted in Joyce, vol. II, p. 118.
55 Applying to register as voters in the *Ballyshannon Herald* of 31 March 1837 were Francis McAneer, Ardara, Innkeeper and John Sheeran, Ardara, Innkeeper.
56 of 4 November 1839.
57 Among others quoted in the *Ballyshannon Herald* of 12 October 1838 as applying for and receiving spirit licences were Patrick Kennedy, Michael Doney and Patrick Shevlin, all of Ardara.

XIII

THE NESBITTS AND WOODHILL HOUSE

For the house of the planter
Is known by the trees.
Austin Clarke.

HE NESBITT RESIDENCE in Ardara was Woodhill House. Leaving the Diamond and Slye's Corner behind we go on to Wood Road. In the mid-1800s the former hotel orchard on the left was owned by John Crumley,[1] and an excise officer named Blakeney Gubbins – whose persecution of poteen-makers, especially the resourceful poteen men of Gortnasillagh, still lingers on in tradition – was living where the Byrne household now reside and where the late Hugh Byrne had his forge.

As we proceed out the Wood Road we note that there were very few dwellings here in the early 1800s – this was all part of the Nesbitt demesne. Where the road to Woodhill and the road to Donegal town bifurcate, the site of the building immediately on your right as you start on to the Woodhill Road, in which the late Johnny Gallagher of the Yellow Banks used to weave tweed, was a gate lodge to the estate. In the big field on the left, belonging to my own family, just across the road from the entrance to the Show Field (the hotel holm) stood the estate's ice-house. The present Wood School was the boys' national school, and further up the road, Wood House, which is my own family home, was the girls' national school – it is marked as such on the 1847-50 Ordnance Survey map. The only other homes out here on the Nesbitt estate, apart from Woodhill House itself, were the house where Paddy Boyle lived, now owned by the Hennigan family, and a little rose-surrounded house at the well, deep in the wood, close to my mother's home, where Eddie Brogan was born. Both Paddy Boyle and Eddie Brogan worked as gardeners on the Nesbitt estate. There was a fresh-water well at both these houses – at Brogan's and at Boyle's – and this is where the townspeople used to get their water. We will refer to this on our way back into Ardara. The only other dwelling on the Nesbitt estate was the second gate lodge on the Donegal town side of the estate, at the bad bend just after you pass Patrick Rourke's house on your way to Donegal town. There is still a gate here on your right; the gate lodge stood beside it and an avenue led over to Woodhill House.

The Nesbitts were first granted land in Ardara on 20 December 1669. They were of Scottish stock; the name Nesbitt is said to have derived from the lands of Nisbet in the shire of Berwick. It is said that in the Civil Wars of the time of Charles I (1625-49), the Nisbets suffered confiscations and death as a result of supporting the royal cause. The first Nisbet we hear of was Philip Nisbet who married sometime before the year 1505. He was succeeded in turn by George, Philip, George and then Alexander. This Alexander Nisbet is said to have been the first of the family to come to Ireland. Alexander had a son named James and it is thought that it was this James Nisbet who was granted land in Ardara in 1669. When the family name changed from Nisbet to Nesbitt is not known, and indeed one cannot even be totally sure of the Scottish ancestry, quoted above, of the Nesbitts.[2]

We first begin to come across references to the Nesbitt name in the first and second quarters of the 17th century in the Inver and Bruckless areas. In a muster roll of the Earl of Annandale's men and arms taken in 1630 the name Andrew Nisbet appears. He was one of only three men who were armed with swords in the whole barony. The Earl of Annandale was an undertaker[3] of 10,000 acres in the barony of Boylagh and Banagh; each undertaker had to show a muster roll of men who could defend the areas which had been confiscated.[4] Andrew Nisbet's name appears again in a 1632 Inquisition as a leaseholder for the quarter-land of Brenter from the Earl of Annandale, and the 1659 census reveals an Andrew Nisbet and a James Nisbet at Brenter. In 1661 a James Nisbet is the parish clerk of Inver and Kilaghtee.

We begin to come across numerous references to the Nesbitt family in other areas of Donegal such as Tullydonnell, near Raphoe, and Greenhills, but we will only concern ourselves here with the Nesbitts of Woodhill, and later on our travels we will refer to the Nesbitts of Kilmacreddon (near Inver) and Bruckless and the Nesbitts of Carricknagore, near Killybegs.

Up until the death of James Murray, the 2nd and last Earl of Annandale, in 1658, it appears that the Nesbitts and other undertakers in Boylagh and Banagh were not landlords but were leaseholders. There was a long legal battle as to who would be heir to the Earl of Annandale and it is likely that fairly soon after his death the Nesbitts purchased their lands from the apparent heirs to the Earl. The Nesbitts of Woodhill do not appear to have been landlords of an extensive estate. In a list of the landowners of Donegal, printed in 1879, at which stage the male line of the Nesbitt family had died out and the Woodhill estate now belonged to the Tredennick family, the total Tredennick estate only amounted to something over 6,000 acres.[5] By comparison the Murray-Stewart estate, which covered most of the Killybegs and present-day Ardara parishes, amounted to over 50,000 acres, while the Conyngham estate, which mostly covered the area north of the Owenea river, consisted of over 122,000 acres. I have borne in mind that the Aighan area of Bruckless and the Loughill area of Loughros Point were no longer part of the estate and that some houses in the village of Ardara had been sold, but these were only small areas which had been lost by 1879. Ardara village was the main bastion of the Nesbitts and they also owned Glenconwell, Kilraine and some townlands in the parishes of Kilcar and Killybegs.

James Nesbitt was given a fee farm grant[6] of Woodhill estate on 20 December 1669. He married Margery, daughter of Andrew Knox, Bishop of Raphoe. There were five sons in the family. The eldest son and heir was the Rev. George Nesbitt. George, who was Rector of Inishkeel from 1696-1742, originally lived at Drumalough, down Loughros Point, and is said to have built Wood House, the house where I was reared, which was part of the Woodhill estate.

A view of Woodhill about 100 years ago (courtesy National Library)

George's eldest son, James, born in about 1700, became the next owner of Woodhill. In 1724 he married a daughter of Colonel John Hamilton of Brownhall, near Ballyshannon. In 1982 an ornamented stone slab came to light on an ivy-covered wall just above the gate of the entrance to the orchard at Woodhill. The slab carries a very well preserved coat of arms of the Nesbitt family and bears the following inscription: "The Lord is a strong towre. The righteous runneth into it and is safe. James Nesbitt Anno Dom 1723." This slab is now standing up against the front wall of Woodhill House.

James was High Sheriff of Co. Donegal in 1771. James's brother, the Rev. Andrew, was Rector of Killybegs from 1739-69. Another brother, Richard, lived at Loughill (Drumalough) on Loughros Point.

In 1760 a blind harper named Arthur O'Neill[7] passed through this area and was entertained by one of the Nesbitts - presumably James of Woodhill, but we cannot be certain - and went with him to a most interesting wedding! He writes: "When at Boylagh, I was invited by a gentleman named Nesbitt, to go with him to a great wedding without my harp, for there were plenty of pipers

The same view in 1991. Though there are more bushes in the
foreground, the wood is almost gone

and fiddlers. There was no expense spared to make it a grand wedding. The gentleman bridegroom's name was M'Gunnigal and the lady's name, O'Donnell. There were as many people present as almost at any fair. All that wished to stay over-night had to sit up, the beds being occupied by scores lying three-na-y'hele [*trí-na-chéile*].

"Mr. Nesbitt and I sat up all night and in the morning he made a remarkable breakfast for the remaining guests. He burned a large quantity of whiskey in a wooden bowl, put a pair of tongs across it when burning, and then he put some canes of sugar-candy on the tongs, which was soon dissolved into the whiskey, and then the party present drank it with bread, for my part I never got a breakfast I liked so well, as at that time I began to be partial to that native cordial. When I left Mr. Nesbitt's, I was almost tired of rambling ... going home I came to Dungannon ... I was then about twenty or twenty-one years of age (being now sixty-seven) and it was in or about the year 1760 I finished my first tour."[8]

This is as good a description of the morning-after-the-night-before as you will get! But what is of interest, too, is that it shows that "Mr. Nesbitt" was a man of the people; in addition it is difficult to see how he could have mixed so freely with the McGonigles and O'Donnells unless he spoke Gaelic.

George Nesbitt, as the eldest son of James, inherited Woodhill House on his father's death. George was born in 1732 and died in 1827 – a long life. George was father of James, whom we will meet later as "Major" Nesbitt. Apart from the Major, George had three other sons and four daughters. Two of the sons died unmarried and without issue; the third son, Richard, did marry but he, too, had no children. The latter lived in Aighan, near Bruckless, and we will hear of him later because he inherited Woodhill House after his brother, the Major's, death.

Of George's four daughters, Mary Frances married the Rev. James Knox, Anne married Galbraith Tredennick, Marcia married Robert Young of Culdaff and Isabella married Capt. John Evans of the Royal Navy. It was the marriages of these daughters which introduce the names Tredennick, Evans, etc, into our later discussion of the Nesbitts.

George made his will in 1819 and died in 1826. His will gives us an interesting insight into the Nesbitt holdings, the family and the man. Here is an edited version: "I, George Nesbitt, of Woodhill in the parish of Killybegs, and County of Donegal ... do order my body to be decently interred in the Churchyard at Ardara alongside my beloved wife, and all my debts, legacies and funeral expenses to be punctually paid. I bequeath to my eldest son James E. Nesbitt all my real estate of the quarterland of Ballyrory and Tullultan in the Parish of Killagher and all my real estate of Ardara,

Woodhill, Drimbaron, Lurganboy, and Kilgolen, together with the corn and cloth mill thereon, lying in the parish of Killybegs, and also my real estate of Largysallagh with the two ballyboes of the Keels together with the corn mill thereon, in the upper part of the parish of Killybegs and also my real estate of Castlecarm, Keenaghen, and Cronarood in the parish of Kilcarr, to have and to hold to the said James E. Nesbitt and his heirs male, & c. & c.... I bequeath to my son Richard W. Nesbitt all my real estate of the quarterland of Aighen with all its subdenominations together with the salmon fishery and corn and cloth mills thereon... I bequeath to my son-in-law Capt. Robert Evans all my real estate commonly known as Cavan in St. John's Point, in the parish of Killaghter.

"I bequeath to my four daughters, Mary F. Knox, Ann Tredennick, Marcia Young, and Isabella Evans £50 each to buy mourning, having paid off their marriage portions...

"I bequeath to my niece Mary Nesbitt of Loughill the sum of £50 she owes me, and to my niece Mary Ramsay alias Conyngham the sum of £20 she borrowed from me... I bequeath to my daughter-in-law Wilhelmina Nesbitt the sum of £40 to buy mourning... I leave to the children of Porter, wife of William, late of Ardara the sum of £50 to be distributed among them at the discretion of my executors... I also leave to the Poorhouse Keepers in the neighbourhood of Ardara the sum of £40... I also leave £30 towards the support of a Sunday-school and buying books for the children in and about Ardara... I also leave all my plate, household furniture, books, and watch to my son James E. Nesbitt and Richard W. Nesbitt, share and share alike, and I hereby appoint them executors of this my last will and testament."

One of the three witnesses to George Nesbitt's will was a Francis Hamilton Nesbitt and we find him writing about poverty in Donegal in the 1830s. We will mention this letter later on.

George was succeeded by his son James Ezekiel, born 20 November 1763, died 3 January 1845. Since his father was a very old man when he died we can take it that James was running affairs in Woodhill for many years prior to his father's death – James was himself, after all, sixty-three years of age when his father died.

James E., "the Major", is the member of the Nesbitt family who stands out most clearly, because he lived a long life in the area and because, since he survived until the middle of the last century, we have folklore stories which involve him. Earlier I mentioned the possible Gaelic-speaking ability of the Nesbitts. This is not surprising because after all they had to be able to communicate with the Gaelic-speaking natives of the area with whom they dealt every day. However their lifestyle was a separate one, mostly confined to their own class. This is exemplified by most of what we can tell about Major Nesbitt. Some of the stories that have come down to us portray him as a kind man, others as an unthoughtful landlord. On the whole, however, most of the stories about the Major have been told in a sympathetic form, indicating that he was well liked by the people. He was a magistrate and Deputy Lieutenant of the county; he served at one stage as High Sheriff of Donegal. In 1836 we find him entertaining Earl Mulgrave, Lord Lieutenant and General Governor of Ireland. Here is a full account of the visit:

"Ardara: The hills were covered with people, extending as far as the eye could reach, and consisting of at least 10,000 persons. They were headed by the Roman Catholic Clergyman, Mr. McGarvey,[9] who was accompanied by Mr Barrett[10] and other gentlemen, who presented an address in the name of the people – to which his Excellency made a gracious reply, which was received with hearty cheers. The assemblage then opened, forming a line at each side, as far as Major Nesbitt's. In the evening the town was illuminated; and the immense number of persons who had assembled, returned to their homes in the most peacable and orderly manner. At the house of the worthy Major Nesbitt, the party were sumptuously entertained; and they remained there till next day.

"The address[11] was presented to his Excellency at Woodhill on Friday morning; soon after he visited the National School-House, lately built by Major Nesbitt, and seemed much pleased with the learning and progress that some children had made under their respected school-master, Mr. Conaghan. His Excellency expressed the great pleasure that he felt at the kind and hospitable reception given to him by the worthy Major Nesbitt, and he left Ardara amid the hearty cheers of the peacable and well-disposed inhabitants."[12]

The *Ballyshannon Herald* of 4 May 1840 carries an account of a three-day race meeting held in Ardara. The races were obviously held on the seashore[13] because on the second day racing had to be postponed owing to

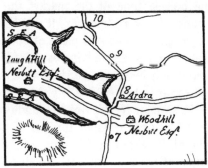

Detail from Taylor & Skinner's map of 1777, showing the two Nesbitt residences

the tide flowing on to the strand. The report concludes as follows: "On Tuesday Major Nesbitt entertained the ladies and gentlemen who attended the races, at his hospitable mansion, Woodhill House. The different gentlemen in the neighbourhood also gave dinner parties during the races. The weather being extremely fine, a vast concourse of fashionables attended, as well as the peasantry. Everything went off peaceably."

The last line of this report would suggest that even while the ascendancy gentlemen were enjoying the horse racing they were still acutely aware that trouble might arise between the "peasantry" and themselves. This interpretation is hardened by our next insight into Major Nesbitt's ways, which takes a very confrontationalist attitude. It was written by a man named Thomas Ainge Devyr in New York in 1882 in a book dealing with life and political movements in south Donegal during the previous fifty years.[14] Unhappy with the yoke under which he saw the people suffering, Devyr, a native of the Donegal town locality, early in his life wrote a book entitled *Our Natural Rights* which was one of the first books to raise the issue of "Land for the People". Deciding that his voice must be heard on a larger stage he moved to England, began writing for a radical newspaper, moved northwards and joined the Chartist movement in Newcastle which organised an open rebellion against the Crown, escaped to America, was quickly in the thick of political battle and started writing again ("The Donegal watch-dog whose weekly utterances carried great weight with the Irish-American masses").[15] He writes:

"Custom"[16]

"Major Nesbit, of Ardara, was the last to enforce this feudal extortion. Cattle sold or exchanged were charged six pence. The Custom man stood at the entrance to the village fair with a book and a cudgel. Then pay six pence or swear there was no trade. It is worthy of notice that the country people who were not his tenants, and who numbered thousands, submitted to this extortion, and that the 'Chapman Billies,' of whom I made one, resisted it. In the busiest time of the market the collector would come round and pronounce the word 'custom'. It was then 'four pence or a fight'. If you refused he caught the end of a piece of goods; then a pull of strength, a volley of expletives, coming to a conclusion of kicks and blows. The custom man was inspired only by some two shillings a day, and though standing the tug bravely for a year or two he finally yielded up the victory.

"This Major Nesbit was the landlord and employer of the men who carried gravel across the moor for four pence a day [see *Our Natural Rights* elsewhere]. He acted in this way, too, when entrusted with the distribution of a cargo of 'coarse oatmeal' donated from England in one of our periodical famines about this time: Roads, bridges and beautifyings on his demesne were made and the labor paid for by small allowances of the coarse oatmeal, a large portion of which became unsound and went to the manure heap along in the autumn, though people perished for want of it during the summer. It had been pleasant to count over his ten or twelve silver pounds every fair night. This pleasure was no more; and, brooding over his loss, the Major hatched a measure of revenge on us. There existed an obsolete law, commanding the liege 'billies' each to pay for a license. In the name of this law he sent the police down upon us, and seized every yard of dry goods exposed for sale, bundled them up, tied them on a cart, and left them under guard for the night preparatory to their consignment next morning to the Custom House in Ballyshannon. It is late; the sergeant and his guard are watching the loaded cart at the barrack door. The Major was implacable; nothing could move him. But sometimes

"'The best-laid schemes o' mice and men gang aft agley.'

"And so it befell with the Major. One of the 'billies' was a crony and a creditor of the sergeant, and paid him a friendly visit on his monotonous watch. The 'mountain dew' had a strong fascination in those regions and in those times – perhaps has yet. At any rate a friendly bottle was produced. Attention could not be fixed at once on the bottle inside and the cart out-

Stone slab bearing the Nesbitt coat of arms

side. Ropes are cutable, and men, inclined to help themselves at least to their own goods, are quick of hand. The Major

"'He counted them at close of day

But when the sun rose, where were they?'

"Nowhere that the Major could find out. And so ended his clutch at the 'Custom'."

Folklore in the Ardara area does not share this portrayal of Major Nesbitt; it is much kinder to him and to the other members of the family. There is no doubt times were hard in the Ardara and south-west Donegal area in general in the 1830s and '40s, but apart from Devyr's article we have no evidence that Major Nesbitt and the other Nesbitts were anything other than sympathetic landlords.

Tradition tells us that on one occasion there was a plague in Ardara and that two sisters of Major Nesbitt came to the village each day and distributed milk and foodstuffs. Jugs and containers were left outside each house by the people, and into these the milk and food were placed. There was a cholera epidemic in Donegal in 1832, but it is likely that the plague referred to here happened well before that year, as by that stage the Major's sisters would have been married for many a day and would have moved elsewhere.

The following story concerning the Major still existed amongst the people in my father's (*obs.* 1982) time and though it shows a deferential attitude, it certainly does not reveal any hostility. When the Major quit the army he received a pension of £1 a day. This he made a present of to the reigning sovereign, who in return granted him the privilege of "a life each year" (some say three lives), that is, that he could each year save one person condemned to be hanged. On one occasion three men, an Englishman, a Scotsman and an Irishman, were to be hanged on the same day in Liverpool. A question arose as to which of the three men was to be hanged first. Then someone in the crowd shouted, "Hang the damned Irishman first." The Major was standing close to the speaker, heard the remark clearly, and felt nettled at the adjective applied to his countryman. When the man was brought out for execution Major Nesbitt went up to the scaffold, caught the Irishman, gave him a kick, and told him to be off. Then turning to the Sheriff he said, "Now you won't hang the damned Irishman first, and there is not a man in England, Ireland or Scotland who can save the other two."

We have mentioned the great fair at Magheramore on our travels. We are told that one year Major Nesbitt officially put a start to the fair by dancing and that his partner was none other than a travelling woman by the name of "Trotty Chonaill".

Tradition tells us that the fair of Magheramore survived into Major

CONGESTED DISTRICTS BOARD.—GENERAL TREDENNICK ESTATE.

FOR SALE
WOODHILL HOUSE & LANDS

THE CONGESTED DISTRICTS BOARD FOR IRELAND are prepared to receive offers for the purchase of the above Premises held in fee-simple free of Tithe and other superior interests.

The Premises consist of a convenient Dwelling-house with Out-offices standing on about eighteen statute acres of land (including a garden and orchard).

Woodhill House was built about twenty-two years ago and is at present in good repair.   The House contains the following apartments :—

ON GROUND FLOOR.---Drawing-room, Dining-room, Study, Kitchen, Cloak-room, Pantry, &c., &c.

ON FIRST FLOOR.---Seven Bedrooms, Bathroom, Lavatory, W.C., &c.

The Offices include the following :---Stabling for four Horses, Cow-house, Coach-house, Harness-rooms, Wash-house, Coal and Turf Houses, Hay and Corn Lofts, and Corn Store, all well built and in a good state of repair.

IN GARDEN :---A Green House and Seed and Fruit Store.

Woodhill lies within about six miles of Glenties Railway Station, and eight miles from Ardara Road Station.

Immediate possession can be given.

For conditions of Sale and order to inspect Premises apply to

THE SECRETARY,
Congested Districts Board,
23, Rutland Square, Dublin.

20th March, 1909.

(3036) Wt. P.460—736. 100. 3/'09.   Printed for His Majesty's Stationery Office by Browne & Nolan, L td., Dublin.

Nesbitt's old age (he died in 1845). For some years before his death the Major was very deaf. A story is told about the workmen who used to labour on Major Nesbitt's estate. They liked to get their wages from the Major just before the fair of Magheramore, so that they could have a good time at the fair. However, besides being deaf, the Major had in his old age developed a reputation for being contrary, and the workmen were afraid to ask him for their pay in case he wouldn't give it to them. One of the workmen thought of a ploy to get money. The Major was a generous man and he never sent a beggarman away from his door without giving him at least a shilling. We know that the Major was deaf in his old age, and possibly, if we are to believe this story, blind as well! The workman came up to the window, dressed in a tunic, and started supposedly playing the fiddle – only he had no fiddle or bow with him, just two bits of sticks. Major Nesbitt was sitting inside the window and saw what he thought was a fiddler ouside. He called on one of the servant girls – she was well aware of the ruse being played by her fellow worker – and asked her who was outside. "Oh, a poor fiddler on his way to the fair of Magheramore," said she. "Give this to him," said the Major, giving her a shilling. Shortly afterwards another of the workmen appeared at the window, pretending to play the tin whistle, and he also went off with a shilling. In turn others of the workmen appeared outside the window as singers, pipers, etc., and all were given a shilling by the Major. Off they all went in good spirits to the fair of Magheramore. They had only just departed when a real fiddler turned up at the Major's window, on his way to the fair. The Major had tired of the "musicians" at this stage and went to the window himself and told the fiddler to clear off. It was a surprised fiddler who left Woodhill on his way to Magheramore, the first time ever he had left without being given a shilling by Major Nesbitt!

Major Nesbitt's deafness is attested to by none other than John O'Donovan, who, visiting him in 1835 in the hope of examining St. Conall's Bell which, of course, was then in the Major's possession, writes: "The Major is most lamentably deaf. I requested of him to open the case (which could be easily done) that we might see if the Bell was gapped or had an inscription on it, but he would not, lest a report might spread that he had got a treasure within it..."[17] Major Nesbitt died in Woodhill on 3 January 1845 and on that night St. Conall's Bell and other valuables were stolen from the big house. We have already heard the saga of how St. Conall's Bell finally ended up in the British Museum.

In the Nesbitt family tree which appears in Amy Young's *Three Hundred Years in Innishowen* Major Nesbitt, though unmarried, has a son, "James Nesbitt, soldier", but of him we know nothing. So when Major Nesbitt died the Woodhill property passed to his brother Richard, Captain Richard William Nesbitt, who was married, and who lived at Hollybrook near the Oyley weir in Bruckless. This is the Richard Nesbitt who offered a reward of £100 for the return of the stolen bell and other valuables from Woodhill. Along with the bell the other objects included a most valuable portable altar studded with precious stones, several gold torques, many gold coins and other ornaments of value. The Rev. G.N. Tredennick of Kildoney was also present in Woodhill on the night of the robbery – he inherited Woodhill House when Richard died three years after the Major, in 1848.

Woodhill House and its surroundings made a deep impression on Lord George Hill when he passed here in 1846 when Richard was the new owner. He writes: "The mountain scenery amongst which Ardara is enbosomed is extremely romantic, and well worth exploring. Near the town is Woodhill, the residence of Richard Nesbitt, Esq. It is luxuriantly clothed with fine and flourishing timber. The demense and environs afford fine vistas disclosing deep bays, mountain glens, and sequestered ravines; and those who have visited the place, must ever retain a very pleasing recollection of it."[18]

Two years later, on 14 January 1848, notice of Richard's death was carried in the *Ballyshannon Herald* as follows: "On the 12th inst., at his seat, Woodhill, near Ardara, county of Donegal, Richard Nesbitt, Esq., Deputy Lieutenant; who, during a long life, enjoyed in an eminent degree the respect, regard and confidence of all classes of the community. For a series of years he was constant in his attendance as a Grand Juror of the County, and laboured to promote public interest with fidelity. In private life he was hospitable and generous; and while his principles were steadfast as a Conservative, he preserved towards all men in politics, liberality of sentiment and charity of heart. As a landlord he bore an excellent character, and in truth his example was in every respect worthy of imitation and esteem."

Ownership of the Woodhill property passed to Richard's sister, Mary Francis, who was married to the Rev. James Knox. She died the following year, 1849, at Culdaff and on her death the property passed to the Rev. George Nesbitt Tredennick, son of Ann Nesbitt, a sister of the Major and Richard who had married Galbraith Tredennick. George Nesbitt Tredennick was born in 1797, entered Trinity College, Dublin, on 1 November 1813 and received his B.A. four years later. He was ordained a clergyman in 1827, and received an M.A. in 1830. He was Vicar of Kilbarron from 1829-72, and died at Killiney on 24 May 1880.

Woodhill House was uninhabited during these years, at least on a permanent basis. T.C. McGinley, writing in 1867 states: "On the road, a little way out of the town is Woodhill House, now untenanted. It belongs at present to the Rev. G. Tredennick, rector of Kildoney, but was formerly the seat of the Nesbitt family."[19]

Before Tredennick's death ownership of the estate had passed to his son, also named the Rev. George Nesbitt Tredennick, who was Vicar of Lismore; in a list of the landowners of Ireland in 1879 ownership of Woodhill is attributed to the Rev. George Tredennick, of Rathronan, Diocese of Lismore, Clonmel, Co. Tipperary.[20]

After 1880 ownership of the Woodhill estate passed to Major General James Richard Knox Tredennick. Major General Tredennick served in the New Zealand war of 1865-66, in the Zulu war of 1879, was Lieutenant Colonel (Colonel 1884) of the Middlesex Regiment from 1880-85, and retired in 1886.[21] He was Deputy Lieutenant of the county and Justice of the Peace and had a Dublin residence as well as Woodhill House.

The original Woodhill House was pulled down by Major General Tredennick "who built a new house to suit himself".[22] The revamped Woodhill House and surroundings continued to hold their charm in the area – from 1893 we read: "Woodhill, the residence of General Tredennick, which, with its thick belt of trees, clothes the immediate surroundings, and makes the town look exceptionally sheltered and picturesque."[23]

When the Congested Districts Board bought the Woodhill estate from Major General Tredennick in the early part of this century we can surely say that it was the end of an era.[24] Woodhill passed from the Nesbitt family, who had first come here in 1669[25] when the village of Ardara would only have consisted of a few basic huts at the river ford. Nowadays Woodhill House is a guest house boasting a first-rate restaurant. In the immortal words of Tennyson:

The older order changeth
Yielding place to new.

Notes

1   Who bought the property now known as the Lobster Pot restaurant, formerly Jim Kennedy's shop, from Major Nesbitt on 24 March 1831.

2   Taken from *Three Hundred Years in Innishowen* by Amy Young (1929). She relied for her family trees on *Burke's Peerage*, some of whose family trees are questionable. Ms. Young raises the possibility that the Nisbet who is said to have been the first to come to south-west Donegal, Alexander, came from Dirleton, but in a recent communication with Dirleton Castle in east Lothian I was told that Sir John Nisbet, who was descended from the Nisbets of Berkshire and who was lord advo-

cate under Charles II, did not purchase the lands in Dirleton until 1663, by which time the Nesbitts had been in south-west Donegal for thirty years. It is likely that "our" Nesbitts came directly from Berkshire.

3   Undertakers: a class of Plantation grantee composed of influential English and Scots who were to undertake the plantation of British settlers on the estates they obtained.

4   With the defeat of the Gaelic chieftains at the Battle of Kinsale in 1602, followed by the Flight of the Earls in 1607, the old Gaelic order had come to an end. The Plantation of Ulster started in 1610. The lands of the departed chieftains were confiscated and made available for plantation purposes. *Tír Chonaill* became part of Co. Donegal and was divided into baronies on the English model (*D.A.* (1971), p. 3). English law was administered by magistrates and assize judges. Brehon law and traditional customs were prohibited.

5   U.H. Hussey de Burgh, *The Landowners of Ireland.*

6   In a fee farm grant you are given a freehold, but you have to pay a rent forever, i.e. a rent is reserved against you and your successors.

7   Arthur O'Neill was born in 1737. At the age of two he punctured his right eye with a knife and his grandmother had him sent everywhere in an effort to save his sight. Had he been left alone it is likely that only the sight of his right eye would have been impaired. At the age of ten, young O'Neill, who was fast losing his sight, began learning the harp. At the age of fifteen he began his travels by striking north-east into Antrim and from thence onwards he was a welcome guest in all the big houses, Gaelic and Anglo-Irish. His description of his first tour of Ireland deals with the interesting people he met in the years leading up to 1760 when he returned home to his parents.

8   C. Milligan Fox, *Annals of the Irish Harper,* pp. 150-51.

9   "Priest" McGarvey, whom we will discuss in detail in Loughill, down Loughros Point.

10   Presumably the Rev. John Barrett, Rector of Inishkeel 1802-44; it was he who gave us the interesting insight into the lifetyle of the people when we were in the Rosbeg area. However, it could have been his son, Rev. Knox Barrett, who was curate of the Inishkeel parish at this time.

11   "TO HIS EXCELLENCY, EARL MUSGRAVE, LORD LIEUTENANT AND GENERAL GOVERNOR OF IRELAND:

We, the inhabitants of the town and vicinity of Ardara, beg to return your Excellency our sincere thanks for the favour you have done us by visiting this part of the county of Donegal. With thankful feelings of gratitude, we acknowledge the many benefits you have already conferred upon us, by promoting the education of the poor, by promptly attending to the wants of the distressed, by supporting all liberal institutions, and by using your best endeavours to do away with all party distinctions from amongst us. Signed on the part of the inhabitants of Ardara and its vicinity – William Barrett, John Cromey." (We referred earlier, at the Wood Road, to the latter; it should read John Cromley.)

12   The *Ballyshannon Herald* 2 September 1836.

13   I think it is likely that these races were held somewhere along the seashore down Loughros Point, since the Nesbitt family owned Loughill House and had other interests down the Point.

14   *The Odd Book of the Nineteenth Century*, p. 91.

15   See "Man from Donegal" by noted Mountcharles author Seamus MacManus in the *Irish Press* newspaper of 3 August 1948.

16   You will remember when we were earlier discussing the fair day in Ardara we noted that permission to hold a fair had been granted to George Nesbitt in 1760 and it was stated that he was to "receive all the usual customs, tolls, etc.".

17   O.S. Letters, p. 119.

18   *Useful Hints to Donegal Tourists*, pp. 36-37.

19   *Cliff Scenery of South-Western Donegal*, p. 153.

20   U.H. Hussey de Burgh, *The Landowners of Ireland*. Woodhill had an acreage of 6,297 and a "valuation" of £1,447. In 1879 others of the Tredennick family owned property near Ballyshannon – John Arnold Tredennick had a very small estate at Camlin Castle near Ballyshannon and William Tredennick had an estate of 2,779 acres.

21   Kelly, *Handbook of the Titled, Landed and Official Classes* (1908).

22   Amy Young, *Three Hundred Years in Innishowen*, p. 195.

23   *The Donegal Highlands*, p. 138. (This was the recast and enlarged edition of the *Donegal Highlands*, by Dr. MacDevitt; the original edition in 1865 does not mention Woodhill House).

24   The entire Tredennick estate was bought by the Congested Districts Board under the Birrel Act of 1909. The estate consisted of 4,736 acres and the total purchase price was £15,932 (Wm. L. Micks, *An Account of the Congested Districts Board*).

25   What was the name of this area before it was renamed "Woodhill" by the Nesbitts? I don't know. We will never know. Woodhill overlooks the Duvoge river; in 1642 there was an area in the quarter of Magumna named Dowragh, which would translate as *Damh Shrath*: the river-holm of the oxen. It is possible that this name applied to the low area along the river below the height on which Woodhill House is built and that there was no specific name for the Woodhill site itself.

XIV

ARDARA: PART 2

WE NOW LEAVE Woodhill House, proceeding back to the Nesbitt Arms Hotel, on our way passing, at the edge of the wood, the spring wells which supplied much of the village in past times. In 1911 Joseph Campbell writes: "I was coming through Ardara wood the other evening just after sunset. There was a delightful smell of wet larch and bracken in the air. The road was dark – indeed, no more than a shadow in the darkness; but a streak of silver light glimmered through from the west side over the mountains and lay on the edge of the wood, and thousands of stars trembled in the branches, touching them with strangeness and beauty. ... I came on a number of women and girls, all laughing and talking together in the half-darkness. I was out of the wood now and almost into the village, and there was light enough to see that they were carrying water – some with one pail, others with two – from the spring well I passed on my way up. This, I believe, is a custom in Ardara (In fact, a 'go of water' is a byword there – 'Many a girl met her man in a go of water!'). The grown girls of the village go out every evening after dark-fall, if the weather happens to be good. They meet at the well, spend half an hour or so chatting and talking together, and then saunter home again in groups through the darkness, carrying their pails, just as I saw them on this particular evening. When I got to the village the windows were nearly all lit up. The white and white-grey houses looked strange and unearthly in the darkness. The doors were open, and one could see a dark figure here and there out taking the air. Over the roofs the stars shone ... and although there was no moon one could see the smoke from the chimneys wavering up into the sky in thin green lines. The fragrance of peat hung heavily on the senses. There wasn't a sound – only a confused murmur of voices, like the wind among aspen-trees, and the faint singing of a fiddle from a house away at the far end of the street. Even the dogs were quiet. I passed through the Diamond, down the long main street next the shore."[1]

This street "over the town" is a very wide street, in contrast to the street "up the town", and its spaciousness has been commented upon before – from 1867 we read: "Ardara stands at the head of Loughross More Bay, and consists of two streets, of about equal length, forming a right angle. The street by which we enter[2] the town is remarkable for its wideness, a circumstance that gives the place an air of cheerfulness. There are two hotels, Maloneys and Brennans, and quite a number of shops. There is a weekly market (Tuesday), which is well attended during the winter months, and at which there is much traffic carried, principally in farm produce."[3]

By now we know that "Maloneys" Hotel is the present-day Nesbitt Arms. Hotels and inns play a large part in the everyday life of the occupants of every small village, but their role as a home-from-home for the traveller passing through has been of even more importance over the years. John Mitchel travelled through Donegal in the summer of 1845 and was accompanied by a friend, John O'Hagan, who kept a diary. They obviously did not have a pleasant journey, neither being impressed by the landscape nor by the overnight accommodation in Ardara. We must remember that Mitchel's account of Donegal is coloured by the horrors of the famine of the 1840s in Ireland. Mitchel wrote: "The most desolate region of all is found in Ulster. As you travel northwards from Killybegs, by way of Ardara, Glenties, and Dunglow, you pass for nearly forty miles through the dreariest region of moor and mountain that is to be found within the five ends of Ireland; – wide tracts of quaking bog, interspersed with countless dismal lakes, intersected by rocky ridges, and traversed by mountain rivers roaring in tawny foam to the sea. The two or three wretched villages that lie along this road give to a traveller an impression of even more dreariness and desolation than the intervening country; a cluster of ragged-looking, windowless hovels, whose inhabitants seem to have gathered themselves from the wastes and huddled together to keep some life and heat in them; a few patches of oats and potatoes surrounding the huts, and looking such a miserable provision for human beings against hunger in the midst of those great brown moors; hardly a slated building to be seen, save one or two constabulary and revenue police stations."[4]

His companion, John O'Hagan,[5] mirrors Mitchel's sentiments. Having walked over the mountain from Glencolumbkille to Ardara he writes: "The way lay through an awfully deep glen [Glengesh]. The mountains on both sides hidden in mist, the bottom of the glen quite invisible, for only a very dim light of the moon penetrated through the thick clouds. The sound of the torrent rushing through it – we, weary and silent, plodding on through the small rain. I never was more oppressed or awe stricken. Got, at long last, to Ardara, after having walked about ten miles during the day, a great part of which was over mountain. Hotel a small public-house, with, you may suppose, rather questionable accommodation; but Donegal travellers must not be choosers. Great turf fire, tea, cursedly bad bread... Beds very clean and dry; got a glorious sleep. (Next day... rain pouring in torrents, and staying in this place is out of the question)."

It is possible that the inn in which Mitchel and O'Hagan stayed was the present Nesbitt Arms Hotel. The noted poet William Allingham[6] from Ballyshannon visited Ardara a few years later, on 28 October 1847, and though he, too, was not enamoured by the landscape he was more impressed than the others by the facilities Ardara offered the traveller: "Set out for Lochrus on Customs duty. Outside car, moors and bare mountains to Ardara, when the groves of Woodhill give a softening. The sun set into a jagged cloud breathing flame from its openings, rested on the dark mountains, disappeared, leaving a gloomy memory which soon faded too. Then the wind blew colder, the road became indistinct, the moors blended into a dim waste. Dine at Ardara, snug little room, adorned with pictures of Christ entering Jerusalem, Mary Queen of Scots, and Byron in a very large turn-down collar, with his arm round the waist of a lady with dark eyes and ringlets. A young naval officer in another room, who smokes cigars. Biddy says with pride, 'O, Ardara's never without a stranger!'"[7]

The inference is that Allingham must have known Biddy fairly well and suggests also that he visited Ardara regularly. There must have been a significant trafficking of goods by boat into Loughros to warrant regular visits by a custom officer; presumably the naval officer was attached to a vessel berthed in Loughros.

In later years the Nesbitt Arms provided comfortable accommodation for the many people who came to fish on the local rivers and lakes. William Harkin, writing in 1897, states: "The 'Nesbitt Arms Hotel' offers every inducement to tourists or anglers, and the scenery is magnificent. Two splendid salmon rivers empty into Loughros Bay."[8]

Philip Geen, writing a few years later in 1904, and who earlier gave us an account of the fair day in Ardara, gives us an insight into the early Nesbitt Arms Hotel when he writes: "Ardara is near the mouths of the Owenea and Owentocker rivers, and is a pretty and interesting town. It is the centre of several industries, and, while there, you may make useful purchases of lace, hosiery, tweeds, or embroidered linens. It was at Ardara that I bought the unique afternoon tea-cloth which all my lady friends go into such raptures over that I anticipate the worker of it has orders that will last her lifetime.

"Mrs. McNelis, of the Nesbitt Arms, personally superintends all that pertains to the comfort of the visitors, and her sons are ever active in arranging for their sport. The two youngest are great car drivers, and are particularly proud of most of the animals they drive, while the eldest son has a store in which is collected a huge variety of cabin-manufactured goods. I think I am within the mark in saying that I saw two waggon loads of tweeds. My purchase of him was of a neat pattern, but bigger men with large ideas could suit themselves with elaborate designs and colours."[9]

Philip Geen did a lot of fishing in the Ardara area and his two gillies were brothers, Pat and Maurice Early. They were two uncles of Tom Early, who lives here in Ardara at the present time and has inherited all his predecessor's wide knowledge of fishing, nature and wildlife. Pat Early was the gillie to Mr. Geen for most of the time. Apparently Mr. Geen often gave Pat his own fishing rod to fish with – on his return to London Mr. Geen writes: "I have often thought of Pat and his love for my rod. He wrote me a letter, which I think so characteristic of him that I add it to this:

'Hillhead
Ardara, Co. Donegal
January 18, 1904.

Dear Geen
If you could come here about the middle of May it would I think be a good time for fishing. Anyhow I will let you know when I think there is a good prospect for fishing. I have had a good day's fishing alone with myself on Oct. 1, 1903, but I only caught three salmon.
I sincerely hope you are well, and wish you a happy new year.
I am your
humble servant Patrick Early.'[10]

In July 1907 Patrick Pearse was in Ardara. He was pleased to find that most of the hotel staff were proficient in Gaelic. From here he sent a postcard picture of the renowned valley of Glengesh to his mother. On the card he has written: "We go through this Glen today on our way to Glencolumbcille, weather not very fine. Scenery magnificent."[11] On 5 July he visited the town school and states: "Most of the children in the town school come from Irish-speaking or partly Irish-speaking homes. The higher classes are taught a little Irish from O'Growney,[12] – translation from Irish into English and '*vice versa*'. Is this the way to grapple with the language in Ard a' Ratha? Attractive *viva voce* teaching in and through Irish for at least half the school day is required for all the classes. The manager and teachers are favourably disposed; by adopting a bold and forward policy *now* they can make Ard a' Ratha Irish-speaking in ten years."[13]

The Nesbitt Arms Hotel was owned by John Byrne and his family when I was a young fellow running around Ardara. The Byrne family then moved to Ashbourne in Co. Meath and the hotel has been run with great success by Connie Molloy and his family for the last few decades.

Up on the Diamond, opposite the Nesbitt Arms, stands the new Ulster Bank, opened in November 1990. The previous building that we all knew so well was razed to the ground at the end of 1989. The Ardara branch of the Ulster Bank was opened in April 1913;[14] prior to this the Ulster Bank used a room once a week in what is now the Nesbitt Arms Hotel. There were I think three[15] front doors in the hotel prior to its being burned on the fair day, 1 February 1919; the door nearest Brennans was used by Patrick J. McNelis in the first decade of this century for bringing in rolls of tweed. It was this room, nearest Brennans, which was used every Tuesday by a representative of the Ulster Bank in Glenties; in the first decade of this century a Mr. Anderson was the representative.

The original Ulster Bank premises consisted of a building known as the "Diamond Lodge" which is believed to have been built in about 1848 by a man named Gallagher who returned home after making his fortune in the gold fields of Ballarat.[16] The premises later came under the control of the Congested Districts Board in connection with the promotion of the Donegal tweed industry.[17] The bank have occupied the premises since 1913 during which time several major extensions and refurbishments have been carried out to the building, and the Ulster Bank has continued to play a major role in the economy of the Ardara area throughout those years.

The bank manager whom I knew best, and that was in his retirement, was Pat Boyle, who was the manager in Ardara from 1957 until 1964. Pat was a writer and had many friends from the literary field who came to visit him, among them the late Brendan Behan and his wife Beatrice. They often retired to the back room of Nancy's Bar, which was then a quieter place than it is now, for a drink and a chat. Beatrice Behan still makes her annual pilgrimage to the back room of Nancy's.

Alas Pat and his wife Teddy are now both deceased. Patrick Boyle's best-known work was the novel *Like Any Other Man*,[18] first published in Great Britain in 1966 and dedicated to Teddy. He also published a number of collections of short stories, his best medium in my opinion, including *At Night All Cats Are Grey*, *The Betrayers* and *All Looks Yellow to the Jaundiced Eye*.

An attempted bank robbery was carried out on the Ulster Bank in Ardara on the 16 June 1921. The bank was searched and the raiders then demanded the keys of the safe, but the demand was refused. The raiders failed to get any money and left the premises. A British government official, then located in the district, witnessed the incident at the bank and noted that the four raiders, travelling on bicycles, hurried off in the direction of Kilclooney. Jumping on his moter-cycle the official made all haste to Glenties R.I.C. Barracks. (The R.I.C. had already been withdrawn from Ardara.) A fully manned and equipped Crossley tender tracked the raiders to the Rosbeg area and in the confrontation which followed one of the raiders, who used the pseudonym "Hennessy," sustained a bullet wound in the leg. Two other men were captured and taken to the Crossley, along with the single casualty. "Hennessy," whose wound was not serious, escaped from hospital, and was back in Rosbeg eleven days later. It was almost two years after the Treaty before the other two captives obtained their freedom.

The four raiders involved in the bank raid were members of the Ardara Flying Column of the Old I.R.A. which was very active at this time. In October 1920 a full-scale attack was carried out on the R.I.C. Barracks in Ardara; the attack was repulsed with the aid of British military who were based at the Mart in the town. Shortly afterwards, in November 1920, a Sinn Féin[19] court being held in a building on the Back Road in Ardara was raided by the British military. In February 1921 the Old I.R.A. carried out a raid on the Ardara Courthouse; records were captured and destroyed. In April 1921 a raid was carried out on the Ardara Post Office, where documents were seized, and in May 1921 the Post Office was again raided and the telegraph machine taken.

Later I will deal with other periods of unrest in the village of Ardara, but for now we will talk of another few buildings of interest in the Diamond area and then we will move on. When I was a child the site below the Ulster Bank, now "Chique Fashions", formerly the Crystal Cinema, was occupied by a long low building (two houses really), roofed with Irish slate which was plastered over with tar. Here lived James "Cooper" Cannon and his brother Harry. Their father, Henry Cannon, a big man who used to wear breeches and long stockings, first came down to live in Ardara from the Muickel Bridge area, up near Dunkineely. He was a carpenter, cooper and wheel-wright. Before moving to the Diamond he occupied the house where the late Con Gillespie once lived – across the archway from the late Johnny Gallagher's – and he had his workshop in the archway. His son, James Cannon, continued the trade of making barrels, churns, etc., and consequently was known as "Cooper" also. A brother of James, Tom, was the grandfather of internationally-known author James Plunkett.[20] A sister of the Cannon family was the mother of the late Johnny Gallagher; anyone who ever heard Johnny's sensitive playing of the violin at midnight mass at Christmas time in Ardara over the years will forever retain the memory.

Below the site of the "Cooper's" house is a large, high building occupied by members of the family of the late Dan Craig, a building which also housed the late Charlie Craig and his family. This house was originally built by a man named Paddy Boyle from Tullycleave, with the aid of two of his daughters, he building and they up and down ladders with hods on their shoulders. He was a stonemason by trade and was known as Paddy "Blue Hawk" – a "hawk" is the term for a plasterer's board, and it is said that he once painted his hawk blue in order to distinguish it from those of his fellow craftsmen, thus earning the nickname. His daughters were named Ann and Helen. They mixed mortar and carried stones up the ladder; they rowed from the Yellow Banks to Liskeraghan slate-quarry, loaded the boats up with the dressed slates from O'Boyle's quarry and then rowed back again to the Banks. Some of these slates still cover part of the roof towards the back of Craig's. *Griffith's Valuations* of 1857 informs us that this site is owned by a Patrick Boyle, that it is unoccupied but that building of the house is "in progress".

Ann Boyle later married John Gilbride, who had resigned from the R.I.C., and they ran a temperance hotel on the premises. In the early 1930s the building became a branch of the National Bank, and was later bought by the Craigs. After serving with her father in the building trade Helen Boyle went to America and later returned and started up a confectionary shop in the premises now occupied by fishing-tackle supplier John McGill. It was she who bought the five stained-glass windows which now stand behind the altar in the Church of the Holy Family, Ardara.

A sister of Paddy "Blue Hawk's" was Nancy Boyle, the original Nancy of Nancy's Bar, and a third daughter of Paddy "Blue Hawk's", Bridget, was the grandmother of publican Patrick Gildea, who kindly supplied me with these interesting details on Paddy "Blue Hawk" from his vast store of knowledge.

Up in the left-hand corner of the Diamond is Tommy Feeney's house; behind it is the site of the first Catholic church built in the village. It was thought to have been erected in the last decades of the 18th century: after 1760 mass houses were common throughout the country; after 1782 they started being built within the walls of towns. Mission closings here were talked of by the older generations;[21] crowds packed not only the little church and its environs, but the entire Diamond. The thousands of lighted candles were then a nine day wonder.[22]

It is generally accepted that Fr. Con Boyle, a native of Lugnagillew, was the first priest to take up residence in the town, shortly after 1800.[23] He lived in, and owned, the house now occupied by Tommy Feeney. Almost the only payment Fr. Boyle got from his parishioners was a stack of corn per household in October. His nephew, Seamus, who spent most of his boyhood in Ardara with Fr. Con, was often one of those who went collecting the corn; his job was holding the horse on the road. A big barn was built at the back of the Diamond, and the corn provided enough meal to supply their wants for a year.

Fr. Con had a standing invitation to go to Nesbitts of Woodhill for dinner every Sunday. it is thought that this friendship started from some good turn Fr. Boyle had done for the Nesbitts. The Nesbitts had his portrait painted and it hung on the wall at Woodhill until the last of the family – General Tredennick – sold out at the beginning of this century. It is said that on the day before the auction a man arrived in the town on a bicycle, and stayed overnight in Gilbride's Hotel (the temperance room). On the following day he attended the auction, purchased the portrait of Fr. Boyle, removed it from its frame and having rolled it up he carried it away on his bicycle.

There was a law-suit over land in the early decades of the 1800s between the Nesbitts and another party in which Fr. Boyle took the side of the Woodhill people. It is possible that his action was unpopular in the district because shortly afterwards he requested the bishop to give him a transfer and he was sent to Clondahorkey, where he later died.

A number of men from Lugnagillew and the surrounding district went to the funeral on horseback. All were dressed in black swallow-tailed coats and castor hats round each of which was tied a wide band of black cloth which hung down their backs. On their way through Meenaroy they met a number of mounted policemen escorting an illicit distiller they had just caught red-handed. While the policemen gazed in wonder at the castor-hatted party the poteen-maker got his chance and urged his fleet-footed steed over a narrow moorland path, where the limbs of the law dared not follow.

This reference to policemen and a poteen-maker takes us to the theme of unrest and especially the implementation of the law in Ardara in the 1800s. The early decades of the 19th century saw trouble in the Ardara area; there was a great deal of discontent throughout the country in general at that time. This was in large measure due to the fact that Catholics, in addition to providing for their own priests and churches, also had to contribute to the upkeep of the Anglican church. Because it was by law the Established church, all tillers of the soil in Ireland had to pay tithes – one-tenth part of their crops – to the Protestant ministers. This period of Irish history is known as the Tithe War. The Tithe Proctor, supported by police and soldiers, descended upon all who refused to pay and seized their cattle if they had any, or any other houshold items, and sold them by auction.

A January 1832 copy of the *Ballyshannon Herald* states: "The Inniskeel Rector cannot procure a shilling [in 1827 the tithes were commuted to a fixed annual payment] though in most cases 2/3 is due. His collectors and bailiffs have been beaten and the people are resolved not to pay unless under compulsion." The *Herald* continues: "On the night of Candlemas Eve lighted brands were placed on all the hills, particularly around the villages of Ardara and Glenties" and adds "The peaceable part of the community much alarmed" (because of the unrest in the area).

That the authorities were concerned about organised unrest, orchestrated by activists, is revealed in a further extract from the *Ballyshannon Herald*: "Large meetings are being held through the county under the pretence of dancing schools, the person acting as both musician and dancing master is in the habit of marching pupils two deep along the road by night. It is lamentable to see the peasants suffer themselves to be lead astray by cunning demagogues, many of whom are travelling through the county."

Presumably as a result of the unrest in the area the Company of the 30th Regiment under Captain Geddes, Lieutenant Waldron and Ensign Wright marched from Enniskillen for posting at Ardara at the beginning of February 1832. How this regiment fared I don't know, but nature did not smile on a later regiment because the *Ballyshannon Herald* states: "Ardara, January 1834, the detachment of the 27th Regiment, stationed at Ardara, under the command of Capt. McPherson marched into Ballyshannon, the barracks in Ardara being unroofed in the late storm.[24]

Earlier, in 1832, we noted that "The Inniskeel Rector cannot procure a shilling" in tithes. In 1832 the rector would have been Rev. John Barrett, whom we have met earlier on our travels. That opposition to the tithes was not solely confined to Catholics is demonstrated by the following example. In September 1838 cattle belonging to the Rev. Early, P.P. of Glenties, were seized and sold for the sum of 12 shillings tithes; the locals held a protest meeting in Glenties and the meeting was presided over by none other than Mr. William Barrett, Attorney, son of the Rector of Inishkeel.[25]

During the mid-1800s, while the police were stationed in the barracks in the area where John Joe Campbell now lives, the law was administered next door in the courthouse, now Eddie Doherty's. Petty Sessions – minor cases much like today's District Court – were held on the last Tuesday of each month. I'm sure you will be as interested as I was in the kind of case brought before the court and the justice meted out.

On 31 July 1855 we find a Glenconwell defendant in court charged with fishing illegally on the Owenea river. Fishing rights on the Owenea in 1855 belonged to William R. Tredennick of Fort William. The court record states: "Defendant did on the night of the 29th or morning of the 30th June last enter upon the River Owenea, Property of Complainant (Tredennick), and was then and there found attempting to take Salmon or Trout therein or therefrom, with a net." The justice meted out to him was that he was fined the sum of £10 and costs, or if in default three months imprisonment. It seems a very harsh sentence. I wonder did it discourage "poaching" in Glenconwell?

That fishing on the Owenea was totally reserved is demonstrated by a case from 28 August 1855 in which a Tullycleave man was in court because he "did enter upon the River Owenea and did then and there fish for Salmon or Trout with a rod and line".

At the same sitting we find a number of local males, presumably spirited young lads, being brought to court by the Rev. George Tredennick of Woodhill for robbing apples from the orchard at Woodhill: "Defendant committed a malicious trespass by entering the complainant's orchard and stealing apples therefrom, on the 5th August inst., at Woodhill." One of the defendants was Owen McNelis of Ardara and the second person was John Boyle, Junior, "of Ardara or Drumbarron". The case was adjourned to the next court.

One comes across numerous incidents of women in court, having been summoned by a Glasgow company because they had not returned muslin in time or had not completed the work. For example: "Defendant[26] is illegally detaining a piece of sewed muslin work beyond the legal time" and "Defendant[27] returned in an unfinished state a piece of sewed muslin work."

On 25 March 1856 we find the Ardara Constabulary bringing a number of intriguing cases to court – firstly a case in which the "Defendant was found winnowing corn on the Public Street of Ardara". The defendant was a Charles Gallagher of Ardara. A Charles Gallagher lived on the Diamond around this time[28] and it is likely that it was he who lived in the Diamond Lodge, now the Ulster Bank. A John Cannon of Ardara was in court because "Defendant's cart was found lying on the Public Street of Ardara." In both these cases the defendant had to pay one shilling and costs. And Henry Strong of Shanaghan was in court because "Defendant's pig was found on 11th March 1856 wandering on the Public Street of Ardara." Again the fine was one shilling and costs.

A court would not be a court without alcohol-related cases. The Ardara Petty Sessions records contain many references to poteen-makers,[29] people making malt without a licence and keeping malt houses without a licence. There is also a number of references to people drinking on the premises coming up to 12 o'clock at night,[30] and numerous cases of people being arrested for being in an intoxicated state on the main street. Possibly the most quixotic case of them all, and the one with which we will conclude our look at the Petty Sessions in Ardara, is one in which a local publican was charged with being drunk on his own licensed premises. After a lengthy hearing it was decided to adjourn the case and in the meantime seek the advice of the Under-Secretary, Dublin Castle.

Not everyone in Ardara had succumbed to the temptation of alcohol, as the *Ballyshannon Herald* of 14 January 1841 reveals: "The Teetotalers of Ardara and its vicinity held a Social in John O'Donnell's spacious house, on Monday, 27th December. Upwards of three hundred of all persuasions sat down to tea. Many of the fair sex (and fairer and more virtuous there are not to be found than in this locality) graced the meeting by their presence, which would do honour to any assembly. There was a splendid band in attendance, conducted by Mr. Cassidy.

"The Chair was taken by their venerated pastor, Rev. Daniel O'Donnell. Mr. Gallagher presented the Rev. Chairman with an address, replete with talent and ability, from the teetotalers of Ardara.

"Many talented gentlemen addressed the assembly in powerful strains of eloquence, during the evening.

"The health of their benevolent and encouraging landlord, Major Nesbitt, was drunk with all due honours.

"The Rev. Mr. O'Donnell vacated the chair at 11 o'clock. Dancing was kept up to a late hour, when the congregated assembly departed, highly delighted with the hilarity of the evening, giving three hearty cheers for her Majesty the Queen, and three for Father Matthew."

Presumably the health of Major Nesbitt was drunk with non-alcoholic beverage!

Popular unrest and dissatisfaction continued into the late 19th and early 20th century. In the fourth quarter of the 19th century the National League were active in the Ardara area. In the course of a letter written on 26 January 1884 to Murray-Stewart, the landlord who lived at the White House in Killybegs and who administered the land of most of this part of south-west Donegal, his agent, Brooke, states: "There is a National League meeting in Ardara on Tuesday, and because there are no Orangemen in this part of the world, I suppose the Government will allow it to come off. I wish they would stop them [i.e. meetings] all everywhere as there is nothing but treason spoken at them all."[31]

Again in 1888 we find Brooke writing to Murray-Stewart, stating: "I sent you a Derry paper yesterday to show you what the National League is doing at Ardara." He goes on to tell how the League in Ardara had sent a deputation of three tenants to him seeking a reduction in rents. He refused the reduction, and, in response, almost no one paid their rents. He then issued a circular saying that he would attend at Ardara on a Tuesday to give the tenants another opportunity to pay. He states that on this day some twenty of the Protestant tenants paid, but not one Roman Catholic. He goes on: "I think and hope, therefore, this will break up the combination," a reference to the fact that the National League, both locally and nationally, contained Catholics and Protestants.

In the first decade of this century we find a body called the United Irish League holding regular meetings in Ardara. On 7 June 1908 they are found sending a postal order for £1 to Gerald O'Reilly, Esq., Lord Mayor of Dublin, as a contribution to the Parnell Monument in the city. The malicious burning of the sacristy of the Roman Catholic church in Ardara on 16 November 1907 produced animated discussions well into the year 1908, but the predominant issue was the continuing dispute between the people and the landed gentry over land and fishing rights. A few examples of the latter are: On 6 September 1908 the secretary of the United Irish League explained that "the deputation appointed at the previous meeting to wait on Dr. O'Donnell, the Lord Bishop of Raphoe, in reference to the Evans evicted tenants dispute, had a most remarkable interview with his Lordship"; 28 March 1909: "The threatened prosecution of the people of Maghera and Laconnell by Brooke, and the obstinacy of the Marques Conyngham by refusing a large number of his tenants the sporting and fishing rights of the Owenea, were ably and clearly explained by Mr. William McGroarty, one of the tenants concerned"; 18 April 1909: A long discussion ensued relating to the grievance of the people of Laconnell and Maghera for a reduction of rent and as to the future purchase of their holdings.

We are inclined to forget, seated in our comfortable homes of the 1990s, that two generations ago, in the early 1900s, people were still striving to gain possession of what we now regard as our natural rights – possession of land and the right to fish the local rivers.

Down along the river-bank lay a cluster of small houses, which I have referred to earlier. Among the people who lived there in living memory are Johnny Grahams, who was a good storyteller – some of his stories are preserved in the Department of Irish Folklore, Dublin[32] – Frank Doogan and Hannah, Peter McTeague, and of course Johnny "Teaguen" had a forge down here. The legendary Donegal fiddler, Johnny Doherty, who is just over ten years dead, was born in one of these little houses, In later years I had the pleasure of listening to Johnny's fiddle-playing and storytelling on many occasions when he was staying with Mickey Brown out in Glenconwell and numerous were the stories I heard starting with the words, "A time that was".

Johnny may be deceased, but living over here in the "West-End" we still have a very accomplished fiddler, John Gallagher. Another noted fiddler who died a number of years ago was Josie "The Post" McHugh. Members of the O'Rourke family of Ardara are also well known for their music, especially their ability to play the fiddle. An earlier member of the O'Rourke family, Jimmy, now deceased, used to live in the little house on the Back Road which had earlier been the Methodist schoolhouse, and is still occupied by Mrs. Rourke, Ned Rourke's widow. Jimmy Rourke was a great storyteller and played the fiddle, and it was on him that the central character in Walt Disney's film *Darby O'Gill and the Little People* was based.

The research for this film was done in and around Ardara in the 1940s by an American named Larry Watkin, who then returned to America and wrote the screenplay which was made into the film. While researching the book Mr. Watkin, who was a novelist, spent a lot of time in the Ardara area, cycling everywhere to get a sense of the atmosphere of the place. In his re-

---

Walt Disney Productions Limited
request the pleasure of your company at a
Reception and Commemorative Supper
to honour
Mr. and Mrs. Walt Disney
at the Mansion House, Dublin
on Wednesday, June 24ᵗʰ, 1959
following the World Premiere of
"Darby O'Gill and the Little People"

THIS CARD ADMITS

Mr. P. C. McGill   (two)

DRESS FORMAL

search he was ably assisted by my late father, Paddy McGill. Having finished, he returned to America and in December 1947 he sent one of his own novels entitled *On Borrowed Time*[33] – "my oldest, most liked book" – to my father, adding, "I'd like to be riding a bike with you right now – will return one day."

The world premiere of *Darby O'Gill and the Little People* was held in Dublin on 24 June 1959, and afterwards there was a reception at the Mansion House in Dublin, hosted by Mr. and Mrs. Walt Disney, which my father and mother attended. And all because of the great storytelling and musical ability of Jimmy Rourke!

I have in my possession a lead-weighted handle of a whipstick which belonged to a man who lived down in one of the little houses beside the river. This man, who presented the whipstick to my father, was known as Donald Rua McGill. A big man with a red beard, in the last century he used to drive a cart to Derry and back, the route of most merchandise coming in to and out of Ardara. The drivers of the wagons were known as "the Derry cartmen". At that time travelling was a dangerous occupation and people were often robbed while going over the mountains to east Donegal. Most of the Derry cartmen carried a lead-weighted whipstick for self preservation. If attacked they were ready to turn their whipsticks on their assailants and, in my father's words, "any man who got a crack of a whipstick lay down and slept for a while nice and quietly on the roadside".

Ardara carts going to Derry travelled in a convoy of from twelve to twenty. Most of them carried money to pay for their goods and they also carried money entrusted to them by commercial travellers who felt it was too dangerous to have on their person as they went from town to town. On one such occasion Ardara cartmen were attacked at *Bealach na gCreach*.[34] They were well prepared and the robbers got a hot reception – more than one of them was left lying dead or unconscious on the road. Dreading that this might be but the spearhead of a bigger attack, the cartmen whipped their horses and went off at full speed. As the fever of battle died in their blood they began to fear a charge of manslaughter, or even of murder. So they

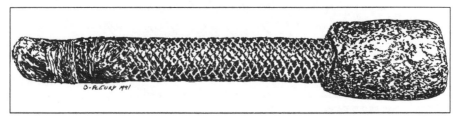

Donald Rua McGill's whipstick

made up their minds to report the matter to Sir Charles Styles[35] of Glenfin. They told him that they had given a very severe beating to robbers at *Bealach na gCreach.* "You didn't give them half enough," he replied. "But, my Lord, we are afraid there are some of them dead," said a cartman. "There's not half enough of them dead," swore Sir Charles. After this incident Ardara cartmen were left alone.

At the west end of Ardara, on the left, stands the Roman Catholic Church of the Holy Family, which was dedicated and officially opened on 15 November 1903. We know of two earlier Catholic churches within the village. The first, which we have already referred to, stood in the left corner of the Diamond; the second was erected in the early 1830s, shortly after the establishment of the Ardara parish in 1829, and stood at the east end of the present graveyard, less than a hundred yards from the present-day church.

The land on which the modern-day church was built was obtained from General Tredennick of Woodhill House at the beginning of this century. The Rev. Peter Kelly, then parish priest of Ardara, was the driving force behind the building of the new church and sadly he died on 18 December 1903, just one month after the official opening.

It is said that the Very Rev. Charles O'Donnell, P.P., who had taken up the administration of the Catholic parish of Ardara in 1867, was the first to introduce a choir into the church – this would have been the church over at the east end of the present graveyard. An amusing story is told about the day the choir first sang in the church. I have mentioned earlier that heavy drinking and fighting with either sticks or fists was quite common in olden times in Ardara. On the day on which the choir first sang in the Ardara chapel among the congregation was a man known as Pádraig Mór. The whole congregation were on their knees during the mass when the choir started up. Pádraig Mór had never heard a choir before and did not understand what was happening. He jumped to his feet. *"Dar priasc!"* says Pádraig Mór, "where's my stick? Let every man be away out of this place or there'll be a bad ending to it all!" Pádraig Mór thought that it was a group of drunken men who had started to sing in the chapel and that they would start fighting at any minute.

The outstanding feature of the Ardara church is the west window, a stained-glass window by the late Evie Hone (1894-1955). She was a member of an outstanding artistic family. A descendant of Joseph Hone (brother of the 18th-century artist Nathaniel Hone – whose works have an international reputation) and probably also of Galyon Hone, the glazier of Kings College Chapel, Cambridge, at eleven she was crippled for several years by polio which had an effect throughout her life. Many, however, later testified to the physical strength she found when working on stained glass. After a spell in London, in 1920 she went to Paris with her lifelong friend, Mainie Jellett, to work with Andre Lhote. His method was insufficiently rigorous for them and until 1931 they made annual visits to and corresponded with Albert Gleizes, who wrote one of the first theoretical books on cubism. In 1924 she held a joint exhibition with Jellett in Dublin but found the public unreceptive.

Her first stained glass commission was for Dundrum church in 1932. She was encouraged by Dutch glassmaker Roland Horst and trained in technique at *An Túr Gloine* by Michael Healy. Hone completed almost fifty commissions, the best known and largest a new east window for Eton College Chapel (1948-52), gained with the assistance of her friend, artist Derek Hill. She is perhaps the greatest 20th century Irish glassworker, her clarity of expression a fusion of her knowledge of cubism, medieval and contemporary glass, mosaics, and, from the 1940s, medieval Irish carvings.[36]

The Rose Window, entitled "Christ Among the Doctors", was commissioned by Patrick Sweeney of New York and completed in 1954. It commemorates Daniel Sweeney (1839-1911), a national school teacher at Beagh, halfway between Ardara and Portnoo and whom we have mentioned earlier in our travels, and his wife Anne, née McGinley (1841-1925). The work was supervised in Ireland by Patrick Sweeney's son, James Johnson Sweeney. He was then the director of the Guggenheim Museum in New York. James Johnson Sweeney's brother, John L. ("Jack") Sweeney (1906-86), was curator of the poetry room in the Lamont Library, Harvard University.[37] Jack Sweeney married Máire MacNeill (1904-87), an illustrious Gaelic scholar.[38] After Jack Sweeney's death in 1986, Máire MacNeill bequeathed their collection of modern art to the National Gallery of Ireland. Her bequest of fourteen pictures and drawings includes works by Pablo Picasso, Giacometti, Paul Klee, Jack B. Yeats and a painting by Evie Hone done in *gouache*, ink and black chalk on board and which is entitled "Study for Christ Among the Doctors" (Ref. No. NGI 7864).

When Christ's parents went up to Jeruselum for the Passover he separated from them and joined in discourse with the learned doctors of the temple. Scolded by his parents, he reminded them of his divine mission (Luke 2: 41-51).

Evie Hone's "Study for Christ among the Doctors" is quite different from the stained-glass work that appears in the chapel at Ardara, in that in her study the four lobes of the painting actually do contain groups of people who represent the doctors in the temple whereas the doctors are not visible in the stained-glass window in Ardara. After completing her sketches Evie Hone decided, in consultation with James Johnson Sweeney, to change the lobes of the window and when he suggested relating them to the Gospels she proposed the symbol of the Evangelists "in the broad traditional manner of a stone cross".[39]

In the Ardara stained-glass window Christ is shown at the centre, his arms raised in exhortation and a scroll on his knees. Above him is King David with his harp and, below, Moses with the two tablets of the decalogue. Being authors of the Psalms and of the Pentateuch respectively they represent the Old Testament.[40] The Evangelists, Matthew, Mark, Luke and John, fill the remaining four panels, but they are shown in their symbolic forms, as living creatures with wings. These symbols have been used in churches since the earliest times. The four symbols are lion, man, eagle and ox. The symbols are linked with the different approaches adopted by the four gospel writers.

Mark starts off his gospel with the story of John the Baptist in the desert, so Mark's symbol is the desert lion. Matthew begins his gospel by tracing the genealogy of Christ; since he takes flight into past ages, he is depicted as a winged man. John is symbolised by the eagle. This is said to be the bird which can fly the highest; John was the one Evangelist who reached the greatest theological heights explaining the Divinity of Christ, so the eagle is a suitable symbol for him. Luke starts off his gospel with the story of Zachary offering sacrifice in the temple. Luke was trying to emphasise the fact that Christ sacrificed his life for mankind. The animal most frequently used in the temple sacrifice was the ox or calf. Accordingly Luke is symbolised by the winged ox.[41]

So the interpretation of the actual window is that the whole work represents the Word of God. The old and the new Testaments, God's word to man, are arranged symbolically in six panels, placed literally about the young Christ.[42]

Derek Hill painted the ox symbol of St. Luke on the Ardara window. The rest of the work was done by Evie Hone. She has stated, in reference to the Ardara church, that she was happier working on a window for a mountain church than doing either the Eton College or Washington cathedral windows. Derek Hill has written that he found it her most beautiful window. Evie Hone has said that the colours of rich green, dark blue, browns and tawny earths that she had used had been inspired by the mosaics that she and Hill had seen together in Ravenna in the spring of 1948. They were colours that suited the grandeur of the northern Celtic landscape where the glass was to live.

As you leave the Ardara chapel, some yards east of the main gate there is another small gate for pedestrians. Just inside this gate is the gravestone over my father's grave. This stone is an exact replica of the cross slab on

Inishkeel island which depicts the figures of monks, swans and the chariot carrying two people. This gravestone is yet another reminder to us that we are still well within the geographical sphere of influence of Inishkeel island and St. Conall.

In times past death was accompanied by the rituals of a wake. Hugh Curran, ex-national teacher of Gortahork, passed on to me a tale which had been told to him by the late Canon Hugh McDyre, P.P., of Cloughaneely. It goes as follows: "A niche on the ruined church of St. Conall Caol on Inishkeel held a skull reputed to be that of the saint. It was customary, when a serious dispute arose between neighbours in the locality, that the disputants swore on the skull to the truth of their evidence. It happened that there was a wake in Ardara and as usual after midnight wake-games were held with the object of keeping the attendants awake. The games were usually in the form of 'question and answer' and a wrong answer entailed a stinging slap or more from a strap on the open palm. During a game a young girl's character was impugned and her vehement and tearful denials were ignored. Taking her shawl she left the wake-house. Alone and in the dark she walked to Inishkeel; the strand was favourable and she crossed to the island church, took the skull from its niche, wrapped it in her shawl and set off for the wake-house. Arriving there she uncovered the skull, placed her hand on it and swore to the falsity of the allegations. In the hushed silence she walked out, intent on returning the skull to Inishkeel. This time she was accompanied by an apologetic audience."[43]

As we leave the Catholic graveyard behind us and continue westwards we remember the deceased members of the entire Ardara community over the years and are reminded of Joseph Campbell's touching account of a funeral in Ardara in the year 1909:

"I was coming into Ardara this morning from the Lochros side, and as I came up to the chapel on the hill I heard the bell tolling. That, I knew, was for a burying: it was only about ten o'clock, and the Angelus does not ring until midday. Farther on I met the funeral procession. It was just coming out of the village. The coffin, a plain deal one covered with rugs, was carried over the well of a side-car, and the relatives and country people walked behind. The road was thick with them – old men in their Sunday homespuns and wide-awakes, their brogues very dusty, as if they had come a long way; younger men with bronzed faces, and ash-plants in their hands; old women in the white frilled caps and coloured shawls peculiar to western Ireland; young married women, girls and children. Most of them walked, but several rode in ass-carts, and three men, I noticed, were on horseback. The tramping of so many feet, the rattle of the wheels and the talk made a great stir on the road, and the movement and colour suggested anything but a funeral. Still one could see that underneath all was a deep and beautiful feeling of sorrow, so different to the black-coated, slow-footed, solemn-faced thing of the towns. As the coffin approached I stood into the side of the road, saluted, and turned back with it the *trí céimeanna na trócaire* [three steps of mercy] as far as the chapel yard."[44]

Proceeding from the Roman Catholic church towards the turn-off for the Loughros Point peninsula we are again reminded of sites associated with early Christianity, reinforcing our earlier concept that most early sites were situated close to the sea. In the large green field on our right just before the road leading off to Loughros Point there is a little hump in the middle of the field. This is the site of an ancient abbey. A few hundred yards to our rear, just behind where Triona Design now exists, there was a standing stone. Tradition tells us that this standing stone was the site of the grave of the monks who lived in the abbey, who were said to have been massacred en masse. Isn't it sad that this standing stone was levelled to the ground within the last ten or fifteen years?

Just north of this area and situated between the Owentocker and Owenea rivers is Kilgole [*cill*: a church; *gabhal*: a fork, used here to indicate the land situated between the fork of the two rivers]. The 1847-50 Ordnance Survey map shows us a spot here marked "Dermot and Grainne's Bed" and an area marked "Site of burial ground". That this "Dermot and Grainne's Bed" represented more than the usual interpretation – a portal tomb (a dolmen) – is suggested by my father's observations from 1937: "Monday 11th October 1937: Accompanied by Christy Byrne, went to see 'Dermot and Grainne's Bed' in Willie Young's land. The place so called may be a small stone circle but as it is overgrown with brushwood it is impossible to say. Willie Young told us that he had heard his mother say that it had one time a large cap-stone in which were two holes facing westwards. Willie while quarrying about twenty yards away discovered a circular hole in the quarry. I myself saw evidence of this on the flags quarried."

The portal tomb is said to have been removed in the early decades of this century in the course of land reclamation. That there was a stone circle or cashel at this site in earlier times, in addition to a portal tomb, is verified by Joseph Campbell, who, writing in 1911, states: "I was watching a rainbow this afternoon – a shimmering ring in the sky between the fort at the mouth of the Owentocker river and Slieve a-Tooey beyond. 'That's a beautiful sight, now,' said a beggar, stopping on the road to have a word with me – the sort of person one meets everywhere in Ireland, friendly, garrulous, inquisitive, very proud of his knowledge of half-secret or hidden things, anxious at all times to air it before strangers. 'We do have a power of them this weather.' He looked into the sky with a queer look, then started humming over the names of the colours to himself in Irish. 'And they say, sir, it's unlucky to pass through a rainbow. Did you ever hear that?'[45]

That the nearby "circular hole in the quarry" was probably a man-made souterrain is suggested by the fact that the late Johnny (Tom) Gallagher informed my father that when Matthew McCullagh lived in Kilgole years ago he pointed out a spot on the north side of the field in which the portal tomb had been situated where there was a hole which lead downwards to a cave.

The "site of burial ground" is located near by, just north-west of the house occupied by Jimmy Gavigan and his sister, Annie. The graveyard wall was carted away over a century ago for building purposes in Ardara. A line of trees runs along the site of the wall and is said to divide the Protestant and Catholic graves. It is likely that this graveyard was used for many centuries by the people living in the original settlement of Ardara, located along the Owentocker river; its siting would again suggest that the original river crossing may have been down here closer to the sea.

The area along the lower stretches of the Owentocker river is known as the *Muirlinn*. This is an aquatic term, derived from *muir*: the sea and *linn*: a pool, and denotes that part of the river which comes under tidal influence. The tide extends up along the *Muirlinn* as far as "the Neas" [*eas*: a water-fall], a fishing spot frequented by generations of Ardara people.

At the Loughros Point junction the building on the right at the corner, now occupied by noted local poet Don Byrne and his family, used to be the Ardara Number Four School – so called because there were three schools already in the village of Ardara when it was erected in 1879. It was the first Catholic school to serve the village. T.C. McGinley, passing through in 1867, makes a note of the need for such a school when he observes of the village: "It has three national schools – two under the patronage of the rector, the third under the management of the Methodist minister. The Catholic element is not represented in the matter of education."[46]

We now proceed down Loughros Point.

Notes

1   *Mearing Stones*, pp. 52-53.
2   T.C. McGinley was coming up from Loughros.
3   T.C. McGinley, *Cliff Scenery of South-Western Donegal*, pp. 153-54.
4   From *The Last Conquest of Ireland (perhaps)*, p. 116 – first published in a

series of letters in the *Southern Citizen* in the United States in 1858; reproduced in the *D.A.* (1970), pp. 161-62.

5   John O'Hagan (1822-1890) was a contributor to *The Nation* newspaper. Born in Newry, his journal was published in eight parts in the *Irish Monthly*, the sections relating to Donegal in the issues of May–September 1913; reproduced in the *D.A.* (1970).

6   Born in Ballyshannon in 1824; after seven unhappy years in a bank he became a customs officer, working initially in Ireland and later in Lymington, England. However his first love was poetry and between 1850 and 1887 he produced twelve volumes of verse, gaining popular recognition in 1854 with the publication of *Day and Night Songs*. In 1851 he started a lifelong friendship with Tennyson, the central figure in his diary.

7   *William Allingham, a Diary,* edited by H. Allingham and D. Radford, p. 40.

8   *North-West Donegal,* p. 79.

9   *Fishing in Ireland,* p. 100.

10   Ibid. p. 106.

11   *D.A.* (1966), p. 72.

12   Eugene O'Growney was born in Co. Meath in 1863. Gaelic was spoken in parts of Meath when he was a child. He was ordained a priest in 1889. He knew that Gaelic could not be revived unless the learners had books, and although he was a professor of Irish in Maynooth College and a scholar of note, he did his best to simplify the task of learning Gaelic by writing and publishing his *Simple Lessons in Irish*. He was one of the founder members of the Gaelic League. In 1894 his health broke down and he was forced to resign his position at Maynooth College to seek a warmer climate. He went to California where he died in 1899 at the age of thirty-six.

13   *An Claidheamh Soluis,* 20 and 27 July 1907.

14   Des Sheridan, *Dearcadh* (1989).

15   Presumably dating back to the original three small houses which stood on the site.

16   *Dearcadh* (1989).

17   Ibid.

18   Robert Baldrick in the *Daily Telegraph* reviewed Pat's novel as follows: "While Patrick Boyle's first novel *Like Any Other Man* is as Irish as they come, it is hard to imagine it getting past the censors in its country of origin. Though, on second thoughts, a story of sexual indulgence punished by total blindness and final ruin might well be considered worth a dozen hellfire sermons. ... Half-way through the novel, I thought that Mr. Boyle would be unable to maintain the pace he had set himself, but the story continues triumphantly to its gory, highly moral climax."

19   The Sinn Féin party had swept to victory in the General Election at the end of 1918 and the first Dáil Éireann met in public assembly on 21 January 1919.

20   Born in Dublin in 1920 his best-known novel, *Strumpet City*, was acclaimed on both sides of the Atlantic. His latest work is entitled *The Circus Animals*.

21   *H.P.A.,* p. 27.

22   Ibid.

23   Dr. Maguire (*H.D.R.*) gives 1802 as the year he became P.P. of Ardara.

24   Quoted in the *D.A.* (1953-54), p. 470.

25   Ibid.

26   A Laconnell woman.

27   A Carn woman.

28   See *Griffith's Valuations* and accompanying maps, 1857. Another Charles Gallagher lived over the town at this time; it may have been he.

29   E.g. Charles Shovelin of Lagunna "was found carrying a certain keg which contained illicit spirits at Drimbarron or Ardara".

30   E.G. "Def. had his house open for the sale of spirituous liquors and a number of persons found drinking therein, at a quarter to 12 o'clock p.m. on the night of 15th May, 1856, at Ardara."

31   Murray-Stewart estate records; now in the National Library, Dublin.

32   Ms. 336, pp. 94-104; written down on 30 March 1937; note especially a long tale called "Robin the Blacksmith"; did the inspiration for this story come from the nearby blacksmith?

33   Doubleday, Doran & Co. Inc., New York, 1937.

34   On the mountain road between Glenties and Ballybofey; an interesting place-name which suggests that robbery and cattle raids were nothing new to its history [derived from *bealach*: a road, a mountain pass, and *creach*: plunder, spoils, booty, especially of cattle]. The name suggests that this route over the mountains has been used since ancient times to drive home the cattle after raids into the land either east or west of the mountains.

At the time of the Derry cartmen poteen was extensively made in the mountainous region of *Bealach na gCreach* and the makers of it often intimidated solitary cartmen into delivering it for them in the towns through which they passed.

35   Sir Charles Styles was a general at Waterloo (1815); he came to Ireland in about 1821 and, offered a choice of sites to build a home, he chose Cloghan because of the salmon leap. The state of his health compelled him to leave Ireland in 1836. (My informant was Liam McMenamin, a native of Glenfinn, recently deceased and a past president of the Co. Donegal Historical Society).

36   Most of the foregoing, and much of what follows on Evie Hone and the Rose Window, comes from *National Gallery of Ireland: Acquisitions 1986-1988*, pp. 75-77.

37   To honour his twenty-four years as curator of the Woodberry Poetry Room in Harvard a poetry reading takes place there annually since his death. In 1990 the Memorial Reading was given jointly by Richard Wilbur, Pulitzer Prize winner and Poet Laureate of the United States, and Irishman Seamus Heaney, Professor of Poetry at Oxford and Boylston Professor of Rhetoric and Oratory at Harvard. Jack L. Sweeney was himself a poet.

38   Whose best-known work is *The Festival of Lughnasa* – a study of the survival of the Celtic festival of the beginning of harvest – published in 1982.

39   *National Gallery of Ireland: Acquisitions 1986-88*, p. 75.

40   James White, former Director, National Gallery, *Dearcadh* (1990), p. 2.

41   Rev. Liam McCaul, P.P., *The Evie Hone Window, a Guide for Tourists* (1984).

42   *Dearcadh*, op. cit.

43   Not everybody used a skull for swearing in the reverential manner in which the woman above used it. In a story (*J.R.S.A.I.*, vol. 43 (1912), p. 136) from Co. Mayo we find a skull being used by a sorceress. The sorceress forces a lady to swear on a skull and makes her take an oath that if she does not obey her commands then all the sins of the soul once dwelling in the skull would be added to her own on the Last Day. We are told (Ottay's *Tour in Connaught*, p. 337) that swearing on a skull was used on exceptionally solemn occasions in the past in Connaught. An oath on a skull and a bunch of keys was of even greater force, the presence of iron adding to the solemnity. (W. Maxwell, *Wild Sports of the West*, vol. II, pp. 64-66.)

44   *Mearing Stones*, pp. 30-31.

45   Ibid. pp. 3-4

46   *The Cliff Scenery of South Western Donegal*, pp. 153-54.

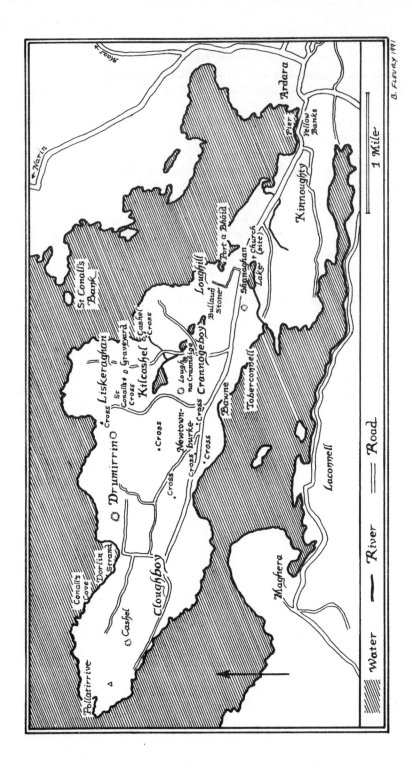

B. FLEURY 1991

Maas-r.

Narin

Ardara

Pier

Yellow Banks

Kilnoughty

St Conall's Bank

Port a Bháid

Shanaghan + Church Lake (site)

Loughill

Bullaun Stone

Conall's Cove

Pollatirrive

Dorlin Strand

Cashel

Cloughboy

Drumirrin

Liskeraghan

Cross

St Conall's Cross

Cross

Kilcashel

Cashel Cross

Cross

Loughan na Cruintóige

Crannogeboy

Newtown-burke

Cross

Cross

Cross

Bawne

Tobercornell

Maghera

Laconnell

1 Mile

Water

River

Road

XV

LOUGHROS POINT

THE LOUGHROS POINT peninsula is always referred to locally as just "the Point". Most natives of Ardara would associate the Point with fishing and with fairly good land. Large amounts of herring were caught in the Point over the years and channel fishing for salmon is still carried on in the short restricted summer season. As a youth I went out fishing with one of the crews from Loughros and witnessed "Henderson's Lights", the mysterious lights which appear to Point fishermen when they are out fishing at night time. Thomas Addi, in his description of fishing at the Owenea, referred to earlier, alluded to salmon fishing by boat in the channel off Loughros Point in 1730.

Tradition tells us of vast catches of herring down the Point, so great that the road for a mile down from the Ardara school would be stacked up on both sides with fish, with nowhere to send them and no facilities to store them, except for the small percentage of the catch which could be carted to Killybegs. That the former reputation of Loughros for herring was justified is verified by *The Belfast and Province of Ulster Directory* for 1910 which informs us that "During the winter months herring of the larger and best quality are caught in Loghros Bay, a quarter of a mile from the village" of Ardara.

Salmon fishing in Loughros remained the preserve of the landlord class until they had to sell up their estates at the beginning of this century. The Loughros fisheries belonged to the Murray (later the Murray-Stewart) estate, but were usually rented out to the Nesbitts. In 1846, the year of the Great Famine, we find R.W. Nesbitt paying £12 per half-year rent for the Loughros fishery and in 1851 William Tredennick payed rent for its use. The fishing was based at two areas, the Crumlin fish-carry, which we will deal with when going down the Laconnell road from which it is more visible, and at "Port a' Waud" [*Port a' bhád; bád*: a boat], which is off to the right of Shanaghan

Lough and is situated next to the Loughill area, which was in possession of the Nesbitt family until it was bought by Fr. McGarvey in 1835.

Loughros is also associated with fairly good land and with good husbandry. Our fishing observer, Thomas Addi, writing in 1730, also makes mention of the land in Loughros. At that time the complete Loughros peninsula was one big farm unit (comprising five *quarters*, or forty *ballyboes*) belonging to the Murray estate. It was leased out at the time to William Conyngham "who paid Mr. Murray but £80 per annum" and he in turn "had set the land to several different tenants for 43 or 44 years at £230 per annum". Addi states that there is "a great deal of good land in it for grain and grazing".[1]

In August of 1755 John Hood mapped out the whole Loughros area for the Murray estate and made observations on the quality of the land. Referring to whether land is arable or not he states that the land at Kinoughty is "indifferent", that at Crimlin[2] and Shanachan is "indifferently good", that at Cranegboy is "mostly very good" and at Clobooy is "good". He also mentions woodland at Crimlin and Drimalagh.

The reputation of Loughros for good potatoes was still much in evidence in the early decades of this century. At fair days in Ardara, the market house being full, old Paddy "Hahill" would have his stand on the Diamond with forty or fifty bags of potatoes. Other Point men situated themselves between the present day Corner Bar and the Post Office and over between Diver's supermarket and John Gallagher's. For a week afterwards carts would leave Ardara with potatoes, bound for Kilcar, Mucross and other places. The potatoes cost 2s a cwt.

As we start down the Point we have the sea immediately to our right. This area, with the pier on the right, is known locally as the the Yellow Banks. We are told that this pier was used in the last century by a family, no longer represented in the area, who used to bring goods up to the Yellow Banks in light boats. These goods were thought to have come from a large ship owned by the family, which would have been anchored out in deep water. The captain of this ship was said to have had a streak of the pirate in him. On one occasion it is said that he sailed to a foreign port in the ship, put aboard the most valuable cargo he could, then ran up sail and flew for England without paying for the goods. In the memory of people who lived earlier in this century it is said that he tried this in the port of New York on one occasion. His reputation had gone before him to America and after he had cleared American waters he was followed by an American warship, which had been watching his movements. He was finally overtaken by the warship and sunk in British waters. Trouble was expected from Britain, but not a word was said. The late Master McGrenra of Laconnell informed my father that two men from Laconnell were in the United States Navy at the time of the sinking of this ship. One was a brother of "Jimmy Sally's" and the other a brother to his father-in-law, Charlie Jimmy McHugh. One of these men was on the American warship that sank the local vessel. It was said that the family who owned and captained the ship had a house almost completed in Ardara, but on the sinking of the ship work stopped and never re-started on it.

This road at the Yellow Banks wasn't always as solid as it is now. The revised 1847-50 Ordnance Survey map describes it as a "causeway", thus indicating that it was a built-up section of road on the water's edge. John Hood's earlier map, of 1755, shows the road to the Point going down through the centre of Drimagha townland and then through the centre of Kinnoughty and on to Shanaghan. It seems that there was an old road through these townlands, further away from the sea than the present road. This was probably the "bridle-path to Loughros Point"[3] which Matthew Stewart took when he first began to preach Wesleyanism down the Point in the late 1700s.

We pass through Kinnoughty, a placename derived from *ceann*, a head, roughly "the highest point of", here indicating a hill, and *ucht* (or *ocht*), a breast, meaning the breast of a hill. Joyce tells us that "Kin-" is the dative of *ceann* used as a nominative[4] and that "-oughty" is *octaighe*, the pleural of *ucht*.[5] A translation of "the breast of a hill" will suffice us here.

Nearby Crumlin translates as *Cruimghlinn* [*crom*: curved; and *glinn*: a genitive form of *gleann*, a glen; the curved glen]. There are about twenty townlands of this name in Ireland and in every one of these places there is a winding glen.[6] Hillsborough in Co. Down was formerly called *Cruimghlinn*. Older estate maps of the area divide this townland into "Irish Crimlin" and "Upper Crimlin"; nearby Shanaghan was divided into Upper and Lower.

We now come to the historic townland of Shanaghan – written as "Seanchan" in the 1659 census of Ireland. Here there used to be a church on the side of the lake and there is still a holy well, dedicated to the memory of Saint Shanaghan. The popular belief is "that a monastery was founded here by St. Conal Caol, and that St. Shanaghan was the first abbot."[7] We are further told that "The Patron of Ardara is Seanachan, one of seven brothers, who were all well-known Irish saints, two others of them being abbots in County Donegal – Garvan was the founder of a monastery near Rathmullan, and Boedan settled at Culdaff."[8] O'Clery's Genealogies give Seanaghan's line of descent as "Seanaghan Dubaith, son of Luighdeach, son of Nathi, son of Dolbaigh, son of Sedna, son of Connla, son of Aonghasa, son of Oilealla Cedaigh, son of Cathaoir Mór". Shanaghan's feast-day is said to be 7 August.

You will remember that in dealing with Conall Caol's pedigree earlier I was sceptical of the family trees given to our early saints. My scepticism will have to surface again now in the case of Shanaghan's genealogy. The argument is the same – it is not possible to accept that a genealogy written down a thousand years after the saint's alleged lifespan can be an accurate one. We are, again, probably dealing with the cult of an early ecclesiastic who established a religious foundation elsewhere and whose reputation was then brought to this area by his later followers.

Earlier I have quoted three references to Shanaghan. We will now have a look at these and other references to see if we can get any pointers as to the origin and associations of the cult of Shanaghan.

The only really relevant clue is in the reference from the O'Clery Genealogies, and it took me a long time to notice its significance. "Seanaghan *Dubaith*" means Seanaghan of *Dubadh*; *Dubad* is the ancient name for Dowth, Co. Meath. So O'Clery's Genealogies is listing the predigree of a St. Senchán known to have been associated with a church at Dowth, Co. Meath; we can only presume that the cult of Senchán which was celebrated at Shanaghan was part of the *wanderkult* of Senchán of Dowth. In a publication dealing with *Sheela-na-gigs* in 1894 a *Sheela-na-gig* is noted at an old church at Dowth, Co. Meath. The person who showed it to the author of the 1894 article referred to it as "Saint Shanahan".[9] How intriguing that a *Sheela-na-gig* – a female fertility symbol, often represented erotically – should be called St. Shanaghan.

Shanaghan is said to have been descended from Lughaidh (Lugdach, Lugaid), who himself had sprung from the race of Cathaoir Mór. The latter was the legendary chief of the Laigin, an ancient tribe who ruled an area in the present-day province of Leinster; the *Annals of the Four Masters* state that he assumed sovereignty of Ireland in the year 120 A.D.[10]

We are told that Cathaoir Mór's descendant, Lughaidh (Lugaid, etc.) had seven sons who were saints;[11] I think we can interpret this loosely as meaning that the cults of these early saints were popular amongst the Laigin and possibly in the Leinster area in general. The seven saints were Mochua (also known as Cronán), Lasrain, Garbhán, Baedán, Baoithán, Ruadhán and our own Senchán.[12]

Of these early saints Mochua (or Cronán – another reminder that these early ecclesiastics were known by a multiplicity of names, possibly generated by their being given a different name in each area to which their cult spread) was venerated at Clondalkin, Co. Dublin; his cult also spread to Scotland and his feast-day was the same in both places – i.e. 6 August, the day before Shanaghan's feast-day. A Lasrian (or Mo-Laisse) is associated with Leighlin,

Co. Carlow - "One of the principal churches of the Laigin ... an ancient establishment";[13] it is possible that he is identical with Laisren (or Mo-Laissi, St. Molaissi) of Devenish island in Co. Fermanagh. Garbhán is associated with a number of areas, principally Kinsealy in Co. Dublin and his cult later spread to the Rathmullan and Killygarvan areas of north-west Donegal - "A cell dedicated to him being established on the Swilly by some monk or monks who came by sea."[14]

We need not deal with all the saints that we have traditionally been told are associated with Shanaghan; suffice to say that their origins are hazy indeed and that their cults spread in various directions.

So what of our very first reference when we arrived here at Shanaghan - "that a monastery was founded here by St. Conal Caol and that St. Shanaghan was the first abbot". Can we establish any direct association between Conall and Shanaghan? Not really. Possibly the cult of Senchán came via the Dallán Forgaill cult, to which the cult of Conall may have been by now attached, from Maighin (Westmeath).

In the earlier chapter on Conall Caol it was noted that the old kingdom of the Ulaid (which equates roughly with present-day Ulster) originally extended down to the mouth of the river Boyne. It would have included Dowth and there must be a possibility that the cult of Senchán became in some way attached to that of Cóelán - known to have associations with east Ulster (Nendrum) and possibly also with south Co. Down - in the general south Down–north Meath area. I think this is the most likely explanation for the Senchán–Conall Caol connection in west Donegal. You will have remembered that it has been suggested that Conall Caol and Cóelán (Móchóe) of Nendrum are one and the same. 22 June is Cóelán's feast-day and on the same day is celebrated the feasts of "The Children of Senchán" and of "The Children of Senán". If we adhere to our earlier-voiced concept that saints who were associated are often grouped together in the lists of feast-days, then I think we can suggest that here we might have an association between Cóelán/Conall and Senchán/Shanaghan.

Later on our travels we will visit St. Conall's well at Aighan near Bruckless. Near by is an area, now called Wood, which used to be called Diriconell (the Oak Wood of Conall). The 1642 list of placenames which gives us "Diriconell" lists a "Seanaghan" next to it;[15] surely further confirmation that the cults of Conall and Senchán travelled in tandem.

There is no part of the old Shanaghan church standing at the present day but the remains of the building have been noted in the last century. T.C. McGinley, while travelling up the Point in the direction of Ardara in 1867, states: "On our way we pass the handsome residence of the parish priest,

Rev. John D. McGarvey. It looks down on a beautiful lake, called Shanaghan Lough from the church of St. Seanchan, whose ruins are still observable upon its eastern shore, close to the roadway. After passing the border of the lake, we enter the village of Shanaghan, also named from the patron saint."[16] John Hood's map of 1755 has a "chappel" marked here. (Incidentally the only other buildings that he has marked in on the Point are a building just on the Ardara side of the chapel in Shanaghan, a building at the site of Loughill House and a building further down the coast at Crannogeboy. This latter was probably the "bawn" which we will refer to later on). The revised 1847-50 Ordnance Survey map has the Shanaghan church marked as "Loghros church and burial ground."

The antiquity of this church is not to be doubted, because in a list of Co. Donegal parishes of 1306-7, along with "Inyskill" (Inishkeel), the "Church de Loghrossce" (Loughros) is also mentioned.[17] This list forms part of "the most ancient ecclesiastical statistics connected with Ireland now remaining"[18] and demonstrates that Loughros was a separate parish, albeit a small one, at this early juncture.[19]

Though originally church land, the five quarters of Loughros were later claimed by the O'Boyle sept; the reason behind their claim, as given to the English authorities after the Plantation of Ulster, makes curious reading at the present day: "the said jurors saie, uppon their oathes, that there are in the said parish five quarters of land called Loughresse, which have auncientlie bine in controversie betwixt the church and the sept of O'Boyle's, and as by tradicon it hath beine delivered, the land originally came to the O'Boyle's, in manner and forme followinge, viz. that the bishop of Raphoe gave it in mortgage to a daughter of one Shewgrie O'Boyle for twentie cowes or tenne markes in monie which hee promised her for the use of her bodie, and that she beinge thereof seized, and, that ever since that time, which [is] beyond the memorie of man, the said land hath successivelie bine and yet is in the possession of the O'Boyle's, but that sithence the departure of the late earle of Tireconnell, the lord bishopp of Raphoe hath receaved the rentes thereof."[20]

We should remember that clerical life in the first centuries of this millenium wasn't as organised as it is now. The resignation of bishops and abbots was a relatively common feature of 12th-13th century Irish ecclesiastical life[21] and, in fact, on 18 May 1198 we find Pope Innocent III writing to the archbishop of Armagh concerning the resignation of the then bishop of Raphoe. He writes: "We are not unmindful that on a former occasion we instructed you to direct our venerable brother the bishop of Raphoe into a resumption of the episcopal office which he had resigned without due process of law..."[22] Church reform in Ireland was soon to take effect.

I cannot say with any certainty when the parish of Loughros ceased. In 1704[23] we find that the priest residing at Loughros is named William O'Boyle, though he appears to be the parish priest of the parish of Lettermacaward, which by now was exercising jurisdiction in these parts.

Dr. Maguire, writing of the Shanaghan church in his *History of the Diocese of Raphoe*, informs us that: "The Inquisition demonstrates that very extensive estates were attached to this monastery, and that, on its extinction, they had reverted as herenach lands to the Bishop of Raphoe. These were not 'termon' lands, however; hence Niall O'Boyle was obliged to seek sanctuary within the church itself, on the occasion of his incursion against his kinsman, Conor, in 1540, as recounted in the Annals. The Mooneys were the herenachs of the Shanaghan church lands, and they were also the most ancient herenachs of a portion of the Inniskeel estates."[24]

The "incursion" referred to above relates to a tragic event which occured in this area between two brothers of the O'Boyle sept, Niall and Conor, in 1540. It has led to a long folk tradition, involving the jealousy of Niall's wife and other influences, but here we will simply reproduce the version given in the *Annals of the Four Masters*:

"The two sons of O'Boyle, Niall Roe and Conor, were in contention and at strife with each other. Niall made an incursion against Conor into Luachras (for Conor had his seat and residence there), and remained that night in ambush in the church of St. Seanchan. Conor next morning went upon the hill adjacent to the church, and Niall and his people sallied forth from the church against him. When Conor saw them approaching him, he ran away to avoid them, as he had with him only a few [and these] persons unfit to bear arms and he proceeded alone down across the strand of Luachras. Niall pursued him as quickly as he was able, and he outran his own people in his eagerness to catch Conor; he overtook him, and they engaged each other vigorously and ferociously, forgetting friendship and relationship. Conor gave Niall a blow on the top of the head, and prostrated him on the ground, and then fled away, severely wounded. The people came up to Niall, who told them to pursue Conor, and that he himself was not in danger of death on that occasion. They did so at his request, and overtook Conor on the borders of a neighbouring lake; and they did not dare to come to blows with him, until they had first knocked him down with the stones which were on the strand of the lake; and when he was prostrated, they struck at him with weapons. And on their return they found Niall dead. There had not been of their tribe, for some time, two of the same ages who were more generally lamented than these two who were slain by each other."[25]

This event has bequeathed us two very interesting placenames. "The hill adjacent to the church" here at Shanaghan is called Dromnafingle [from *druim*: a ridge; *fionghal*: signifies the murder of a relative or clansman]. Internecine killing was considered so great a crime among the ancient Irish that a curse was believed to alight on the murderer and his race. However, this belief appears to have been forgotten in later centuries and, in fact, some years prior to the killing of Niall and Conor there was a similar incident in this area – the *Annals of the Four Masters* tell us that in the year 1509 "O'Boyle (Edmond Boy, the son of Niall) was slain at night, with one cast of a javelin, at Luachros, by Conor Oge O'Boyle."[26]

The "neighbouring lake" on the borders of which Conor was killed is named Lough Warvaneill. It is situated in Tullybeg, between Ardara and Maas. The name Warvaneill would seem more appropriate for a lake in Sussex or the Lake District until we realise that Lough Warvaneill translates simply as *Loch Mharbhadh Niall*, the Lake of the Killing of Niall. Thus do the actions of our ancestors leave an indelible mark on the nomenclature of our landscape.

The 1847-50 Ordnance Survey map indicates two villages in Shanaghan: Shanaghan Lower, into the right before coming to the lake and Shanaghan Upper, well into the left and also on the Ardara side of the lake. This latter is probably the group of houses which T.C. McGinley referred to in 1867 when, in coming up the Point, he stated: "After passing the border of the lake, we enter the village of Shanaghan". The single structure marked at this site on John Hood's map of 1755 may represent the village of Shanaghan Upper.

A road goes off to the left well before Shanaghan Lough and leads down to the sea at Ballyganny, an apt placename which translates directly as *Baile an Ghainimh*[27] [*gaineamh*: sand; the townland (or place) of sand]. Ballyganny is dominated by a huge expanse of sand which becomes exposed when the tide goes out.

Interestingly enough the sand on this strand, which was always fairly dark, is now becoming lighter in colour. This is explained by the fact that brighter coloured sand is being carried in over the bar mouth and deposited here at Ballyganny. If you had a chronological series of aerial views of the whole Ardara coastline you would notice that the great sand dunes over at Magheramore towards Rosbeg are gradually being carried away by the current and are being deposited over on the Point side of Loughros More Bay. In addition some of the sand is being carried in here into Loughros Beg Bay and deposited at Ballyganny.

The present-day alteration taking place in the silhouette of the sand dunes over on the Rosbeg side of Loughros More Bay is but the latest, if most obvious, manifestation of the continuing change which goes on in our landscape, much of which we are oblivious to. Thankfully there are those whose scholarship and research afford us a glimpse of earlier changes in the terrain which would otherwise be hidden from us. Writing of bog-covered sand dunes over on the Rosbeg side of the bay Frank Mitchell, that most illuminating of interpreters of our landscape, writes:

"On the north, Dawros, side of the bay, opposite Maghera, are fossil dunes, buried by blanket-bog, and the alignments of these dunes show that when they were forming, the wind was coming from a south-westerly direction. We talk about post-glacial changes in climate, but there was clear evidence of a change in general wind direction at some time in the past. I took a sample for radiocarbon determination from the base of the peat, and the answer was an age of 4200 years. This sample killed two birds with one stone; first it said the wind change took place more than 4000 years ago; and second it said that by that date the surface of the dune had become sufficiently waterlogged for peat to start to form on it. This is one of Ireland's oldest dates for the beginning of blanket-bog formation."[28]

Presently there is much discussion of the possible climate changes which we might expect in this country due to the "greenhouse effect". For the interested reader I would recommend a recent (1992) government publication *Climate Change: Studies On The Implications for Ireland.*

Half-way along Shanaghan Lough a road goes off to the right. This brings us up to Hilltown, which is part of Loughill (or Drumalough) townland. Hilltown is now uninhabited; it is a place I like to walk in, as it has a calm and serene atmosphere. In addition it is well coated with trees and bushes, which give it a luxurious feel despite its being so close to the sea. There is a large bullaun stone immediately behind the house which used to be occupied by the late Ephraim Ritchie; this bullaun stone was known locally as "the barley hole". We will discuss bullauns in more detail at Maghera.

Further along the main road we associate Loughill House with firstly the Nesbitts and then Fr. McGarvey. A number of generations of the Nesbitt family lived here at Drumalough (Loughill). Since I have dedicated a chapter to the Nesbitts earlier we will not dwell on the family again, but we will speak of Fr. McGarvey.

The first mention we have of Fr. McGarvey in Ardara is from tradition. In 1832 a terrible cholera epidemic swept through western Europe and North America. The *Ballyshannon Herald* carries numerous references to its spread in Donegal in 1832-35. Fr. McGarvey then lived in the house now occupied by Baskin's Supermarket adjacent to the bridge in Ardara. One morning, in the early hours, he looked out and saw the local doctor (whose name is not known) leaning over the bridge. An hour or so later the doctor was still in the same position and there wasn't a sign of life in the village. Dressing hurriedly Fr. McGarvey came out and enquired from the doctor if anything unusual had happened. "Father," he replied, "it couldn't be much worse; the plague has struck. I have been out all night attending people. This disease is so frightfully contagious that I cannot return to my lodgings which, so far, have not been affected." "This is my job as much as yours," replied Fr. McGarvey. "Come and stay in my house and, with God's help, we'll fight it together." So they did and with careful segregation and good nursing few lives were lost in Ardara. Fr. McGarvey and the doctor came through the whole ordeal unscathed.

Fr. McGarvey is said to have been a very careful man with his money. When he purchased Loughill House and farm in 1835 the old house was said to have been in poor condition, but its new owner had no intention of wasting money in improving it. He was friendly with Murray-Stewart, the landlord, who paid him a visit on one occasion. The visitor knocked at the open door through which thick smoke was rushing from the kitchen. A voice from within bade him enter, but a fit of coughing stayed his progress. "Bend low," said the voice, "and it won't be so bad." The landlord obeyed and then sure enough he saw the speaker, Fr. McGarvey, sitting quite comfortably by

"The Barley Hole"

the fireside under his low ceiling of smoke. The priest was surprised and de-lighted when he recognised his visitor, whom he entertained in the parlour, though it was little better than the kitchen. "My dear Mr. McGarvey," said the landlord, "I'm sorry to see you living under such poor conditions which I shall do my best to remedy. You require a new house suited to your exalted position. On Monday morning I will send you horses, carts, quarrymen and masons, and before long you'll have a home where you can sit in comfort." Young Murray-Stewart kept his word and in a few months Fr. McGarvey was the occupant of a large two-storey house which remains to this day.

The Loughill farm contained some of the best land in the parish and soon Fr. McGarvey was engaged in farming on a large scale. (The Murray-Stewart rental book for 1849 shows us that Fr. McGarvey's rental was £24 for the year, whereas the other people living in Loughill were only paying rent of £1 – £2 ; this reflected the size of his farm.) As well as breeding and rearing cattle he was a well-known dealer at the local fairs. No greater compliment could be paid to a cattle man than to say he was "as good a judge as Fr. McGarvey". On Saturdays and eves of religious holidays he usually heard confessions in or around his own house. Young active people attending for confessions felt they were expected to help with whatever farm work was in progress, and many of them did. During the harvest the confessional was usually the open hay field or the corn field. He preferred payment in kind, a sheep, a lamb or a pig for services such as baptisms, marriages, etc. Pigs seemed to have been the most common method of payment for marriages. He also took up sheep farming and leased land on the mountain townlands of Meenaboll and Meenagoland. Many traditional stories have come down to us of his economy and industry, but there was never a whisper that he was neglectful of his religious duties. He was a man of the people and they liked him. If he made an entry in a book, the records have never been found.

Among the Protestant population "Priest McGarvey" was highly respected and popular. He was often the only priest in the extensive parish of Ardara, which included Downstrands. Tradition remembers him riding his horse on a Sunday morning across Sandfield to the little church at Mullyvea. However, the abiding memory of him that persists in the folklore of Loughros Point is of his economy. I recently asked a hale and hearty octogenarian, resident in the Point, about this aspect of Fr. Mc Garvey's personality and he replied "you could work for him all day and in the evening he wouldn't give you as much corn as you'd take home in the turn-ups of your trousers". Which goes to prove that oral lore isn't *always* benign in its adjudication of past people and events!

We now come to the townland of Crannogeboy [*crannóg*: a lake dwelling made of wood; *buidhe*: yellow, tawny]. Presumably when the timber of which the structure was made became seasoned and old it gave the *crannóg* a yellowish appearance. Once in the townland of Crannogeboy, if we take the Kilcashel road up the hill to the right it brings us to where *Loch na Crannóige* (the lake of the crannóg) used to be, now a dried-up lake. A *crannóg* is a type of lake or lakeside settlement, the term being derived from *crann*, the Irish word for a tree, this being a reference to the amount of timber used in its construction. Lake and lakeside dwellings are known from all over the world and they were built in the manner that best suited the terrain and the environment. Many hundreds are known in Ireland. They most frequently come to light when through one cause or another the water level is lowered. When the surrounding water has been lowered or drained away the *crannógs* appear as mounds in marshy or boggy areas. Traditionally they are associated with the Early Christian period and in function they were defensive, or at any rate separated from the mainland, though occasional traces of a causeway have been found. They were single homesteads and, judging by some of the excavated examples, were occupied by a wealthy class. They are frequently mentioned in the annals and other early historic sources.[29]

Irish chieftains of well-known families generally occupied *crannógs*.[30] The crannóg here at Crannogeboy has always been associated with the premier family of this area historically, the O'Boyles, and indeed it has been suggested that the actual name Crannogeboy is derived from *Crannóg Uí Bhaoill*, O'Boyle's *crannóg*, but this is incorrect.

T. C. McGinley, writing in 1867, states: "The crannóg stood on an island in a small lake; this island was a solid rock, artificially enlarged by a pile of large, rough stones, built up at one end. There is no lake, however, to be found there at the present day, as that which formerly existed was drained about two years ago; and what was, till recently, a bed of mud at the bottom of a pond, many feet deep, is now a solid turf bank."[31]

In 1952, in a letter to the Co. Donegal Historical Society, the late Tommy Mulhern gave a vivid account of the history of this *crannóg*. The Mulhern family have lived in Crannogeboy for many generations and Tommy's cousin Sylvie and his family still reside in Crannogeboy. (Sylvie it was who first showed me the site of the *crannóg*, as it is difficult to find nowadays.) Tommy Mulhern writes: "The building would appear from description to have been on or rather built up to a small rocky island. It was reached by a causeway of stepping stones; as these stones were a kind of freestone they were carried away by the local people for sharpening axes and knives, etc.; however there are a few still available. As these stepping stones were about six inches thick some of them are almost worn through. The lake was known as Loch na Cran. It was drained about 1866 and the surrounding land re-claimed for tillage. A subsequent generation cut this land away for turf and the place became more or less a swamp again. About seven or eight years ago this place was drained again and the place is now practically dry land. The remains of the building were there until about fifty years ago. At that time, two men got permission from the then owner of the land to dig for treasure on condition that they built a fence. They found no treasure, but they built a fence, so that no trace of the building now remains on the sur-face.

"In the surrounding area, during turf-cutting operations, there were sev-eral finds including butter, glass beads and a battle axe. I remember seeing some of the beads years ago. But in the course of the passing years they got lost or mislaid. I have been trying to trace the battle axe and I believe it to be the one sent to the National Museum from Ardara some years ago. There was a local tradition amongst an older generation of this *crannóg* being used as a sanctuary, when he was in disgrace, by one of the O'Boyles, the site of whose castle was about a mile from here."

The Donegal Archaeological Survey states that "a number of stone axe-heads and three saddle querns have been found on the mound".[32] In 1954 Tommy Mulhern donated a saddle quern, which had been found at the site of the *crannóg*, to the Historical Society's museum in Rossnowlagh. The two common types of quern used in the past for grinding cereals are the saddle quern and the rotary quern. Before the potato came into general use it was customary for families to grind their own cereals for home consumption. The saddle quern is the oldest type; from 1928 we read: "The oldest form of quern, which may go back to the Bronze Age, is the saddle quern, so called

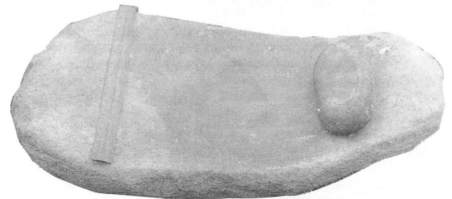

The saddle quern complete with its "rubber" stone, which
Tommy Mulhern donated to the Rossnowlagh Museum

from the shape of the lower stone. It is a long rectangular slab of rough stone, upon which the upper stone,[33] a smaller block with a flat base, is rubbed backward and forward."[34] The more recent view of the dating of saddle querns is that "the manufacture and use of saddle querns in Ireland appear to date largely to the prehistoric period. This is so because the saddle quern was made obsolescent by the introduction of the rotary quern sometime in the last few centuries BC (Caulfield 1978. 130)"[35] and "There is no dating evidence for the saddle quern: it is likely to belong to any stage between the Neolithic and the last few centuries BC when, according to Caulfield[36] (1978,130) the type may have been replaced by the more efficient rotary quern."[37]

The relevance of these statements for us is that though this *crannóg* is identified with the O'Boyle sept, who were at their prime in this area in the 14th-17th centuries, this site, where stone axe-heads and saddle querns have been found, must have been inhabited in the Iron Age, before the time of Christ.

If you continue on down past the site of the *crannóg* you come to Kilcashel graveyard on the left. The name Kilcashel is self-explanatory [*cill*: a church; *caiseal*: a stone enclosure]. The cashel is an almost circular area enclosed by a stone wall, which survives up to about 1 m. in height; it is located on a knoll of limestone away down to our right, at the edge of the sea. You will identify this raised area, which is surrounded on three sides by the sea, from the little bushes which are growing all over it. On the south-east

Kilcashel cross

side of the cashel there is a small stone with a plain Latin cross with T-bar ending carved on one face. This land formerly belonged to the late Joe Blain, who was the only one who knew of the existence of this little cross for many years and who kept a close eye on it; it is now in the equally good care of the Morrow family who farm here. The little cross slab is just 11.5" inches in height and about 8.5" in width.

Kilcashel graveyard is still used. Even though "burial ground" is marked on an earlier map[38] at the site of St. Shanaghan's church, which we visited earlier, there is no evidence nowadays that there ever was a graveyard in Shanaghan. It has been suggested in the past that this graveyard at Kilcashel was the graveyard for the Shanaghan church. Dr. Maguire, in referring to the Kilcashel graveyard, states: "Neither ruin nor tradition points to the existence of any church within or close to the enclosure. This was obviously the most ancient Christian burial-place in the district, and was attached to St. Shanaghan's Abbey."[39] However, I think it likely that a graveyard was attached to the Shanaghan church in earlier times, just as the presence of the word *cill* here at Kilcashel would suggest that in fact there had been an early church here. The presence of St. Conall's cross just a hundred yards due west of the graveyard would also support the suggestion that there had been an early church here, as it would be more likely that such a cross

St. Conall's cross

would be erected close to the old *cill*. The Donegal Archaeological Survey team, in discussing the enclosure formed by the modern graveyard stone wall, state that "traces of older enclosing walls are visible in places".[40] But the strongest evidence that there was a church (*cill*) here comes from T.C. McGinley, writing in 1867, who states: "Kilcashel is ... beautifully situated on the side of a rocky hill, clothed with soft fresh verdure, and rising above the southern margin of Luachros Mór Bay. The ruins of the church are still traceable, and the place is even yet used as a burial ground. Near it stands the cross of St. Conal."[41]

This cross, situated just over the hill behind the graveyard, is a crude cross-shaped slab, 1.57 m. in height. Of most interest is that it has little embryonic arms, indicating that its makers were leaving the stage of just incising crosses on slabs and were now beginning to shape the slabs into actual crosses. (The other numerous "crosses" down the Point, which we will be describing soon, are simply slabs of stone which have crosses incised on them.) The south face of St. Conall's cross bears a ringed cross, the arms and stem of which terminate in a crosslet.

When you stand on the hill behind the graveyard close to St. Conall's cross, and look over towards Rosbeg and Carn, the sandbank over near Carn is known as Connall's Bank (*Oitir Chonaill*).[42] We have mentioned this sandbank earlier, when discussing the *turas*; the proximity of St. Conall's cross to the sandbank in the middle of Loughros More Bay would support the old tradition that this was the route by which St. Conall used to cross over to Glencolumbkille, a route supposedly followed in later years by people doing the long *turas* from Inishkeel over to Laconnell and Glencolumbkille.

We now leave this north coast of the Point, return to the main road at Crannogeboy, walk down a small slip-road past Gallagher's house towards the sea on the south side of Crannogeboy and come to Toberconnell [St. Conall's well; *tobar*: a well]. No tradition or ritual pertains to this well nowadays, but its presence here on the Laconnell side of the Point would again support the old belief that people passed this way when doing the long Inishkeel–Glencolumbkille *turas*. Nevertheless, it is also possible that this well and the numerous cross slabs on the Point latterly formed part of a *turas* confined to the Point peninsula. This is the view to which I would incline. Since we know by now that Loughros was an ancient parish, it is likely that this ecclesiastical unit had its own separate *turas* sites here on the Point peninsula.

A coastguard station and a Protestant school were located down here in the vicinity of Toberconnell in the middle of the last century. The Catholic school was a little further down the main road, opposite to where the present national school[43] is situated and there was a Wesleyan School down at the end of the Point in Drimirrin. T.C. McGinley, writing in 1867, refers to these schools when giving us his impressions of the Point: "On arriving at the coastguard boat-port we find ourselves in the village of Crannog Buidhe. It is inhabited principally by coastguards, the cottages in which they reside being rented from William Walker, Esq., who occupies a house in the same village. And here I may be permitted to observe, that the tourist will find Mr. Walker and the Luachross coastguards exceedingly accommodating and obliging. There are two national schools (male and female) under the respective management of the parish priest and the rector. There is a third national school farther down, of which the Methodist minister is the patron. Thus are all three demoninations represented in the Point. The dwelling-houses observable here are substantial and cheerful looking. Their appearance at short intervals along the road leading to the extreme end of this peninsula tends to render the walk thither an exceedingly pleasant one, while the fine views to be had of the lofty cliffs of Sliabh Toiadh just opposite, furnish an additional charm, and make the downward tour still more gratifying to the lover of the sublime and beautiful in nature."[44]

I would certainly agree with his latter sentiment; the scenery here, especially the play of light on mountain, sea and sand, is spectacular. In addition his observation of houses at short intervals along the road confirms an impression that the Point used to be quite densely populated; mid-19th century maps suggest that the Loughros peninsula was heavily populated at that time, especially at Crannogeboy and further down at the village of Cloghboy.[45]

One comes across numerous references, both oral and written, to O'Boyle's castle in Crannogeboy. This was a separate identity from the *crannóg*. Presumably it was to it that Dr. McParlan was referring in 1802 when he states: "At Lough Rus, town of Cranaghboy, are the ruins of an ancient building, said to have belonged to the O'Boyles."[46] On past the Crannogeboy national school, down right against the sea on your left, on Donal Gallagher's land, is a large walled structure. This is often thought of as being O'Boyle's castle, but these walls are more likely the remains of a "bawn" erected just after the Plantation of Ulster, in the early 1600s.

Pynner's Survey of 1618-19 found that a strong bawn of lime and stone had been built in the Proportion of Monargan. This Proportion included the Loughros area. It had few British tenants, but a great many Irish dwelt upon the lands. In 1622 it belonged to Sir Thomas Chichester and a wooden house had been erected inside the bawn. There were but two British men. The bawn was a strongly built enclosure of lime and stone inside of which the undertaker[47] had his homestead. The rectangular ruins (130' x 80') on the lands of Donal Gallagher, Stonebrook (the very name of this area, Stonebrook, suggests a strong Plantation influence) are believed to be the remains of the Monargan bawn.[48] This is probably the building which is marked on John Hood's map of 1755 and at which the road down Loughros Point seems to end. Donal Gallagher, who owns the land here, points to a place opposite the entrance to the bawn as the site of the O'Boyle castle. It is a spot roughly circular, like the remains of a fort. There was an old cannon in this field said to be of a type similar to that on Kiltoorish island.[49] Whether it came from the bawn or the castle no one knew. Well over a century ago it was used as a test of strength on summer Sunday evenings by young men who gathered from a wide area: the pasture suffered as a result. Then one night Donal Gallagher, grandfather of the present owner, got the assistance of a neighbour and buried it. It has never since been seen.

The Ordnance Survey map of 1847-50 shows us two ringforts in the townland of Crannogeboy, one down to your left just after passing Shanaghan lake, just inside the Crannogeboy boundary, and the other up on top of Drumacrolly Hill. No significant trace of either now survives. We still have the remnants of a few cashels in other townlands in the Point and the mid and lower parts of the peninsula are very rich in cross-inscribed slabs. We will now detail these artefacts, paying particular attention to the cross slabs.

Behind the late Maurice Heekin's house in Crannogeboy stands a slab 1 m. high x .5 m. wide; it has a Greek cross incised on each face, the ends of the crosses terminating in a T-bar. It lies against a fence behind Maurice's house. I was saddened by Maurice's death, which occured in recent years, as I had often visited him and brought other people to see the little cross slab. There are the remains of a few rotary querns embedded in the wall in front of Maurice's house.

Liskeraghan has the remains of a cashel, over near the Drimirrin boundary. What remains is an almost circular area enclosed by a grassed-over stone wall. The spot is close to and south-west of Liskeraghan strand.

Newtownburke (Burkestown) has three cross slabs. The first of these stands behind the ruins of the house formerly occupied by Paddy "Bradden" Shovlin.[50] This slab is just over 1 m. high. On one face is a Latin cross with T-bar terminals; a cross on the other side is nearer in shape to the Greek form. It also has T-bar terminals. The late Paddy "Bradden" senior uncovered it while making a drain close to his house in 1875.[51] Failing to notice that the flag bore markings he brought it home to fill a depression in the kitchen floor, under the dresser. Some time later while his mother was energetically scrubbing the new flag the cross "appeared before her eyes".

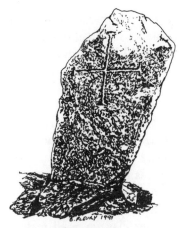

The Crannogeboy cross

Newtownburke cross 1

Newtownburke cross 2

Newtownburke cross 3

Cloughboy cross 1

Cloughboy cross 2

Thinking she had witnessed a miracle she called in her neighbours, a few of whom were quick to solve the mystery – boulder clay had obscured the lines of the cross – much to the disappointment of old Mrs. Shovlin. The slab was removed from the kitchen and erected at the spot where it was found, and there it still stands.

The second Newtownburke cross slab stands beside a wire fence on Newtownburke hill. It is .7 m. in height. There is a Greek cross with T-bar endings on each face. The third Newtownburke cross slab stands on top of a grass-covered mound close to the road, on the south side. It is a trapezoidal-shaped slab. A Latin cross with T-bar endings is inscribed on both sides. This slab was dug up about the beginning of the century, at the spot where it now stands, by the late John Breslin of Liskeraghan and the late Thomas Carlin and others, while searching for boulder clay for road making.[52] The first few sods they turned revealed the cross slab which they placed in an upright position, and ever since the site has been regarded with reverential respect.

Cloghboy has two cross-inscribed slabs. These had gone unnoticed until the late Paddy Rua Gallagher pointed them out.[53] One is cut on the smooth face of a low crag close to the old road on the late Paddy Rua's grazing land. It is a Latin cross with T-bar terminals. The second cross slab is a rough flagstone bearing four small crosses, near the late Paddy Rua's house. It appears to be part of a larger slab. It is decorated on both sides: on one side is a single Latin cross with T-bar terminals and on the other side there are three smaller Latin crosses, two of which have T-bar terminals. It is said that it originally came from an unknown location in the townland of Newtownburke. The Gallagher family continue to care for these artefacts.

Cloghboy also has the remains of a cashel; it is a subcircular area enclosed by a collapsed stone wall; a modern square structure is built of stones taken from the cashel, on the east side; at the south-east corner the beginnings of a modern wall runs off the cashel. A gap of 2.7 m. to the west seems to have been the original entrance.[54]

In Drimirrin a more recent structure has been built on the site of a cashel. If you start at the Dorlinn strand and walk back along the coast towards Ardara you will come upon it. It is a D-shaped modern stone enclosure which is built on the remains (and probably from the same material) of a destroyed cashel.[55] With its high wall it's a good place to shelter if you happen to be walking along the coast and a sudden squall of rain comes on.

Drimirrin also has a cross slab. This is situated close to the Drimirrin–Liskeraghan boundary, about 150 yards north-west of the Liskeraghan houses. Being in a remote area it was not known outside the immediate neighbourhood, and even there it was forgotten about for many a year.[56] Sloe and bramble hid it from view. The late John Shovlin (Liskeraghan) was about the only one who knew of its whereabouts, and shortly before his death he hacked away the bushes that obscured it and brought it into view. It leans against a roughly built stone stile known as "the Altar". It is .87 m. high. On the north face is a cross with a circle to the top and two-thirds of a circle to the base. The cross-bar is thicker than the shaft and there is a small circular depression at the junction.[57] There is no tradition other than that it is believed mass was celebrated at "the Altar."

I will not attempt to date the cross slabs in the Point. However their presence in such numbers would seem to point to very intensive early ecclesiastical activity in the area. Professor Michael Herity of U.C.D., in discussing similar type cross slabs – "small slabs, many with simple incised decoration, or tiny free-standing crosses"[58] – in the western end of the large glen of Glencolumbkille, states that they "would appear to have a date in the sixth or early seventh centuries".[59]

Isabel Crozier, discussing the Newtownburke cross slabs in 1938, states: "As to the type of cross with terminal cross-bars, which appears on all these Newtownburke cross-slabs, it would seem to be originally an early Christian type. It also recalls the heraldic Cross Potent. ... It is also to be found in Egypt on the Walls of the Ramesseum at Thebes.[60] Rude cross-slabs of the Newtownburke type are difficult to date with certainty, and nothing is known locally of their history, neither do we know if there was ever a church or graveyard or even a 'kileen' in the townland."[61]

Drimirrin cross slab

Why are there so many cross-inscribed slabs in the Point? More precisely, they are confined to the middle third of the peninsula. Across from Newtownburke on the opposite shore of Loughros Beg Bay is Laconnell; the linear proximity of Laconnell gives rise to the belief that the Newtownburke and other cross slabs in the Point were part of a long *turas* which started on Inishkeel island and continued over to Laconnell and into Glencolumbkille, a return journey of some 50 kms. A number of the cross slabs close to the waterline (the little one at Kilcashel and the one nearest Laconnell) could be interpreted as entry and exit points on to and from the peninsula for those doing the long *turas*. That the Newtownburke slabs are cross inscribed on both sides would indicate that the penitent was met by a cross as he or she approached each "station", irrespective of whether he or she was on the outward half or the return leg of the *turas*. That is what one would expect.

Though folklore from the Glencolumbkille area supports the concept of the long Inishkeel–Glencolumbkille *turas* I had always doubted it myself. I must admit, however, that though the return journey would entail a long trek along the bay and over the mountains the concept of a long *turas* was an established fact in earlier times - there was a tradition in the Laconnell area in the recent past of people going to pray at St. Catherine's well at Killybegs and people from all over west Donegal trekked to Lough Derg. Yet one question that I would put forward against the concept of the Inishkeel–Glencolumbkille *turas* is that, bearing in mind the numbers of cross slabs which have survived in the Point, why has not one cross slab been preserved or unearthed on the *turas* route between Inishkeel and the Point and from Laconnell until one reaches the outskirts of Glencolumbkille?

A possible answer is that the cross slabs in the Point were on the route of a *turas* performed between Inishkeel and Glencolumbkille in very early times, that this *turas* fell into abeyance and that the Point cross slabs may have been preserved because a later *turas* confined to the Point itself developed around them. The more common type of *turas* is usually confined to the environs of an early Christian monastery or hermitage; there is no evidence that such existed in the Newtownburke area and this diminishes the argument for a *turas* confined solely to this part of the Point. We have noted before, however, that Loughros was an ecclesiastical unit - a parish - in former times and the peninsula in general may well have had its own *turas*. Enrí Ó Muirgheasa, writing in 1936, suggests that there was a *turas* performed in the Point and writes: "The *turas*, now discontinued, I believe, went from Tobar Chonaill round by Cloch Buidhe, Druim Miotain and Cill Chaisil."[62]

There is certainly no doubting the importance of this area from an early ecclesiastical point of view. We would do well to remember that the area known as the "five quarters of Loughros" was originally church land, but mortgaged long before the Plantation to the O'Boyle family.

We now leave the subject of cross slabs and continue our tour towards the end of the Point.

One of the aims of the Plantation of Ulster was to get people to live in towns or nucleated settlements. Cloghboy seems to have been the main nucleated settlement in the "five quarters of Loughros". The 1847-50 Ordnance Survey map shows a lot of houses in Cloghboy, all along the road on the right.[63] The Rev. John Barrett, writing in 1821 (you will remember that he was answering questions, part of a survey, in which the answers have survived but not the questions), stated: "The only town is Glenties; the principal villages are Narin and Cloghboy. I know of no other consisting of twenty houses contiguous." No mention of Ardara! I wonder what was the question.

The townlands of Cloghboy and Drimirrin both extend down to the very end of the Point, Cloghboy on the southern side and Drimirrin on the northern. The big sea pool at the end of Loughros Point is called Pollatirrive [*tarbh*: a bull; the hole of the bull, the bull's chasm]. There is an overhanging precipice from which a bull is said to have fallen in the past right down into the dark pit below. And is said to have been taken up alive again!

The terrain here towards the end of the Point is rocky. Some of this rock has been of use to the locals over the years. T.C. McGinley, writing in 1867, states: "The rocks of Luachross consist principally of mica slate, overlying the gneiss formation.[64] At a former period it supplied this part of Donegal with slates for roofing, called Boylagh slates. At present the quarrying is confined to the raising of flags for paving purposes."[65] When the Drimirrin Methodist school was built in 1864 (some say 1857) stones quarried at nearby Whitefield at a cost of £5 were the principal material used. Incidentally when the building was renovated during the Second World War timber from the wrecked ship *Aurora* was used for roofing and flooring.[66]

The wrecking of the *Aurora* reminds us that rocky headlands like Loughros Point held danger for maritime traffic all down the years. The following story is told about a massacre of sailors which took place at the very end of the Point. Many years ago a ship was wrecked off Loughros. The shipwrecked sailors landed at the end of the Point; they wore long hair down their backs and spoke in a foreign tongue. The Point people attacked them with "grapes", forks, spades and shovels. One of the strangers must have been an Irishman, for when attacked he shouted in Gaelic, "*Caitliceach mise, ná mharbhuigidh mé*" ("I'm a Catholic, don't kill me"). The tradition is that all were killed and buried at a spot still pointed out at the extreme end of Loughros Point.

Just west of the Dorlinn strand (*Trá Bán*) is a little cove called Conall's cove; it is likely that this is another reference to St. Conall Caol, but it is also possible that it was named after a local man. I think we would be wiser not to ascribe this little cove to St. Conall Caol of Inishkeel, no more than we would suggest that the cove next to it, Nancy's cove, is named after Nancy's Bar in Ardara!

John Hood, writing of this shoreline and the surrounding areas in 1755, states: "The Shores of Lochris[67] point except about half of Drimerhin and Clobooy are generally covered over with good Wrack fit for Kelp or Manure, as is also the other Shore as far down as Lakonnel and Machry Marein.[68] In Drimerhin and Clobooy, they complain of a Distemper incident to Black Cattle called the Cruppan which obliges them to send 'em off to the Mountains every now and then, during the Summer season which is the case in some measure in other farms in ye point."

One comes across numerous references to this cattle disease called "the cruppan" in earlier books. Dr. McParlan, writing in 1802, states: "The cattle feeding for twelve months on those mountains, or most of the coarse farms, are seized with a disorder here called 'the cruppan'[69] which is most probably a corruption of the cripple; for the cattle do become crippled, as if by rheumatic pains; in a more advanced and aggravated state of the disorder they are totally deprived of the use of their limbs; the hair on the back stares; it becomes a favourite resort of the flies; at length an atrophy succeeds, and death. This disorder, however, is cured by removing the cattle to sweet soils; if, however, the cattle should remain a year on this very soil, which cures the cruppan, it induces another not inferior in malignity, called the 'galar'.[70] Cattle, which die of the 'galar', when opened are found to have the gall-bladder enlarged, and skin black. It would seem then, that the 'galar' is a jaundice."[71]

John Hood's earlier assertion that the cure for the cruppan was "to send 'em off to the Mountains every now and then" caused a lot of problems for me until I realised that he was mistaken and that he was mixing up the cure for the cruppan with the ancient tradition of sending cattle off to summer pasturage in the mountains, a practice still carried on throughout Europe and known as transhumance, or in Ireland booleying (*buailtearacht*); we will deal with this concept shortly.

Dr. McParlan was correct. Cruppan was not cured by sending cattle to the mountains, it was caused by cattle having to graze on the hard mountain grasses. Up in the mountains behind Maghera we have an area called

Croagh a'Cruppan and near by is a lake called *Lough na Cruppan*. This would indicate that here was one of the areas where cattle left to graze developed the cruppan. However they also, as John Hood correctly pointed out, developed the cruppan on the much more low-lying Loughros Point. The cruppan was, in fact, a deficiency disease resulting from a lack of phosphorus; it does not occur nowadays because of the use of artificial fertilizers. The hard mountain grasses and the equally harsh sedge grasses of the Point predisposed to the cruppan. Dr. McParlan, who was a member of the Royal Dublin Society,[72] and therefore keenly interested in the welfare of animals, investigated further and discovered that the cattle grazed mostly on what he called "keeb" grasses, the *"keebdu"*, the *"keebroe"*, etc. – "the keebdu, from November till March, is the chief food of the outlying cattle", he states.[73] "Keeb" translates as the Gaelic word *cíb*: sedge. "Keedu" is *cíb dhubh* (*dubh*: black), common sedge, *Carex nigra*.[74] "Keebroe" is *cíb rua*, brown sedge, *Carex disticha*.[75] There are fifty-five different types of sedge. It is of interest at this juncture to point out that the placename Loughros derives from *luachair*: sedge or rushes, and *ros*: a peninsula, the peninsula of the sedges or rushes.

The cure for cattle suffering from the cruppan was to bring them to graze on rich sandy soil – the "sweet soils" referred to by McParlan – but if left here too long they developed a cobalt deficiency, presumably the *galar* referred to by McParlan. Animals grazing on sandy soils nowadays can suffer from cobalt deficiency but the farmer can now dust his land with cobalt. Previous generations of farmers had to walk the tightrope between their cattle developing the cruppan or a cobalt deficiency.

To give the exhausted lowland grazing areas a rest, and because palatable grass grew on the highlands during the summer months, animals were brought off to the mountains every year – the practice of transhumance (*buailtearacht*). The survey which went with John Hood's map of 1755 shows us not only the lowland areas which comprise the "five quarters of Loughros" but also indicates the appropriate mountain areas to which each lowland area sent its cattle during the summer.

The cattle were not just brought up to the mountains and left there. In Ardara preparations for migration to the mountain booley started about 12 May, "Old May Day".[76] When the crops had been planted by late spring, the people living along the shoreline rounded up their cattle, packed some of their household utensils and set off for mountain pastures. It was customary for two or three families, especially those who were related, to travel and "booley" together.

When the lively cavalcade reached its destination in the mountains willing hands set to work to put things in order for the duration of the booleying period. The sod cabins, used during previous years, were again made habitable. Firewood and turf were collected. The cattle were turned loose to roam and graze over the moorland pastures. As soon as the necessary tasks were performed, all returned to their homes by the shore except the young women who were to look after the cattle. During the months they spent up in the mountains these young women were kept busy. They had to round up the cows morning and evening for milking. They had to churn milk and make butter. There was wool to be carded and spun.[77] It is said that the carding and spinning of lint – to be used in bandages – was a very remunerative occupation in the mountain booleys during the Napoleonic Wars, so much so that one woman is said to have made the price of a farm of land spinning lint in the sheeling. There was knitting to be done and there were garments to be made. The afternoon of Sunday brought a pleasant respite – boys and girls from the neighbouring valleys made their way to the mountain cabins to spend the evening in dancing, music and song.[78]

While they were up on the summer pastures the people had little to eat. Mostly they survived by drinking milk and astonishingly they also drank blood which they look out of the cattle. To do this they used a little instrument called a *tuagh chuisle* – this is the term used by a man[79] from Meenacurrin, above Maghera, in 1940. A *tuagh cuisleann* is a lancet and it can be identified as a veterinary three-bladed lancet known in English as a fleam; a *tuagh cuisleann* translates directly from Gaelic as a "vein axe". A vein in the animal's neck was compressed until it swelled with blood and the *tuagh cuisleann* was then driven into the vein with the tap of a piece of wood.[80] The blood was then allowed to congeal in a tub, could be preserved for some days by salting and was then boiled up, mixed with butter and eaten in the mountain booley. It thus served as a type of flesh-meat. The earliest reference in English to this custom in Ireland dates from 1571: "Their kyne they lett bloode, which grown to gelly they bake and overspredd with butter, and soe eate yt in lumpes."[81]

When I first learned of the practice of cattle being regularly bled on the mountains during the booleying season I found it difficult to accept that the reason for its origin was solely dietary – that the people needed the blood as food. I felt that originally there must have been a physiological reason to do with the health of the cattle and that the habit of the people in baking the blood and eating it was secondary to some forgotten or unknown reason for bleeding the cattle for the cattles' sake. Folklore[82] from another area of Donegal suggests that the bleeding was a cure for a cattle disease called "red murrain" (red water, *mún fola*), but this is incorrect – the traditional cure in this area for red murrain, which is a tic-borne disease caused by a parasite, was to boil up the little sour sticks of the bog-myrtle (in Gaelic *roideog, Myrica gale*) bush (which grew in profusion in the Meenakillew curragh when I was a child) and give the water to the cattle to drink.

Possibly the origin for the practice might be explained as follows. The red blood corpuscles in our blood carry oxygen around our body; when a person moves from a low-lying area to an area of high altitude, where oxygen is scarcer, the red blood corpuscles in their bloodstream increase greatly – this results in their being able to move the less available oxygen around their body more quickly and efficiently, thereby making up for the relative lack of oxygen. If they return to the lowlands after some time they would have a super-efficient system of transporting blood gases in their body – an increased concentration of the transport medium (red blood corpuscles) and, now, a normal supply of oxygen. This physiological change caused by high altitudes underlies the reason why athletes go off for "altitude training" for some weeks before major sports events such as the Olympics. However the effect is temporary – the "thick" mountain blood soon returns to normal at lower altitudes. It is possible that cattle brought from the lowlands showed signs of distress after some time on the high mountains, because their blood was becoming "too thick"; therefore some blood was taken off the cattle on a regular basis. In humans a condition called Polycythaemia Rubra Vera exists in which the blood becomes "too thick" and the only solution is to remove a pint or two of blood at usual, often monthly, intervals. This is still done at the present day. This is my theory as to the original reason for the bleeding of cattle while on the mountain during the summer, a reason forgotten or not understood by the later generations.[83] However all this might be absolute balderdash. The difference in altitude between highlands and lowlands might not be great enough in Ireland to cause problems to cattle. Possibly the reason for bleeding the cattle was solely dietary. But I'll leave in my theory as an act of mischief and as a topic of discussion.

Now, if you have finished your culinary delight of baked cows' blood mixed with butter, we will conclude our discussion on booleying. Towards the end of September preparations were made for a return to the lowlands. Mountain grass was getting withered and dry. Nights were getting long and cold. Another important consideration in bringing the season to an end just then was the approach of the great fair of Magheramore which would be held in the early days of the following month.[84]

The practice of booleying was supported by the old Gaelic land system of rundale. The use of the rundale system meant that until the early 1800s there can have been few land boundaries erected by man. It is noticeable in

Ireland that rivers and watersheds play a major part in delimiting boundaries and that areas or parishes tend to be physical entities.

People lived in little clusters, or "clachans", of houses, sometimes a dozen or so together, but often the groups of houses were much smaller – just three or four. The houses were clustered without plan or order and never strung together end-to-end, generally in some sheltered hollow in the richest part of the townland, though they might be disposed along a road with some semblance of regularity. They were essentially communities of related families bound together in "friendship" – the word "friend" means a blood relation in Ireland. The system of agriculture they worked was an open field system; the arable land was unenclosed and each holder had a scattered patch here and there. There are cases on record where one man held thirty-two different patches, or again where twenty-six people had shares in a field of half an acre. Between the cultivated patches ran waste strips (mearings), often as much as three yards wide.

The hillside above had neither fence nor ditch, just a wide open space over which the cattle and sheep of the townland roamed at will unless accompanied by a herder. There was, however, an arrangement that the number of animals one might graze was in proportion to the rent one paid. Since there were no ditches or fences cattle had to be herded most of the time – this was one of the drawbacks. There were no roads up in the hills, just cattle paths.

The rundale system naturally led to fights, trespasses, disputes and assaults, yet the people were reluctant to abandon it. In the end they were forced to in the 1800s when "squaring" of land was brought in by the landlords. The "squaring" of land meant simply that the landlords decided that the most economically viable way to use the land was to create rectangular land divisions, generally placing the house or living quarters right in the middle of the square. Captain John Pitt Kennedy, writing in 1838, states: "As the comfort and the profits of the farmer materially depend on the shape of the farm and the distribution of the buildings ... the nearer the shape of the farm comes to a square and the nearer the buildings are placed to the centre the better."[87]

The squaring, or consolidation, of farms and the wiping out of rural villages became general all over Ireland from 1838. The initiative came from the landlords and their agents. The chief motive unquestionably was to increase the value of the rents and to establish a tenantry that would be better able and more likely to pay their rents promptly. One method of consolidation was by adding to a farm the adjacent lots of a tenant whose tenancy had expired. The tenancy might cease simply by eviction, or by the tenant being encouraged to emigrate, the landlord arranging his passage.[88]

In this area the old rundale system was replaced by consolidated holdings in the shape of narrow oblongs stretching from the bottom of the valleys to the mountain ridges above.[89] The old village, which had nestled in its sheltered hollow, perhaps for centuries, was now abandoned and its occupants obliged to transfer their belongings to an isolated homestead on their new holdings. Many of the whitewashed cottages, with their roofs of thatch, that dotted our countryside until recent times, were erected at the time of the "squaring".[90] To the tenant it was a greater blessing than he ever anticipated. A consolidated holding tended to improve his husbandry and his new house, spacious and well-lighted, was a vast improvement on the miserable hovel in which he had lived in the overcrowded old village. The breaking up of these insanitary clusters went a long way towards ending the fever epidemics that periodically ravaged the country.[91]

These fever epidemics claimed many lives over the centuries. But it was the growing famine conditions prevailing in Ireland during the actual years of the land changes detailed above, culminating in the Great Famine of 1846, which cast one of the greatest shadows of all over the chequered history of the Irish people. There was distress in west Donegal as early as the first years of the 1830s; in 1831 we find one of the Nesbitts, F.E. Nesbitt – from the Bruckless area it would appear – writing to James Dombrain, General Inspector of the Coastguard, concerning the shortage of food. In a covering note, dated 19 February 1831, Dombrain describes the writer as "one of the most respected gentlemen in Donegal" and refers to the letter as "corroboration of other accounts". Here is what Nesbitt wrote: "As I know you [i.e. Dombrain] take an interest in anything connected with Ireland, I think it advisable to tell you that we are in a dreadful State in this part of the coast for want of Provisions. Potatoes are now selling in Ardara at 5d a stone, and oatmeal at 20d the peck of ten pounds, more than double the usual price paid at this early season of the year, and there is every appearance of their being still higher.

"I freighted a smack recently to bring Potatoes from Port a vad; the crew was attacked by a Mob and obliged to put to Sea. She then tried Pulahiney and was served in the same way, and latterly went to Killala where the skipper was robbed of £44 and the crew very badly treated, and they have returned to Bruckless without either Money or Potatoes. And what makes it worse, they were intended to be sold in small quantities for the immediate relief of our neighbours."[92]

The "Port a vad" referred to above is of course *Port a' bhád*, on the north coast of Loughros Point, near Loughill. Remember I made the point in starting our tour that Loughros was famous for its potatoes, so conditions must have been critical in 1831 when the crew who had come to get just one smack-full of potatoes were "attacked by a mob and obliged to put to sea".

It appears that by the beginning of the 19th century potatoes had become the staple diet of the people throughout Ireland. Of local interest are Rev. John Barrett's answers to the 1821 survey in which he states: "Potatoes with milk for four months, potatoes with only salt too frequently for the remaining eight months"; presumably the question he had been asked concerned the diet of the people. If so it paints a bleak picture.

Cecil Woodham-Smith in her classic book on the famine, *The Great Hunger*,[93] also voices the view that the potato now dominated the diet of the people. She writes: "In the backward areas where famine struck hardest, cooking any food other than the potato had become a lost art. Charles Trevelyan, of the British Treasury, writing at the time stated: 'There is scarcely a woman of the peasant class in the West of Ireland whose culinary art exceeds the boiling of a potato. Bread is scarcely ever seen, and an oven is unknown'; and Father Matthew, the celebrated apostle of temperance, ... whose knowledge of Ireland was unmatched, wrote, 'The potato deluge during the past twenty years has swept away all other food from our cottagers and sunk into oblivion their knowledge of cookery'."[94]

Possibly these views are too simplistic; Cecil Woodham-Smith continues: "Routh writing to Trevelyan on January 1st 1846, told him that the Irish people did not regard wheat, oats and barley as food – they were grown to pay the rent and to pay the rent was the first necessity of life in Ireland. It would be a desperate man who ate up his rent, with the certainty before him of eviction and 'death by slow torture'."[95]

Over twenty failures of the potato crop are known to have taken place in Ireland in the century before the Great Famine. These were due to various causes, such as frost, rot and curl. The first fully recorded outbreak of blight took place in the New World in 1842, when potatoes along the Atlantic coast of North America, from Nova Scotia to Boston, were destroyed.[96] This attack was followed in Europe by the serious outbreak of 1845 and the total loss of 1846. Blight is caused by a fungus called *Phytophthora infestans*. Blight is with us still. Every year since 1845 in potato fields throughout the northern hemisphere the blight fungus has been present, waiting only for the right weather conditions to multiply with fearful rapidity. In September 1845 blight made its appearance in this country: it turned the potato fields of Ireland black almost overnight. People struggled through the winter, but the following year, 1846, saw widespread famine.

Cecil Woodham-Smith states: "At Lochrus, near Ardara, the people had been starving from August 25 [1846] onwards; the district was mountainous, no grain was ever grown, and the only food was potatoes, which were entirely lost. Mr. Moore, a coastguard officer [at Crannogeboy], managed to obtain some meal from Sligo, but only enough for one-third of the people. 'I never saw anything like it,' he [Mr. Moore] wrote,[97] 'and I hope I never will. People came 18 miles for a little meal, which I could not give. 14 tons, all but one bag, went in a day. Unless the Government send a supply of food the people must inevitably die of starvation.'"[98]

There are a number of references to Mr. Moore, the coastguard officer at Crannogeboy, in the minutes book of the Glenties Board of Guardians during the period. He learned that two ships, the revenue cruiser *Racer* and the *Warrior*, were available at Sligo to bring supplies, but neither could berth at Loughros so it was decided to bring them into Portnoo from which the Glenties area could also be supplied.[99]

Tradition has preserved many disconnected references to the hunger, starvation and death of that tragic period. A woman, earning 3d a day at road work, was found dead of starvation on a heap of stones on the Wood Road in Ardara. So many people died of fever in one district that the same coffin was used for a number of burials, having been brought back on each occasion to await the next victim. Fever patients were nursed by people who had already survived three attacks and were now immune. People walked to Killybegs, to Dunkineely and even to Donegal town in the hope of being able to buy a small quantity of meal. A new scheme – soup kitchens for feeding the people – was devised in January 1847. There was a soup kitchen established at Boyds of Lacaduff (here in Drimirrin) and there were other soup kitchens at Clooney, Woodhill House, Brackey and Meenavalley House.[100]

The question is often asked – how could people living along a coast rich in cockles, mussels and other shellfish and with the sea itself teeming with fish be in such want of food? My own view would be that firstly the beds of shellfish would soon have become exhausted and would not have had a chance to regenerate because of the constant picking. Secondly, we must remember that fishing was in the hands of the landlords – we have already noted that the various Loughros fisheries were rented annually from the Murray-Stewart estate by the Nesbitts. Accordingly it would appear that the "peasantry" did not have the means to catch a steady supply of fish. For hard evidence of this we again go back to Rev. J. Barrett's answers of 1821 when he observes: "Very little fish is taken in this District ... only a few small boats ... if the weather be not very fine, no boat will venture from the shore ... I learn that herring have been, of late years, frequently on this coast, but were not taken for want of nets."

I will not dwell on the famine period any longer, but it is well for us to remember this harrowing episode in our history which occured not all that long ago, and it should make us, as a nation, more aware of the needs of people in other parts of the world when famine strikes their homelands.

As we retrace our steps up the Point we will dwell on the derivation of some of the remaining placenames as we go along.

The spelling of Drimirrin has changed little since 1642 at which time it appears as "Drum-irryn" and again as the "½ vil' de Drumrryn al' Drumrryn"[101] It derives from *Druim Fiorin* - the "F" drops out under neuter aspiration[102] - and translates as "the ridge of the long coarse grass". Its derivation, allied to that of the Point in general [Loughros, the peninsula of the sedges (rushes)], is relevant to our earlier discussion on the cause of "the cruppan".

Liskeraghan (1642, Liskeroghan) might[103] translate as *Lios* (the enclosure or ringfort) - *caer* (a berry of any kind) - *ach* (a suffix to a noun, denoting 'abounding in') - *an* (a diminutive), "the enclosure of the numerous small berries". Liskeraghan still has the remains of a ringfort.

Cloghboy is *Cloch Buí*, the "yellow" stone. You need not translate *buí* too directly - there are a number of rivers in west Donegal (including the one coming down Granny Glen) which are named "Owenwee", i.e. *Abhainn bhuí*, the yellow river, and in these cases the word *buí* reflects the dark peaty water which these rivers carry down from the mountains.

Before we leave the lower Point I'd better mention "the Dorlinn strand", marked *Trá bán* (the white beach) on maps. The word "dorlinn" probably originated from *dorn*, a fist (a *dornálaí* is a boxer); "dornóges" are round stones,[104] literally fist-shaped stones. However there is another term - *turlinn* - which is presumably interchangeable with *dorlinn* and possibly originated from the word *dorn* too. Joyce interprets a *turlinn* for us and his words are a readymade description of the Dorlinn strand: *"Tuirlinn*, a sea-beach of large stones, 'a boulder beach' (Mac Neill). Above high water is the *tuirlinn*; between high and low water is commonly an ordinary smooth beach (O'Donovan)."[105]

Burkestown or Newtownburke is the great enigma of Loughros Point placenames, because we have no idea where the name came from. I cannot trace anybody called Burke having lived here. The name obviously intrigued my father, in his time, because years ago he wrote to the village of Ardara, near Pittsburg, Pennysylvania, enquiring whether any Burkes lived there - his reasoning obviously being that the "missing" Burkes of the Point might have been instrumental in the founding of the American Ardara. But only one Burke lived there and his origins lay elsewhere. I presume that Newtownburke is a post-Plantation name, just like nearby Stonebrook.

The Gaelic name for Burkestown is *Baile na Gaoithe* - the windy town -

and there is no reason to doubt that this is the original, proper name. As an item of interest, I would add that a placename – "Ballaghmonterboill"– in the 1642 list cannot be identified at the present day; it is possible that if its proper form were *Baile Muintir Uí Bhaoill* – Boylestown – it may have been corrupted to Burkestown. Burkestown is surrounded by sites of former O'Boyle strongholds. However this is only conjecture.

Our two remaining townlands in the Point – Longfield and Loughill (also called Drumalough) – which are side by side have a common origin [*Leamh-choill*, the yew wood]. At first glance this is difficult to accept. However the name "Leawinkill" (*Leamh-choill*) appears in the 1642 list next to "Kiilcashell"; the names Longfield and Loughill do not appear. "Drumlogh", interestingly, does.[106] Again we rely on Joyce: "An elm wood was called *Leamhchoill* and this compound, subject to various alterations, exists at the present day, showing where these woods formerly flourished. The usual anglicised forms are Laughill ... and Loughill. ... But the most curious transformation is Longfield."[107] He continues: *"Leamhchoill* ... is generally transformed into the complete English word Longfield.... The conversion of *choill* into *field* seems a strange transformation, but every step in the process is accounted for..."[108] So it appears that in earlier times the main topographical features of the Longfield–Loughill (Drumalough) area were a yew wood, a ridge (*druim*) and a lake (*loch*).

By now we should be out of the Point and back on the Ardara-Killybegs road.

Notes

1   Public Records Office of Northern Ireland: D.2860/25/3.
2   I have retained his spelling of placenames.
3   *H.P.A.*, p. 31.
4   vol. III, p. 434.
5   Ibid p. 528.
6   Joyce, vol. I, p. 430.
7   *H.D.R.*, vol. I, p. 276.
8   Ibid. p. 258.
9   *J.R.S.A.I.*, vol. 4 (5th series), vol. XXIV (consec. series) (1894), p. 80.
10   vol. I, pp. 102-103.
11   *M.O.D.*, 6 August, p. 213.
12   Ó Riain's *Corpus* lists (p. 41): "Secht meic Lugada; Lasran, Boetan, Garban, Baethin, Senchan, Ruadan, Cronan qui & Mochua Cluana Dolcain." The same genealogy is repeated a number of times in the *Corpus*, Seanaghan being written as

"Senchada" (p. 77), "Senchan" (p. 99), "Senchain" (p. 177) and "Seanch Dubaid" (p. 41).

13 Kenney, p. 450.

14 *Donegal Democrat*, 17 June 1988.

15 Inq., 30 Car. I.

16 *The Cliff Scenery of South Western Donegal*, pp. 152-53.

17 *D.A.* (1974), pp. 66-67.

18 Ibid.

19 The 12th-century church reform in Ireland had meant, among other things, the establishment of the present diocesan system. Then followed – especially here in the north-west – through most of the 13th century, the new parish structuring, resulting in the parochial system that prevailed up till recent centuries, and in many cases, to this very day. (*D.A.* (1974), p. 68.)

20 Appendix (Escheated lands) to the Inquisitions, Ultonia, Vol. II.

21 Ó Gallochóir, *Essays*, p. 53.

22 Ibid. p. 50.

23 County Sessions held in Raphoe, 11 July 1704.

24 vol. I, p. 259.

25 vol. V, p. 1455 -57.

26 vol. V, pp. 1302-3.

27 Grammatically *Baile Na Gainimhe* would seem more correct, but this is not how it is pronounced. On maps it is often written as "Bellaganny", but Ballyganny is the local pronunciation.

28 *The Way That I Followed*, p. 100.

29 Kelly, *Early Christian Ireland*, p. 298.

30 *U.J.A.*, vol. 5 (1942), p. 14.

31 *The Cliff Scenery of South Western Donegal*, p. 150.

32 p. 104.

33 "the rubber"

34 R.A.S. Macalister, *The Archaeology of Ireland*, p. 193.

35 *J.R.S.A.I.*, vol. III (1981), p. 102.

36 See "Proceedings of the Society of Antiquaries of Scotland," vol. 109 (1977-78), pp. 129-39, where, in discussing Atlantic Scotland, Caulfield states: "the replacement of the saddle by the rotary quern is a clearly identifiable Iron Age phenomenon in that region."

37 *J.R.S.A.I.*, vol. III (1983), p. 146.

38 O.S. 1847-50.

39 *H.D.R.*, vol. II, p. 277.

40 *Archaeological Survey of County Donegal* (1983).

41 *The Cliff Scenery of South Western Donegal*, p. 150.

42 This sandbank has become much smaller in recent years. Formerly there were many stones in it, which acted as a magnet for accumulating sand. But many of the stones have been taken away by tractor for building purposes and consequently the

bank is disappearing. It was known to the fishermen as a place that the tide never covered and I'm told (by John McNelis, Sandfield) that in former years the off-shore salmon fishermen built a hut on it. The reputation of this bank as a place which the tide didn't cover is probably the basis for the folktales about Conall crossing the bay, falling asleep, but not getting wet.

43   The present Crannogeboy national school was built in 1944; it replaced an earlier school, the remains of which are still to be seen immediately opposite. The latter school is shown on the O.S. map of 1847-50. This map also shows us the "National School" down beside Toberconnell, "Loughros Female N.S." down at the end of Cloghboy and the "Wesleyan School" over at Drimirrin.

44   *The Cliff Scenery of South Western Donegal*, pp. 150-51.

45   Remember the Rev. John Barrett's observation on Cloghboy when we were in the Rosbeg area.

46   *Statistical Survey of the County of Donegal*, p. 102.

47   i.e. those who had undertaken to develop plantations in Ireland.

48   *H.P.A.*, p. 46.

49   *H.P.A.*, p. 47.

50   Who was a noted *seanchaí*; material recorded from him is housed with the Dept. of Irish Folklore, Belfield, ms. 418.

51   *D.A.* (1963), p. 24.

52   Ibid. p. 249.

53   Ibid. p. 250.

54   *A.S.D.*, p. 129.

55   Ibid. p. 137.

56   *D.A.* (1963), p. 250.

57   *A.S.D.*, p. 263.

58   "Lateinische Kultur im VIII", *Jahrhundert*, p. 121.

59   Ibid.

60   See Rt. Rev. Bishop Graves, "Similar Forms of the Christian Cross on Ancient Monuments in Egypt and Ireland," *J.R.S.A.I.*, vol. 20 (1891), p. 346.

61   *J.R.S.A.I.*, vol. 48, p. 221.

62   *Béaloideas*, vol. VI, no.11, p. 151.

63   This map also shows us the Loughros female national school situated on the first road to the right after you have turned off towards the Dorlinns.

64   The Loughros area was surveyed by members of the Irish Branch of the Geological Survey of the United Kingdom, under the directorship of Sir Edward Hull, between the years 1881-84, on a scale of 6" to 1 mile, and the result published in 1888 on sheet 23 of the Geological Survey Map.

65   *The Cliff Scenery of South Western Donegal*, p. 151.

66   This school finally closed in 1969. There was an even older school in this area, "Miss Beattie's".

67   I have retained his spelling of placenames and his frequent capitals.

68   i.e. Maghera.

69   The Gaelic word *crupán* means "a shrinking".

70   The Gaelic word *galar* denotes sickness, disease or distemper.

71   *Statistical Survey of the County of Donegal*, pp. 44-45.

72   R.D.S., Ballsbridge, Dublin.

73   *Statistical Survey of the County of Donegal*, p. 45.

74   *Carex L Nigra (L) Reichard (C. goodenowii)*.

75   *Carex L. disticha Hudson*.

76   *H.P.A.*, p. 75.

77   *D.A.* (1975-76), p. 133.

78   *H.P.A.*, p. 76.

79   Séamus Ó Híghne, *Mín a' Churraoin, i n-aice le Ard a' Rátha, 9 Lughnasa 1936: i mBéaloideas* (1940), *iml.* X, *uim.* 1-11, p. 100.

80   A.T. Lucas, *Cattle in Ancient Ireland*, p. 210.

81   From *Two Bokes of the Histories of Ireland* by Edmund Campion; quoted in *Cattle in Ancient Ireland*, p. 202.

82   Dept. of Irish Folklore ms. 1773, pp. 10-11, quoted in *Cattle in Ancient Ireland*, p. 214.

83   Or possibly I'm on the wrong track altogether. The difference in altitude wouldn't be that great. I wonder were the cows bled in places such as Switzerland, where the practice of summer pasturage is still carried on?

84   *H.P.A.*, p. 76.

85   Jean M. Graham, "South-west Donegal in the seventeenth century," *Irish Geography*, vol. VI, no. 2 (1970), p. 136.

86   E. Estyn Evans, *Irish Heritage*, 4th ed. (1944), pp. 47-50; much of my insight into rundale comes from this excellent book.

87   Quoted in *D.A.* (1948), p. 116.

88   *D.A.* (1948), p. 116.

89   *H.P.A.*, p. 78.

90   Ibid. p. 79.

91   Ibid. p. 78.

92   Quoted in the *D.A.* (1960), pp. 264-65; the original letter is in the Public Records Office, Dublin.

93   *The Great Hunger, Ireland 1845-49*, London (1962).

94   Ibid. p. 76.

95   Ibid.

96   Ibid. p. 94.

97   Mr. Moore to Stephens, 22 September 1846, Comm. Corr. I, p. 96.

98   *The Great Hunger*, p. 116

99   *H.P.A.*, p. 95.

100 Ibid. p. 93.

101 Inq., 30 Car. I.

102 Joyce, vol. III, p. 327.

103 Dónall Mac Giolla Easpaig, our adviser on Narin, translates Liskeraghan as

Lios Ciaracháin, interpreting the latter as a personal name and adding that "the original diphthong - ia - regularly gives a short e sound under certain conditions in Donegal Irish."

104 Joyce, vol. III, p. 309.
105 Ibid. p. 595.
106 Inq., 30 Car. I.
107 Joyce, vol. I, p. 509.
108 Ibid. pp. 39-40.

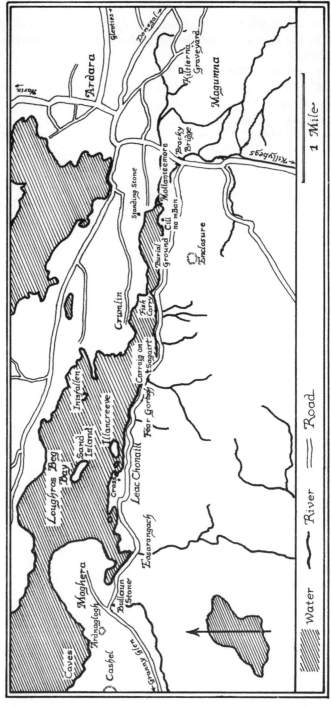

Water
River
Road

1 Mile

B. FLEURY 1991

XVI

FROM LOUGHROS TO MAGHERA

L EAVING THE POINT we turn right in the direction of Killybegs and pass along with the townland of Drimaha[1] on our right. On 21 May 1921, during the Black and Tan war, an R.I.C. patrol was ambushed on this stretch of road and a Constable Hunt was wounded.

Shortly, just before the factory-shop of John Molloy (Ardara) Ltd. on the left, a road goes off to the right and another off to the left. The little road to the right brings us down to the Loughros Beg inlet. There was a salmon weir here in the last century. If, standing at the water's edge, we look up at the long fields on the right with their fences running down from the top of Kinnoughty hill, we see a standing stone down towards the bottom of one of these fields. This stone is 1.64 m. high; at its west end is a second slab .8 m. high. As the earlier Ordnance Survey maps only record one stone it may be that this second slab is a broken part of the first.[2] It is said[3] that a cross was visible on the south side but that it was gone by 1847. No trace of a cross now exists on either stone. This stone is on the Loughros Point peninsula and it has been suggested in the past that because there had been a cross incised on it that it may have been connected with the other cross slabs down the Point and may have formed part of a *turas* done on the Point.

The old name for the large drumlin on the left, which we all knew as Paddy Heron's sand-pit, is Mollanteemore [*Mul (Mullach) an tigh mhóir*: the height of the big house]. The name is said to have originated from a large wooden structure which occupied the summit of the mound in the days of the Fianna and which was used by them as a summer residence while hunting on the hills of *Tír Bógaine*. The malicious burning of the house and the foul murder of those within, mostly women, has led to a long local legend involving this place and Finn and the Fianna. Space does not permit us to retell it here. That this intriguing legend was not the creation of a local *seanchaí* in more recent times is attested to by the fact that as far back as

1642 we come across the placename *Molanty Mac Cuell* – the height of Finn Mac Cumhail's residence.

Mollanteemore is in the townland of Edergole, a placename in which one of the root words is *gabhal*: a fork, just as at Kilgole, between the Owenea and Owentocker rivers, which we discussed earlier. *Gabhal*, old Irish *gabul*, derives from the verb *gabh*: to take;[4] it is often applied to river-forks. The land enclosed by two branches of a river was often designated by the compound *Eadar-ghabhal*[5] [*eadar*: between, (a place) between two (river) prongs]. Edergole is situated between the Duvoge [*Dubh óg*: small black river – just as at Sheskinmore earlier] and Brackey rivers, which empty side by side into Loughros Beg estuary.

Back on the main road, the minor route going off to the left leads over to Magumna and Woodhill House. Initially I had been puzzled that when earlier travellers had passed through Ardara, on their way to Killybegs, they sometimes referred to Magumna and Kiltierna, suggesting that they passed through or close to these areas, which are well east of the present road. Our old friend, Dr. Pococke, passing through here in 1752, states: "We ... soon had Lochrasbeg bay to the west ... we came to Mugurry [i.e. Magumna] on the entrance [presumably the "Nick"] between the mountain in the middle."[6] Earlier, in 1730, Thomas Addi writes: "Magumna is a fine spot of ground, all under grain and hay. It contains about 20 or 25 acres and is one Ballyboe. I look upon it to be worth about £9 or £10 per annum. Kiltarney [*sic*] is a large farm, very improvable, but is at present in very bad order and boggy. If it were well drained there would be a good quantity of meadow in the farthest end of it."[7]

My puzzlement was resolved when I realised that the earlier road from Killybegs to Ardara followed a path which was much more easterly than the present road and went through Magumna. John Hood's map of 1755 shows the road from Killybegs turning at right angles through Edergole and into Magumna where it is marked "Road to Glenfin".[8] About forty perches west of the Edergole-Magumna boundary a road branches off to "Magheramore" – another reminder that in earlier times all roads lead to the great fair of Magheramore. The "Magheramore" road went up over Drumbarron hill and down at the Diamond into Ardara. The 1847-50 Ordnance Survey map shows the old road running eastwards of the then established present road.

Magumna translates as *Mag Omna*. *Mag*, usually translated as "a plain", can denote a long-settled place and can signify permanent pasture;[9] this might be of relevance in making the case that nearby Kiltierna is an ancient ecclesiastical centre. [*Omna*: an oak or just a tree-trunk; *Mag Omna*: the plain of the oak tree.] In early literature there are many variations of the genitive pleural of *omna* – *omne, omnadha, omnaí*, etc. Possibly *Mag Omne* – "of the oak trees" – is correct. There may be much more to the deciphering of this placename than meets the eye. I have seen it translated as *Má Gamhna* [*má*: a plain; *gamhna*: gen. pl. of *gamhain*, a calf, the plain of the calves]. However this does not fit with local pronunciation. I'll stick with *Mag Omna*. It is written as Moygumna in the Inquisitions of 1642.

An 1813-14 estate map shows trees inside the north-east boundary of Magumna; this seems to be a continuation of the Woodhill planting. In later years the eastern part of Magumna was rented from the Murray estate by the Nesbitts. This part of Magumna is still referred to by locals as "the Major's hill", after Major Nesbitt. In 1846, the year of the Great Famine, east Magumna was rented out to R.W. Nesbitt and twelve householders were paying rent to the Murray-Stewart estate for west Magumna. There were five families of Boyles, two Carlins, one McTague, Bridget Meehan, Daniel Herroran (Heron), Niel Brisland (Breslin) and Edward Molloy. The latter's farm was much the most extensive; he was paying between £10 and £11 in rent, while the other households were just paying £1 or £2.

An earlier survey and book of maps of the Murray estate by John Bell, land surveyor in 1749, includes a map (No. 24) of the "Magumney, Killterney and Moegh" areas. It refers to "The Hill or part called Magumna ... a part of Magumna called Moegh ... and Kilterney – the part called Muney". The whole area is referred to as a mixture of "Arable meadow and green pasture, pasturable mountain for grazing, shrubs and stones, black bogs and black mountain". This describes very well the landscape starting at Magumna and extending up over Kiltierna and into the mountain above Mullinacloy. And what is this mountain called? This is "Muney" mountain [*An Maoineach*, derived from *maoin*: wealth, riches; *An Maoineach*: the mountain abounding in natural riches or wealth].

The bounteous nature of this mountain was extolled in a Gaelic poem of the mid-18th century, entitled *Moladh Shliabh Maoineach*, composed by a noted Ardara poet of the time, Eoghan Óg Mhac Niallghuis (Owen McNelis).[10] In recent years there has been some confusion about the exact location of *Sliabh Maoineach*. This is it. Eddie Brogan, a sprightly eighty-four years of age and the oldest inhabitant to live in its shadow up here in Mullinacloy, concurs and adds that "the older people called it Muney or Money mountain".[11]

Below *Sliabh Maoineach* and overlooking Magumna is the now disused but very well-kept graveyard of Kiltierna. [*Cill Tighernach*: the church of Tighernach]. Its origin has been lost in the mists of antiquity and there is no trace now of an ancient church. It has been suggested that Kiltierna is a

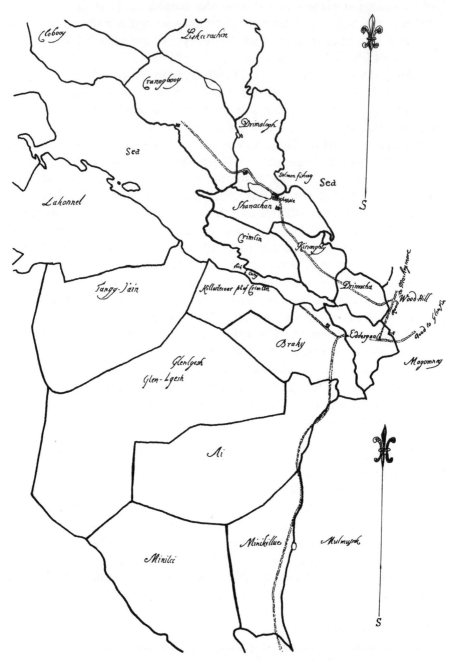

An artist's impression of John Hood's map of 1755; the original is in the
National Library

fairly modern graveyard, that no early *cill* (church) ever existed here and that the name Kiltierna derives from *Ár dTiarna*, the Gaelic term for Our Lord; Kiltierna: the church of Our Lord.[12] Dr. Maguire, writing in 1920, in discussing the prohibition on Catholics celebrating mass in Loughros Point in post-Plantation times, refers to the fact that after being expelled from Loughros the Catholic clergy initially celebrated mass at Killasteever (on the road to Laconnell and yet to be visited) and states: "With the suppression of the O'Boyle chieftancy, the dispersion of that long-dominant sept, and the continued usurpation of their lands, shrines, and even graveyards, Loughross, with all its grand memorials of sanctity and prowess, had to be abandoned. Then a plain, unpretentious church was constructed a short distance to the south side of Ardara village under the title of *Cill-Tighearna*, or Church of Our Lord. The Killtierny graveyard, which surrounded the old church, is now rarely resorted to for interments, but, little over a half century ago, it was the chief burial ground for this whole extensive and populous district."[13]

However, I incline to the view that Kiltierna is probably the site of an early ecclesiastic settlement. We have already referred to the name Kiltierna appearing in correspondence and surveys in the 1700s. In 1642 "Kilterny" appears as part of the proportion of "Moynargan"; it seems likely that if the placename "Kilterny" was that established by 1642 then its origin must have predated the Plantation. I think it probable, then, that there was an early *cill* founded here and that the name celebrates the cult of a St. Tighernach, possibly Tighernach of Clones. In the 7th century the religious community in Clones was quite powerful; their influence certainly reached into east Donegal[14] and it could be suggested that the cult of Tighernach of Clones could have spread as far west as this. The community of Clones was under the influence of powerful Armagh, but towards the end of the 7th century they won free of Armagh by submission to Kildare.[15] I mention this to remind you again that the cults of various saints were promulgated depending on which cults the mother monastery espoused.

The *Annals of the Four Masters* inform us that St. Tighernach, Bishop of *Cluain-Eois* (Clones), died on 4 April 548 A.D.[16] The *Félire Oengusso* traces his pedigree back through seven generations to Daire *barrach*, son of Cathaír Mór, the legendary chief of the Laighin (Leinster-men) whom we referred to earlier when discussing St. Shanaghan.[17] In recent years Tighernach of Clones is listed[18] as one of the *Uí Bairrche*[19] saints. There is also a Kiltierney in Co. Fermanagh.

Near Lough Melvin (ancient name *Loch Meilge*) in Co. Leitrim was located a place named *Doire Meille*. At 4 November in the *Martyrology of Donegal* we read: "Tighernach, of Doire-Melle. Mella was the name of his mother, and she was the mother also of Cainnech the priest." If we accept, as was suggested along the Gweebarra estuary, that Cainnech was a hypocoristic form of Colmcille, then the cult of Tighernach may have accompanied that of Colmcille in Co. Leitrim. There is a further pointer to a Columban association in Ó Riain's *Corpus*[20] reference to "Eithne & Mell i nDaire Melle" (Colmcille's mother was named Eithne). If the cult of Tighernach accompanied that of Cainnech in Co. Leitrim it may well have done so here in west Donegal as well.

The cult of Dallán Forgaill was also celebrated in Co. Leitrim – at *Glenn Dalláin*, situated at Glencar on the borders of counties Leitrim and Sligo. I think it likely that the cults of Tighernach and Dallán travelled in Leitrim via the Colmcille cult and that the latter was also the vehicle for the spread of the Tighernach cult to this area.

The most prominent tombstone in Kiltierna graveyard is that erected to the memory of the Rev. John Gallagher, P.P. of Kilcar, who died in 1847. He was born in the townland of Brackey, close to Kiltierna. Fr. Gallagher was intensely fond of his native place and his interment in the solitude of Kiltierna was in fulfilment of his dying wish. That his body was carried back here from Kilcar demonstrates the esteem in which Kiltierna was held by the older generations. Thankfully there are those in the present-day community who share this esteem and who keep the old graveyard in very good condition.

Now back to the main road and over the Brackey bridge. There was a corn mill and a "mill race" on the river here in the last century. A map of Old Brackey – a separate entity from New Brackey – by Murry Babington, in 1813-14, drawn for the Murray estate, shows the mill among other local features.

A man of the Protestant denomination, called *an Clarcach Mór* (Big Clarke), who was of giant stature and had great strength and of whom many stories are told, once lived in Brackey. He was immensely popular among his mainly Catholic neighbours. One story tells of how in earlier times it was customary for farmers from the Ardara and Glenties districts to go to Ballina (Co. Mayo) fair to buy stock. On one occasion two local men went to the Ballina fair, accompanied by *an Clarcach Mór*. They were separated from the latter for a while and were intimidated by some local men – remember that fighting was an inevitable part of fair days. The two men escaped, found *an Clarcach Mór* and then returned with speed to the scene of the action and stated: "We are here now, prepared not only to meet the strongest men in Ballina, but the best that can be produced in the province of Connacht." And, of course, with the aid of *an Clarcach Mór* they were invincible.

We now proceed down towards Laconnell and Maghera. John Hood's map of 1755 shows that just a short stretch of road existed at that time, going down towards the sea and ending before Killasteever. The 1847-50 Ordnance Survey map shows a road in patches to Laconnell and Maghera, but there was no continuous road. A letter to Murray-Stewart from his agent, Brooke, of 12 June 1893 states: "The Congested Districts Board are going to complete the road along the coast to Maghera."[21]

The first place of note down this road is the site of an old graveyard at Killasteever. This graveyard is marked, down close to the sea, on the 1847-50 Ordnance Survey map. Dr. Maguire in his *History of the Diocese of Raphoe* has stated that mass was celebrated here for some time after Catholic services were prohibited in Loughros Point and before the supposed move to Kiltierna and the later move to the first Catholic church in Ardara village. The "Burial Ground" marked on the second and third editions of the Ordnance Survey maps survives as a wedge-shaped, stone-walled enclosure.[22] There is no evidence of its former use.

There is a very large stone-walled enclosure up on the hill behind Killasteever. This large enclosure is bisected by the boundary wall between the townlands of Killasteever and Scadaman. It is irregularly shaped and its internal dimensions are 61.6 m. north–south and 57.2 m. east–west[23] – so it certainly is big. The exact function of this type of very large drystone-walled enclosure is unknown, but its very size appears to preclude the possibility of a domestic function and it was probably of defensive if not of military significance. It is more easily approached by climbing the hill behind Brackey school, at the entrance to Glengesh Pass. Local tradition tells us that this enclosure and "the castle" high above Maghera village, at Granny Glen, acted as barracks at these mountain passes and were used as signal stations to alert the inhabitants of the flat countryside stretching away to the north when enemies approached. Folklore strongly connects them with Mollanteemore.

A professional archaeologist would be wary of attempting to date this large hilltop enclosure, but might be predisposed to a date somewhere in the middle ages. As an amateur I might be excused for attempting to give it an earlier date and my reason is as follows: the townland of Killasteever, in which half of the enclosure lies, translates as *Cill Lios Diamhair*, a most interesting name [derived from *cill*: a church; *lios*: an enclosure or ringfort; and *diamhair*: recess, solitude, related to the word *dithreabhach*, a hermit, eremite (a hermit, especially of Christian solitaries from the 3rd century onwards)]. It is likely, then, that in the early days of Christianity this place down here along the coast was the site of an early Christian hermitage. We have discussed before how many of the early Christians sought to get away to very remote areas on their own. We can well imagine one of their number travelling along the coast and coming up Loughros Beg Bay and starting his early foundation at this spot. Since this early hermitage is celebrated in the name *Cill Lios Diamhair* it is likely that the *lios*, which presumably refers to the large enclosure on the hill above, is also of ancient origin.

Next we come to Mullanacarry [from *mullán*, a diminutive of *mullach* and meaning the top of a low hill; and *cora*: a weir (a word we met early in our travels at Doochary, *Dubh Choraidh*), *Mullán na coraidh*: hillock of the weir].[24] All the older maps show a "fish carry" between Mullanacarry on this side and Crumlin Point (*Gob na Coraidh*) on the Loughros side of the estuary. This fish carry was used by the landlords over the years; presumably it was part of the Loughros fishery which the Nesbitts rented from the Murray estate. It was crude, but effective, and certainly wouldn't be allowed nowadays. A wall was built out into the channel from both sides of the estuary, leaving a gap in the middle. There was probably a box-like structure, similar to the one noted at the Owenea earlier, in place in the channel. As the tide receded the fish were caught in the "box". Of course the landlord could do as he wished – when this whole area was regranted to the Earl of Annandale, John Murray of Cockpool, in 1629 (it had been granted earlier in 1620, but proper use had not been made of the grant, and it was regranted to Murray by the king in 1629, paying double the rent that had been arranged in 1620), he was granted "Free fishing and taking of salmon, herring, cod, and all other kinds of fish in the creeks and the weirs."

Next we come to Garrowchuill [*garbh*: rough; *coill*: a wood; the rough wood]. A story about St. Conall is told in this area: "One day, on his way back from Glencolumbkille, Conall was coming over the hill at Garrowchuill and he was being pursued by enemies. Exhausted from the pursuit he crossed the estuary at Laconnell, and, having evaded his pursuers, he lay down on the sand and slept. The tide came in, but miraculously the area where Conall was lying rose up under him and remained dry as the tidal waters flowed around. This spot, where Conall slept as the tide came in, has remained elevated ever since and is still visible as a small island."

The mountainous terrain between Barkillew [*Barr Coilleadh*: the top or highest part of the wood] and Laconnell [*Leac Chonaill*: Conall's flagstone] bears many reminders of religious activity in earlier times, presumably dating to the time of the Penal Laws, when priests were persecuted and often sought refuge in areas such as this. However it should also be borne in mind that the practice of celebrating mass in the open air in Ireland appears to be very ancient.[25] The mountain between Barkillew and Laconnell is called

Croaghataggart [*Croagh a' tSagairt*: the mountain of the priest]; the stream which runs down from this hill and which divides the townland of Barkillew from that of Laconnell is called Sruhaunnaheglise [*Sruthán na hEaglaise*: the streamlet of the church]; down at the roadside, at the very bottom of the stream, just beside the sea, is a rock called *Carraig an tSagairt*: the priest's rock. Mass is said to have been celebrated at this rock for a period after the prohibition of Catholic services in Loughros Point. The disused altar-slab later became embedded in clay and gravel and overgrown with moss; it was uncovered about a century ago, and while Fr. McGarvey and some men were raising it from its place to set it up on a more commanding position as an object of interest and veneration it was accidently broken and remains in that condition to the present time. Finally, estate maps of the 1813-14 period show a shrubbery marked along the shore here and this "garden" is called Caarreenteggurt [*Garraí an tSagairt*: the priest's garden].

East of the *Sruthán na hEaglaise* rivulet is a second stream which flows down from Barkillew to the sea. In former times the land running down the hillside between these two streams was known as Teangavane, a name which was often given to a long lick of land such as this, the appropriate original Gaelic wording being *An Teanga Mheáin* the middle tongue (of land). This tongue-shaped unit of land is clearly visible if you look across from Loughros Point.

As we enter Laconnell townland, making our way towards the village of Laconnell, we should bear in mind that there was no completed road along this coast until the end of the last century. Earlier travellers on this stretch of coastline had to negotiate the *féar gortach* – hungry grass, quaking grass, *Briza media* – a mountain grass supposed to cause hunger-weakness when trodden on. An area of *féar gortach* is marked on the earlier Ordnance Survey maps just before the village of Laconnell. The following is a fanciful description of the *féar gortach*, from 1897: "The *Féar-Gortha*, or Hungry Grass, is believed to grow in certain spots, and whoever has the bad luck to tread on this baneful fairy herb is liable to be stricken down with the mysterious complaint. The symptoms, which come on suddenly, are complete prostration, preceded by a general feeling of weakness, the sufferer sinks down, and, if assistance is not at hand, he perishes. It is believed that if food be partaken of in the open air and the fragments remaining be not thrown as an offering to the 'good folk' (fairies) that they will mark their displeasure by causing a crop of 'hungry grass' to arise on the spot and produce the effects described. Fortunately the cure is as simple as the malady is mysterious. Oatcake is the specific, or, in its absence, a few grains of oatmeal. The wary traveller who knows the dangers of the road, carries in his pocket a small piece of oatcake, not intended as food, but as a charm against the *Féar Gortha*."[26]

As we continue along this road, with its lovely views of Loughros Beg Bay and the Point, we note the small island of Inishfallen just off the point of Ballyganny. This rock has the bare remains of a cashel on it. A socketed bronze axe-head was found[27] on this island in December 1939 and is now in the National Museum in Dublin.

Further out in the bay is a flat sandy island, mapped as "Sand Island", but known locally as *Oileán Mhachaire* (Maghera island). Though off the coast of Laconnell it is said to have derived its name because the Maghera warren, now greatly diminished by coastal erosion, originally snaked up the bay and into close proximity to *Oileán Mhachaire*. Consequently the Maghera people regarded the bent [or more correctly Marram, *Ammophila arenaria*, in Gaelic *Muiríneach* (*muir*, the sea)], used in thatching, which grew on the island as being their preserve. The size of this sandy island has also been greatly reduced by tidal currents in recents years. On the north-eastern side of the island are the remains of a portal tomb. This monument was known locally as *Cloch a' Bhean* (interpret this name at your peril!). Four of the large megaliths making up the remains of the tomb used to be visible, but on a recent visit I found that only one large slab is now visible above the sand. This large flat stone, over 2 m. long, has a cup-mark on it.

An Teangaidh Rua *with Loughros Beg Bay in the background*

Back on the road, on a steep incline on our right, between the road and the sea below, is an interesting stone lying flat on the ground – it bears a depression very suggestive of a man's large footprint. This is regarded locally as being the footprint of St. Conall. The last time I viewed it the weather had been very wet and the incline was so slippery that I was afraid I would fall and leave my own impression on the rocks below!

Well up on the hill on the other side of the road is another rock bearing a less well-defined impression of a man's footprint. The spot is known as *Mallán na mBráthar*, the hillside of the friar [*mala*: an incline; *mallán* usually denotes a hillside sloping down to the sea, as in this case]. This precipitous mountainside is alive with interesting names; every nook and cranny has its own identity. The stream tumbling down the hillside just east of *Mallán na mBráthar* is known as *Sruthán Mala Gabhar*, the rivulet of the hillside of the goats. The projecting nature of the rock formation jutting out from the mountainside a few metres east of the stream is well captured by its name, *An Teangaidh Rua*, "the strong tongue" [the Gaelic word *rua* usually translated as "red", "russet", is best interpreted as "wild", "rough", "strong", when used in a topographical sense]. "The rocky spur" would be the most apt non-literal translation here. Possibly the most interesting placename in the area is attached to a rocky cliff deep in the mountains here, known as *Screig a' Phréachán*, the crag of the crows. This cliff face is known to give back an echo; the older generation tells us that when the local men were on the mountain with their sheep and shouting instructions to their dogs their voices rebounded off the cliff and boomeranged back to them, sounding like the raucous screeching of crows.

It is regretable that as our rural areas become more denuded of people and fewer men spend their days on the mountain with their sheepdogs, many of the older names which give our mountains and valleys a personality and a voice of their own will be lost forever.

Stone said to bear
St. Conall's footprint

Leac Chonail

By its very name we associate Laconnell with St. Conall. It is said that he frequently rested and prayed at the stone (*leac*) which gives the area its name. This rock is down a little road to the right towards the sea, opposite some of the Laconnell houses on the left. A small cross is carved on the south-western face, near the base, of a natural rock outcrop. The top and base of the cross have T-bars but the arms are indistinct. A holy well, associated with St. Conall, was located in a field to the west, but it is now filled in. Near by, carved on an erratic boulder, is a rock-basin .25 m. in diameter and .15 m. deep.[28] Another holy well existed on Illancreeve island just off the coast of Laconnell, but it also has dried up or has been filled in.

The late Master McGrenra of Laconnell forwarded information regarding local beliefs about St. Conall to the Irish Folklore Commission[29] in Dublin in the 1930s. Stating that the flagstone is located about 300 yards from the Laconnell national school, where he taught for many years, he notes that the *leac* is held in great veneration locally. He also mentions the presence of a *Leabaigh Chonaill* (St. Conall's Bed) in Glencolumbkille and says that local tradition states that Conall had slept for seven years on this bed. This bed "is a hollow in a rock and is said to have been made by the impression of St. Conall's body". Master McGrenra also refers to the tradition of Conall having to do penance for a great sin and relates the story about how he would not be forgiven until the birds of the air had brought out their young in the palm of his hand. Having spent seven years sleeping on the "bed" in Glencolumbkille, Conall awoke to find the surrounding area littered with egg shells and young birds nesting in the palm of his hand. He states that St. Conall's feast-day is 22 May and that it is believed locally that St. Conall visits the island of Inishkeel every year on 1 June and remains until 12 September. It is during this period that the *turas* to Inishkeel is made. He notes that there is scarcely a family in the parishes of Ardara, Glenties or Glencolumbkille that does not number a Conall among its members, that the name has come down from olden days and that sometimes it takes the form of Con or Condy.

The facilities at the school where Master McGrenra[30] taught were not always so good; the following appraisal of the school was made by a schools' inspector in 1855: "A thatched hovel; light very bad, one window only, which consists of four nine-inch panes; the poorest house I have ever seen used for a school. Furniture middling; no arithmetical tablets; no blackboard; one large map. Time-table fair, no sale stock; order of children good; school very filthy. Teacher not trained; class 3; method of teaching skilful and intelligent; examines sensibly; he is the master of the worst school I have ever been in ... and yet his manners, appearance and conversation are rather superior. He walks six Irish miles to school and six home again every day. When the pupils come first they know no English, and it takes them a long time before they can master a phrase or two. The school is situated at the base of a chain of mountains through the whole extent of which English is scarcely known. When the children go home in the evening they have to unlearn the learning of the day, and speak Irish again to their relatives, to return with Irish only on their tongue to school in the morning."[31]

Between Laconnel and Maghera we pass by the spectacular waterfall of Easaranca. What does the name mean? T.C. McGinley, passing by here in 1867, gives us the clue; he writes: "We also notice a beautiful cascade, called Eas-rangach (the wrinkled cataract), descending from a great height, tumbling down the mountain steep, over Lia-Conaill, and breaking itself into a thousand fragments ere it reaches the bottom."[32] The name derives from *eas*: a waterfall, and *rangach* (or *reangach*): wrinkled; the wrinkled waterfall. Standing here on the roadside you can only see the lower reaches of the waterfall, but from a distance, such as from Loughros, you can observe it snaking down the whole mountainside like a wrinkle.

We have no evidence as to when the more permanent village of Maghera first came into existence, but we do know of human activity in this area since

Easaranca. A wild day, spray everywhere

very early times. People inhabited the nearby sand dunes from prehistoric times; we will discuss this later. It also appears that one or more major battles were fought here at Slivetooey early in our history – as far back as 291 A.D. we are told of "three battles at Sliabh Toadh"[33] and in 610 A.D. we are informed that "after Maelcobha, son of Aedh, son of Ainmire, had been three years in the sovereignty of Ireland, he was slain by Suibhne Meann, in the battle of Sliabh Toadh".[34] There is no reason to doubt that "Sliabh Toadh" equates with Slivetooey here at Maghera, especially as Maelcobha, slain in the latter battle, was a member of the Cenél Conaill of *Tír Chonaill.*

The village of Maghera may well have grown up around the early ecclesiastical foundation known as *Cill Chreaghaill;* Kilcraghy graveyard, where in the past skeletons have been exposed by blowing sand, is located west of Maghera village. The land has been tilled here and the original extent of the site is not clear; a rise 16.7 m. x 12.7 m. and up to 1 m. in height survives.[35] When this land was first brought into cultivation well over a generation ago, it is said the workers discovered the foundation of a number of circular structures "like large lime kilns".[36] They were probably the remains of early Christian cells. The bullaun stone which used to be at Peter McGill's and which is now lying beside the fence on your left-hand side just as you enter Maghera village may have belonged to this site.

Bullaun stones are not uncommon in Ireland; they are usually large blocks of the boulder type, in which round depressions have been made artificially. They may also occur on natural rock surfaces. The high percentage of association between bullauns and early ecclesiastical sites leads one to believe that they were used in connection with the pounding of cereals[37], herbs and roots in such establishments.

There exists a large body of folklore associated with bullauns and often where two hollows occur on the same stone they are traditionally believed to be the imprint of the knees of a saint (as at Derryleconnell, near Doochary, where our travels started). Water which has collected in bullaun stones is often used as a cure for warts and other ailments.

The most informed piece of writing on bullaun stones in Ireland appeared in the Journal of the Royal Society of Antiquaries of Ireland of 1959[38] and its author, Liam Price, suggests that the introduction of the use of these rock basins or bullauns as mortars into Ireland was due to the coming of early Christian immigrants from British to Irish monastic communities. In the opening half of the 6th century the relation between the British and Irish churches was that of master and disciple. Many British monks came to Ireland, travelling along the sea routes. It is thought that these ecclesiastics introduced features of ordinary Roman civilised life into the country.

Christians from post-Roman Britain are believed to have come to Irish monasteries in considerable numbers and they may have brought with them methods of preparing food which were not in use in Ireland; a new species of barley, which had to be ground or pounded to remove the grain from the husk, came into general use in post-Roman times. It is suggested that the Irish bullauns were mortars and were used by these early ecclesiastics. For that reason they are often associated with very early church sites. When we were discussing the *crannóg* at Crannogeboy we mentioned that rotary querns were an early[39] form of grinding stone; however in the 6th century they may still have been comparatively rare and expensive implements and the rock basin, which cost nothing, may then have come into common use. Perhaps the increasing introduction of the quern may explain how it came about that as early as the 12th century (when people had forgotten the original use for the rock basins) some of the rock basins had come to be regarded as having supernatural powers; they may have ceased to be used for any kind of grinding as soon as the use of rotary querns became general. Once a rock basin was abandoned it would fill with water and belief in the healing properties of the water might give rise to legend.

It might be suggested also that these bullaun stones were used as baptismal fonts, but in fact it was not until the 9th century that fonts came into general use; in Ireland the practice of the early saints was to administer baptism in rivers or springs.

As you walk over behind the village of Maghera, going in the direction of the sandhills, the strand and the Maghera caves, you pass a high circular mound. Known as Ardnaglogh [*árd*: high; *cloch*: a stone; the height of the stones] the site consists of a massive mound of sand and stone roughly flat-

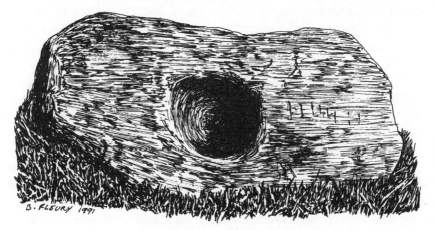

The Maghera bullaun stone

topped with steep sides and vegetated over. The mound is 7 to 8 m. in height, with a basal diameter of 39 m. There has been much speculation about the nature of this site. It has been suggested as the site of a ringfort, a burial place and a motte-and-bailey.[40] The mound would certainly seem to have been built by the hands of man. In earlier times a few local men began digging at the mound with spades, but stopped and covered it up again on discovering numerous skulls and other bones. Earlier this century the stones of two huts were still visible on top of the mound and two arrow-heads have been found here.[41] It certainly is a site that deserves professional archaeological excavation.

The mound is best viewed from a ridge on Slievetooey mountain at the back of Maghera village, and having made the ascent of this first part of the mountain you will come upon "Maghera castle", as it is called locally, and which is in reality the remains of a cashel. The site is located on the top of a knoll in an exposed but naturally defensible position. Much of the cashel wall still survives, except on the north and north-eastern sides where the natural slope may have precluded the need for a wall; there is a definite entrance to the south-south-west.[42]

Most visitors to Maghera come to see the caves. You walk out behind the village towards the sea, past the big mound, past the sand dunes, on to the beach, and then proceed beneath the cliff face on the left. At times the caves are difficult to see and difficult to enter, because the entrances can be almost choked up with blown sand. It goes without saying that the tide must be out; don't get caught by the incoming tide!

The entrance to the cave nearest Maghera is now blocked up with sand; inside it was known to be very lofty and spacious, with branches going off into quite a number of passages which penetrated under the cliff. The next cave, the best known, is called *Uaimh na nDaonaidh*, the cave of the people. T.C. McGinley recalls why the cave was given this name: "It would hold about five or six hundred persons. In the time of Cromwell's wars in this country, a multitude of people took refuge here to escape the indiscriminate slaughter to which they were sure to become victims if they fell into the hands of that merciless conqueror. They were betrayed, however, and his myrmidons slew in this cave upwards of five hundred persons, including women and children. Out of the entire number who sought shelter and safety here, one man only escaped. He had concealed himself on a projecting ledge, which is still observable near the roof of the cavern. From his dark retreat he witnessed, unobserved, the cold-blooded massacre of his friends below, until not a soul was left of the thousands [sic] who had flocked thither in the vain hope of eluding the Cromwellian bayonet-points. The floor

Mound at Ardnaglogh

A collapsed section of the cashel high above Maghera

is of sand – in common with the rest of the caves – and it is said that human bones are not unfrequently brought to the surface."[43]

The legend of the slaughter of so many people here at Maghera probably has a basis in fact. The massacre most likely took place at the time of the rebellion of 1641. This rising was an inevitable result of the Plantations of twenty and thirty years before. Earlier, when discussing the O'Boyle sept, I mentioned that Turlough Rua O'Boyle of Kiltoorish, his son and his brother were early in the field. Initially the English were taken by surprise by the 1641 rebellion. Colonel Audley Mervyn, one of the English officers operating in this area, in a report to the House of Commons on 4 June 1642, refers to the outbreak of the rebellion the previous October: "The suddennesse of our surprisall, and the nature of it, was so unexpected, that the inhabitants could scarcely believe themselves prisoners, though in their chaines, and the Irish servant which over-night was undressing his master in duty, the next morning was stripping master and mistris with a too-officious tyranny."[44]

The Planter regiments had their revenge. Tradition tells us that they came down into Loughros Point and devastated the whole area; people were thrown to their deaths at Pollatarrive at the end of the Point. It is said that the soldiers were about to leave Loughros when they saw a wisp of smoke across the bay. They went over to Maghera in boats and discovered the people in the cave. It is said that the fire had been lit to warm a woman in childbirth; the story fits with the climatic conditions, for it is known that there was deep snow on the ground in the month of December 1641.[45] People were put to death, also, in other parts of the parish – around Aighe and Glengesh.

Slaughter was widespread; a large number of people were massacred while hiding in a cave on Arranmore island off the north-west coast of Donegal in November 1641; the Governor of Letterkenny "gathered together on a Sunday morning fifty-three poor people most of them women and children and caused them to be thrown off the bridge into the river and drowned them all."[46] Colonel Mervyn's report lists one atrocity after another – e.g. "Sir Robert Stewart ... march'd up to Castle-derge, burnt all the enemies country and killed divers, brought four hundred cowes, then marched up over against Glenfin, burnt that country and kil'd divers." Most of the soldiers were Laggan volunteers. Thousands of innocents were slaughtered. It is, therefore, not surprising that this harrowing phase of Irish history has left an indelible mark on the folklore of the people.

Another cave here at Maghera is called *Uaimh a' Dorchadais*, the cave of darkness. It goes quite a way in under the cliff. A tradition is told concerning this cave that a party of people once visited the caves, provided with a blind fiddler for entertainment, who had his dog as a companion. The visitors loitered too long in the dark aisles of the cave and forgot about the incoming tide. Suddenly the cry went up "the tide is rushing in"; the poor fiddler, playing his fiddle deep in the bowels of the cave, was forgotten by the party in their rush to get out of the cave. The tide closed in and he played on. Tradition tells us that a month later he was heard, still playing the fiddle, four miles inland from the cave in the Glencolumbkille direction. He was never seen again. Some add that the dog came out at Glencolumbkille.

On our way back from the caves it is well to remember that the sandhills and sand dunes here were the site of the earliest habitation by man in the Maghera area. If you stand at the base of one of the sand dunes and notice a band of black soil running along the face of the dune, then you are looking at the discoloured soil which has been left by an ancient people who lived here and who built fires and cooked their food among the sandhills. The resulting debris from the firesides is the black band before you in the face of the sand dune. These areas are called kitchen middens. Excavation of them reveals many artefacts associated with man's early existence. It is also thought that whereas the more enterprising members of Neolithic man moved inland and began to clear the forests (and build the great tombs) some of the less ambitious remained near the coast and moved from one kitchen midden site to another. These sites generally have shown an abundance of shells of edible molluscs, indicating that the inhabitants mostly depended on sea-fare for nourishment.

Under what conditions did these shore dwellers live? We can speculate, but only that. In a few cases they may have had huts, but generally they lived in temporary shelters, probably tents, made of the skins of the animals they caught, and more often than not merely grouped round a fire in the open air. They lived principally on shellfish which they gathered on the rocks. They cooked them on a fire made of wood on some large flat stones in a rough vessel of pottery, or, perhaps, even adopted the more primitive method of heating pebbles red-hot in the fire, then dropping them into a vessel of water until the water boiled and cooked their food.[47]

Another ancient method of cooking was whereby stones heated in the fire were dropped into a sunken water-filled trough in the ground; these ancient cooking places – known as *fulachta fiadh* in early Irish literature – were invariably sited close to water sources and are thought to date from the first millenium B.C.

Though kitchen middens are among the earliest remains which we possess of the Mesolitic and Neolithic Ages they would of course have been used at periodic intervals by people in the later stages of our history. Some of these shore heaps which contain nothing but shells might be as recent as the last century when it was still the custom for inland people to go to the shore, a day or two each year, to collect "strand meat".[48] Cockles, mussels, periwinkles, etc. were gathered and boiled on the site. Only the edible parts were taken home.

The person who collected the greatest number of archaeological artefacts from the Maghera sand dunes was a Dr. d'Evelyn, of Ballymena, at the turn of this century. Dr. d'Evelyn first visited Maghera in 1896. Because of his kindness to the fishermen and their families and the treatment he gave them for any ailment they suffered he became so friendly with them that subsequently any flint or other type of object that became exposed in the sandhills over the years was sent to him by post. Dr. d'Evelyn continued to visit Maghera for the next four decades. He subsequently donated all the finds from the area to the Ulster Museum in Belfast. His collection demonstrates to us the varied number of people who have lived in and passed by these sand dunes over the centuries. He collected over 2,000 worked flints, fragments of early pottery, early flint axes and flint scrapers, arrow-heads, one polished stone axe, disc stones, numerous bronze pins, bronze penannular brooches, a possible bronze bracelet, a bronze finger ring, bronze clasps, a small strap of gold broken off some ornament and his collection also included later artefacts such as a silver coin of George III and a "gun-money" half-crown of James II, dated March 1690.[49]

Maghera was for many generations the home of a distinguished branch of the O'Boyle family. It is said that whenever an importance or respectability was claimed for a meeting, a sports contest or a horse race, the last word to enforce conviction of the success of the event was that the O'Boyles of

Bronze "Omega" ring-pin found in the Maghera sand dunes, now in the National Museum. Circular and penannular, its everted terminals taking the form of stylised birds' heads (after J.R.S.A.I, 1961)

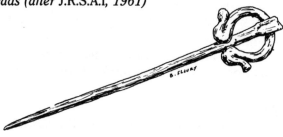

Maghera were there: *"Bhí an saol mhóir ann agus Baoilligh an Mhachaire."*

The O'Boyle name became extinct in Maghera about 1915. Tradition says that this was caused by a curse which hung over earlier generations of the family since they had lured a crippled ship to its doom by lighting welcoming fires on the sea cliffs. Soon the vessel was astride a sunken reef with water pouring in fore and aft. The first survivor to swim ashore was killed by a blow of a club. All the others turned back and were drowned in the raging sea. The broken ship with most of its cargo fell to the wreckers. The spoils having been divided, the worst was yet to come, for the sea refused to accept the body of the murdered sailor. Again and again the tide deposited it close to the scene of the foul deed. Even when it was buried deep in the sand (for no one wanted it close to his house or land) the turbulent waves washed it up. At last a messenger was sent for a holy monk who prayed long and fervently over the open grave in which was stretched the corpse. He asked those present to gaze on that poor dead face and ask the pardon of God for their terrible deed. "For," said he, "everyone who shared in the spoils is as guilty as the one who struck the death blow and a day may come when there will not be one of their descendants left in the area."

This type of story is also told of Cornwall and of many other parts of the world where people often depended on shipwrecks for their survival.

Mrs. Nellie McNelis of Glenconwell, who died in 1956 at the age of ninety, was the last survivor of the O'Boyles of Maghera born in the old homestead. She was born in 1866 and her grandfather, Turlogh O'Boyle, whom she remembered, was a nephew of the last Fr. O'Boyle, whose name, she thought, was Seamus. Her only two brothers, Edward and James, emigrated to America in their youth and never returned. The O'Boyles of Owenteshna, with those of Curraghafeehan[50] and Lugnagillew, are descended from the Maghera family.

A remarkable relic of the O'Boyles of Maghera – *buabhall Uí Bhaoill* – still exists in the village. It is an old bugle-horn, said to have belonged to the O'Boyles. It is held in safe keeping in the home of Mrs. Kitty McGill (Dan Bhrían's) in Maghera. The Gaelic word *buabhall* means a wild ox or a horn, so presumably the bugle is the horn of a wild ox. There is indecipherable lettering, possibly names, on it and it is said that one of its later uses was in the time of Fr. Seamus O'Boyle, mentioned above, when it was employed to call people when mass was about to be celebrated. Nowadays the youngest of the household, ten-year-old Brian Óg McGill, has developed the art of producing a loud resonant sound from the horn.

Not all of the O'Boyles of Donegal and the rest of Ulster are descended from the ancient Donegal branch; many are also descended from another and equally ancient line, the Síol (a race, a clan) Baoill of Cenél Eoghain. There are many earlier references to this family and as late as 1470 we find a reference to them when the *Annals of Ulster* mention the *Coillte Síola Baoil* (O'Boyles' Woods) somewhere in the west of the present Co. Tyrone.[51]

The village of Maghera is situated at the base of Slievetooey (*Sliabh Thuaidh*, the northern mountain), pronounced with three syllables – Sliabh-a-Tooey. This large mountain range extends from Maghera almost as far as Glencolumbkille. It is sad to relate that one of the last golden eagles in this area met its death at Meenachurrin,[52] on this mountain range, earlier this century. Dr. d'Evelyn, the archaeologist of Maghera, writing in 1933, refers to "Slieve-a-Tooey, where the last of the golden eagles met its doom, recently, in a rabbit trap".[53] The eagle had alighted to feed on the carcass of a sheep. After its death it was stuffed; what a derisory end for this great bird. Its mate was later shot on the top of *Screig a'Bheithigh* [*screig*: a precipice; *beithíoch*: an animal], the area up behind the cliff face on your left going up Granny Glen. The precipice on your right here is known as *Screig an Iolair*; [*iolar*, an eagle], surely confirmation that this area was a traditional habitat of the golden eagle.

Brian Óg McGill with buabhall Uí Bhaoill. *The mouthpiece is missing.*

In 1924 Arthur W. Fox published a lovely book about the golden eagle entitled *Haunts of the Eagle – Man and Wild Nature in Donegal.* He had come to Donegal on numerous occasions hoping to catch a glimpse of this great bird. And he had been successful – he had witnessed a golden eagle at close quarters at Glenveagh and he also saw the two golden eagles which used to nest at *Sliabh Thuaidh.* One of these eagles he had seen at *Sliabh Liag* and he had seen its mate at Teelin.

He even came here to try and sight the nesting place of the two eagles on *Sliabh Thuaidh* but he was out of luck. He writes: "Before I left County Donegal I made up my mind to visit the last nesting-place of the golden eagle within its boundaries, the lonely and not easily accessible peak of Slieve-a-Tooey, which frowns over the narrow and wildly grand inlet of Loughros Beg. ... Below boomed the sea, rolling up the narrow inlet. ... The scattered grouse went scudding along the summits uttering their staccato cry of alarm; now and then the whistle of a solitary curlew pierced the still air, and once a snipe rose from a patch of marshy ground, beating his feathered drum as he darted away to a securer refuge. Now and then I caught the low note of the wheatear, as he was beginning to feel the migrant call to other lands within him. But the eagles, I saw no more; neither he nor his mate deigned to put in an appearance to gladden my eyes."[54]

However, he had sighted a golden eagle earlier at Glenveagh,[55] and I think his description is worth reproducing: "Suddenly the speck dropped downwards, taking two or three wide circles and growing larger every moment. Then down it came sheer, gripping in its pitiless talons something still struggling vainly to escape, till it alighted on a spot within a few yards from my hiding place. ... When the royal bird was almost on the ground his wings seemed to stretch to the width of almost six feet; when he had folded them around his sturdy body he appeared to stand almost three feet above the ground. To me, at least, it was a wonderful sight, so utterly unlike most of the pictures in books. It was a male bird just emerged from the moulting season and in fine plumage, deeply brown, with his tail slightly white-barred beneath, while his golden head and breast shone vividly in the lustrous light. His beak was bright yellow at the base, but horn-coloured throughout the rest of its length, his talons were dull yellow, his sturdy legs were brown and feathered from end to end. His hazel eyes flashed fearless glances around him."[56]

Let us hope that sights such as this are not a thing of the past in Donegal. I'm told that efforts are being made to reintroduce the golden eagle to the county.

You can continue up this road past Maghera, through spectacular Granny

Glen, past Lagunna, on to Port and then into Glencolumbkille. It is a very interesting drive, though far more pleasant to walk out to Port and spend a few days tenting, in splendid isolation, watching the waves rolling in.

Many people find the name "Granny Glen" an interesting placename and wonder what it means. Granny derives from the Gaelic word *grean* which means the bottom of a river or the gravel or coarse sand in such a bottom. It is always sounded short – *gran. Greanach*, the adjective form with the suffix *-ach* (which when placed after a noun such as *grean* conveys a sense of "full of", "abounding in"), signifies gravelly. T.C. McGinley, passing by here in 1867, calls it "Greanaighe, i.e., the gravelly glen".[57] The area appears in the proportions of 1642 as "Greannagh"; a "Drumgrineagh" is also noted in 1642 and might represent the highest point of Granny.

I would suggest that the name originally derived from the gravelly bottom of the river[58] which runs through the glen rather than from any gravelly nature of the valley itself. Before the present little road which hugs one side of the precipitous mountain was built people travelled through here by adhering to the river bank. Coming here in 1909 Joseph Campbell writes: "Bearing south by the Owenea river from Maghery, we strike up through Maum[59] gorge. Outside Maghery we come on two men – one of them a thin, wizened old fellow with no teeth; the other a youngish man, very raggedly dressed, with dark hair and features like an Italian. The old man tells us in Irish to keep up by the river-bed, and we can't possibly lose our direction. A quarter of a mile further on we meet another man. He repeats what the old man told us, viz., to keep to the river-bottom, and to cut up then by the fall at the head of Maum to Laguna."[60]

It would appear that a road up the side of Granny was being constructed in 1909 because Campbell refers to "a point where the track ends in the heather, and where a squad of navvies is engaged laying down a foundation of brushwood and stones to carry it further into the hills."[61]

As we descend from the top of Granny towards Maghera we will reflect very briefly on a few of the placenames we have mentioned here. Port is locally pronounced Purt and must have been one of the most unsafe places in Ireland to bring in a small boat. It is difficult to be sure of the correct interpretation of Lagunna. The first part of the name is simple enough – *log*: a hollow, here indicating a hollow surrounded by hills, which describes the siting of Lagunna admirably. The name is written "Lagenae" in 1642 and in 1835 John O'Donovan interpreted the second part of the word as a personal name and called it *Lag Eanna*, Enda's Hollow. There is a local suggestion that the name may have derived from Lagunna's propensity, because of its hollow shape, to retain whatever the elements rained down on it – e.g. water, snow – for a longish period and that the placename should be interpreted as *An Log a Choinneas* [from *coinnigh*: to keep; the hollow which retains water, snow, etc. for long periods]. However, in the name of the nearby mountain of Cnocuna we are dealing with the same termination as in Lagunna, so this makes the local suggestion unlikely to be correct, though it is interesting.

Dónal Mac Giolla Easpaig, on whose expertise we have relied earlier, gives us his views on this most difficult of placenames: "Although the meaning of the second element of this name is not known, there can be little doubt about its form; both local and documentary evidence point to either Onna or Unna. It cannot be linked to either *coinne* or *connadh* as some have suggested. This element Onna occurs in a number of other names in the vicinity: Cnoc Onna, of which there are two, one above Lagunna, and one outside Carrick above a lake called Loch Onna. I have not been able to find any noun resembling this element. My own suggestion is that Onna is a personal name, possibly mythological."

Maghera translates as *An Mhachaire*; *machaire* is a derivative of *magh*,[62] a plain, a level district and describes very well this flat area in the shadow of *Sliabh Thuaidh*. The nature of the terrain underfoot is not uniform here and this is reflected in the 1642 names for the area – Magheryerdogh al' Magheryruvye al' Magheryreogh, the former presumably being *Machaire Dumhcha*, the plain of the sandhills and the latter two being interpreted as *Machaire Fhraoich*, the plain of the heather; altogether an apt description of the area.

Finally, we leave Maghera with an excerpt which describes the atmosphere here at the beginning of this century: "The dark green bulk of Slieve-a-Tooey rising like a wall behind, a wisp of cloud lying lightly upon its carn. The village of Maghery, a mere clachan of unmortared stone and rainbeaten straw, huddling at its foot. A shepherd's whistle, a cry in torrential Gaelic, or the bleat of a sheep coming from it now and again, only to accentuate the elemental quiet and wonder of the place."[63]

Notes

1   *Druim a' Chátha* (*cáith*, g.s. *cátha*: chaff): the ridge of the chaff, a winnowing place. A polished stone axe-head has been found at Drimaha.

2   *A.S.D.*, p. 280.

3   Ordnance Survey, Hill Drawing Antiquity Books, ms. books 1-25, compiled 1845-48 by Thomas Fagan, book 21, p. 39.

4   Joyce, vol. I, p. 529.

5   Ibid.

6   *Dr. Pococke's Irish Tour*, p. 68.

7   Public Records Office of Northern Ireland: D/2860/25/3.

8   In the Grand Jury presentments of 7 April 1767, £31 10s was awarded to George and Wm. Nesbitt "to build a bridge of two arches over the Adrige (al) River"; £45 10s was awarded "to build four bridges over four rivers in the lands of Cashel, consisting of one arch each". On 28 March 1768, £36 1s 6d was awarded to George and Wm. Nesbitt "to make 78 perches of road from Addregole to Drumbarron at 9/3d per perch". Presumably this was the new road being made; it was a time of much road building.

9   *D.A.* (1987), p. 7.

10   See Énrí Ó Muirgheasa, *Dhá Chéad de Cheoltaibh Uladh,* pp. 410-11; see also pp. 184-85.

11   *Mullach na cloiche* or possibly *Mullán na cloiche. Mullach*: the top, summit; *Mullán,* a little summit, is a diminutive of *mullach* and is generally applied to the top of a low, gently sloping hill; since this height is dominated by *Sliabh Maoineach* at its rear *mullán* is probably correct; *na cloiche*: of the stone, *cloch*: a stone.

Near by is Maogh, derived from *magh*, a plain. This might seem a strange place-name for this elevated terrain but the actual area enclosed in Maogh is mostly the land extending from Ardvalley over to Monargan and is not really precipitous.

Finally Ardvalley, *Ard Bhaile* [*árd*: high], should be interpreted more as "the high place" than "the high town". The Gaelic word *baile* is now understood to mean a town, or townland, but in its original acceptation it denoted simply *locus* – place or situation (Joyce, vol. I, p. 347). Its application to mean townlands – without any reference at all to habitation – is as old as the 12th century (Joyce, p. 349). In modern times the word is usually translated "town".

12   The Gaelic word *tigherna* means "a lord"; it is derived from *tig(h)*, a house; the word appears in the old Welsh form *tigirn* and the Cornish *teyrn*.

13   *H.D.R.,* vol. I, p. 280.

14   *D.A.* (1987), p. 11.

15   Ibid. p. 12.

16   vol. I, pp. 186-87.

17   110, 112; quoted in Kenney, p. 387.

18   *Corpus*, pp. 59, 199.

19   An early tribe who occupied lands in the south-east of this country.

20   p. 155.

21   Murray-Stewart Estate Papers, National Library.

22   *A.S.D.*, p. 316.

23   Ibid. p. 118.

24   Joyce, vol. I, p. 118.

25   Ibid.

26   Hugh Allingham, *Captain Cuellar's Adventures in Ulster and Connacht.*

27   By a member of the Craig family, Shanaghan.

28   *A.S.D.*, p. 280.

29   Now the Dept. of Irish Folklore; ms. 948, pp. 21-23, Seamus MacGrianna, Laconnell.

30   Mr. James P. McGrenra, who was appointed U.S. Attorney General by President Truman in 1952, was a relative of the late Master McGrenra. The former Attorney General's father, Patrick McGrenra, known locally as "Pat Bán", was a native of Termon near Letterkenny.

31   Reproduced in *D.A.* (1956), p. 104.

32   *The Cliff Scenery of South Western Donegal*, p. 149.

33   *A.F.M.*, vol. I, pp. 122-23.

34   Ibid. pp. 236-37.

35   *A.S.D.*, p. 137.

36   *H.P.A.*, p. 25.

37   As recently as the early decades of this century a bullaun stone at Laconnall was used for pounding barley for Christmas broth.

38   pp. 161-89.

39   Replacing the even earlier saddle quern.

40   *A.S.D.*, p. 61.

41   *J.R.S.A.I.*, vol. 3 (7th series), vol. LXIII consec series (1933), pp. 88-100.

42   *A.S.D.*, p. 149.

43   *The Cliff Scenery of South Western Donegal*, p. 148.

44   Reproduced in Sir J. Gilbert's *Contemporary History of Affairs In Ireland*, pp. 464-75; report relates to the counties of Donegal, Tyrone, Fermanagh and Londonderry.

45   Colonel Mervyn's report, ibid, pp. 470-72.

46   Ó Gallachóir, *Essays*, p. 88.

47   *J.R.S.A.I.*, vol. 44 (1914), p. 207.

48   *H.P.A.*, p. 88.

49   *J.R.S.A.I.*, vol. 3 (7th series), vol. LXIII consec. series (1933), pp. 88-110.

50   Near Dunkineely; a very interesting placename – *Curragh a' Phíocháin* [*curragh*: a marsh; a hoarseness in the throat is known as *píochán* in Gaelic]. It could be suggested that the marsh gave rise to this ailment, but another explanation, and the more likely one, is that the wind blowing through a crevice by the river here produced a long plaintive wail. Earlier generations were very conscious of sounds they heard in the night – "fairy voices" carried in the wind.

51   *D.A.* (1973), pp. 322-23.

52   Translates as *Mín a' Chuirrín*, the smooth (*mín*) field of the little *curragh* or marsh.

53   *J.R.S.A.I.*, vol. 3 (7th series), vol. LXIII consec. series (1933), p. 88.

54   *Haunts of the Eagle*, p. 40, p. 48.

55   In north-west Donegal; now a National Park and well worth visiting.

56   *Haunts of the Eagle*, pp. 15-19.

57   *The Cliff Scenery of South Western Donegal*, p. 149.

58   The Owenwee: *An Abhainn bhuí*, the yellow river.

59   *Madhm*: burst, rout, chasm, break, a break or pass in a mountain, a high mountain pass.

60   *Mearing Stones*, pp. 14-15.

61   Ibid. p. 15.

62   Interestingly enough, from this word *magh* come the Gaelic words *amuigh* (*i maigh*) – outside, and *amach* (*i magh*) – out; it appears to suggest a spaciousness, which I suppose is synonomous to the human mind with being out-of-doors.

63   *Mearing Stones*, p. 3.

XVII

"UP THE NICK"

REJOINING THE ARDARA-Killybegs road we continue through the townland of Brackey. Older maps divide the area into Old Brackey or Brackey Beg and New Brackey or Brackey More. Old Brackey is roughly lower Brackey. In 1642 we find the following places listed, in this order: Brackaghbegg, Brackaghmore, Derygall, Caman, Cashell, Ahagh. The first two placenames refer, of course, to Brackey, Derygall is Edergole, Caman is very likely the present-day Common, Cashell is Cashel and Ahagh is present-day Aighe.

Brackey I would translate as *An Bhreacaigh* since the root word appears to be *breac*, which means speckled[1] or parti-coloured. As land, especially hillsides or dry upland, often presents a speckled or spotted appearance, caused by different kinds of vegetation, or by the varying colours of the soil or of rocks, this word is of very frequent occurence in local names.[2] *An Bhreacaigh*,[3] then, means speckled land or multifaced terrain. In 1755 John Hood describes the land at Brackey as "indifferent" and mentions that there is substantial woodland here – this woodland with its changing hues may have contributed to the varied appearance of the area.

There is an old burial place in lower Brackey called *Cill na mBan*, the Church of the Women. We know nothing definite of its history. Perhaps it was an early ecclesiastical site peopled by females. In local folklore the site features in the legend in which so many of the womenfolk of Finn and the Fianna were burned to death at *Mul an Tigh Mhóir* in nearby Edergole; it is said that the Fianna buried the remains of their loved ones here at *Cill na mBan*.

Arriving at Common bridge we find a road going off to the right to Glengesh and Glencolumbkille; we continue on the road to the left and proceed through the townland of Common. This, I suggest, is the area called Caman in 1642. The placenames Common or Caman do not appear on

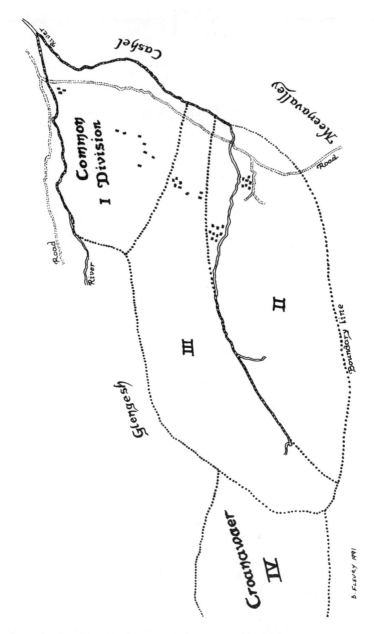

The four divisions of Aighe townland in 1831. By this time the road has been built on the present-day course, nearer the houses than the old road. (An artist's impression after an estate map in the National Library)

earlier maps – neither on John Hood's maps of 1755 nor Murray Babington's of 1813-14; Common then appeared to be part of Aighe townland. The Gaelic word *camán* means a bend, but usually denotes a hurling or camogie stick, used to strike the ball while playing these games. The sport of hurling has been played since very ancient times in Ireland and we often find it referred to in old epic tales. The terrain here is relatively flat and it is possible that there was a tradition of playing hurling here from early times. It is unlikely that the placename Common would denote a centuries old use of this area for commonage, such as for grazing, since the ancient Irish rundale system allowed livestock to wander freely and therefore specific, isolated, areas of commonage would have been unknown. Possibly, then, Common is a name applied in more anglicised recent times to this area which used to be part of the old Aighe townland and part of which was formerly called *Camán*, a place where sports were played. I'm aware that the mountain extending over towards Glengesh is now called "Common Mountain", but, as I've stated earlier, all this area appears as part of Aighe in earlier maps.

To our left is the Aighe river and on the far bank is the townland of Cashel. You would be surprised if Cashel did not have the remains of a stone enclosure (a cashel) and indeed it had the remains of two up until the recent past; nowadays there is just the one. This cashel consists of a subcircular platform 33.5 m. in diameter and from .5 m. to 3.3 m. above the surrounding land.[4] Stones are incorporated into the edges of the platform but probably most of them have been taken to build the adjacent field walls.

Common also has the remains of a cashel[5] – a subcircular area enclosed for the most part by a collapsed stone wall; the interior has been planted with conifers. Common, also, used to have a second stone fort.

We now approach the bottom of the steep incline locally called "the Nick" and pass into the townland of Aighe. Earlier travellers and cartographers refer to this mountain pass as the "Neck of the Ballagh" – *bealach* is the Gaelic word for a road or way and the term "Neck of the Ballagh" merely refers to the fact that the gap through the mountains here is narrow, reminding one of the narrowness of the neck in the human body. Presumably "the Neck" gradually changed to the pronunciation "the Nick" (appropriate enough – a nick in the mountains which allowed passage) and this name was taken up by the locals.

Until a few hundred years ago, of course, the road did not follow its present path but came along away over to our left, alternating between the holms of Aighe (present day Common) and Cashel and went up through the pass hugging the left-hand side of the hill. This is verified by folklore from the Aighe area – *"Ní raibh bealach ar bith fríd an Fhaithche san am sin; ar*

a' Chaiseal a bhí an bealach – There was no road through Aighe at that
time; the road was in Cashel." I believe that the habitation pattern in this
area over the latter centuries was that the people built their homes in an elevated position – for security reasons – on the hillside on our right and used
the river valley below, which was easily observable and through which travellers passed, for tillage and husbandry.

Because of the mountainous nature of the terrain here I had great difficulty coming to terms with the meaning of the placename Aighe [*An
Fhaithche*: a hurling field or any level green field in which games are cele-
brated]. The name seemed inappropriate. *An Fhaithche* is a very old placename. In front of ancient Irish residences there was usually a level green
plot, used for various purposes – for games and exercises, for the reception
of visitors, etc. – called *an fhaithche*. Ancient Irish writers frequently mention the *faithche* in connection with the king's or chieftain's fort.[6] The word
is often used to denote a hurling field. I searched for other meanings for the
placename Aighe. Did it spring from the word *aghaidh*, the Gaelic for "face",
reflecting the high position (head, face) that Aighe holds overlooking the
valley here? Did it come from the Gaelic word *faighdhe*, meaning help or
succour, possibly indicating that the mountains here offered succour and
refuge – this suggestion will crop up later – to people fleeing from tyranny
over the centuries? In addition there is an old Gaelic word *aighe*,[7] which can
mean a hill; surely appropriate and its pronunciation sounds exactly the
same as we pronounce Aighe nowadays. Finally, however, I settled for *An
Fhaithche*; if, as I believe, the river valley below was used for playing hurling
(*camán*) from ancient times – and the older maps suggest that this valley
was formerly part of Aighe – then this flat area used for sporting occasions
may be the reason that Aighe should be correctly interpreted as *An
Fhaithche*. In folklore from this area there is frequent mention of the words
"*amuigh ar an fhaithche*", confirming that this is the correct interpretation
of the placename Aighe.

Though I will deal with Aighe and later, Glengesh, separately, I see these
two mountain valleys as geographically and culturally identical. If we take
the mountain range here as being horse-shoe shaped, with the Cuntaman
(*Ceann na mBeann*) as the apex, then Aighe and Glengesh are the two end-
points of the horse-shoe. The mountain range between them was not a dividing factor; rather it was common to them and in the days before roads
nothing was thought of going across the mountain. In addition men from the
two valleys intermingled while tending to their animals "on the hill". Happy
was the man "on the hill" with his dog.

Aighe, like Glengesh, remained Gaelic in lifestyle when the old order had faded away elsewhere. Folklore from the area reflects a stubbornness on the part of the inhabitants to accept English rule in later centuries and place-names here cause us to remember acts of tyranny which were carried out against the people.

Penal Laws can be said to have started in the parish of Ardara in May 1611,[8] the date on which the native population had to leave the lands now assigned to British undertakers and servitors and betake themselves to the most inhospitable parts of the country. Protestant clergy were given charge of all churches, church lands and cemeteries. Deprived of their churches, nothing remained for the priests and their flock but to assemble at convenient and suitable places for worship in the open air.

Dr. Maguire, writing in 1920, informs us that when the priests had to seek a hiding place, "The wild, untraversed recess of bleak mountain, thence called Aighe (Refuge), was chosen, and a substantial, rude dwelling was there constructed, very appropriately designated *Cró-na-Cleire* (the Hut or Hovel of the Clergy), a name still preserved in the local topography."[9] It still is. *Screag an Aifrinn* (the rocky ledge where mass was said) and *Uaigh a' tSagairt* (the priest's grave) are the names of other places in this locality which have their roots in the days of religious persecution.

Poll a' Mhurdair (Murder Hole), in nearby Cashel, is a reminder of the massacres which took place in this area in 1641. Earlier Aighe people pointed to a spot in the Nick where one man was found alive after the terror had passed. *Poll na Giorra*, over in the valley of Glengesh, is pointed out as the spot where another 1641 massacre took place. A number of people of all ages were in hiding there when one of their number, a child, died. Owing to the risk of going into the open, burial was postponed. Soon a pair of ravens with their hoarse cry, signifying death, appeared circling overhead. The soldiers, too, hearing the ravens' call, hurried to the spot to investigate and left not even one survivor.[10]

In the local placename *Mullan a' Tairbh*, the hillock of the bull, we have a reminder of the tithe troubles of the early 19th century. Tradition from Aighe asserts that even if only one householder hadn't paid his tithes the bailiffs would still come into a townland and take all the cattle. One day Seamus Mór Mac a'Ghoill (Big Seamus McGill), who was living up on *An tArd Bhán* (here, up on our right), saw the bailiff and his helpers down below going off with all the Aighe cattle, including his own – even though he had paid his tithe. He took pursuit and catching up with them he took a hold of his own three-year-old bull by the horns. The bailiff struck the bull with his stick, but Seamus Mór, who had a reputation for great strength, held on. Suddenly the horns came away in Seamus's hands and the young bull charged off homewards, followed by all the other Aighe cattle. The bailiff and his helpers slunk off, watched by Seamus Mór, still holding the bull's horns in his hands and standing on the spot thereafter known as *Mullan a' Tairbh*.

Aighe is a stronghold of the McGill sept, of which Seamus Mór was a member and of which I am proud to be numbered. Tradition tells us that the first McGill to come to this general area was a *Dinnsí Buí na nGabair* (Yellow Denis of the Goats; did he have a sallow complexion?) who is said to have come to the Glengesh area from Antrim about 1660. After a few generations all the pockets of this whole mountainous area of south-west Donegal had their representation of McGills. Of the twenty householders in Aighe in 1857[11] eight were McGills.

We now continue our travels. After going up and over the Nick the road levels out and we have Meenakillew on our right and Meenavalley on our left. The Gaelic word *mín*, written "meen" in English, is very prevalent in Donegal and is usually applied to a comparatively smooth and fertile green area – with rushes growing through the green – on the face of a mountain or in the midst of coarse, rugged hilly land.[12] *Mín* originally meant fine or smooth. Meenakillew translates as *Mín a' Choilleadh*, the mountain field of the wood, and Meenavalley as *Mín a' Bhealaigh*, the mountain field of the road or pass – we are actually travelling along this road now. Up behind Meenakillew is Meenateia, *Mín a' tSeighe*, the mountain field of the wild deer. The word *séig/séigh* noted by Joyce as indicating a wild deer has changed little from that – *ség*[13] – used to describe wild deer in the ancient *Cormac's Glossary*.[14] *Fia* is the modern word.

Towards the top of Mulmosog peak, on your left you'll spot a conspicuous white rock; this is called the *Gearran*[15] *Bán*: the white horse. It serves as an indelible reminder of another episode which is said to have occurred during Penal times. Relentlessly pursued by soldiers the priest, who was on his travels from place to place saying mass, had his horse shot from under him at the *Gearran Bán* and was himself wounded. Tradition tells us that he was later captured and put to death. There are grounds, though, for believing that the name *Gearran Bán* might be a throwback to a much older time-frame. There are a few other places in Ireland which bear this name and they are situated in mountaineous areas overlooking a path, just as this site does; examples are those at Barnesmore Gap between Ballybofey and Donegal town and at the Curlew mountains in north Connacht. These *Gearran Bán* areas were associated from very early times with bands of outlaws who survived by plundering traffic going through the mountain passes.

J.C. MacDonagh, writing in 1946, informs us that "the Garran Bán ... bears a close resemblance to the Centaur of Greek mythology ... half-man, half-horse, but whereas the Greek monstrosity was a kindly creature our Celtic Centaurs were under a 'Geasa' or spiritual obligation to eat the first Christian they met in morning canters".[16] The *Garran Bán* legends go back into the mists of time; in his evaluation of a study of a *Garran Bán* site in Connacht MacDonagh notes that the author concludes that "the Garran Bán of this (Connacht) locality was the focal point for two eras of pre-history – (a) the era prior to the introduction of written record and (b) the folk version of all time which lies beyond the memory of living man".

Ancient Ireland had a well-defined tribal and territorial system and it is likely that the *Garran Bán* outlaws were grouping of individuals who had been cast out by their own tribe. Most immigrants from a tribe sought the protection of the chieftain of another clan. These immigrants – a comparatively despised class – were known as *Fuidhir*.[17] Other immigrants may have banded together to become outlaws of the wild mountain passes. Little of their early history is known but in the more recent past – 1544 – the Lord Deputy informed King Henry VIII of a remote wilderness in Munster called *Cnoc-an-Garran-Bán* where "dwelt a sept of thieves and outlaws called 'ye olde Eville Children'".[18]

In 1583 Sir Henry Sidney recorded his march through Connacht and states: "I marched on the craggy mountains of the Curlieus, a passage bad enough, where I chased and chastised the ancient outlaws of that quarter called the Garran Ban."[19]

The *Garran Bán* site at the Curlews provided a most intriguing description of its inhabitants: "There was only one class that wasn't bested by the clansmen; them was the horse thieves of the Garran Ban, the wans in the woods above in the mountains ... no wan but the robbers themselves could find their way in and out of them wildernesses. Every class of outlaw joined them, men put out of their land by the power of the clansmen, Gallows' birds escaped out of the halter; bondsmen running away from their slavery on the land ... that robber clan was better manged than them with Lords over them ... they had their fairs ... they had their tradesmen of their own ... and cow doctors and a sight of oulde black knowledge that's now lost forever. They had a cure for every class of ailment in man or baste. ... Faith, the people, the downtrodden, labouring man would be in a bad way in the time of the clansmen's wars but for the kindness of the Garran Ban outlaws."[20]

It is likely that the formerly wooded mountains of the Mulmosog and Meenakillew areas were home to such a band of outlaws in the distant past.

My father was born here at Meenakillew in 1897 and in his memory, here in the place of his birth, I will relate a few of his observations on dress styles and related subjects. On Sundays the elderly men whom my father remembered in the early years of this century wore skirted jackets with two buttons in the middle of the back. His father had told him that this style owed its origin to military jackets, where the buttons were used to hold up a military belt. Their hats were black with a shallow crown having a narrow ribbon around it. A dickey bow was sometimes worn around the neck.

On working days the country man wore a large grey flannel shirt-shaped garment instead of a jacket. It hung down over his hips and was light and roomy enough for working in. Of the two vents over his hips one was usually tied in a knot. He didn't remember any of these later than 1920.

Most women wore black shawls of a honeycomb pattern. He remembered young university students who would arrive home from Dublin in the dress-style of the period, but like the girls of the neighbourhood wore the black shawl to fair and church during their holiday.

My father added that Paddy Antoine, the travelling tailor who made his father's suit in 1880, possessed a copy of the *Annals of the Four Masters* which he carried on his rounds and which he read and explained to his audience after his day's work was finished. All the journeymen tailors were not as serious minded as Paddy Antoine. Some of them were noted liars, in a humorous sense. As a rule, if they were strangers in an area, they boasted of their exploits in foreign parts and especially their heroism in wars. One man claimed to have spent years in China where he saw a large field, the size of the parish of Ardara, and in which were stacked all the old moons which had ever crossed the sky since time began. Nice!

In the 1930s my father visited an old man, John Mór McGill, then aged eighty-two years, who lived in the area over towards Glengesh and sat chatting to him at his fireside one Sunday evening. He noted that all the time John Mór talked there was a faraway look in his eyes; he lamented the passing of the old times and the old ways and stated that in the present world life was very lonesome for an old man. In his young days each household was almost entirely self-supporting. There was no drapery shop in Ardara; woollens and linens were made in the home. My father was shown towels of the most intricate pattern which were spun and woven locally – about seventy years before – and a small roll of indigo blue flannel. Fifty years earlier two suit-lengths of this material were made in the house. John Mór got one tailored for a Sunday suit and the other length was left aside until he should require another, but the first suit had lasted him ever since and the suit length was still tied to the couple (a pair of rafters in a thatched house).

We leave my father's reminiscences and continue in a more harsh vein.

The whole Mulmosog mountain area, including Meenavalley and extending back over the top of Mulmosog hill to Meentinadea and Crucknagapple behind, was the scene of extensive land changes – exploitation might be a truer term – in the mid-1800s. The *Ballyshannon Herald* newspapers of 1840 and 1841 carry long reports of social occasions held at Mulmosog House (later Meenavalley House) to which local dignitaries had been invited to witness the land improvements. From 21 August 1840 we read: "The above place [Mulmosog], the property of Captain Harcourt [who had this land leased from the Murray estate] was the scene of great festivity. It was occasioned by Mr. Houghton, his enterprising agent, having sent cards of invitation to a large number of the surrounding gentry and clergy, etc., to witness the great improvement that had been effected there for the last two years, in reclaiming a hitherto barren mountain, consisting of 860 acres, and bringing it into a high state of cultivation, and that they might be partakers at the festive board of a sumptuous entertainment, got up in the good old English style of hospitability." At the festive dinner Mr. Murray, the landlord, was eulogised for having established schools on his estate to promote the education of his tenantry.

The following year, 27 August 1841 (*Ballyshannon Herald*), we are told that the 860 acres were almost a perfect waste until they came under the management of Mr. Houghton two or three years earlier, that there were seven tenants upon them, who paid in all £12 of rent, "which was sufficiently high, if viewed relatively, not to the inert capabilities of the soil, but to its actual produce"; that Mr. Houghton paid the tenants for what is termed "the goodwill" of the land, instead of ejecting them, and that "the whole estate was without shelter and without a fence and that the occupants, when conveying their scanty produce to market had to carry it on their backs, often wading knee-deep in mud, and always through streams, until they got far beyond its limits".

One would think to read all this that Mr. Houghton did not evict the tenants and that he was in fact about to improve their poor circumstances. Admittedly they weren't evicted penniless, but they certainly had to go – they were made "an offer they couldn't refuse" to use a phrase from *The Godfather*. The Crucknagapple tenants were paid £200 and the Meentinadea tenants £220 13s 4d. between them. How the Crucknagapple tenants disposed of their wealth I have never heard, but the tenants dispossessed from Meentinadea proceeded to buy pieces of moorland from the occupants of the townlands of Monargan, Glencoagh[21] and upper Gortnacart.

Now, unhindered, the great experiment went on. Mr. Houghton began to construct first-rate roads and to have the land divided into large fields by the building of substantial fences. "An elegant and commodious dwelling-house, with a walled garden attached," was erected. Soon a hundred acres were put under oats, twenty under potatoes, a smaller portion under clover, etc. A large stock of cows, native and Durham, was initiated and pigs which were of the Berkshire breed and horses of the Suffolk breed were introduced.

When the management changed in 1847 the new agent, Mr. Wilson, immediately intensified efforts to strip holdings and get tenants[22] off the land in this area and throughout the whole Murray-Stewart estate, extending in towards Killybegs and Kilcar. In an 1848 Murray-Stewart estate account book there is an expense of £23 12s 9d: "expenses while ejecting refractory tenants – 16 men extra and the carriage of the luggage of 60 soldiers and 40 constabulary". Squaring of the land started in earnest in 1849. In 1850 we note a "widow Bridget Cunningham evicted from her farm at Kille" (Kill, between Killybegs and Kilcar). Her arrears amounted to £26 14s 11d.

It became common practice to give people money to go to America, so that their lands could be taken possession of. In the 1857-58 estate records we find the landlord paying numerous passages to America – the price was between £3 and £3 10s. In 1864 the landlord paid £13 1s 1d to "outfit Donchey Breslin's wife and children leaving for America".

The whole land question in Ireland in the 1800s is a difficult and complex one and I will not attempt to address it further. But before leaving the subject completely I would like to share with you one entry in the Murray-Stewart estate papers which always haunts me. On 26 October 1893 Brooke, Murray-Stewart's agent, wrote to Todd, the solicitor, stating: "I will want you to prosecute a boy called Pat Conaghan of Meenakillew for taking a hare in a snare on Meenavalley farm on which the game is reserved to Mr. Murray-Stewart." Such was life for the people of this district at that time!

As we move out of this area we pass, on our left, the Meenavalley school, which finally closed its doors in 1973. There had been a school here from at least the early 1840s and the 1847-50 Ordnance Survey map shows a national school on this site; it also shows the large Mulmosog House (now Meenavalley House) on the hill above, surrounded by a large walled garden. Seán Beag Ó Gaibhtheachain of Common was one of the first teachers at Meenavalley; it is said that with the aid of a pen and coloured inks he drew pound notes that deceived Wilson, the landlord's agent whom we have heard of earlier, at the White House (Murray-Stewart's house) in Killybegs.

A schools' inspector, who visited here in 1855, states: "This school is situated in an exceedingly wild valley in the heart of the mountains, far away from towns, and attended exclusively by children of the mountaineers."[23] Such, later, as my father.

With such a strong history of displacement of people in the previous century one doesn't wonder that nationalist fever ran high in this area in the years after the Easter Rising of 1916. The first tricolour seen in this locality was flown from the chimney of a derelict building adjacent to Meenavalley school in mid-August 1917; it was removed a few days later by a Constable Chapman from Ardara. At this time organising of a local column of the Old I.R.A. started in earnest and drilling was practised in secluded places. There was a number of incidents in the Black and Tan war – on 11 September 1920 Meenavalley House was burned and on 15 September 1920 the main road at Meenavalley was cut.

But we now leave the parish of Ardara and go to Bruckless, the site of another well dedicated to St. Conall; then we will take a quick run through Killybegs on our way to Kilcar and Glencolumbkille, where there are further wells dedicated to St. Conall. So, for the time being, we continue on the Ardara-Killybegs road:

From Killybegs to Ardara is seven Irish miles,
'Tis there the blackbirds whistle and the mating cuckoos call.
Beyond the fields the green sea glints, above the heaven smiles,
On all the white boreens that thread the glens of Donegal.[24]

Notes

1   The Gaelic word for a trout is *breac*, derived from the speckled skin of the trout.

2   Joyce, vol. II, p. 288.

3   *An Breac-aigh*: the termination *-aigh* is the Gaelic oblique form of that commonest of all Gaelic terminations *-ach* and conveys a sense of "full of", "abounding in".

4   *A.S.D.*, pp. 126-27.

5   Ibid. p. 131.

6   Joyce, vol. I, p. 296.

7   Edward O'Reilly, *An Irish-English Dictionary* (1864).

8   *H.P.A.*, p. 60.

9   *H.D.R.*, vol. I, p. 279.

10   *H.P.A.*, p. 54.

11   *Griffith's Valuations*, p. 24: in addition there were four Gallaghers, two Gavigans, two Shevlins (Shovlins), one Keeney, one Bresland (Breslin), one Maloney and one Gillespie – all common west-Donegal names.

12   Joyce, vol. II, p. 400.

13   Joyce, vol. III, pp. 502-3.

14 *Sanas Cormaic* (*sanas*, a secret), a glossary of Old Irish words and names written by Cormac mac Cuilennáin *c.* 900 A.D.

15 A gelding, nag, hack, a horse – as opposed to *capall*, a mare.

16 *Ballybofey Civic Week*. MacDonagh was the prime mover behind the founding of the Co. Donegal Historical Society in 1946.

17 *Fuidh* (*h*) *ir*: "A member of an inferior class in the early Irish social organisation. The etymology is *fo-dír*, interpreted as 'in the tribe but not of the blood,' or 'belonging to the lower grades of the kindred.' (*Dictionary of the Irish Language*, R.I.A.)

18 MacDonagh, *Ballybofey Civic Week*.

19 Ibid.

20 Ibid.

21 The part of Glencoagh purchased by one or two of the Meentinadea families is the present day Glendoan. As land had not been divided by this time each tenant in Glencoagh had a claim to the Glendoan moor, so each was entitled to get a share of the purchase price, which was staggered over a number of years, the instalments being paid on 26 December each year. On that date the Glendoan tenants (two in later years; only one originally) went to Glencoagh with the money. As the sum was small it was not considered worth dividing amongst the tenants of Glencoagh, so all agreed to spend the money on food and drink for a party in which the people of both townlands participated. The feast sometimes went on for three days and the Glendoan people remained until it ended.

22 Many of the older "boolies", high up in the mountains, had became occupied in the half-century before 1800.

23 *D.A.* (1953), p. 104.

24 This verse is from a poem called "A Road of Ireland" from a collection entitled *The Cloister and Other Poems*, by the Rev. Charles L. O'Donnell, C.S.C., printed by the Macmillan Company in New York in 1922. Rev. O'Donnell was professor of English literature at the University of Notre Dame in Indiana. His father was Neil O'Donnell, who was a son of Charlie Mhici O'Donnell of Altnagapple (over behind Mulmosog mountain) and his mother was a daughter of Peter O'Donnell of Cullion, Killybegs. It would seem from another verse in the poem that his father and mother knew each other before emigrating to America. The writer visited his ancestral home at Altnagapple on a number of occasions in the early decades of this century. He later became president of Notre Dame University.

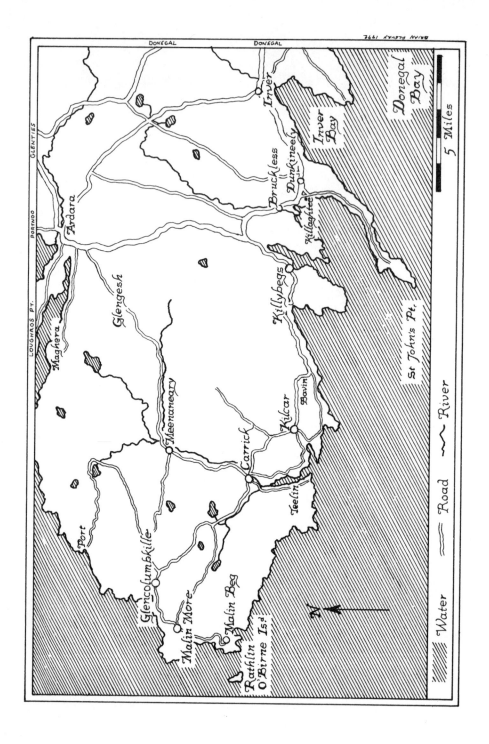

Donegal Bay

Inver Bay

St John's Pt.

Inver

Bruckless

Dunkineely

Killaghtee

Killybegs

Bavin

Kilcar

Carrick

Teelin

Donegal

Donegal

Glengesh

Meenaneary

Maghera

Ardara

GLENTIES

PORTNOO

LOUGHROS PT.

Port

Glencolumbkille

Malin More

Malin Beg

Rathlin
O'Birne Isd.

N

Water /////
Road =====
River ⌒⌒⌒

5 Miles

XVIII

BRUCKLESS AND ST. CONALL

FTER LEAVING THE Ardara-Killybegs road at the "Five Points" and
having joined the main Killybegs–Donegal town road, a short drive
takes us to the outskirts of the village of Bruckless.[1] Here, where
there is a group of houses on the left, you walk up the lane beside the
Milltown Bar, owned by Mary Murrin, and following this track for a good distance you come to St. Conall's well and bed. A *turas* is still carried on here,
involving the well and bed and an area known as the *Relig*[2] which is across
on the other side of the laneway. These old sites are in the townland of
Aighan.[3] Possibly you might remember that Aighan also had a strong connection with the Nesbitt family over the years – they owned property here
until 1847. In the will of George Nesbitt of Woodhill, of 1819, he left to his
son Richard W. Nesbitt "all my real estate of the quarterland of Aighen with
all its subdenominations together with the salmon fishery and corn and cloth
mills thereon".[4] A Nesbitt mill was situated at Hollybrook, at the time in the
possession of the Nesbitts. Hollybrook House stood immediately to the south
of the railway line where it crossed the river Oyley.[5]

The *Relig* consists of an elevated oblong area 31.8 m. x 21 m.[6] There is a
small rock-cliff running along the north-west side of it. At a part of this cliff
face there is a D-shaped dressed piece of rock jutting out, forming a seat-like
feature. In the *Archaeological Survey of County Donegal* this rock is incor-
rectly labelled St. Conall's bed; in fact it is known as "the table" and forms
part of the *turas*; St. Conall's bed is further along up the lane-way on the
right, past St. Conall's well. In the *Reilly* is another stone - also used in the
turas – which is called "the chair".

Denis Verschoyle writes that "It appears that the Relig was in the nature of
a Cillin, or church of the early Christian period which did not become a
parish church in the 12th century. There are quite a number of such sites,
which are usually associated with burial grounds, in South Donegal..."[7]

Unbaptised children were later buried at these places. The early use of this site is supported by the tradition that "three great saints, bishops and confessors, were interred in this *relig* side by side".[8]

There is a number of cairns of stones – which play their part in the *turas* – within the *Relig*. The largest of these cairns is called "the altar". On top of the altar is a cross-inscribed slab, .59 m. x .35 m. This is decorated on both faces. Face A has a Greek bar cross with a thin line forming a second cross inside the first. There is a circle at the centre of the bar cross. There is an X design in each of the quarters formed by the bar cross. Face B has a thin line Greek cross with a circle at the centre.[9] Also on the altar is a slab with a U-shaped notch and another one like it where one side of the notch is broken off, with three small perforations in it.

A *turas* is still practiced here and can only be done on the seven[10] days of June 23-29. Here is how Mary Murrin, who lives near by, described the ritual of the *turas* to me: "First you kneel at St. Conall's well and say the Creed; then you make three circuits of the well, clockwise, saying three Our Fathers, Hail Marys and Glorias on each circuit. You then leave the well, starting fifteen decades of the rosary as you go and walk down to the *Relig*. You walk around the whole outside perimeter of the *Relig*, clockwise, three

At the altar in the relig, *soaked through*

times and then, if you haven't your fifteen decades finished, you can go in and finish them at the front of the altar. You then say three Our Fathers, Hail Marys and Glorias when kneeling at the altar and when saying these prayers you place your right wrist in the U-shaped notch in one of the stones which is erected on the altar and the tips of the middle three fingers of the left hand in the little perforations that are in the other long erect slab of stone. You can now make your wish, i.e. make a request which you hope will be granted. You then rise and say three Our Fathers, Hail Marys and Glorias going clockwise around each cairn of stones; you then sit at the chair stone, facing in the Killybegs direction and say three Our Fathers, Hail Marys and Glorias. You then kneel at the table stone and say three Our Fathers, Hail Marys and Glorias; votive offerings are sometimes left here. You then go further up the lane past the well, saying Our Fathers, Hail Marys and Glorias as you go along, to St. Conall's bed which is on a little cliff-face further up the lane, on the right-hand side. You have to enter the bed from the Croagh (upper) side; you stretch out on the bed, turn around three times and say an Act of Contrition and conclude with three Our Fathers, Hail Marys and Glorias; you then get up and leave the bed from the lower side. On the way back down the lane-way you can lift water from the well and take it home."

In former times clay was also taken home from the vicinity of the well. At the present day you either have to start or finish the *turas* with prayers in

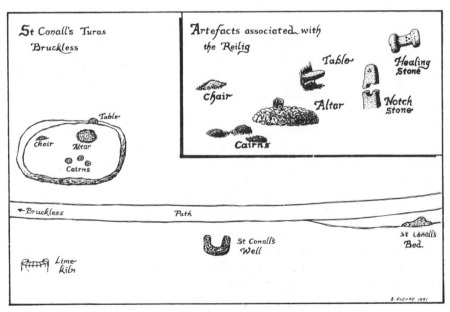

St. Conall's turas, *Bruckless*

the Roman Catholic church of Saints Joseph and Conall in Bruckless, but this practice is of fairly recent origin. Another practice which has disappeared is that of spending the whole night lying on St. Conall's bed. In the early decades of this century it was common for a person to spend the night lying on the cold rock, a practice which surely demonstrates a great belief in the power of the *turas* at this site.

There is a number of interesting points about this *turas*. The first is that it is only done on the seven days starting on mid-summer's night, possibly suggesting an ancient tradition of well-worship at the well now known as St. Conall's, in which the power of the well was at its strongest around the time of the pagan mid-summer festival.

The second very interesting point is how, while praying at the altar in the *Relig*, you have to put your right wrist in the stone with the U-shaped notch and the middle three fingers of your left hand in the little depressions in the other stone. In former times, when the "healing stone" was still at this site, you held it in your right hand while you rested your right wrist in the U-shaped notch and you then made your request.

Dr. Maguire, writing in 1920, states: "A noticable feature of this pilgrimage to St. Conal's Well, at the present day, is the extraordinary faith that brings women from long distances."[11] With reference to the role of the perforated stone in the *turas* here and the former popularity of the *turas* among women, I am reminded very much of the practice that used to be carried out on the historic island of Inishmurray, off the Sligo coast. This island is now uninhabited and has very well preserved features of an early Christian settlement. W. Fraser, writing in 1896, states: "On the island of Inismurray are two stones with perforations; the first stone is at the south-side of the principal church and is especially resorted to by the female inhabitants of the island; a Latin cross is inscribed on its face, and the centre of the cross expands into a small sized circle, such as often occurs on early Irish crosses. On its eastern face are two holes, large enough to admit the entrance of a thumb into each, and these holes extend through the sides of the stone, where they expand into openings sufficient to admit the rest of the fingers of the hand. In praying at the stone, which is practiced by women approaching their confinement, in the hope of securing a favourable result, they kneel, and inserting their thumbs into the smaller apertures, firmly grasp the stone with the rest of the fingers placed in the corresponding side openings. The natives of the island assert as a proof of its efficacy that death resulting from childbirth is unknown amongst them."[12]

The healing stone which used to be kept in the U-shaped notch in one of the slabs on the altar at Bruckless was taken away to a sick person some twenty or thirty years ago and has not been seen since. W.H. Patterson visited the *Reilig* in 1870 and his observations make interesting reading: "The most interesting object in connection with the *Relig*, however, is the healing, or medicinal, or magic stone. This is a dark brown-coloured stone, measuring 5 inches long, and 3 inches thick, in shape and size somewhat like an ordinary 'dumb-bell'. This stone is regarded in the neighbourhood with the highest reverence, and is considered to have a most powerful effect in curing all kinds of diseases. The sick person desiring to make use of the stone has it brought to his house, where it is retained till it is no longer required in which case it is returned to the *Relig*, or till a more urgent case arises in the neighbourhood, when the stone is transferred from the one patient to the other.

"When not in use, the stone is kept in a hollow or mortise of the broken cross, on the top of the cairn at the *Relig*, of course exposed to all weathers; it has no custodian, but any person on going to borrow it gives notice to some of the families living near, so that it is always known where the stone is; and to return it is a matter of duty. When I visited 'the *Relig*', the stone was away with some sick person; but my friend, having found out where it was, sent for it, so that the next morning I had an opportunity of seeing and making a drawing of it; the stone was then returned to the patient. A letter

The healing stone, in its position on top of a slab on the altar. I am indebted to Denis Verschoyle who, from South Africa, sent me this reproduction taken from a now very faded photograph which he took in 1929. I am not aware of any other extant photograph of the stone

written from Bruckless, Sept. 16, 1870, tells me that the stone is at present 'out' with a different invalid from the one who allowed me to see it. I was not able to learn in what way the stone is used, as the people seemed rather unwilling to speak on this subject, and they carefully conceal from their clergy all about the taking of the stone or 'going through the station'."

Referring to St. Conall's well Mr. Patterson states: "The well is surrounded by a low wall of uncemented stones. It is now small and shallow; but the spring is copious, and the overflow forms a small rill, which flows down the sloping ground to the bottom of the glen. No thorn tree overshadows the little basin, but the brambles, which grow over and around it, have their branches decorated with rags and shreds of various colours, fragments of clothing, etc - some fresh, as if placed there but yesterday; others bleached and faded by the sun and rain. These shreds are votive offerings, left to propitiate the genius of the well, here personified as Saint Conall, by those who visit this place to 'do stations', and to pray for the relief from bodily and mental ills. I learned that here, as in other parts of Ireland, the Roman Catholic clergy discourage as much as possible this resorting to the holy wells, and that the persons who come here are careful to hide the fact from their clergymen.

"This practice is no doubt the continuation of a Pagan observance, and one which has been made the subject of repressive laws at various times in these countries."

He continues: "It is, however, believed in the neighbourhood that Saint Conall, who was one of the earliest Christian missionaries in Tyrconnell, in the fifth or beginning of the sixth century (probably finding this well an object of veneration among the Pagan inhabitants) blessed it, and endowed it with healing powers, erected a stone cross near it, and established a church or oratory."[13]

Mr. Patterson also mentions a large bullaun stone which at that time was built into the corner of a fence in an adjoining field; at the present day there is a large bullaun stone in the yard of a nearby house. The presence of these bullaun stones[14] - or possible they are the one stone - so close to the *Relig* would point to this site as being that of an early Christian foundation and supports the view that a church originally stood here.

Denis Verschoyle, a lifelong student of urban and regional history, a native of this area, and now living in South Africa, writing about St. Conall states: "His Bed and Well near the Relig in Aighan townland are well known, but I have found further evidence of his sojourn there in the inquisition of 1642; here there is reference to Derriconnell in the quarter of Aighan, and this I think can be identified with a place called Wood which was listed as a townland on its own in the Tithe Roll of 1834; it lies in the northern corner of the present townland of Aighan; this Oak Wood of Conal confirms the saint's association with this district."[15]

It is of interest, and I have pointed this out earlier when at Shanaghan, near Ardara, that listed next to "Diriconell" here at Aighan in the 1642 list is a place called Seanaghan, surely proof that the cults of Conall and that of Seanaghan (Senchán) travelled hand in hand.

Earlier Mr. Patterson referred to pieces of clothing being attached to brambles at St. Conall's well. This is a manifestation of one of the old beliefs that still surface despite the Christianising of well-worship. Long before the time of Christ wells were venerated. Spring wells were basic to survival. To secure the continued supply of this essential – water – it was an easy step to the worship of the well and to suppose some indwelling spirit.[16] This is especially feasible if we take it that the people who first came to this country came from warmer climes where water was scarce. Bushes, especially thorns, which hung over or surrounded the wells were also seen as having special powers. The pieces of clothing noted on the branches here by Mr. Patterson are associated with the very old belief that a disease can be transferred from man to a tree or bush. You transfer your illness in a scrap of your clothing to the bush on to which you tie it.[17] In recent years I have seen pieces of clothing tied to branches of trees on the path up to St. Conall's well here and the practice is still carried on at other well sites that I know.

Another surviving practice in well worship is the leaving of votive offerings. Metal – e.g. coins – is preferable; this is white magic and a very ancient idea; the metal offering and its potency is likely to go back to the first introduction of metal and the uncanny power that it gives to its possessors.[18]

Devotion to stones also manifested itself in the practice of the *turas* and of well worship; this is evident in the use of healing stones – such as the stone which used to be on the altar at the *Relig,* the healing stones which were rotated in a hole on the altar on Inishkeel island and the large stone with white strata through it which used to be passed around the body three times on the Inishkeel *turas.*

Finally I would mention that of course it is *de rigeur* to walk in a clockwise direction when doing a *turas*: the next station, or place of veneration, must always be to your right-hand side as you approach it. You must always always walk around each cairn of stones or "station" in a sun-wise, or right-handed direction. You must go round in the track of the sun - in a deiseal direction; in Gaelic *deas* means south and to the right. Anti-clockwise circumambulation is known as "withershins" and is considered unlucky, even evil.[19] The rationale behind deiseal circumambulation seems to have been simply that the movement echoed that of the sun. It reflected the once universally felt need to live in harmony with cosmic forces, represented in this case by the sun as the ultimate generator of life.[20] To go in a clockwise direction was to identify with the sun's diurnal course, regarded as life-enhancing and bringing luck; withershins circumambulation was identified with the sun's nocturnal course and signified death and misfortune.[21] These associations are deep-seated and universal.

An intriguing point of interest is that when a person sneezes, in which case one would exclaim in English "Bless you!" it was traditional in the Gaelic language to exclaim "*Deiseal!* " Further evidence that right was good.

We have strayed a little here but I thought it important that you get a feel of the ancient influences which are still at play in the present-day *turas*.

We now leave the *Relig*. I must add that we are not the first to have enjoyed touring around viewing the sites associated with St. Conall; an earlier traveller who covered much of the same terrain as we have ourselves, writes: "I have not mentioned the wild flowers of Donegal; in no other county of Ireland do they grow in such profusion. I shall always remember the *Relig* at Bruckless in the month of May, a sea of bluebells, golden whin and hawthorn; the purple drifts of wild thyme at Narin, during the hot days of summer; walking barefoot along the shores of Gweebarra Bay on a carpet of flowers (yellow lady Bedstraw, heartsease, pink centaury, trefoil and the tiny blue gentian); the hills heather clad, with harebells and bushes of myrtle, and bordering the grey walls, long lines of purple loosestrife, foxglove and meadowsweet. The flowers, the soft Atlantic air and the kindly, courteous people, make a Donegal holiday a treasured memory."[22]

Notes

1   From *broc*: a badger; *lusca*: a cave, a subterranean cavity, here indicating a badger's sett. The correct anglicised form is Brocklusk; the last "k" is dropped through what is called "laziness" in utterance. (Joyce, vol. III, p. 150)

You might be interesting in Giraldus Cambrensis's extraordinary 12th century account of badgers making their sett: "The badger, or melot, is also found here. It is an unclean animal and tends to bite, frequenting rocky and mountaineous places. Scraping and digging with its feet it makes for itself holes under the ground as places of refuge and defence. Some of them are born to serve by nature. Lying on their backs, they pile on their bellies soil that has been dug by others [i.e. other badgers]. Then clutching it with their four feet, and holding a piece of wood across their mouths, they are dragged out of the hole with their burdens, by others who pull backwards while holding on here and there to the wood with their teeth. Anyone that sees them is astonished." (*The Topography of Ireland,* p. 29.)

2   Early Latin texts use the word *reliquiae* to describe a relic. The word was borrowed into Gaelic in the form *reilic*, but curiously enough it is not usually applied to a relic in Ireland but to a cemetery, modern Irish *reilig* (*J.R.S.A.I.*, vol. 116 (1986), p. 6). The word can be spelt *reilig* or *roilig* and was also applied to a church or churchyard as well as its usual application – a graveyard. This would support the concept that there was an early chuch here.

3   Aighan is usually interpreted as a diminutive of a placename we have met before – *An Fhaithche* – a level green on which sports are played. I am not convinced that that is correct. Denis Verschoyle ventures the opinion that "from the various spelling in surveys, inquisitions, deeds and vestry records, *Aghaidh Chaoin* might be the correct original. This would translate as 'Fair Face' and might describe the appearance of the terrain here. The present English pronunciation of Aighan would be close to the Donegal Gaelic pronunciation of *Aghaidh Chaoin*." That a probable early Christian site associated now with St. Conall is situated in Aighan makes me wonder if the name might not have an ecclesiastical basis. It is pronounced "ay-hin" by the local people. Could it have been an early Patrician site associated with a member of St. Patrick's household, his cook Aithcen (*A.F.M.*, vol. 1, p. 137)? In Ó Riain's *Corpus*, also, the latter is associated with St. Patrick as "*Aithchen a firchuic*" (Aithchen, his cook). Ó Riain states that "The saint's name should read Aíthgen." The modern spelling of his name would be Aíthghen. Was Aighan a very early Christian site founded by missionaries who came by boat from east Co. Down? St. Aíthghen is known to have been associated with the church of Both Domnaig near Strabane, Co. Tyrone.

4   See p. 226.

5   Derived from the Gaelic word *aill*: a precipice, a cliff.

6   *A.S.D.*, p. 241.

7   *D.A.* (1958), p. 44.

8   *H.D.R.*, vol. II, p. 111.

9   *A.S.D.*, p. 241.

10   The *Claidheamh Soluis* of 1 April 1899 says nine days.

11   *H.D.R.*, vol. II, p. 112.

12   *J.R.S.A.I.*, vol. 6 (5th series), vol. XXVI consec series (1896), pp. 166-67.

13   *J.R.S.A.I.*, vol. 2 (1870-71), pp. 466-70.

14   I have been unable to find the bullaun stone in a fence; possibly it was removed and is the same stone which is behind a nearby house.

15   *D.A.* (1961), p. 52.

16   Daphne Pochin Mould, *Irish Pilgrimage*, p. 56.

17   Ibid. p. 87.

18   Ibid.

19   Bord, J. and C., *Sacred Waters*, p. 81.

20   Ibid. p. 82.

21 Ibid.
22 Isabel Crozier, *D.A.* (1957), p.70.

XIX

INVER AND THE NESBITTS

W E HAVE ALREADY noted that Aighan remained the property of the Nesbitts of Woodhill until 1847. Along the coast at Kilmacreddon, near Inver, lived another branch of the family. Andrew Nesbitt held the lands of Kilmacreddon from the Earl of Annandale as early as 1621 and an old document, found[1] in one of the walls of Kilmacreddon House earlier this century, states that in 1665 the Nesbitts had purchased Kilmacreddon, consisting of 667 acres, from the Earl of Annandale. Kilmacreddon House is now no more – it has been razed to the ground. Interestingly enough, there had been an inscription cut with a diamond on one of the back windows of the second floor stating that the house was painted and glazed in 1774 by Alexander Campbell of Strabane.

This branch of the Nesbitt family have left their stamp indelibly marked on Irish history because of their activities in whale fishing. In the year 1736[2] a Lieutenant Samuel Chaplain, quartered at Gibraltar, who had been formerly employed in the Greenland whale fishery, was informed by a Captain Nesbitt, a colleague, that whales abounded in the spring of each year off the northwest coast of Ireland, particularly in the counties Sligo and Donegal. Chaplain resigned his commission and came to Ireland with a view to fishing for whales. He established a settlement on St. John's Point. Apparently Chaplain was not particularly successful, only catching two whales in a matter of eight years. After his death it is said that Chaplain's brother continued the whale fishery, also with little success.

The likely reason why only two whales had been caught when there is evidence that many whales were sighted along the coast is given by James Fairley, the author of *Irish Whales and Whaling*: "The bulk of whales sighted were almost certainly rorquals, probably mainly finners, and with the primitive methods of the time it would have been virtually impossible to secure one of these meteoric monsters. The only baleen whales available which Chaplain could have had any chance of holding were the slow-swim-ming nordcapers and these were scarce in Irish waters. His enterprise had been doomed to a very limited measure of success all along."[3]

Though there wasn't much success with whales the fishermen also hunted for basking sharks, which they called "sun-fish". Following is a description from as early as 1739 of fishing the "sun-fish" – the inoffensive and, if unmo-lested, lethargic basking shark (*Cetorhinus maximus*) – off the coast of Killybegs; it is likely that the local fishermen, especially the Nesbitts, were in the habit of hunting basking sharks before Chaplain arrived on the scene. Here is the vivid account: "They are taken in the Hot Season in the Months of June and July, in this manner. – As they sleep on the Surface of the Sea, they are Discovered by their Fin, which being extended above the Water, re-sembles the Sail of a Boat. They lye in this posture, til the Fishermen, making up to them, strike them with their Harpoon Irons. Whereupon they dart down to the Bottom and rolling on the Ground, work the Harpoon deeper into the wound. Then being irritated, they rise again to the Surface and shoot away with an incredible Velocity Dragging the Boat after them ... and they bear away to sea sometimes for Leagues; til at last Dying, they Float on the surface till the fishermen come along their side, and cut out the Liver, which affords several Barrels of Oyl. In this dangerous war with these smaller Leviathans, it is necessary to have 100 Fathoms of small Cord fixt to the End of the Harpoon, to give it play: and for a man to stand by the Gunnell of the Boat, with an hatchet, to cut the Rope in Case of any stop of its running off, or the Fish's emerging too suddenly; either of which Accidents might overset the Boat."[4]

The next important attempt at whale fishing was made by Thomas Nesbitt of Kilmacreddon, in association with his brother Andrew, Paul and James Benson, merchants, and Acheson Irwin, gentleman. (Major Nesbitt of Woodhill's mother, Catherine, was a daughter of John Irwin of Drumsillagh, County Leitrim; the latter died at Woodhill House. Acheson Irwin was his son and therefore a brother of Major Nesbitt's mother.) In 1759 Thomas, who appears to have been the prime mover throughout, went to London and purchased a vessel of some 130 or 140 tons, costing £1,340; he had the ship fitted up for the purpose and had five boats made "of a new construction". Eight men, experienced in fishing for whales in the Greenland fisheries and in flensing, were employed in each of the five boats. Early in 1760 they com-menced work. They approached several whales and struck at them fre-quently but without effect, for their harpoons failed to enter. Eventually they succeeded in killing one; the carcass was towed ashore, flensed (i.e. cut up), the blubber placed in casks and since there was no manufactory for the bone or blubber in this country sent to London. Unfortunately, however, it must not have been treated correctly because we are told that "not being properly managed, it turned to very little account".[5]

In 1761 work was resumed. Five new harpooners were employed, the best that could be obtained – a Dutchman, two Danes, one Englishman and a Scot. All their best efforts proved unsuccessful; not one whale was caught that year.

With the poor return in actual whales caught since their venture had started, Thomas Nesbitt had been acutely aware that the equipment which they were using was not effective. As a result he invented a swivel gun which discharged both harpoons and lances with considerable force into the body of the whale. Credit for the invention of the gun harpoon is generally given to Svend Foyn, a Norwegian, who brought out his invention as late as 1864.[6] However the introduction of a gun harpoon by Thomas Nesbitt in the 18th century is most worthy of being noted because it must have been one of the earliest uses of explosives for this purpose.[7]

Things now appeared to pick up because in 1762 three whales were caught and in 1763 five whales were struck into, though three were lost "by the baddness of the ropes."[8]

But expenses were building up and in November 1763 the Nesbitt group petitioned the Irish House of Commons for a grant to help defray their growing debts. The size of the whale population off our coast at that time can be gauged by the testimony of one of the petitioners, Alexander Ellis, "mariner" – possibly the captain of the Nesbitt vessel – who, it is reported in the records, told the Irish House of Commons Committee that he had seen "above one hundred whales in a day (off the Donegal coast); he thinks more than he has seen in a season in Greenland, where he was formerly employed in the fishery".[9] One of the difficulties the petition to the Commons stressed was the lack of proper facilities to "render" the blubber in Ireland at that time. The House of Common's Committee granted a sum of £2,000 to the Nesbitts to erect warehouses and boilers; this grant was later reduced to £1,500 and later again to just £1,000.

Despite the Nesbitt ship, the *Bustle*, being forced from her moorings and then stranded during a great storm in early April 1765[10] the whale fishing appears to have been relatively successful throughout the following years. This success is highlighted in the following press reports from May and June of 1776: "By letters from the County of Donegal we have an Account, that Mr. Thomas Nesbitt killed and brought in-to Port on 11st inst. a large Whale; and as many others now appear on the Coast, there is Reason to hope for a successful Season in that Fishery"[11] and "We hear from Port, in the County of Donegal, that Mr. Thomas Nesbitt, had brought in a Whale there, which measured 63 Feet in length."[12]

In *Irish Whales and Whaling* we read that in the manuscripts of the Dublin-based Medico-Philosophical Society, dating from 1756 to 1772, appears the following: "LARGE WHALE – There was lately killed on the N.W. coast of this Kingdom, in the Bay of Enver near Donegal, a large whale, 62 feet long, 15 feet deep as it lay; its tongue filled eleven hogsheads. The Whalebone is computed to be worth 8 or 900 pounds. The blubber filled 62 rum puncheons."[13]

Arthur Young in his tour of Ireland passed this way in August 1776 and was most impressed by Thomas Nesbitt and his gun harpoon; he was obviously an eye witness to its use. He writes: "From many experiments, he brought the operation to such perfection, that, for some years, he never missed a whale, nor failed of holding her by the harpoon. ... When the harpoon is fired into the whale, it sinks to the bottom with great velocity, but immediately comes up, and lays on the surface, lashing it with tail and fins for half or three quarters of an hour, in which time he fires lances into it, to dispatch it, and when killed, it sinks for 48 hours, where he leaves a boat, or a cask, as a buoy to mark the place, to be ready there when the whale rises,

The old graveyard at Inver where Thomas Nesbitt the whaler is buried

that they may tow it into harbour, according as the wind lays."[14]

Whaling was a hazardous business and in fact the whale fishing seems to have come to an end after an accident in which two men were killed. We have referred to this incident earlier, when we were at Eden, near Rosbeg. Dr. McParlan, writing in 1802, states that the incident happened about twenty years before that. One of the whales gave Mr. Nesbitt's boat a whisk of its tail and shattered it to pieces. Two men were lost[15] and only the bravery of Mr. Hamilton of Eden saved many lives including that of Mr. Nesbitt, who was the last picked out of the waves. This put an end to his whale fishing.

This accident and the story of whaling in these waters may seem to us to belong to a distant era; yet until recent times Port (Inver) fishermen painted the bottom of their boats red to frighten off whales. It was said locally that a whale would "drink" a small boat while taking a gulp of fish; a local man[16] has stated that a boat on which he was a crew member had encountered a whale while fishing in Inver bay and that the whale had nearly "drunk" their boat. I found this phraseology particularly interesting.

Thomas Nesbitt himself died on 15 December 1801, aged seventy-nine years, and was buried in the old graveyard at Inver. Within a few decades his lands had passed to new owners – in 1833 we read of the impending sale of "all the estate and interests of the late Thomas Nesbitt, Esq., of Kilmacreddon", including his "lands of Clonroad or Clonrod in the Parish of Kilcar", "now held by John Smith, Esq."[17] (Smith had leased the lands in 1814 for thirty-one years).

By this time the Kilmacreddon Nesbitts' interests in this area may have lessened, but that of the Woodhill Nesbitts had not. In 1839 we are informed as follows: "That excellent gentleman, Major Nesbitt, with his accustomed liberality, has this season employed a number of the poor on his estate in building a pier at Bruckless port, which will be very serviceable to the fishermen along the coast."[18]

As we retrace our steps from Inver back towards Bruckless, passing through Dunkineely and going in the direction of Killybegs, you must forgive me if I drag you off at Bruckless for a minute down to the old church of Killaghtee.[19] Within the adjoining graveyard here stands a most interesting ancient decorated stone slab, *c.* 1.75 m. in height and .75 m. in width.[20] On the west face at the top is carved a Maltese cross inside a circle. At the centre of the cross are two concentric small circles. A small D-shaped notch is cut on the upper arm of the cross. Of most interest on this stone is the triquetra knot (said to represent the Holy Trinity) which is present on the slab below the cross. In the study of stone sculpture this cross slab represents a stage when people were developing from the earlier inscribed slabs, which are mere engravings (in other words the outline, such as the shape of a cross, was just scraped out on the stone), to this more developed work where the stone surrounding the design was pared away so that the design stands out in relief.

Writing in 1940 Françoise Henry, who was obviously impressed, gives us her opinion of this cross slab: "The big slab which stands in the churchyard of Killaghtee, in Donegal, brings us one step further. There, we pass beyond the stage of mere engraving. The notion of relief appears, combined with an imposing monumental feeling. It proceeds from the same art as the Clonamery or Fore doorways, and draws, as they do, its chief effect from the juxtaposition of the rough stone, hammered into shape with a few masterly strokes, and the smooth surface where the design appears in low, infinitely delicate relief. But the sculptor who made the Killaghtee slab showed an even greater sensitiveness, inventing the slightly concave disc, giving a hardly perceptible curve to the arms of the cross, and boldly putting a trifold knot on one side of the slab, which might have upset the whole composition, yet successfully avoids doing so. This knot stands most probably for a symbol of the Trinity..."[21]

Killaghtee cross slab

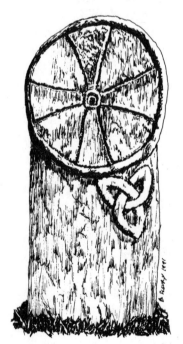

Old court cross base (after P. Ó hÉailidhe)

Françoise Henry concludes her assessment of the Kilaghtee slab by interpreting the notch in the upper arm of the cross as another Christian symbol, known as a Chi-Rho, but as I would be very wary of this conclusion I do not intend to introduce the subject of Chi-Rho symbolism here.

The triquetra knot is thought to be an early symbol of the Trinity. It occurs elsewhere. On the west face of a cross base at Oldcourt, near Bray, Co. Wicklow, is a representation of a very lightly carved triquetra knot with a large horned animal on each side, facing the triquetra, presumably guarding the symbol of the Trinity. From the excellent publication *Figures from the Past* we read that a triquetra knot is also to be found "with a horseman on the shaft of the Bealin Cross which can be dated by an inscription to about 800 A.D. (Henry 1965,143), and on the shaft below the encircled cross on one face of the early finely-carved cross-slab on Inis MacDara, Co. Galway."[22]

In a reference to the Bealin cross shaft[23] the point has been made that a Christian significance should not necessarily be read into a triquetra knot and that it was frequently used as ornamentation in various media of the period – e.g. it appears in a secular context to decorate the expanded ends of penannular brooches. However it seems safe to interpret the Killaghtee triquetra in a purely Christian context.

Now we move on; this whole area, extending from Inver through to Bruckless and including St. John's Point, is very rich in archaeological and ecclesiastical sites, but, thankfully, it is also rich in enthusiastic local historians and I will leave it in their capable hands to keep the traditions and architecture of these sites before the public. We go to Killybegs for a very brief visit.

Notes

1   By the late Dan Fisher, while living in Kilmacreddon House.

2   *J.R.S.A.I.*, vol. 98, part 1 (1968), p. 32.

3   *Irish Wales and Whaling*, p. 122.

4   In 1739 Rev. William Henry penned a little-known work, *Hints towards a natural and typographical history of the countys Sligoe, Donegal, Fermanagh and Lough Erne*; this excerpt from it is quoted in *Irish Whales and Whaling*, pp. 119-120.

5   *Irish Whales and Whaling*, p. 123.

6   Ivan T. Sanderson, *Follow the Whale* (1956), p. 296.

7   Arthur E. J. Went, "Whaling from Ireland," *J.R.S.A.I.*, vol. 98 (1968), p. 36.

8   *Irish Whales and Whaling*, p. 126.

9   Irish House of Commons Report, 1763-64.

10   *Irish Whales and Whaling*, p. 127.

11   The *Freeman's Journal*, 22 May 1776.

12   Ibid. 14 June 1776.

13   p. 126.

14   *A Tour in Ireland*, vol. I, p. 184.

15   This unfortunate loss of life pales in comparison to what followed in the Bruckless area in 1813. On 12 February 1813 a terrible storm blew up. Twenty fishing boats were smashed to pieces and the lives of forty-three fishermen were lost. The greatest loss of life appears to have been among fishermen from the Teelin and Malinbeg areas. "The Great Drowning at Bruckless" has never been forgotten.

16   The late Hugh Cunningham.

17   The *Ballyshannon Herald*, 28 September 1833.

18   Ibid. 30 August 1839.

19   *Cill Leacht Aoidhe*: the church (*cill*) of the flagstone (*leacht*) of Hugh (*Aoidhe*). You might remember that when dealing with St. Mary's church on Inishkeel island I mentioned this church at Killaghtee; see "Notes on Transitional Architectural Fragments in Co. Donegal," *U.J.A.*, vol. 27 (1964), pp. 133-36.

20   *A.S.D.*, p. 244.

21   *Irish Art in the Early Christian Period*, p. 55.

22   *Figures from the Past*, ed. Etienne Rynne, pp. 98-110. A parallel for this motif of two horned animals (possibly oxen) guarding the symbol of the Trinity can be seen in the church of S. Appollinaire in Classe, Ravenna, dating to the 5th-6th century, where a pair of peacocks guard a Chi-Rho.

23   *J.R.S.A.I.*, vol. 110 (1980), p. 13.

XX

KILLYBEGS

The harbour lights of Killybegs
Look out to an open sea,
Where powder and wine in Spanish
kegs
Came over in "ninety-three"

Red Hugh he was the chieftain bold
And high his word in Spain,
Where never a don his beads that told
But cursed the English main.[1]

A
S WE PASS quickly through Killybegs we will confine our observations mostly to people and clans which we have met earlier on our travels. It was from Killybegs that the ill-fated *Girona* sailed in October 1588, carrying many of the former crew of the *Duquesa Santa Ana* which had earlier gone aground near Rosbeg. Here at Killybegs is the grave of T.C. MacGinley, whose book, *The Cliff Scenery of South Western Donegal*, we have frequently referred to. In 1872, while principal of Croagh national school, near Dunkineely, this very able man wrote a textbook of general biology which was adopted by the schools' authorities of Kensington and Chelsea.

Killybegs is now our premier fishing port but its main role in Irish history is that for long it was the chief port-of-call for emissaries from Spain, whose rulers were supportive of the rebellious Irish chieftains because of their common interest – the defeat, or at least the harassment, of the English. The port of Killybegs played a prominent role in the communications between Spain and Ireland in the decades before and after the fateful Battle of Kinsale in 1602. It was known to the Spanish as "Calbeque", very close in pronunciation to the Gaelic name *Na Cealla Beaga*.[2]

Prior to the defeat at Kinsale the Spanish messengers would have regarded Killybegs as a safe haven because of the protection afforded them by

Red Hugh O'Donnell, chief of Tír Chonaill from 1592-1602. In November 1596 Alonso de Cobos, an envoy from the king, arrived in Killybegs. He was met by Niall O'Boyle, bishop of Raphoe from 1591-1611 and who, on his death on 6 February 1611, was interred on historic Inishkeel island. Bishop O'Boyle then resided at Killybegs and he duly brought de Cobos to Lifford "where O'Donnell then was". Later, when de Cobos disembarked from Killybegs for Spain we are told that "O'Donnell's people gave him plenty of flesh meat in the ship, large hinds and white-fleeced sheep. He was ready for the east wind whenever it should come."[3]

In the same year, 1596, we find Bishop O'Boyle writing to the King of Spain "from his manor of Killybegs"[4] thanking him for the aid he was about to send.

In April 1597 Don Roderigo de Vayen was sent by the king of Spain to confer with the Irish. He landed at Killybegs and went to Donegal "where O'Donnell then was". There he was entertained most generously, and on his departure he was given presents of hounds and horses – *con 7 each* – for his royal master.[5]

In the spring of 1600 two ships came from Spain, under the command of Ferdinand de Barranova. They were laden with materials of war and "knowing that the northern chiefs were then at enmity with the English they put into the harbour of Killybegs".[6]

On 3 January 1602 a combined force of Spaniards and the Gaelic chieftains were defeated at Kinsale, Co. Cork, by the English. On 6 January 1602 Hugh O'Donnell left for Spain to seek further assistance from King Philip III. Later that year, after sixteen days of illness, he died on 10 September at the age of twenty-nine. "It was in the palace of the King of Spain himself in the town of Simancas he died. His body was then taken to Valladolid, to the King's Court, in a four-wheeled hearse, with great numbers of State officers, of the Council, and of the royal guard all round it, with blazing torches and bright flambeaux of beautiful waxlights blazing all round on each side of it. He was buried after that in the chapter of the monastery of St. Francis with great honour and respect and in the most solemn manner any Gael ever before had been interred."[7] Indeed the memory of Hugh O'Donnell still burns brightly in the hearts of Donegal people at home and abroad even up to the present day.

Here in Killybegs we have the remarkable gravestone of the chieftain of one of the clans most loyal to the O'Donnells, the MacSweeneys of Banagh. Earlier, when dealing with the O'Boyle sept at Kiltoorish, we noted that this branch of the MacSweeneys came from north Connacht at the beginning of the 15th century and dislodged the O'Boyles from this part of present-day west Donegal. When discussing the O'Boyles I made much of their support for Red Hugh O'Donnell when he rose from his sick-bed in April 1592 and summoned his greatest allies; among those who also answered the call immediately was *mac Suibhne thíre bóghaine*;[8] most likely this was Donnchadh Dubh Mac Suibhne who was the last MacSweeney Banagh to be inaugurated Chief of Banagh, in 1588, and who died in 1633.[9]

The Killybegs tombstone is said to have been placed over the grave of an earlier MacSweeney chieftain, Niall Mór, who died in 1524 A.D. The Four Masters, in their notice of his death, are lavish in their praise of him: "Mac Sweeny of Tir-Boghaine (Niall More, the son of Owen), a constable[10] of hardiest hand and heroism, of boldest heart and counsel, best at withholding and attacking,[11] best in hospitality and prowess, who had the most numerous troops, and most vigorous passes of any man of his own fair tribe, died, after Unction and Penance, in his own castle of Rathain, on the 14th of December."[12]

The tomb-slab is said to have lain over his grave at *Fan an Chartha* friary, at Ballysaggart, near the MacSweeney stronghold at Rahan on St. John's Point, near Dunkineely, until it was removed to Killybegs in 1868. It is now set against the exterior face of the west gable of St. Mary's Catholic church

The grave slab of Niall Mór

in Killybegs. We are told that it was removed from its original site because though "known and admired by the peasantry ... it was trodden over by children, and the young men used to try their strength at lifting it".[13] The Rev. Stephens P.P. who removed it to Killybegs in 1868 stated that he did so "to protect it from the careless step of the passer-by, from the decaying hand of time, and the falling debris of the old building, and the more to perpetuate and hand down to posterity the fame of this fine old warrior, of whom the annalist has supplied such a noble character."[14]

That the slab should remain outside, as it is now, exposed to the elements, is open to question. Comparisons of engravings[15] taken around the time of its removal with its appearance now suggest that the designs on it have faded due to weathering. When Rev. Stephens originally relocated it he had it fixed securely in the south wall, inside the nave of St. Mary's church.[16]

The sandstone slab is trapezoid in shape, measuring 1.98 m. by .72 m. tapering to .46 m.[17] The surface of the slab is divided into nine panels by one vertical and four horizontal broad bands of plaited mouldings. The panels are carved with various foliate and animal patterns, some of which resemble those found on medieval Irish leatherwork.[18] In the upper left-hand of the slab, as you look at it, is a figure, helmeted and plumed, holding a battle-axe in his right hand and a sword hanging by his left side. He is wearing a garment reaching to his knees and a pisane collar i.e. a mail defence over his neck and shoulders. The figure is undoubtedly the representation of a gallowglass. Diagonally above and below the gallowglass are two very weathered animal-like figures. The other panels contain a variety of figures, animals and designs.[19] The slab seems to be related to some monuments of the west of Scotland[20] and to another slab at Doe Castle, in north-west Donegal – another stronghold of the MacSweeneys.

By now we have established that the O'Boyles and MacSweeneys were trusted allies of Red Hugh O'Donnell; their violent rejection of English rule did not end with the departure and subsequent death of Red Hugh. We have already noted[21] that Turlogh Rua O'Boyle and his family were active around Donegal town on the outbreak of hostilities in the Rebellion of 1641. The MacSweeneys of Banagh were also up in arms – a number of the sept were named by English sources of the time as being rebels – and we are also informed by an English source that in November 1641 "the Mac Swynes [MacSweeneys] and the O'Boyles were encountered about Kilbegge ... in which skirmish the best Mac Swyne was killed".[22]

Ultimately, however, the history of Killybegs is a maritime one. The patron saint of the town is St. Catherine, who is regarded as the patron of seafarers. Tradition represents the village as dedicated to her from the 6th century,[23] but it is likely that her cult was introduced to this area by later sea-borne visitors. The name Catherine is not Irish; it comes from the Greek word *catharos*, signifying pure. It is said that St. Catherine suffered martyrdom in her native Egypt in the 4th century; the St. Catherine honoured at Killybegs is known as Catherine of Egypt or Catherine of Alexandria.[24]

Her intercession was surely sought in 1513 when the town was attacked by pirates while the MacSweeneys and presumably the O'Boyles, too, were off supporting O'Donnell. The annalists inform us that "Owen O'Malley came by night with the crews of three ships into the harbour of Killybegs; and the chieftains of the country being all at that time in O'Donnell's army, they plundered and burned the town, and took many prisoners in it. They were overtaken by a storm [on their return], so that they were compelled to remain on the coast of the country; and they lighted fires and torches close to their ships. A youthful stripling of the MacSweeneys, i.e. Brian, and the sons of Brian, son of the Bishop O'Gallagher, and a party of farmers and shepherds, overtook them, and attacked them courageously, and slew Owen O'Malley, and five or six score along with him, and also captured two of their ships and rescued from them the prisoners they had taken, through the miracles of God and St. Catherine, whose town they had profaned."[25]

In 1627 Killybegs was visited by a different class of pirate who, to use today's terminology, "had their money made" and were obviously well received by the local inhabitants, if viewed less kindly by the English authorities. A flurry of letters between the authorities in Donegal[26] and the authorities in Dublin Castle in April and May of 1627 tell us of the arrival of these visitors to Killybegs; we hear of the coming of Captain Claes Campane, obviously a well-known pirate, with his ships. The first ship to arrive is supported by two other ships and later by four more.

At first it is thought that they are invaders from abroad. Then they announce themselves as ships of Captain Campane, the pirate. Campane claims to have the king's protection. The English authorities initially disbelieve that it is Captain Campane the pirate, then realise that it is and become intent on capturing him. But Campane informs the authorities that he has "already a pardon from the States of Holland and a protection from the King of England which came lately to my hands upon the coast of Barbary by one Captain Harrison. I will do no damage but merely require provisions for which I will pay largely."

We are told in the correspondence that "his men drink so much on shore with loose women and he himself so much on the ship that twenty good men could cut all their throats: Campane's men do not come ashore armed except with knives to cut their meat and are always drunk."

Obviously the hostelries in Killybegs weren't complaining, as we are informed that "Campane and his men spent £1,000 to £1,500[27] there, all in Barbary ducats and Spanish silver."

Two brothers, James and William Hamilton, respectively High Constable and Minister of Killybegs, entertained Campane and his men, supplied them and in fact showed Campane's pilot the instruction they had received from the authorities to arrest some of the crew; they informed their superiors that they did not have "sufficient power at the right moment" to arrest the pirates.

By mid-May Campane had left Killybegs and we are told that "He went for Amsterdam, going round Scotland. He is said to have £6,000 or £7,000 on board in gold, silver, and jewels."[28]

Perhaps those Errol Flynn films of pirate ships sailing up and down the Barbary coast, which are shown on television on Sunday afternoons, won't seem so incredible after reading about these interesting visitors to Killybegs in the 1600s!

We have heard earlier in our travels of the Woodhill Nesbitts and the whaling Nesbitts at Kilmacreddon; there was also a branch of the Nesbitt family living at Carricknagore, across from the harbour at Killybegs. A letter written on 14 March 1674 indicates that a John Nesbitt settled in Killybegs just prior to this and that he was soon, like all good Killybegs men, on the high seas; it states: "There is one Captain John Nisbet, who lived formerly at Lisneskey, in the County of Fermanagh; this man left Lisneskey 7 or 8 years since, and came to live at Killebegs in the Barony of Boylagh and Bannagh, in the County of Dunnegall in Ulster, (a corporation you know right well). This man, Captain Nisbet, since he came to Killebegs hath fraught out several vessels to France and Holland, &c. with such merchandize as the countrey afforded. And in September last he fraught out a vessel of about 70 Tuns, laden with butter, tallow and hides, for France which was to bring back French wines."[29]

Local tradition associates the Carricknagore Nesbitts with the whaling enterprise; it may have been that the Carricknagore and Kilmacreddon Nesbitts were the same family and that Port (Inver) was more suitable for bringing in whale carcasses than Killybegs.[30] The whales would have been brought in at Inver at high tide and cut up on the strand when the water had receded. The blubber and whale bones were very likely exported in a ship from the port of Killybegs, so that both places were prominently identified with the work.

The likely Nesbitt ship, the *Bustle*, which we noted going aground in a storm in April 1765, is listed in the first Lloyd's Register of Shipping in 1764. It appears as "Port: L.pool. To Port: Killybegs."[31] In other words she ran between Killybegs, Nesbitts' base, and Liverpool – by 1762 Liverpool was the largest whaling port on the west coast.[32]

Having referred again, here at Killybegs, to the Nesbitt family, we must not lose sight of the fact that over the years the landlords for most of the present-day parishes of Ardara, Killybegs and Kilcar were the Murray family, whose estate was later to become the Murray-Stewart estate. The agent for the Murray estate lived in the "White House" in Killybegs; sadly this house was demolished just a few years ago. Many a decision which greatly affected the lives of the people hereabouts was taken within its walls. It was to this house that my paternal great, great-grandfather, who died of old age in 1848, came to purchase from the landlord, for £14, the fifty-acre mountain farm at Meenakillew on the Ardara-Killybegs road, on which my father was reared.

The thatch was almost all blown off the "White House" during a hurricane in 1743. The great storms of 1801 ("Mc Dowell's night") and 1839 (*"Óiche na Gaoithe Mhóire"*)[33] are enshrined in the folklore of the maritime people of the Killybegs area. Luckily we have a letter available with an interestingly written account of the 1743 storm. It reads: "We have had the most terrible hurricane last month that was ever heard of in this place. Any ships that were in the harbour drove ashore and bulged prodigiously. The housess all torn, the tennement possesd by John Waren now by Jno McIlwaine is totally the ground. He has given it up on the account he's not able to rebuild it. It left little thatch on the White House forby many others, the custom house that was slated ruind intirly, whole stacks of grain quite carried off . ... Since the storm began there were three ships cast away on Boyla, I here a great many of the men lost ..."[34]

Ainge Devyr,[35] whom we referred to earlier because of his writing about Major Nesbitt of Woodhill still charging a "custom" or "toll" on fair days, lived for some time at Killybegs – presumably about 1830-40. In his book[36] he frequently rages against injustices and speaks out for the "small man" against his oppressors, but when dealing with his tenure in Killybegs he shows very little empathy with the local "mountain men" and comes across as a stranger among the very people whose cause, in his writings, he claims to champion. He refers a number of times to the countrymen coming in from surrounding areas, and their propensity for fighting with blackthorn sticks – "adventurers from the mountain," he calls them.

One particular skirmish he describes graphically: "... a party of the adventurers attended the annual Regatta at Killybegs. I am keeping store there, and some friends come to visit me and see the Regatta. Intending to return immediately, their jaunting cars are at the door." Admitting that his friends and he have been drinking and are "all very merry ... and singing too, it must be confessed," he adds that then "along came the adventurers from the mountain". The "adventurers" make off with the jaunting cars, but Devyr's party manage to drive them back and recapture the cars, but then the "adventurers" go and find reinforcements and return. Devyr goes on to state: "It did not suit my purpose at all to make enemies of the clans around where I lived; so I tried to persuade this man [the leader] to 'let us have peace'. I did not make much progress for he understood little English and I understood less Irish." The fighting restarted and "their friends in the neighbourhood were numerous and we were comparative strangers. The street soon became crowded, and the jaunting cars, with my visitors, were at a stand still. In my store were scythes for sale – each a two handed sword." Devyr then, incredibly, goes on to describe how his wife's brother and he rushed back to his store, armed themselves with a scythe each and rushed into the crowd and managed to escort his visitors a safe distance and "the scythes brought us home again, safe and sound". Obviously this action wasn't too popular because he finishes by stating: "Some weeks after, six of those men waylaid me in the 'Nick of the Balloch', a mountain pass, on my way to the yarn market of Ardara – wounded me dangerously, and only for one generous young fellow in the gang who took me under his protection, probably would have killed me outright."[37]

How quiet the regatta days of later years in Killybegs seem after reading this account!

Notes

1   From a poem entitled "Killybegs" by Rev. Charles O'Donnell.
2   "The little cells", a reference to the early Christian structures which would have originally stood here. Though these are now no more, the outline of similar beehive cells can still be traced within the parish of Killybegs at *Srath na gCeall* (the river holm of the cells) close to the Roughra river in the mountainous area of Tieveskeelta, between Killybegs and Ardara (O.S. map, sheet no. 19). See *D.A.* (1973), pp. 292-94.

In latter times the Gaelic-speaking inhabitants of the surrounding areas didn't talk of going to *Na Cealla Beaga*; they always abbreviated it and spoke of going to *na gCeall* ("*ag dul na gCeall*").
3   Lughaidh Ó Cléirigh, *Beatha Aodha Ruaidh Uí Dhomhnaill*, The Life of Hugh Roe O'Donnell, Prince of Tirconnell (1586-1602), pp. 118-19.
4   Ibid. p. LXXX.

5   Ibid. pp. 134-35.
6   Ibid. p. CXVI.
7   Ibid. pp. 324-27.
8   Ibid. p. 38.
9   Ó Gallachóir, *Essays*, p. 21.
10 This seems a strange word to use to describe a Gaelic chieftan, but the Gaelic word in the original text is similar – *consabal*.
11 Witholding and attacking, i.e. the most judicious in deciding when it was best to retreat, or keep from action, and when to join battle with the enemy.
12 *A.F.M.*, vol. V, pp. 1372-75.
13 *J.R.S.A.I.*, vol. 12 (1872), p. 129.
14 *Illustrated Handbook of South-Western Donegal* (1872), p. 37.
15 Ibid. facing p. 35 and *J.R.S.A.I.*, vol. 12 (1872), p. 128.
16 *Illustrated Handbook of South-Western Donegal*, p. 37.
17 *A.S.D.*, p. 329.
18 John Hunt, *Irish Medieval Figure Sculpture 1200-1600*, vol. 1, p. 133.
19 Below the gallowglass figure the second panel contains two opposing beasts separated by a narrow double strand of interlace; each stands on stylised foliage, the stem of which emanates from the beasts' backs. The third panel contains three interlace designs; the fourth panel contains two bowed clasping figures, apparently in combat, which are flanked by weathered designs, one an interlace knot. Right-hand side: the upper panel contains two cusped ogival ovals with paterae. The second and third panels are filled with interlace designs. The upper part of the fourth panel contains two sets of four, apparently naked, inter-locking figures and lower part contains an interlace knot. The fifth panel contains a stylised vine leaf design. (*A.S.D.*, p. 330.)
20 *Irish Medieval Figure Sculpture*, p. 133.
21 p. 148.
22 Relation of Colonel Audley Mervyn, 1642, quoted in Sir J. Gilbert's *Contemporary History of Affairs in Ireland*, p. 470.
23 *H.D.R.*, vol. II, p. 94.
24 C. Conaghan, *History and Antiquities of Killybegs*, p. 24.
25 *A.F.M.*, vol. V, pp. 1322-23.
26 Sir Basil Brooke.
27 Actually written "1,000L. to 1,500L".
28 See Calendar of State papers of Ireland, 1625-32.
29 Written by William Hamilton, Londonderry, to his cousin in London: reprinted in *Irish Minstrelsy* by James Hardiman, M.R.I.A., vol. 1, pp. 370-76.
30 The late Charlie Conaghan in his book *History and Antiquities of Killybegs* states that there was a tradition of a whaling station at two Killybegs locations – Walker's Bay and Towneysligo – and that "until recently there were to be found in various locations in the area whale bones"; he suggests that the location of the whaling station was changed from Inver to this area after Thomas Nesbitt of

Kilmacreddon had abandoned whaling.

31   Fairley, *Irish Whales and Whaling*, p. 127.

32   Ibid. p. 125.

33   This storm raged into the continent of Europe, wreaking havoc in its path and is said to be the tempest described at Yarmouth by Charles Dickens in *David Copperfield* – "for it is still remembered down there, as the greatest ever known to blow upon that coast".

34   Broughton and Cally Papers, Irish Correspondence 1673-1761; 447+, H.M. Register House, Edinburgh; 508: "Letter from Henry McCulloch to Alexander Murray of Broughton, K. beggs, March 17, 1743". I have not interfered with the text.

35   Presumably the surname was originally "Diver", a common Donegal name.

36   *The Odd Book of the Nineteenth Century.*

37   Ibid. pp. 106-7.

XXI

KILCAR

AFTER A FEW miles we pass the beautiful beach at Fintra, on our left, and continue along an elevated section of road which affords spectacular views across Donegal Bay to the mountains of Sligo and Mayo. The first townland met with in Kilcar parish is Kill [*cill*: a church]. Énrí Ó Muirgheasa, writing in 1936, states: "Here on the slope of the rugged hill north of the road was a Holy Well, now almost closed up. Some 20 or 30 yards lower down was an old graveyard, the site, no doubt, of the *cill* or church. When the plot was cultivated many years ago bones were dug up on the spot. No saint's name is remembered in connection with well or church, nor do the oldest people about remember having seen stations performed there."[1]

Possibly this site was associated with the ecclesiastic foundation at nearby Bavin, the remnants of which still survive. Here we have St. Ciarán's well. For the casual passer-by possibly the most interesting object at Bavan is the painted, carved wooden statue,[2] depicting St. Ciarán, which stands on the left-hand side of the road beside St. Ciarán's well.

Again we quote Énrí Ó Muirgheasa, now writing of St. Ciarán's well: "Stations are still made there on the 5th March, which proves that he is the same St. Ciaran who is patron of Ossory, known in our Martyrologies as St. Ciaran of Saighir, and generally supposed to be earlier than St. Patrick's time. He is commemorated by churches in Argyleshire and in the Island of Islay in Scotland, on the coast of Cornwall and in Connemara, all of which would point to his using the sea as a highway on his missionary labours."[3]

Here we are dealing with the traditional view. Nowadays, with our more revisionist attitudes, we would suggest that St. Ciarán did not himself travel by boat to all these places; rather was his cult introduced to these areas on its own or in the company of the cult of other early saints with whom he was associated. One such was St. Carthach, the saint who has given this parish its name – Kilcar, *Cill Charthaigh*, but often written *Cill Chartha*.

Traditionally it has been believed that St. Carthach himself ministered in the Kilcar area. Local folklore says that St. Carthach was a Munster bishop who came here to do penance for his sins; that the Munstermen, on discovering his retreat, wished him to return home but that he would not go.[4] However, in St. Carthach it is likely that we are dealing with another *wanderkult* and that his cult (devotion to him) was brought to this area, in the company of the cult of St. Ciarán, by later, now forgotten, ecclesiastics. Let us examine this possibility.

Between Leinster and Munster lay the very ancient kingdom of a people called the Osseirge, from whom comes the name of the present-day diocese of Ossory; their patron saint was Ciarán, whose monastic church was at Saigir, now Seirkieran near Birr, in Co. Offaly. Saigir may have been a pagan sanctuary – it is said that a perpetual fire was kept burning there.[5] The Osseirge, later Osraige, are represented as relying on Ciarán for victory over the Leinstermen, who trusted in Brigid, another pagan diety of perpetual fire, later to become adopted as the Christian St. Brigid. Ciarán is generally associated with the very first phase of the spread of Christianity in Ireland; indeed it is claimed that he preceded St. Patrick. We are told that when Ciarán yielded his spirit he dedicated his congregation to God and to Carthach.[6]

Ciarán's feast-day is 5 March; on the same day we have the feast-day of Carthach, bishop, *alumnus*[7] of Ciarán of Saighir. We are informed that he was son of Aenghus, son of Nadfraoich, king of Munster.[8] The *Félire Oengusso* written in metrical verse, confirms the association between Ciarán and Carthach:[9]

> *Roleblaing, ní balbdae,*
> *a clú tar sál sairde*
> *Ciarthach rígdae rúamach*
> *Ciarán slúagach Saigre.*

which translates as:

> Unsilently their renown
> has sprung over the eastern sea:
> Carthach royal, city-possessing
> Ciarán the hostful of Saigir.

It is interesting that Carthach is here spelt Ciarthach, reflecting the view that Carthach is said to have belonged to the Ciarraige, an ancient people of north Kerry, descendants of Ciar. And of course the name Ciar is very similar to that of Carthach's mentor, Ciarán. I have made the point frequently that the study of early saints is most difficult. If I tell you that the cult of Carthach was better known as that of Mo-Chutu[10]/Mo-Chuta/Mo-Chuda and that he has also been given the alias Cuimmíne[11] then I think you will appreciate the point! There are many difficulties in studying the cult of Carthach/Mo-Chuta, not least that Carthach is associated with Ciarán – who is said to have been a very early Christian – and yet the annalists place Mo-Chuta's death at *c.* 637 A.D. The genealogies[12] associate Mo-Chuta with the Sil Fergusa, a branch of the Ciarraige of modern-day Co. Kerry.

I wonder how the Kilcar Gaelic football team would have felt over the years – when drawn against a Kerry team in the Gaeltacht championship – if they had known that their patron, St. Carthach, hailed from the opposition camp!

We are told that there were ecclesiastic foundations dedicated to St. Carthach at Druimfertain, now Carbury, Co. Kildare, at *Inis Uachtair* in Lough Sheelin and here at Kilcar.[13] Again it has to be said that it is unlikely that St. Carthach himself ministered in all these places in addition to succeeding Ciarán at Saighir. Rather have we here evidence of the spread of the cult of St. Carthach northwards. How did devotion to these far-off saints,

St Ciarán, Bavan

Carthach and Ciarán of Ossory, reach this part of south-west Donegal? To try to answer that question we enter uncertain territory. Here is a possible explanation.

St. Náile (St. Naul), who has given his name to Inver (*Inbhear Náile*), which we visited a short time ago and where we discussed whaling, is given the same pedigree[14] as St. Carthach; it is alleged that they were brothers. Náile is also celebrated at Kinawley (*Cill Náile*), Co. Fermanagh – a holy well in the parish is called *Tobar Náile* – and it is written that he was a successor of St. Molaisse as abbot at Devenish, Co. Fermanagh.[15] We have to be very wary of these assertions. What we can be certain of is that Devenish had become a very powerful monastic centre by the 7th century and that it was trying to extend its influence elsewhere. We have touched on this subject before , indicating that the great monastic centres of the 7th century were in competition with each other in advancing their spheres of influence. It is probable that Devenish had secured control over Inver and "was actively engaged in seeking control over other churches around Donegal Bay"[16] in the 7th century. It is possible that the cults of Náile, his "brother" Carthach and Carthach's mentor, Ciarán, came to this area via the influence of the Devenish monastery.

Now, back to Bavan. Énrí Ó Muirgheasa, writing in 1936, has already informed us that at that time stations were still performed in the proximity of St. Ciarán's well on 5 March. He continues: "the *turus* embraces the little green plot surrounded by a low circular fence about a dozen yards below the well, locally known as the 'graveyard'. The station begins at a stone structure within this plot, locally called 'the altar'. ... There can be little doubt that this plot was the site of St. Ciaran's Church."[17]

The rough, rocky valley extending southwards from St. Ciarán's roadside well towards the sea at Shalwy contains the remains of a number of very large court tombs, one at Bavan proper, one at Shalwy and one at Croaghbeg lower down the valley. They are visible from the side of the road, especially through binoculars; better again to don a pair of wellingtons with which to negotiate the soft terrain and walk down. These tombs are of massive construction and the lintels above the entrance to the lower two tombs are particularly impressive.

These huge tombs have been excavated and finds have included planoconvex knives, leaf-shaped arrow-heads, fragments of a shale bracelet and Neolithic sherds, including fragments of a decorated heavy-rimmed vessel.[18] At Bavan also are two former standing stones now collapsed.[19] A large cairn has been recorded near to these, but it had been removed even by 1847.[20]

Two matters of interest spring to mind here at Bavan. The first is that here we have an example of the predeliction of early Christian missionaries to establish their ecclesiastic foundations close to the site of earlier pagan megalithic tombs. And the second is the old nugget – why were these tombs built in such wet, boggy terrain? Could these early peoples not have picked drier sites in which to place their dead? The answer to this question is that when these great tombs were erected some 5,000 years ago the blanket bog which now covers so much of west Donegal would not have been so profuse; the land here would have been of better quality and drier.

Although the first stages of peat development started *c.* 9,000 years ago[21] – around the same time as man's arrival in this country – bog growth was originally confined to the lower areas, but upland peat had certainly started to form before 4,000 years ago[22] and its spread continued into the present millenium. Gradually much of the west of Ireland became smothered in the blanket bog which is such a feature of our landscape nowadays. In its advance it covered over much of Neolithic man's field systems and the investigation of some of the dividing walls – both stone and earthen – of these ancient field systems which have come to light in recent years, particularly in Co. Mayo, is one of the most exciting developments in present-day Irish archaeology.

We now proceed towards Kilcar village, our destination being the well in its vicinity which is dedicated to St. Conall.

Entering Kilcar village St. Carthach's Roman Catholic church is on the right; it was built in 1903–4. Alistair Rowan, in his book *Buildings of North-*

One of the mighty Bavan–Shalwy megalithic tombs

West Ulster, describes it thus: "After endless tower-and-hall or T-plan chur-ches with minimal detail inside and out, St. Cartha's seems wonderful. Of course it cannot really merit such an adjective but it *is* good, especially inside. ... It has a stone front in what the *Irish Builder* calls a Romanesque style; inside, Byzantine might be a better description, for the church has a basilican plan with four arcades on weighty Tuscan columns stepping down the aisles. The space feels big, metropolitan, and perhaps again too grand for the countryside, but grand it certainly is, solid and satisfying."[23]

On a hill at the far end of the village and overlooking it is the old church of St. Carthach; appropriately this area is called Churchtown. On the hillside immediately behind the old church are three holy wells – one dedicated to St. Carthach, one dedicated to the Blessed Virgin and the other to St. Conall.

Énrí Ó Muirgheasa, writing in 1936, states: "Crowds of pilgrims still make the station or *turas*. It begins in the old ruined church of St. Carthach, after which the pilgrim makes three circuits of each of the three wells, and then finishes up at the 'altar' in the old church."[24]

The pilgrimage date is 4 March,[25] but few remember it nowadays. The McDevitts of Churchtown, living near by, are the authority on this *turas* – Michael McDevitt of the past generation and now his son Charlie. The

Looking down on St. Carthach's church at Kilcar. The cairn of stones in the foreground is the site of St. Conall's well.

McDevitts have kept a kind eye on the area over the years and made sure that no harm has come to the old artefacts. Charlie McDevitt describes the *turas* as follows: "You start at the tombstone at the bottom of the right-hand side of the old graveyard and say the Creed; then you say seven Our Fathers, Hail Marys and Glorias. You then leave this area, starting to say the fifteen decades of the rosary as you go and proceed in the direction of St. Carthach's well; you would generally try and have about five decades of the rosary said before you reach the well. You go around St. Carthach's well in a clockwise direction three times, saying seven Our Fathers, Hail Marys and Glorias.

"At St. Carthach's well there is a large round stone with an indentation in it; people used this stone to cure back problems. If you walked around St. Carthach's well in a sunwise direction three times carrying this stone behind your back it was supposed to cure backache.

"You then leave St. Carthach's well, resuming where you had interrupted the fifteen decades of the rosary and go to St. Conall's well. You walk around St. Conall's well in a clockwise direction three times, saying seven Our Fathers, Hail Marys and Glorias. Having resumed the fifteen decades of the rosary you go to St. Mary's well and repeat the pattern. Having finished these prayers and having completed the fifteen decades on the way down you end the *turas* back at the tombstone in the graveyard; you can then say prayers for your intentions."

Charlie McDevitt states that at some time in the past there was a big storm at Inver and many people perished (he is referring here to the Bruckless drownings of 1813); one boat from *Clad na gCaorach*, on the Kilcar side of Teelin Bay, was washed to safety; the crew had a bottle of water from St. Carthach's well in the boat. It was customary for fishermen to come and do the *turas* here and to bring a bottle of water from the well to carry in their boats for safety.

It is of interest that even though devotion to St. Carthach and his teacher, St. Ciarán, remained dominant in this area over the centuries the cult of St. Conall Caol still managed to survive in the shape of the holy well dedicated to him at this spot. Whether Conall's cult here predated or came after the cults of Ciarán and Carthach is open to conjecture. Very often when an artefact – such as a well in this case – associated with a particular saint survives in an area dominated by the cult of another saint or saints it can be interpreted as the remnant of an earlier cult which was adopted into the trappings of the practice of the later cult(s).

A number of placenames have been applied to the Kilcar area over the years. In the earliest list[26] of parishes which we have, dating from the years

1306-7, Kilcar is written as "Killcarchyt". In 1608 we read of "the parish church of Kilcharr. There is in this church a parson only."[27] In a list of place-names in 1642[28] we come across the names "Kilkeran al'[29] Kilkarhan" and, later in the list, "Kilkeran". This cements the Ciarán-Carthach connection further and suggests that Kilcar was also known in the past as Kilciarán. In 1610 a patent was granted to Alexander Dunbar investing him with the ownership of "Kilkerhan" and this we take to be the site of the old church of St. Carthach at Churchtown.[30]

Though Kilcar[31] is the name of this parish Keenaghan is the name of the townland in which the village of Kilcar stands. The placename Keenaghan derives from the Gaelic *caonachan*, a diminutive of *caonach*, moss, and is applied to mossy land. In 1632 we read that "Onora ny Galchoir, a meere Irishwoman, and her under-tenants, beinge meere Irish, and such as are not of the English or British descent or sirname, held the half-quarter of Kynaghan, in the proporcion of Killkeran."[32]

Bridgetown[33] is another name applied to Kilcar village. Estate maps of 1813-14 have the village as Bridge-Town and show the Kilcar river bridged between Keenaghan and "Ballinteampul" (Ballintemple, Churchtown).

The townland of Keenaghan, including the village of Kilcar, belonged for many years to the Nesbitts and later the Tredennicks of Woodhill, Ardara. When the Kilcar fair was established it is said that the fair green was given by the Nesbitts out of Kilcar village estate. There were two entrances to the fair green, one of which was used in the early years of the fair as a tollgate (shades of what Ainge Devyr was writing about earlier at Magheramore) and the lower gate, at "The Piper's Rest", was the exit gate.

Fairs were at first held quarterly, then a monthly fair was decided upon. The fair was held on the 26th of each month. Some of the larger fairs spread out over three days – this applied particularly to the October fair of each year. This was the great annual pig fair and the most important of the Kilcar fairs of the period from the 1870s until 1914-15. Pig rearing in Kilcar and Glencolumbkille was a recognised industry in those days. Every household had one or two pigs which were kept for the full twelve months – immense animals weighing upwards of 3 cwts. Over a thousand such pigs were each year disposed of at the October fair at Kilcar. The buyers were usually from the Donegal town area; the pigs were later driven to Derry and sold as pork in the English midlands. Even in the early part of this century the pig industry was the means whereby many small farmers paid their rent and rates. Gradually the industry died out; nowadays I'm sure there aren't many pigs in the combined parishes of Kilcar and Glencolumbkille.

Enough of fairs; we now cross over to Glencolumbkille, an area rich in historic lore and artefacts and where further remnants of the cult of St. Conall persist. On our way we pass through the village of Carrick, gateway to the spectacular sea-cliff scenery of *Bunglas* and *Sliabh Liag* and also the entry point to tranquil, historic Teelin.

Notes

1   *Béaloideas*, vol. VI, no. 11 (1936), p. 146.
2   Erected by the late John Byrne of Malinmore, Glencolumbkille.
3   *Béaloideas*, op. cit., p. 147.
4   Ibid. p. 148.
5   Kenney, p. 316.
6   *M.O.D.*, 5 March, p. 65.
7   Pupil or student, though it can mean foster-child.
8   *M.O.D.*, 5 March, pp. 64-65.
9   Felire Oengusso, ed. Whitley Stokes, p. 80.
10 Ó Riain, *Corpus*, p. 131.
11 Ibid. p. 132.
12 Ibid. pp. 21, 194.
13 *M.O.D.*, 5 March, pp. 64-65.
14 "He was son of Aenghus, (son of Nadfraech, son of Corc, son of Lughaidh), who was king of Munster." *M.O.D.*, 27 January, pp. 28-29. In Ó Riain's *Corpus* his genealogy is given as Naoile m. Aengusa or slicht Cuirc m. Aengusa no Luigdeach and in the Recensio Metrica (*Corpus*, Ó Riain) he is given a Sil Eimir genealogy:
>   "Naili Mac Aengois na n-each,
>   ua do Chorc mor Mac Luigdeach
>   Mic Oilella an ga lethain
>   Mic Fiacha móir Muillethain."
15 *M.O.D.*, 27 January, pp. 28-29.
16 *D.A.* (1987), p. 11.
17 *Béaloideas*, vol. VI, no. 11, p. 147.
18 Flanagan and Flanagan, *U.J.A.*, ser. 3, vol. 29 (1966), pp. 16-38; see also *A.S.D.*, pp. 16, 20, 20.
19 *A.S.D.*, p. 77.
20 Ibid. p. 78.
21 Mitchell, *Reading the Irish Landscape*, p. 91.
22 Ibid. p. 122.
23 p. 326.
24 *Béaloideas*, vol. VI, no. 11, p. 147.
25 Énrí Ó Muirgheasa puts forward this suggestion as the reason why the *turas* was not done on Carthach's feast-say, 5 March: "A probable explanation of this is

that the people of the Kilcar district found it too much to do both stations (i.e. the one at Bavan and this one) in one day, and that it was arranged for them by some one in authority that St. Carthach's *turas* could be done on the preceding day. The old Irish day, however, began at sunset, so that after sunset on the 4th would count as St. Carthach's festival, and very probably his *turas* was at first performed only at this time, but gradually came to be regarded as lawfully done any time during the 4th."

26   *D.A.* (1974), pp. 66-67.

27   Ms. Rawlinson A. 237, the Bodleian Library, Oxford.

28   Inq., 30 Car. I.

29   i.e. alias = or.

30   *H.D.R.*, vol. II, p. 36.

31   Out the Towney road is another area which is a reminder of St. Carthach. This is Cruckarra: *Cnoc Chartha*; it appears in the 1642 lists as Knockarra. Earlier we noted that Ciarán and Carthach are associated with Ossory. It is of interest that Ossory hill in the Co. Kilkenny parish of Jerpointwest, in the diocese of Ossory, is known in Gaelic as *Cnoc na gCárthach* (see Owen O'Kelly, *The Place-Names of Co. Kilkenny*).

32   Inq., 18, 19 Car. I.

33   Kilcar is still frequently referred to as *Baile 'n Droichid* rather than *Cill Chartha* by native Gaelic speakers from the surrounding areas.

—————— XXII ——————

GLENCOLUMBKILLE

GLENCOLUMBKILLE IS AN archaeologist's delight; it numbers a wonderful concentration of megalithic tombs, cross slabs – many beautifully decorated – enclosures, churches and a souterrain among its attractions. The megalithic tombs of this area are spectacular and indeed are of special interest because their characteristics raise so many of the difficult questions pertaining to the function of megalithic tombs. The Farranmacbride court tomb has the largest court of all the court tombs in Ireland and begs the unanswerable question – what type of ritual was held within the court as part of the burial process? When was the ritual held? Was it held as part of each burial? Was it held at certain times of the year and, to develop this question slightly more, were bodies kept in store elsewhere until times of the year which were deemed particularly auspicious for placement, with its accompanying ritual, in the chambers of the tomb? The presence of two orthostats decorated with curvilinear ornament in the well preserved and partly reconstructed court tomb of Cloghanmore in the Malinmore valley raises questions of the role of decorated stones in the function of our megalithic tombs.

Among the many artefacts in the Malinmore valley is a field containing a group of six portal tomb chambers – a cemetery of portal tombs – almost in a line. This site poses further questions: were the chambers originally all incorporated in one long cairn, did a cemetery of portal tombs have a different role than the single portal tombs (dolmens) with which we are more familiar in the landscape, etc. etc? All beautifully difficult questions – to which I certainly cannot provide the answers. Ah! to know the thinking which governed the everyday lives and ritual of our Neolithic ancestors.

The valley of Glencolumbkille contains numerous little stone crosses, cross-inscribed slabs and pillar stones decorated with intricate designs – but not figures of people – many of them associated with the *turas* devoted to the pre-eminent saint of this area, Colmcille (hence the name Glencolumb-kille: *Gleann Cholm Cille*, Colmcille's Glen). This fine *turas* is still practiced by many people, takes about three hours to complete, is usually done early in the morning and can be done any day, but is especially popular on Colmcille's feast-day, 9 June. There was also a tradition of doing it on three successive Fridays.

One of the most interesting decorated pillar stones in the valley is situated on a rocky prominence close to the Protestant church. Suggesting a 9th century date for this decoration, Peter Harbison, whose writings I relied upon heavily in our discussion of the cross slabs on Inishkeel island, states: "a 9th century date for this stone could give rise to the possibility that it – and some of the other decorated stones in the valley – may be stone imitations of metal shrines containing the relics of St. Columba (Colmcille), perhaps brought to the valley by Diarmait, abbot of Iona, when he carried the reliquaries of St. Columba to Ireland in 830, or by his successor Indrechtach, when he brought further relics of the saint to Ireland in 849, as the *Annals of Ulster* (Hennessy 1887) tell us."[1]

Continuing his discussion of this and the other decorated stones in the valley Peter Harbison concludes: "Most of the other features on these monuments ... would be difficult to parallel in the 7th century, and fit much better into a context of the period after 800, so that a date in the 9th century, and in some instances close to its second quarter, would seem to be the most appropriate for many of the monuments."[2]

However, pride of place in any discussion about the numerous stones in this valley must go to Michael Herity, professor of archaeology at University College Dublin and a frequent visitor to this area. In a recent treatise in a German publication he concludes that the decorated slabs and pillars in Glencolumbkille divide into two very different series; he states that a date of *c.* 700 has been argued for the pillar stones on the eastern side of the valley, whereas the western group of small slabs, many with simple incised decoration, or tiny free-standing crosses, appear to have a date in the 6th or early 7th centuries. He notes the presence of what appears to be a tomb-shrine, *Leaba Cholmcille*, at the north end of St. Colmcille's Chapel and argues that the difference between the eastern and western stones in the valley suggests the existence of an earlier *turas* around the simple western stones which was later extended eastwards to include the pillar stones when they were erected.[3]

It would be an uneasy conclusion to come to if you were to deduce from the presence of a *Leaba Cholmcille* and a St. Colmcille's Chapel, at the site of what appears to be an early hermitage[4] here in the west of the valley, that

Colmcille himself visited the valley or played a part in the spread of Christianity here. The presence of a tomb-shrine is an integral part of the spread of any cult and it is likely that *Leaba Cholmcille,* "ostensibly a tomb-shrine"[5], played a part in cementing the cult of Colmcille here.

Possibly the initial pattern of Christianity here in Glencolumbkille was that there were early hermitages in this area founded by a number of different early saints and that the cult of Colmcille was introduced here at a later stage, finally becoming the predominant cult. Rev. Dr. John Silke, the foremost authority on the introduction of Christianity to the area encompassed by present-day Donegal, in 1987 remarked that before the end of the 7th century while "Armagh's claim extended to Sliabh Liag" that "the Columban tide was already sweeping away memory of the older episcopal foundations ... westwards to Glencolumbkille and Sliabh Liag."[6] Liam Price, in discussing much the same subject as far back as 1941, theorises that "There were primitive Christian communities here, not connected with St. Columba. ... Later monks of the Columban order settled in the Glen. ... Perhaps they took existing traditions and made Columcille the central figure in them instead of some less important saint."[7]

Unease about any possible role that Colmcille himself might have played in the introduction of Christianity to this area is based on the fact that so far no early references connecting Colmcille to the glen have come to light. The major traditions asserting Colmcille's presence here do not appear until 1532 when Manus O'Donnell recorded them in his wonderful book *Betha Colaim Chille.* There is no mention of Glencolumbkille in Adamnán's *Life of St. Columba* (Colmcille), written much earlier, about 685 A.D. In fact the first mention of Glencolumbkille as a placename appears to be in the *Annals of Loch Cé* ,[8] written in about 1530. Surprisingly, in view of the fact that the cult of Colmcille would have been well established by then in this area, Glencolumbkille is referred to as merely "Glend" in the earliest list of parishes of the diocese of Raphoe, dated 1306-7.[9]

Apart from folklore perhaps the greatest argument for Colmcille's own presence in the glen is the high level of workmanship and intricacy of design on the pillar stones here. The sheer quality of these artefacts must surely be attributed to the presence here of a powerful early ecclesiastic – possibly the pillar stones were erected to mark the route of a very early *turas* carried out by pilgrims coming to the glen to honour the memory of this early ecclesiastic – and who is to say that this powerful personage was not indeed Colmcille? Colmcille was and remains a giant of the early church. Much has been written about him and I believe that other works are in progress. So here, in this area which is a shrine to his memory, we will, instead of developing on the theme of Colmcille, content ourselves with a brief look at the other figures who might possibly be associated with the early Christianity of this place.

Across from Malinbeg, on Rathlin O'Birne island, are the remains of an early monastic settlement;[10] the 5th century St. Assicus is associated with the island. Bishop Assicus is said to have been a coppersmith in the service of St. Patrick and had been in charge of a religious community at Elphin, Co. Roscommon. It is said that having exiled himself as a hermit for seven years on the island he was eventually induced to return but died on the way and was buried at *Ráith Cungi*, Racoon, near Ballintra.[11] The holy well on the island has been variously attributed to St. Naal (*Náile*), St. Ciarán and St. Assicus.[12] The small church on the island has also been referred to as Templecavan and it is likely that this island foundation would have been associated with Temple Cavan on the mainland at Malinbeg. This mainland church has been translated as *Tampoll Caoivan*[13] (St. Kevin's church) and also as "St. Ciaran's ruined chapel".[14] So here we have a plethora of saints making claims to a very small area, possibly suggesting that efforts were made to introduce the cults of various saints at different times. The Patrician claim, embodied by Assicus,[15] seems strongest.

Assicus (Tassach) is said to have administered the communion to St. Patrick in his final illness. This is commemorated in the *Féleire Oengusso*, at April 14th, as follows:

"Inrig espoc Tassach
Dobert odonanic
Corp Crist inrig firbailc
La comainn do Patraic."

which translates as

"The royal bishop Tassach
Gave, when he came
The body of Christ, the King truly powerful,
As communion, to Patrick."

On top of magnificent Slieve League [*Sliabh Liag*, formerly written as *Sliabh Liac*, the mountain of the flagstones; *leac*: a flagstone] are the remains of an early church and holy well dedicated to St. Aodh Mac Bricc, who died in 588.[16] Tradition tells us that he is buried at *Ráith Cungi*, near Ballintra, with his contemporary Bishop Assicus, who is recorded as having spent a while as a hermit on this mountainside also.[17] We are told that he "wandered through Munster and Connacht and northwards to Loch Eirne and very many miracles are attributed to him".[18] But here, too, we are possibly dealing with a *wanderkult*, in which, after his cult had become established in various areas, he was given a local pedigree in each area in order to cement his supposed local origins. Pádraig Ó Riain, Professor of Irish at University College Cork and an acknowledged expert on the study of early Irish hagiography, states: "Aed m. Bricc, for instance, whose principal church was in Mide, is given a Ceinél Fhiachach pedigree[19] because of the location of his church at Rahugh (Ráth Aedo), Co. Westmeath, but is also assigned to the Ceinél Bógaine because Sliabh Liac, which is associated with him, lay within their territory."[20] Aodh Mac Bricc's reputation as a patron through whose supernatural aid headaches might be cured have ensured his lasting fame.[21] He was known as the *sui-liag*, the "master-physician."[22] A poem written in Latin by an Irish monk in the 8th century and preserved in the Monastery of Reichenau on an island in Bodensee (formerly Lake Constance) on the German-Swiss border extols his ability to cure head-aches.[23] In his *Life*, probably a 12th century[24] composition, we are told that a man with a violent headache came to Aodh Mac Bricc and begged the saint's intercession. He prayed, the man's pain disappeared, but the method of obtaining relief was that the headache was transferred to the cranium of Aodh Mac Bricc himself![25]

Local man Pádraig Ó Beirn, writing of Mac Bricc and *Sliabh Liag* in 1972, states: "A Holy Well and Church ascribed to him were the scenes of extensive local devotion and an annual pilgrimage in former times. The pilgrimage was undoubtedly very old. It is mentioned by O'Donovan in his Ordnance Survey Letters of the year 1835 relating to Donegal. Indeed he reports that, at that time, the pilgrimage had ceased but it was later revived and held in comparatively recent times."[26]

Doubt could be cast on John O'Donovan's 1835 observation that at that time the *turas* on *Sliabh Liag* had ceased. A mere ten years later, in 1845, climbers on *Sliabh Liag* witnessed people doing the *turas*; one of them writes: "When near the top, we came on a man and woman who were making stations, at a holy well that is here, for the man's health. The man spoke very little English. I was a good deal amused at his incredulity that we should have ascended the mountain for no other purpose that to see the view. During the whole time we were on the mountain we saw the pair of them go from cross to cross (there was an immense number of stone crosses, very rudely put up), with the Rosary in their hand, saying their prayers."[27]

Now we descend *Sliabh Liag* and return to the valley of Glencolumbkille. The oldest surviving Christian building in the glen is said to be the little oratory – it looks like a *cró* that sheep would seek shelter in during very inclement weather – called St. Fanad's cell, in the townland of Kilaned (*Cill*

Fhanaid).[28] Who is this St. Fanad? I don't know, but I will put forward a very tentative suggestion. In the *Martyrology of Donegal* the feast-day of Aodh Mac Bricc is given as 10 November; on the previous day, 9 November, we have the feast-day of "Aedhnat, daughter of Loichén". Again, earlier in the year at 4 January, we have the feast day of "Aedh, Bishop" and "Fiadhnat, Virgin". Different feast days can be given to the same saints in different locations, possibly explaining the November and January dates. If we adhere to our principle that saints associated with the same place are often celebrated within forty-eight hours of one another in the calendar of saints we might here have an association between Aodh Mac Bricc (Aodh, Bishop) and a female St. Aedhnat (Fiadhnat).

Our excuse for having come to Glencolumbkille is that it contains vestiges of the cult of St. Conall Caol. Here at Kilaned there is a holy well dedicated to St. Conall. No tradition attaches to it now. On the other side of the valley stand a number of cross-pillars associated with the *turas* of St. Conall – one near *Cill an Spáinnigh* (the Spaniard's Church) in Cloghan, one further up the hill in Drum townland and another in Haughey's garden in Cloghan. Along the side of a minor road, just past Haughey's, is a well dedicated to St.

St. Fanad's cell, said to be the oldest remaining ecclesiastical structure in the valley of Glencolumbkille.

Conall. Professor Herity, in his guidebook *Gleanncholmcille*, states: "Local tradition says that these slabs formed part of a *turas* performed from St. Conall's foundation at Inishkeel, 25km over the mountains to the north-east, together with a terminal slab near the sea-coast at Doonalt. The route is marked by a cross-inscribed boulder at Laconnell (*Leac Chonaill*) near Ardara and by cross-slabs at Newtownburke closer to Inishkeel."

He continues: "A short *Turas Chonaill* was also performed from Cill an Spáinnigh, with stations at the cross-pillar in Drum, at *Bun na nDrungán* between Drum and Kinnakillew to the north-east, and at the cross-slab beside Cill an Spáinnigh in Cloghan. It ended with the pilgrims drinking water from St. Conall's Well in Cloghan."[29]

The *turas* of St. Conall is no longer performed here. Over a century ago a child was drowned in St. Conall's well in Cloghan and it is very likely that this incident played a large part in its discontinuation.

Folklore from this area confirms the carrying out of a long linear *turas* from Glencolumbkille to Inishkeel and also mirrors the tradition, obviously commonly held and which we have aired before, of why St. Conall first sought out Inishkeel island. Peigí ní Ghadhra, from here at Cloghan, speaking in 1940 at the age of eighty-seven, states: "I do not know where St.

*Tailor and historian
Seán Ó hEinne in
his home in
Glencolumbkille*

Conall was born, neither do the people who came before me; but they did know that he was a 'pet' who would never do what his people told him; he was a rascal through and through. One day he and his father were out beside the house and apparently his father asked him to do something he did not wish to do; he simply turned and struck his father a blow on top of the head. Whatever kind of an instrument he held in his hand, he felled his father instantly. When he saw what he had done remorse struck him and he had no peace day or night until he could find five priests to whom he could tell his terrible story and to try and get forgiveness.

"He went off one day to find the priests. When he was making for the place in which they were he met two of them, an old priest and a young priest. He went to them and told them his story and said he would like to go to confession to them. The old priest asked the young priest to hear his confession, but the latter refused and the old priest had to bring him with him and hear his confession. The old priest, when he had heard his confession, said that he would never get forgiveness from God until he went out to a desert island far away from his people and remain there until the birds of the air would come and make a nest in the palm of his hand and would raise their young there.

"The poor fellow returned home and he very downcast, because he had never thought the crime he had committed was so bad until he heard the judgement that was put on him. He left the following morning, early, and he was walking on and on until he came to Inishkeel. This little island is at Gweebarra, so near land that one can walk out to it at low tide. He went out there and decided to do his penance there. He was on the island for a long time without having anything to eat or drink but whatever seafood he could collect on the rocks. He made a shelter for himself of large rocks on the island and when night came he would rest there. He spent a long time like that, but the birds of the air showed no sign of coming near him to make their nests in the palm of his hand.

"At last, one very hot day in summer, he went to the highest point of the island; he stretched himself on his side on the top of the height and with the heat of the sun he soon fell asleep. The old people said he slept for seven years. When the birds found him asleep they came and made a nest in the palm of his hand and hatched their young and then went off. He awoke and when he looked he saw the little nest in the palm of his hand and the shells in it. He then saw what had happened when he was asleep and knew that he had made his peace with God. He made up his mind, then, that he would become a priest and it is said that having become a priest he returned to Inishkeel and made the *turas* which can be seen to the present day.

"It was customary for the people of Glencolumbkille to go to Inishkeel long ago and to make the *turas*, or walk the *turas*, and there are old women still living who walked it as often as they have fingers or toes. It is said that St. Conall came from Inishkeel to Glencolumbkille and that is the time he made the *turas* which is there on the north side of the Glen."[30]

The tradition, which we heard earlier, of the sand miraculously rising up and keeping Conall dry from the incoming tide as he slept, fatigued, on the strand in Loughros Beg Bay on his way from Glencolumbkille to Inishkeel is also retold here in Glencolumbkille.[31]

These folktales are examples of the great wealth of tradition and history of the Glencolumbkille area which has been preserved over the years and in the last half-century by none more so than An Dochtúir Seán Ó hEochaidh, now resident at Gortahork, and Seán Ó hEinne. At the present day, because of the drive of the very active local development group, based at *Foras Cultuir Uladh*, allied to the archaeological skills of Professor Michael Herity, the future of the culture of Glencolumbkille seems assured.

We now take our departure from *Glend Colaim Cilli*[32] and proceed along the mountain road towards Glengesh.

Notes

1   *BAR* British Series 152 (1986), p. 66.
2   Ibid.
3   Herity, "The Antiquity of *An Turas* (the Pilgrimage Round) in Ireland," *Lateinische Kultur im VIII. Jahrhundert*, pp. 95-143.
4   *J.R.S.A.I.*, vol. II (7th series), vol. LXXI consec series (1941), p. 87; Herity, op. cit., p. 104.
5   Herity, "The Antiquity of *An Turas* (the Pilgrimage Round) in Ireland," op. cit., p. 98.
6   *D.A.* (1987), pp. 7-8.
7   *J.R.S.A.I.*, op. cit., p. 87.
8   Ibid. p. 80.
9   *D.A.* (1974), pp. 66-67.
10   It contains an irregular outer enclosure and an inner enclosure which incorporates two wells, two stone huts or cells, on oratory, a probable church, a kiln, six cross-inscribed slabs, three upright slabs and other buildings. (Walsh, *J.R.S.A.I.*, vol. 13 (1983), pp. 53-66.) See also Herity, *Gleanncholmchille*, pp. 41-43.
11   *J.R.S.A.I.*, vol. 113-114 (1983-84), p. 54.
12   *Béaloideas*, vol. VI, no. 11. (1936), p. 150.
13   Fagan, *Hill Drawing Antiquity Books*, 1845-48, book no. 20, p. 24.

14   *Béaloideas* op. cit.

15   Assicus was known as Tassach (Herity, *Gleanncholmcille*, p. 41). In Ó Riain's *Corpus* we find a number of references to him having been a craftsman in the service of St. Patrick:

    (a) "Tri primcherda hEreann .i. Tassach la Patric...tri epscuip in sin"

    (b) "A trí cerdda Essiu 7 Biti 7 Tassach"

    (c) "A thri cerda, fa mor rath

        "Aissmiti, Tairill, Tasach."

In naming the members of Patrick's family the *A.F.M.* list (vol. I, pp. 136-37) "His three artificers, of great endowment, Aesbuite, Tairill, and Tasach" and a note (pp. 138-39) informs us that only Tasach has been identified – "he was the patron saint of Rath-Cholptha, now Raholp village, near Saul, in the county of Down." It is no surprise that the other two could not be identified with a particular church because Ó Riain informs us (*Corpus*, p. 213) that Aesbuite is a fusion of Essiu and Biti and that Tairill is a complete fabrication. As I have stated before, the study of early saints is treacherous ground indeed.

16   *M.O.D.*, 10 November, pp. 302-3: his orbit is also given under 589 and 595; see also *A.F.M* at year 588.

17   *D.A.* (1972), p. 157.

18   Ibid. p. 156.

19   "Epscop Aed m. Bricc m. Cormaic m. Crimthaind m. Fiachach m. Néill Noigiallaig ut supra." (*Corpus*, p. 4) and, *Corpus*, p. 87:

"Epscop Aeda mac Bric bind,

mic Corbmaic caoim mic Cremthainn

mic Fiachra[d] feil an fiadaigh,

mac sein Neill Naoigiallaigh."

([d]: Fiachach).

His mother belonged to the Múscraige Tíre of north Tipperary (*Corpus*, p. 190, and introduction p. XXXV).

20   *Corpus*, p. XV of the introduction.

21   Kenney, p. 393.

22   Quoted in Kenney, p. 393, who states in a footnote: "So in a fragmentary Life of Brigit, Rawlinson B 512 ff 31-5ᵛ."

23   Reproduced in Joyce, vol. II, p. 87. We are told that the Latin is "very barbarous" and that "we may assume that the writer merely transcribed it, and that its composition may be referred to a still earlier date."

24   Kenney, p. 393.

25   Quoted in Joyce, vol. II, pp. 86-87.

26   *D.A.* (1972), p. 156.

27   From the diary of John O'Hagan who accompanied John Mitchel in Donegal in 1845; reprinted in the *D.A.* (1970), pp. 167-68.

28   *J.R.S.A.I.*, vol. 11 (7th series), vol. LXXI consec series (1941), p. 85.

29   p. 37. I have not reproduced the drawings of any of the stones associated with

Turas Chonaill; these are all well displayed in Professor Herity's guidebook, which is an essential companion on any visit to Glencolumbkille.

30   Dept. of Irish Folklore, Belfield, ms. 972, pp. 462-65.

31   Ibid., Belfield, ms. 143, pp. 1826-27. (Seamus Uí Cuinneagain, aged twenty-four years, from Malin in Glencolumbkille, taken down from him on 9 January 1936.)

32   *Betha Colaim Chille* (1918 ed. p. 26 item 40).

XXIII

DOWN GLENGESH

"A day on a hilltop is worth a week by the sea."
Ruskin.

As we travel along the road from Glencolumbkille towards Glengesh – always pronounced "Glenish" by locals – we should remember that this road is a veritable motorway compared to the routes of travel that existed in past times. In a report[1] on the distress of the people of Glencolumbkille in 1822, William Hume, among other observations, comments on the lack of roads.[2] He later writes: "I find the distress of this parish much greater than I at first imagined. ... Upwards of 100 families are, at this moment, from age, sickness, or some bodily infirmity, unable to provide for their wants, besides others who are willing to work, but have no employment; indeed the situation of the poor in this parish is very miserable. ... The manufacture of flannel, which, some years since, was carried on here to a considerable extent, has latterly declined very much, as well as linen – both from want of encouragement; the poor not having the means of procuring wheels, looms, or even the raw material."[3] Commenting on the "traffic of illicit distillation" in the area one of the reasons he puts forward to explain it is "the inability of the people, from the want of roads to convey their produce from the parish to a market, being obliged to convert it, by manufacture, into a portable compass."[4]

The poor condition of the roads is given prominence in another report from the Glencolumbkille parish around the same time. In 1821 John Ewing observes: "[The] roads [are] horribly bad – not a perch of good road in the parish. The first step to be taken for the improvement of this parish is to make roads or at least a road into it. At present a wheel car with half a load could not enter the parish on any side whatever. People from the interior cannot come in here for flannel, butter or fish."[5]

Passing through Meenaneary[6] and Crove, and continuing towards Glengesh, we remain with our theme of roads in earlier times. William Lithgow, a celebrated Scottish pilgrim, journeyed through Ireland in 1619 and his account, written in Elizabethan English, is certainly descriptive and should make anyone appreciate the pot-holed roads of today! He writes (read each Elizabethan English ſ as an s): "And this I dare avow, there are more riverſ, lakeſ, brookſ, ſtrandſ, quagmireſ, bogſ and mariſheſ, in thiſ country, than in all Chriſtendome beſideſ; for travelling there in the winter, all my dayly ſolace was ſinke downe comfort, whileſ boggy-plunging deepeſ kiſſing my horſe belly; whileſ overmired ſaddle, body and all; and often or ever ſet a ſwiming, in great danger, both I and my guideſ of our liveſ; that for cloudy and ſourtayne-bred perilſ, I waſ never before reduced to ſuch a ſloting laborinth. Conſidering that in five monthſ ſpace, I quite ſpoyled ſix horſeſ, and myſelf aſ tyred aſ the worſt of them."[7]

Road conditions had improved greatly by the time Arthur Young toured Ireland in 1776-79, but he too had his uneasy moments, as witnessed by the following excerpt: "I had often heard of roads being made over such quaking bogs, that they move under a carriage, but could scarcely credit it; I was, however, convinced now, for in several places, every step the horse set, moved a full yard of the ground in perfect heaves."[8]

Not everyone who toured Ireland in those early days travelled on horse-back or in a carriage. A young French *émigré* named De Latocnaye travelled through Ireland in 1796-97 and elected to walk. A description of the few accessories he carried with him makes interesting reading: "He carried his luggage in a handkerchief, which he fixed upon the top of his cane-sword. It consisted of a powder-bag made with a woman's glove, a razor, some thread, needles, scissors, a comb kept in a pair of dancing-pumps, a pair of silk stockings, a pair of breeches fine enough to be rolled into a lump as big as a man's fist, two very fine shirts, three cravats, three handkerchiefs, and his travelling dress. When invited to stay in a genteel house this young aristocrat had, therefore, the satisfaction of being able to enter the parlour with his hair powdered and with his white stockings on, just as if, as he says, he had been travelling at his ease in a coach with trunks and a complete wardrobe. The Frenchman who journeyed through Ireland for over six months in such an agreeable fashion also carried an umbrella, an object which he tells us excited curiosity everywhere and made people laugh in a way that seemed to him absurd. But umbrellas, although then in general use in Paris, were still looked upon in parts of England as effeminate, so that in Ireland, where they can have been seen less often, they were very naturally still greater objects of ridicule."[9]

In Ireland there were few new roads until the reign of James I (1603-25). Continued warfare had prevented much progress in domestic arts, and Irish chieftains almost invariably selected inaccessible sites for strongholds and residences. Besides, there was the very important consideration that facilities of communication would be more advantageous to the enemy than to the lightly armed Irish troops; we can therefore understand why there was no significant road building until after the Flight of the Earls in 1607.

That is not to say that there hadn't been a road system in earlier Ireland – there had. There was a system of ancient highways in pre-Christian Ireland. In low-lying bogland the foundations of the road were often of oak timbers and a number of these roads across bogs have come to light in recent years. By the 2nd century A.D. five great highways were probing into each province of Ireland from the capital seat at Tara. These great roads from Tara showed Ireland's acceptance of the Roman idea of a road as an agent of central political power. In the middle ages this idea fell away and the destruction of roads was often a weapon used to impede English troops and force them into the perils of forest and bog.

Early in the 17th century the English devised a new system of road building in this country. In 1613 an Act (11 Jas. I, cap. 7) was passed in the Irish Parliament by which the duty of repairing the highways was thrown on the parishes in which the roads were situated.[10] By this enactment every householder and cottage labourer (not being a hired servant by the year) inhabiting the parish was obliged to give a fixed period of six days labour every year at road making. Every person with a plough was to supply a cart with horses or oxen. This might all sound very well but we learn that "Compulsory labour on the roads, however, was always grudgingly given. The cottiers supplied their feeblest members and their worst horses and cars. Work was begun late and finished early, and its quality was very indifferent."[11] Despite this the statute labour system continued to be the sole means of repairing the roads for one hundred and fifty years.

In 1763 the passage of the First Grand Jury Act (5 Geo. III, cap. 14) introduced the Presentment system of road building.[12] As we have noted earlier[13] in our travels this soon led to the expansion and improvement of the road network here in south-west Donegal. The Grand Jury, the equivalent of the present-day County Council, was made up of members of the gentry and though the Presentment–Grand Jury system of road-making was prone to corruption, favouritism and jobbery[14] it seems to have served Donegal well enough.

In 1809, also in the time of George III (1760-1820), an act was passed whereby passengers and travellers of all descriptions were obliged to take the left hand side of the road under a penalty of 10s, the half to go to the informer and the remainder to some local charity.

This stretch of road between Carrick–Glencolumbkille and Glengesh on which we are now caused plenty of problems to a traveller of almost a hundred years ago – Stephen Gwynn. Writing in 1899, he states: "The road from Carrick follows the course of the Glen river north, then crosses by a bridge and turns to the east, then north again; but it is so lonely a moor that even the map supplied at Carrick hotel – an example of cartography not much more trustworthy than a West African Boundary Commissioner's – cannot mislead you. For about six miles the road rises slowly, and on a dry day, especially with wind behind, it could all be ridden. Then it turns straight to the left, up a long straight mile, perfectly hopeless to ride. Beyond that is a drop to a valley, where a road comes in from Glen, and then it goes up again like the side of a house, and when you get to the top you meet the only C.T.C. warning post known to me in Ireland. This is Glen Gesh hill, at the head of a valley which runs down to Ardara, and is probably the steepest piece of roadway in use for any considerable wheeled traffic in these islands. It is very carefully engineered, and a part of it can be ridden, but the beginning and end of it nobody but an idiot would attempt."[15]

The road which "comes in from Glen" – referred to above – is the road which goes off to the left here at Leamagowra, about a mile before Glengesh, and runs over behind the mountains to join the road which goes through Maghera and up Granny Glen, at Largnaseara. This road then continues out to the isolated rocky inlet of Port[16] and you can then also continue on to Glencolumbkille.

The placenames of this high plateau extending from Leamagowra out towards Port are determined by the mountainous terrain and especially by the rivers which, having run down from the peaks, wend a relatively flat, if tortuous, course along here. Leamagowra itself is translated *Léim a' Ghabhra*, the leap or pass of the goats (*gabhar:* a goat); the word *léim*, a leap, is often used to designate spots where animals were in the habit of passing – especially a narrow part of a river where they crossed by bounding from one bank to the other.[17] The river – which also gives its name to a townland (Owenteshna) – flowing through here is called *Abhainn tSeascinne*, the river of the *seascann*[18] or marsh. The road continues over through Stravally, *Srath Bhealaigh* – again appropriately named – the river holm (*srath*)[19] of the road or pass (*bealach*). The roads meet at Largnaseara, *Leargaidh-na-Saorthach*, the hillside (*learg*) of the *saerhachs* or freeholders (*saor:* free) – land which was held free of rent or duty of any kind.[20] This placename is written as "Lerganasirragh" in 1642[21] and a fuller account of its meaning would involve us getting embroiled in the old Gaelic system of land tenure, a subject best avoided here.

Over near Port is another placename derived from a river – Straboy, *Srath*

Buidhe, the yellow river-holm. Here we are reminded of a poignant event which occurred in the year 1576, involving a member of the O'Boyle clan and noted by the Four Masters. That the annalists recorded it is another reminder, as if we needed one, of the esteem in which the O'Boyle clan was held. It reads: "The daughter of O'Boyle, Siubhán Óg, daughter of Turlough, who was son of Niall, was drowned on St. James's day, as she was learning to swim, in the river of *Srath-Buidhe*."[22] This is a sad reference, but an intriguing one in the sense that we sometimes think that swimming is a fairly modern leisure activity and yet here we had – in 1576 – this young lady learning to swim ("*ag foghlaim snámha*").

But enough of our straying; now back to the approaches to Glengesh.

Since in this book we are travellers ourselves, we will have a brief look at the deep impression that Glengesh has made on earlier travellers. T.C. McGinley, writing in 1867, states: "A work professing to treat of the topography of South-Western Donegal would not be complete without some notice of the remarkable valley of Glengesh. ... The road leading from Carrick to Ardara runs through it; and a tourist, finding himself at Straboy, might, if he were so minded, select that route to Ardara in preference to climbing the steeps of Sliabh Toaidh. The road from Straboy leads along by the constabulary barrack[23] until it joins, near Crove, the highway from Carrick to Ardara. At this point, the two ridges which form the glen, first branch out from each

Glengesh valley

other, leaving a deep narrow defile lying along for two miles between them. Standing here, the tourist has within his view, stretching away from beneath his feet, one of the wildest and most remarkable glens in all Ireland, perhaps in the whole world." Referring to the valley below he adds: "The houses are all built low, and have their roofs always secured with ropes thrown over them, and tightened by weights at either end. These precautions are necessary, as the wind sometimes rolls down that narrow gorge with the force of a hurricane."[24]

A traveller, writing in 1872, states: "It is decidedly one of the grandest and wildest passes in Ireland. I have met with nothing to surpass it for its wild and natural beauty. The entrance to this magnificent pass is guarded by two high mountains of stern and rugged appearance. ... In the winter season the torrents that rush down these precipices lend additional attractions to this lovely scene. And far away as we can see there is no human habitation, but all around a dismal waste of rock, where the storm-king reigns at times in all his unabated fury."[25]

Another visitor, coming up through Glengesh Pass in 1887, writes: "Glengesh, which is not far from Ardara, is one of the sweetest glens I ever saw. ... We ascended for a mile and a half in gradual windings, between two smooth slopes of fertile land. The bottom, vividly green, was sprinkled here with busy groups, making and carrying what seemed excellent hay. Hay in September sounds strange; but we found it often still left in the fields. Every turn in the road made a picture, framed between these two verdant sides, of the distant Rosses, and the mountains beyond. ... On the top of Glengesh we sat down to eat and drink, blessing the little mountains stream and the baker of Ardara [do you remember her buying bread from this baker in Ardara earlier[26] in our travels], and looking back on a view which I can see still with shut eyes, and remember as one of the lovely visions that we carry away with us – forever."[27]

Perhaps our old friend Joseph Campbell has written my favourite reference to Glengesh when he writes poetically: "Darkness and austerity – those are the notes I carry away from this wild glen. Its lines have something of the splendid bareness of early architecture; its colour suggests time-stained walls, with quiet aisles and mouldering altars where one might kneel and dream away an existence. When you meet a stranger going the road that winds through it, like a coil of incense suspended in mid-air, you expect him to look at you out of eyes full of wonder, and to speak to you in half-chanted and serious words, stopping not, turning neither to left nor right, but faring on, a symbol of pilgrimage:

"*Le solus a chroidhe,*

Fann agus tuirseach
Go deireadh a shlighe."[28]

The atmosphere which Campbell creates, of the age-old mystery of this place, brings us to our next topic – the meaning of the placename Glengesh. In Gaelic it is called *Gleann na Geise*, the valley (*gleann*) of the *geis*; a fascinating name. The Gaelic word *geas* or *geis* means "tabu" or "prohibition", the infringement of which led to misfortune or even death. The custom of tabu or *geis* (pl. *geasa*) is found in the very early Celtic tales. The Celtic *geis* was a prohibition forbidding a person to do, or enjoining him to do, certain things. The following excerpt enlarges on the subject: "In the oldest Irish tales the meaning of *geis* seems to have been limited to an injunction against doing a specific thing, 'a rule of prohibition under penalty of ill luck for its infraction...' or 'an absolute prohibition from doing certain things.' Cuchulainn, the hero of the Ulster cycle, was under many *geasa*, among them not to go to a cooking-hearth and consume the food prepared there, and never to eat the flesh of a dog. Infraction of these prohibitions brought about his death. The ancient tale of Conaire, *The Destruction of Da Derga's Hostel*, has *geis* as its central motive, and Conaire, caught up in a mesh of conflicting *geasa*, which he violates one after the other, is finally doomed. There were, too, many instances of *geasa* connected with sacred places and objects, which served to protect the sanctity of kingship. Tara, the seat of the high kings of Ireland and the symbol of the sacred authority of kingship, was a place steeped in *geasa*. No hero's arms could be brought into Tara after sunset; no one could go to Tara to banquet after sunset; no fire could be kindled in Ireland during the special feast of Tara; and no king could assume the sovereignty of Ireland at Tara until he first wore the *nasc niadh* (champion's chain) around his neck."[29]

The nature of *geis* took many forms in early Irish literature; and in the older tales the injunction clearly came from the supernatural force. The *geis* imposed by fate or God was virtually the only limitation placed upon the otherwise invincible heroes of these tales.[30] The author of our earlier excerpt concludes: "The evidence of *geis* as a singular feature of the old heroic life is so extensive in the Irish sagas, laws and historical tracts that it may be considered a characteristic element of early Irish literature."[31]

Further afield there is a *geis* present in the early Anglo-Saxon poem *Beowulf* in lines 168-69, and "although it is not necessary to seek any specific origin of the use of *Beowulf* of so common a primitive custom as tabu," it is well to remember that "The Anglo-Saxons were recipients of the wealth of native Irish custom, myth and story through the medium of the Irish Christian missionaries" and "the meaning of the lines can be enriched by recognizing the nature and prevalence of the custom of *geis* in the early Irish lore, which formed part of the literary heritage of the *Beowulf*-poet and was available to him for appropriation."[32]

Closer to home we learn that "Among the *geasa* or 'prohibitions' of the king of Tír Eoghain was one, very necessary for warlike tribes living side by side, forbidding him to make war against the king of Tír Chonaill.[33] This, if faithfully observed, would have changed the whole future not only of both tribes, but perhaps of the entire nation."[34]

The word *geis* continued into later Gaelic literature and in a tale taken from the *Book of Fermoy*, a codex of the 15th century, the language of which is Early Modern Irish, we find a couple playing *fidchell* (chess) out on the green ("*ar an fhaithche*"[35]) and the word *geis* is uttered a number of times – e.g. "*Geis* to him (*Geis do*)," she said, "unless he play *fidchell* with me for stakes." But the male won the game and in his victory puts a *geis* on the girl – "And *geis* on thee,"[36] said he, "if thou eat food in Ireland until thou procure the warrior's wand which Cúrói son of Dare had in his hand when taking possession of Ireland and the great world, and fetch it to me here."[37]

In "Glengesh" we have a name going back into the mists of time. If we remember that *geis* meant a tabu or prohibition, the infringement of which led to misfortune or even death, then Glengesh must have been a very forbidding place in early times. This was a place to avoid. Early man in this area of south-west Donegal possibly believed that if he descended into the misty chasm below, or, alternatively, ventured into the mouth of the valley below and started to ascend the cloud-covered peaks in the hope of crossing the mountain barrier, then it was likely he would never be seen again. And so this valley was tabu, a place to avoid. Near by, above Aighe, is a cliff-face known as *Alt na nDeamhain*, the precipice of the demons [*deamhan*: a demon], another screeching reminder of the fear this area must have struck in the hearts of early man. This latter cliff features in local epic tales of Finn and the Fianna.

Coming here from Glencolumbkille we have noted a few references to the road from Glen going around by Port. It would appear that in earlier times the traffic from Glen to the Ardara came via the Port track and down at Granny Glen. Though this latter valley is almost as forbidding as Glengesh it must have been considered as more benign by earlier man. Perhaps the proximity of the sea to it was a reassuring factor.

Below Glengesh the townland at the entrance to the valley is called Scadaman, appropriately named because the Gaelic word *sceadaman* means "throat" and here indicates the narrowing approach to the steep-walled glen.

This whole area of Glengesh and Scadaman, and the areas east and west of Glengesh, being Gaelic speaking, are rich in oral tradition and folklore. Historic Inishkeel island is prominent in many of the stories, not least because of the part it played over the years in the lives, deaths and burials of the people here. Tradition tells us that in the last century old Seán Cormac O'Heena of Stravelley helped to carry a corpse from Owenteshna for burial on Inishkeel island. The reverence in which Inishkeel was held by the older generations is further exemplified by the following story told to *Cú Uladh* by Eamonn Óg McGill of Glengesh in 1902; it refers to the slaughter of people in this area at the time of the Cromwellian wars – a subject we have referred to earlier.[38] It goes as follows: "Cromwell and his soldiers came to this area and they killed everyone they came upon, including men, women and children. Anyone who could fled before the advancing army, but one man stayed behind in Glengesh because his wife had died and her body was in the coffin [*faoi bhord'*], ready to be brought to Inishkeel island for interment. The man 'waked' her overnight and in the morning he hitched up his cart, put his wife's coffin on the cart, an set off for Inishkeel, where St. Conall and many other saints were buried. He hadn't gone far when Cromwell's army, with Cromwell himself at the head of it, came upon him. Cromwell enquired from

One of the landmarks of Glengesh, on your right coming down, is Carraig Na Sróine *(srón: a nose). The apex is called* An Storrúil Árd *(storrúil: strong, bold).*

him what was in the cart and he replied that it was his dead wife in the coffin and that he had to bury her himself as he had no assistance because everybody else had fled. Cromwell took pity on him and allowed him to proceed, but cautioned him not to look behind him and to keep his eyes straight in front of him until he reached Inishkeel island and to pay no attention to any sights he might see as he went on his way. And this is what the man did."[39]

An earlier member of my own tribe, An Bráthair 'ac a'Ghioll (Friar[40] McGill), who lived in the 1700s, plays a large part in the folklore of this area. It is said that he was born in the Glengesh-Aighe area and that he attended a school at Kilraine, which is situated between Ardara and Glenties. Some years later he became a student at a Paris college, from which he graduated to Rome and from whence he returned as a wandering friar to the mountain areas of south-west Donegal.

We are told that in his early student days, while travelling in Europe, he was struck by a fever; he became very ill and was on death's door. He began to rave and imagined that he was standing on the bank of a well which is still at the bottom of Glengesh, at the side of the road. Though he was parched with thirst he was unable to reach the water; he thought that if he could just get one drink out of the well he would improve. Finally he imagined that someone came to his aid and brought him a vessel full of cool water from the well and that he drank his fill out of it; his thirst was slaked and his fever disappeared. On his return to his own area he went as soon as possible to the Glengesh well and drank his fill of water from it; he then blessed the well. In later times it is said that there was a *turas* to this well.

We must remember that these folktales came down to us through the medium of the Gaelic language; the following little story is my own favourite involving An Bráthair 'ac a'Ghoill and I have decided to tell it in Gaelic for two reasons - firstly because I don't think it translates well and secondly I would like to record it in Gaelic in memory of the older generations who lived in this area and who preserved the Gaelic language, its customs and its oral traditions. Many *seanchaithe* spent the last moments of their lives in reciting Gaelic poetry, so that it might be saved and handed down to later generations; there were many instances of old people in the Aighe-Glengesh area reciting their favourite Gaelic poems to their own family and neighbours when the candles were being lighted at their deathbed. This is how the story involving An Bráthair 'ach a' Ghoill goes:

"*Bhí daoine múintearach de'n Bhráthair 'na gchómhnuidhe amuigh ar an Fháithche. Lánamháin phósta a bhí ionnta. Ní raibh aon duine cloinne aca na gheibheadh a gcuid páistí uilig bás nuair a rugtaoi iad. Bhí duine*

*cloinne le bheith ann a truip seo agus cuireadh sgéala chuig an Bhráthair.
Rugadh an páiste, agus ní rabh ann acht go rabh faill baisteadh tuatha a
thabhairt dó go bhfhuair sé bás, d'réir chosamhlacht. Sgairteach ar a'
Bhráithair.*

*"D'fhág sé an páiste 'na luighe ar thábla, chuir salann ina bhéal agus
thosuigh a' léigheamh ós a chionn. Ní raibh a bhfad gur chaith an páiste
an salann as a bhéal agus thosuigh a' sgreadaigh. Ní raibh cumadh ar bith
báis ansin air.*

*"'Bí cúramach fá dtaoibh dó anois,' arsa an Bhráthair, 'ná thug mise
amach as faoi ascall na Maighdine Muire é.'"*

When An Bráthair 'ac a'Ghoill died his body, like so many other from the
area, was carried by the Glengesh people to Inishkeel island and interred
there. His grave on the island was well known to the older generations from
the fact that the stone was broken diagonally across. The site is now unknown, but if the recumbent crucifixion slab just outside St. Conall's church
on the Inishkeel island is not 9th century and can be ascribed a much later
date, possibly 18th century, then it might well mark the grave of An Bráthair
'ac a'Ghoill.

As we start our descent into the valley I should mention that a number of
placenames subdivide the actual Glengesh area itself. We will use some of
the older maps of the region to elucidate them. The high peak and moorland
on our left, above the valley and extending over towards Leamagowra, is
"Croaghavehy" [*cruach*, a stack, here indicating a stack-shaped mountain;
beithíoch: an animal (a horse, cow, etc.); *Cruach a'Bheithigh*: an area used
for grazing stock, presumably brought up from the valley below]. As we start
our descent, but well before the S-bend, the pitted, sparsely covered moorland in front of us and on our right is "Meelrhudd" [this name probably derives from *maol*: bald; *ruaiteach:* rough moorland], appropriately named.
This area extends down to include the first houses on the right side of the
valley. The whole upper third of the left side of the valley is marked
"Boluey" on an 1831 estate map; this area extends across to the right side of
the valley below "Meelrhudd". It is pronounced "Bulowen" locally and translates as *Baile Eoin*, a personal name, Owen's Town.

The area where most of the houses are congregated at the present day, in
the centre of the valley, in Glengesh proper, is marked "Shanwella" i.e. *Sean
Bhaile*, Oldtown. This contained twelve houses in the early decades of the
last century. At the same time there was a grouping of eleven houses close
together at the actual *caiseal* (stone enclosure) in Ballycashel, *Baile an
Chaisil*, below *Sean Bhaile*. This cashel, which stood behind the home of
Eamonn Óg McGill, the storyteller we have mentioned earlier, is no more.

We should not be surprised that maps drawn in the early decades of the last century show groupings of houses built closely together. Land had not yet been divided out and people lived in clachans.

As we exit from Glengesh we note that the last houses over on the right of the valley, in *An Céidradh*, are located in the townland of Common. This area is marked "Aiye or Aiyea" on Montgomery's 1831 estate map, reinforcing the view expressed earlier that present-day Common was originally part of Aighe.

Scadaman is the townland just below Glengesh. Earlier we noted that it translates directly as "throat", indicating the entry to Glengesh valley. Over on our left a blind gorge comes to an abrupt end up against a cliff-face; this part of Scadaman bears the interesting name of *"Bráid a' Sceadamain"*, literally "the throat (*bráid*) of the throat" and surely conveys a sense of a gradual narrowing finally ending in inaccessibility. This inaccessibility led to the setting up of the best-known landmark in Bráid, a mass rock, sited at *Mallaigh na hAltóra*. This well-hidden area was shrewdly chosen as a site for celebrating mass during the era of religious persecution.

Brackey national school is on the side of the road, on our left, just before

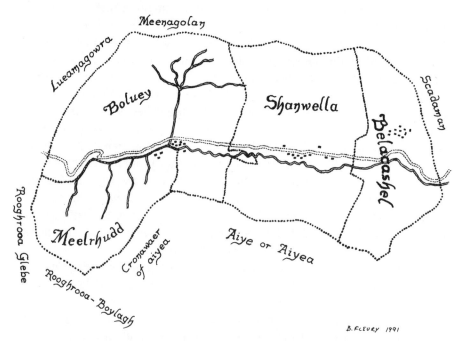

Glengesh in 1831; note the clusters of houses.
(An artist's impression of an estate map in the National Library)

we leave the townland of Scadaman. The present building was erected in 1932, but earlier schools existed both on the present site and beside it. One of the first teachers at Brackey was a man known as "Humpy Campbell";[42] he later taught in Meentinadea.[43] He also followed the occupation of dressing and lettering flagstones for graves. This he carried on during school hours and rows of inscribed flagstones stood around the room. Campbell and his family lived in an adjoining room behind the school and kept a number of hens which were allowed to roam through the class picking up crumbs. This old building was demolished in the third quarter of the last century.

A letter from Arthur Brooke,[44] the Murray-Stewart agent in Killybegs, relating to the Brackey school and written in 1876, focuses our attention on the conflict at that time in the field of education between the establishment and the emerging power of the Catholic Church. On 1 July 1876 Brooke wrote[45] to the Rev. Charles O'Donnell P.P. of Ardara regarding rebuilding of the school at Brackey. Fr. O'Donnell had apparently commenced the work without asking the landlord's permission as was necessary in those days. But it appears that Fr. O'Donnell was of the opinion that there was no necessity for this permission, as he was under the impression that there were 20sq. perches of land at Brackey set aside for this purpose when the previous building was being erected. This was denied by Brooke and it appears that Fr. O'Donnell had written him a rather sharp reply, calling him a bigot and a tyrant, terms which Brooke resented very much.

Brooke sent the correspondence to Murray-Stewart, including a letter he had received from Rev. Fr. McGarvey, now at Milford,[46] which stated that there were no 20 sq. perches for a school site at Brackey and that the previous school had been built by the curate and himself out of funds raised by themselves. Continuing his letter Brooke says: "It is doubtless very humiliating to him to have to stop the building of the school at the bidding of an agent, his parishioners most probably knowing the cause, and with them as you are no doubt aware, a priest is all powerful..."

He continues: "but I am inclined to fancy the real reason of his wrath in this – there is a growing desire on the part of the Roman Catholic Hierarchy to have the exlusive control of the education of the people ... my idea is that it is not your place to assist them in their endeavours to keep the people in the state of moral and political bondage in which they now are, opposed as it is to all that we hold right, and also to all recent legislation on the subject of education."

Brooke repeated his previous offer to Fr. O'Donnell of leasing him 20 sq. perches of Murray-Stewart property at Brackey; it appears Fr. O'Donnell agreed and the work of rebuilding was continued.

However we will not leave this hauntingly beautiful area on such an acrimonious note; instead we will remind ourselves of an earlier traveller's observations, made in 1887, on a schoolhouse situated on the road we have just passed, between Carrick and Glengesh. She writes: "But this one [school] was a good-sized cottage, and out of it poured at least a dozen healthy-looking children – bare-footed, bare-headed, but with clean faces and sturdy brown limbs. Nothing strikes one more in Donegal – or, indeed throughout Ireland – than the exceeding wholesomeness of the children. Ragged they may be, that and half-starved, but they are seldom either crippled or diseased. They can run like hares, and spring like wild cats; they look up at you fearlessly with their big, bright, Irish eyes, and grin at you with their dazzling white teeth, till you laugh in spite of yourself, and they laugh back again, as if, in spite of all this misery, life were a capital joke."[47]

We now rejoin the Killybegs–Ardara road and our travels are almost at an end. I hope when you are finishing this *turas* that the weather is more kind to you than it was to the traveller who, descending from Glengesh in 1899, wrote: "From the bottom of the hill is a slope of four miles into Ardara, most of which can be coasted. There are probably beautiful views along the whole road; but I travelled it very tired and heavy-laden on a dismal day with a nor'-wester driving sleety rain at me on the last day of May, and glad I was to see a great fire in the inn at Ardara."[48]

I'll take my hint from that and stop off in one of Ardara's twelve "inns". Take my word for it, there's nothing like a drop of the black stuff after a day on the mountains. Or perhaps you'd prefer to continue on to Inishkeel island and complete your *turas* in honour of St. Conall.

I hope you have enjoyed our tour. I have deliberately used over and over again the written word of people who have travelled these roads in bygone days, people who are now deceased. I think it is interesting to note their impressions and compare them with our own as we pass through the same countryside. Above all their writings should keep us aware of the brevity of our human lives in comparison to the landscape and Mother Earth, which though coated in equally transient outer layers display a resourcefulness and underplayed resilience which we humans are incapable of.

Mark! how all things swerve
From their known course, or vanish like a dream;
Another language spreads from coast to coast;
Only perchance some melancholy Stream
And indignant Hills old names preserve
When laws, and creeds, and people all are lost!

W. Wordsworth

Notes

1   Reports of the Committee for the Relief of the Distressed Districts in Ireland, appointed at a General Meeting held at the City of London Tavern, on 7 May 1822; with an Appendix (London: 1823).

2   Ibid. p. 68, writing from Glen on 14 August 1822.

3   Ibid. p. 84, writing from Glen on 14 September 1822.

4   Though these observations (which I have edited) of William Hume appear sympathetic enough, folklore from the Glencolumbkille area does not remember "Lord Hume" kindly; there are many stories of his oppressive nature and of his clashes with the local Catholic priest, Fr. Ferry, who stayed in Una ní Leín's (Lyons) in Kilaned. Folklore records the end of his role as an oppressor as follows: "One day Lord Hume was coming into Glen down Cashel hill on horseback; he fell off the horse, had to be carried home on a stretcher and he never walked a step again." (Seán Ó hEinne.)

5   John Ewing, for the North-West Society. Box 21/XII/1, pp. 1-4, Royal Irish Academy.

6   Where we join the road from Carrick.

7   Quoted in Richard Twiss, *A Tour in Ireland in 1775*, pp. 173-74.

8   *A Tour in Ireland*, vol. I, p. 177.

9   Quoted in Constantia Maxwell, *Country and Town in Ireland under the Georges*.

10   *Ulster Folklife*, vol. 10 (1964), p. 73.

11   Constantia Maxwell, *Country and Town in Ireland under the Georges*, p. 287.

12   *Ulster Folklife*, vol. 10 (1964), p. 74.

13   p. 38.

14   *Ulster Folklife*, vol. 10 (1964), p. 76.

15   *Highways and Byways in Donegal and Antrim*, p. 76.

16   See pp. 322.

17   Joyce, vol. II, p. 317.

18   We encountered this word earlier when we visited the Sheskinmore (*An tSeascainn Mhór*) wildlife sanctuary.

19   In pronunciation a "t" is usually inserted between the "s" and "r" and so you get Stravally, Strabane, etc.

20   Joyce, vol. II, p. 483.

21   Inq., 30 Car. I.

22   *A.F.M.*, vol. V, pp. 1684-85.

23   The gaunt remains of this R.I.C. barracks, destroyed by the Old I.R.A. on 17 April 1920, are still visible.

24   *The Cliff Scenery of South Western Donegal*, pp. 154-55.

25   Monsignor Stephens, *Illustrated Handbook of South-Western Donegal*, pp. 114-15.

26   See p. 206.

27   Craik, *An Unknown Country*, pp. 160-61.

28   *Mearing Stones*, p. 5.

29   *J.R.S.A.I.*, vol. 85 (1955), p. 189.

30   Ibid.

31   Ibid.

32   Ibid. p. 190.

33   This *geis* appears in the *Book of Rights*, p. 267.

34   *Beatha Aodha Ruaidh Ui Dhomhnaill* (ed. 1895), p. XVIII.

35   Remember our earlier discussion on the placename Aighe, *An Fhaithche.*

36   *"Ocus geis fort."*

37   See *Ériu*, vol. III (1907), pp. 149-73.

38   pp. 314-16.

39   Peadar Mac Fhionnlaoigh, a native of Breenagh, Glenswilly; written in *An Claidheamh Soluis, iml. III, uimh 50 (22 Feabhra 1902), pp. 829-30.* I've translated this story from its Gaelic original.

40   *Bráthair*, which literally signifies a brother, is used to denote a *friar*; the word *friar* itself is the French *frère*, a brother, Latin *frater*. All three words, *bráthair*, *frater* and *brother* are only modified forms of the same original. (Joyce, vol. II, p. 96.)

41   *"Deirtear gur cúpla an Bráthair 'ac a'Ghoill agus fear an Aird Bháin ar an Fhaithche."*

42   He taught here in 1850-53 and possibly earlier. 1855-58: Hugh McGarvey. 1859: George Boyle. 1860: Dan Sweeney of Beagh and John Brogan, Hillhead, Ardara. 1861: John Brogan. 1863 John Brogan was transferred to Laconnell national school to replace Joseph Bradden, Doohill, Ardara, who took over at Brackey.

43   From 1855-59: replaced in Meentinadea in 1859 by James Roddy.

44   Approximately 10,000 letters written by Arthur Brooke make up part of the Murray-Stewart estate records which were salvaged in an outhouse in Killybegs and forwarded to the National Library in Dublin in 1948 (See *D.A.* (1948), pp. 140-43). These extensive records would provide excellent source material for anyone interested in a study of social conditions and conflict in south-west Donegal in the last century.

45   Murray-Stewart estate records, National Library, ms. 4273, p. 381; Brooke writes: "There was an old school house on the road to Glengesh ... some time ago the house fell, and several weeks since it came to my knowledge that Mr. O'Donnell had begun to rebuild it. I visited the place upon the day I heard this and found that the foundations of a new house were laid on ground adjoining the old site."

46   Do you remember at Loughill, Loughros Point, I told the story of the landlord, Murray-Stewart, building a new house for "Priest" McGarvey? On 21 June we find Brooke writing to Fr. McGarvey at Milford concerning his property at Loughill and elsewhere in the parish. Brooke maintained that the new Loughill house was built in its entirety by the landlord, whose agent at the time was G.V. Wilson, and that Wilson had paid for everything, and that it was his horses which drew the cut stone.

47 Craik, *An Unknown Country*, p. 161.

48 Stephen Gwynn, *Highways and Byways in Donegal and Antrim*, p. 78.

BIBLIOGRAPHY

Adamnán, *The Life of St. Columba, Founder of Hy*, ed. William Reeves D.D., Dublin (1857).

Allingham, Hugh, *Captain Cuellar's Adventures in Ulster and Connacht*, Ballyshannon (1897).

Allingham, H. and Radford, D. *William Allingham, A Diary*, Macmillan & Co. (1907).

Anderson, G. *Scotland in Early Christian Times* (1881).

Archdall, M. *Monasticon Hibernicum* (1873).

Auden, W.H. (ed.) *In the Eye of the Storm* (1976).

Bord, Janet and Colin, *Sacred Waters*, Paladin (1986).

Borlase, W.C. *Dolmens of Ireland*, 13 vols. (-1897).

British Archaeological Reports, British Series 152.

Byrne, F.J. *Irish Kings and High-Kings*, London (1973).

Campbell, Joseph, *Mearing Stones*, Maunsell & Co. (1911).

Cambrensis, Giraldus, *The First Version of the Topography of Ireland*, trans. John O'Meara, Dundalk (1951).

Cannon, Karl, *A Tour of Lettermacaward* (1985).

Cassidy, Patrick Sarsfield, *The Borrowed Bride*, Holt Bros. (1892).

Colgan, John, *Acta Sanctorum*, Louvain (1645); Dublin (1948).

Colgan, John, *Trias Thaumaturga* (1647).

Conaghan, Charles, "History and Antiquities of Killybegs," *Donegal Democrat* (1974).

Craik, Dinah Mary, *An Unknown Country*, Macmillan (1887).

Cuppagh, Judith, *Archaeological Survey of the Dingle Peninsula* (1986).

De Burgh, U.H. Hussey, *The Landowners of Ireland* (1878).

Devyr, Thomas Ainge, *The Odd Book of the Nineteenth Century*, New York (1882).

Dillon, Myles, *Early Irish Society*, Dublin (1954).

Dillon, Myles (ed.) *Lebor na Cert: The Book of Rights*, Irish Texts Society (1962; 1984).

Doherty, William James, *Inis-Owen and Tirconnell*, Dublin (1895).

Donatus, Sister Mary, *Beasts and Birds in the Lives of the Early Irish Saints*, Philadelphia (1934).

Ellacombe, H.T. *Church Bells of Devon*, Exeter (1872).

Evans, E. Estyn, *Irish Heritage*, Dundalgan Press (1944).

Fairley, James, *Irish Whales and Whaling*, Blackstaff (1981).

Fallon, Niall, *The Armada in Ireland*, London (1978).

Flanagan, L.N.W. *Ireland's Armada Legacy*, Gill and Macmillan (1988).

Floyd, Michael, *The Face of Ireland*, London (1948).

Fox, Arthur W. *Haunts of the Eagle*, Methuen (1924).

Fox, C. Milligan, *Annals of the Irish Harpers*, London (1911).

Geen, Philip, *Fishing in Ireland,* Fisher Unwin (1904).

Gibbon, Monk, *The Seals,* Jonathan Cape (1935).

Gwynn, Stephen, *Highways and Byways in Donegal and Antrim,* London (1899).

Harbison, Peter, *Pre-Christian Ireland,* Thames and Hudson (1988).

Hardiman, James, "Irish Minstrelsy," M.R.I.A. vol. I, London (1831).

Harkin, William, *Scenery and Antiquities of North-West Donegal,* Londonderry (1893).

Henry, Françoise, *Irish Art in the Early Christian Period,* Methuen (1940).

Henry, Françoise, *Irish Art in the Early Christian Period to AD800,* Methuen (1965).

Heraughty, Patrick, *Inishmurray, Ancient Monastic Island,* O'Brien (1982).

Herity, Michael, *Gleanncholumcille,* Elo Press (1990).

Hill, Lord George, *Useful Hints to Donegal Tourists* (1845).

Hogan, Edmund, S.J. *Onomasticon Goedelicum,* Dublin and London (1910).

Hogan, James, "The Tricha Cét and Related Land Measures," P.R.I.A. (1929).

Hunt, John, *Irish Medieval Figure Sculpture 1200-1600,* vol. I (1974).

Joyce, P.W. *The Origin and History of the Irish Names of Places,* vol. I (6th ed.), vol. II, vol. III (Dublin: 1891; 1893; 1913).

Keenan, Padraic, *Clonallon Parish: Its Annals and Antiquities,* Newry (1942).

Kelly, *Handbook of the Titled, Landed and Official Classes,* London (1908).

Kenney, James F. *The Sources for the Early History of Ireland: Ecclesiastical,* Dublin (1979).

Lacy, Brian, *Archaeological Survey of County Donegal,* Lifford (1983).

Leask, Harold G. *Irish Churches and Monastic Buildings,* vol. I, Dundalgan Press (1955).

Lehner, Albert and Berschin, Walter, *Lateinische Kultur im VIII Jahrhundert,* Eos verlag Erzabtei (1989).

Leslie, J.B. *Raphoe Clergy and Parishes,* Enniskillen (1940).

Lewis, Samuel, *A Topographical Dictionary of Ireland,* vol. I, London (1837).

Lockhart, Oliver, "Methodism in Ardara" (1982).

Lucas, A.T. *Cattle in Ancient Ireland,* Boethius Press (1989).

Macalister, R.A.S. *The Archaeology of Ireland,* Methuen (1928).

Macalister, R.A.S. *Ancient Ireland,* Methuen (1935).

McCaul, Rev. Liam, "The Evie Hone Window: A Guide for Tourists" (1984).

McCracken, Eileen, *The Irish Woods Since Tudor Times,* David & Charles (1971).

MacDevitt, Rev. John, *The Donegal Highlands,* Dublin (1865); revised ed. 1893.

MacDevitt, Rev. John, *The Most Rev. James MacDevitt, D.D. Bishop of Raphoe. A Memoir,* M.H. Gill & Son (1880).

MacGill, Patrick, *The Rat-Pit,* London (1915).

McGill, P.J., F.R.S.A.I. *History of the Parish of Ardara,* Ballyshannon (1970; 1976).

MacGinley, Thomas Colin, *The Cliff Scenery of South-Western Donegal* (1867).

McParlan, Dr. James, *Statistical Survey of the County of Donegal,* Dublin (1802).

Maguire, Very Rev. E. *A History of the Diocese of Raphoe,* 2 vols., Dublin (1920).

Maxwell, Constantia, *Country and Town in Ireland under the Georges,* Dundalgan Press (1949).

Micks, Wm. L. *An Account of the Congested Districts Board* (1925).

Mitchell, Frank, *Reading the Irish Landscape,* Criterion Press (1986).

Mitchell, Frank, *The Way that I Followed* (1990).

Mould, Daphne Pochin, *Irish Pilgrimage,* Dublin (1955).

Murray, John, *Handbook for Travellers in Ireland,* London (1864).

National Gallery of Ireland, Acquisition 1986-88, Dublin (1988).

Ní Catháin, Proinseas and Richter, Michael (eds.) *Ireland and Europa,* Klett-Cotta (1984).

Ó Cléirigh, Lughaidh, *Beatha Aodha Ruaidh Ui Dhomhnaill: The Life of Hugh Roe O'Donnell, Prince of Tirconnell,* ed. Rev. Denis Murphy, Dublin (1895).

O'Donnell, Rev. Charles L. *The Cloister and Other Poems,* New York (1922).

O'Donnell, Manus, *Betha Colaim Chille, Life of Columcille,* edited and translated by A. O'Kelleher and G. Schoepperle, Illinois University Press (1918).

O'Donnell, Terence O.F.M. (ed.) *Father John Colgan O.F.M. 1592-1658: Essays in Commemoration of the Third Centenary of His Death,* Assisi Press (1959).

O'Donovan, John LL.D. M.R.I.A. *The Martyrology of Donegal: A Calender of the Saints of Ireland,* ed. Todd and Reeves, Dublin (1864).

O'Donovan, John LL.D. M.R.I.A. *Annala Rioghachta Eireann: Annals of the Kingdom of Ireland* by the Four Masters, Dublin (1856; 1990).

O'Kelly, Michael J. *Early Ireland,* Cambridge University Press (1986).

Ó Muirgheasa, Énrí, *Céad de Cheoltú Ulaidh,* Dublin (1915).

Ó Muirgheasa, Énrí, *Dhá Chéad de Cheoltaibh Uladh,* Dublin (1934).

Ó Riain, Padraig (ed.) *Corpus Genealogiarum Sanctorum Hiberniae,* Dublin (1985).

Ó Riain, de Brun and Ó Coileain (eds.), *Folia Gadelica,* Cork University Press (1983).

The Parliamentary Gazetter of Ireland 1844-45, Dublin, London, Edinburgh (1846).

Pender, S. (ed.) "The O'Clery Book of Genealogies," *Analecta Hibernica* No. 18, Dublin (1951).

Pococke, Richard Dr. *Dr. Pococke's Irish Tour,* G.T. Stokes (1891).

Powell, T.G.E. *The Celts,* London (1960).

Praeger, Robert Lloyd, *The Way that I Went,* Allen Figgis (1969).

Quiggin, *A Dialect of Donegal,* Cambridge University Press (1906).

Ray, Simon (ed.) *The Orange Dove of Fiji,* Hutchinson (1989).

Raftery, Joseph, *Prehistoric Ireland,* B.T. Batsford (1951).

Reeves, William D.D. M.R.I.A. *Ecclesiastical Antiquities of Down, Connor and Dromore,* Hodges and Smith (1847).

Reeves, W. and Todd, J.H. *The Martyrology of Donegal: A Calender of the Saints of Ireland,* Dubin (1864).

Robins, F.W. *The Story of the Bridge,* Cornish Press (1948).

Rowan, Alastair, *Buildings of North-West Ulster* (1979).

Ryan, Michael (ed.) *Ireland and Insular Art A.D. 500-1200,* R. I. A. (1987).

Rynne, Etienne (ed.) *Figures from the Past.*, Glendale; Royal Society of Antiquaries of Ireland (1987).

Sanderson, Ivan T. *Follow the Whale,* Cassell & Co. (1958).

Shrubsole, Edgar S. *The Land of Lakes* (4th ed.), William Cate, nd.

Smith and Harris, *The Antient and Present State of the County of Down* (1744).

Sténuit, Robert, *Treasures of the Armada,* David & Charles (1972).

Stephens, Rev. *Illustrated Handbook of South-Western Donegal* (1872).

Stokes, Whitley (ed.) *Felire Oengusso,* London (1905).

Twiss, Richard, *A Tour in Ireland in 1775,* Dublin (1776).

Waddington, T.A.J. *Guide to Donegal and the N.W. of Ireland,* York nd.

Walker, Joseph C. *A Memoir of the Armour and Weapons of the Irish,* Dublin (1788).

Walker, Joseph C. *Historical Memoirs of the Irish Bards,* Dublin (1786).

Walsh, Rev. P. *The Placenames of Westmeath,* Dublin (1957).

Woodham-Smith, Cecil, *The Great Hunger,* Hamish Hamilton (1962).

Young, Amy, *Three Hundred Years in Innishowen,* Linenhall Press (1929).

Young, Arthur, *A Tour in Ireland,* vol. I (1776).

INDEX